Reading the Modern British and Irish Novel 1890–1930

READING THE NOVEL

General Editor: **Daniel R. Schwarz**

The aim of this series is to provide practical introductions to reading the novel in the British, Irish, and American traditions.

Also by Daniel R. Schwarz:

Broadway Boogie Woogie: Damon Runyon and the Making of New York City Culture (2003)

Rereading Conrad (2001)

Imagining the Holocaust (1999; rev. edn. 2000)

Reconfiguring Modernism: Explorations in the Relationship Between Modern Art and Modern Literature (1997)

Narrative and Representation in the Poetry of Wallace Stevens: "A Tune Beyond Us, Yet Ourselves" (1993)

The Case for a Humanistic Poetics (1991)

The Transformation of the English Novel, 1890–1930: Studies in Hardy, Conrad, Joyce, Lawrence, Forster, and Woolf (1989; rev. edn. 1995)

Reading Joyce's "Ulysses" (1987; Centenary edn. 2004)

The Humanistic Heritage: Critical Theories of the English Novel from James to Hillis Miller (1986; rev. edn. 1989)

Conrad: The Later Fiction (1982)

Conrad: "Almayer's Folly" to "Under Western Eyes" (1980)

Disraeli's Fiction (1979)

As editor:

The Early Novels of Benjamin Disraeli, 6 vols (Consulting Editor, forthcoming, 2004)

Conrad's The Secret Sharer (Bedford Case Studies in Contemporary Criticism, 1997)

Joyce's The Dead (Bedford Case Studies in Contemporary Criticism, 1994)

Narrative and Culture (with Janice Carlisle, 1994)

Reading the Modern British and Irish Novel 1890–1930

Daniel R. Schwarz

Blackwell
Publishing

BLACKWELL PUBLISHING
350 Main Street, Malden, MA 02148-5020, USA
108 Cowley Road, Oxford OX4 1JF, UK
550 Swanston Street, Carlton, Victoria 3053, Australia

First published 2005 by Blackwell Publishing Ltd

Library of Congress Cataloging-in-Publication Data

Schwarz, Daniel R.
Reading the modern British and Irish novel, 1890–1930 / Daniel R. Schwarz.
p. cm. – (Reading the novel ; 1)
Includes bibliographical references and index.
ISBN 0-631-22621-4 (hardcover : alk. paper) – ISBN 0-631-22622-2
(pbk. : alk. paper)
1. English fiction–20th century–History and criticism. 2. Modernism
(Literature)–Great Britain. I. Title. II. Series.
PR888.M63S395 2005
823′.91209112–dc22
2003026896

A catalogue record for this title is available from the British Library.

Set in 10/12.5pt Minion
by Graphicraft Limited, Hong Kong
Printed and bound in the United Kingdom
by TJ International, Padstow, Cornwall

The publisher's policy is to use permanent paper from mills that operate a sustainable
forestry policy, and which has been manufactured from pulp processed using acid-free
and elementary chlorine-free practices. Furthermore, the publisher ensures that the text
paper and cover board used have met acceptable environmental accreditation standards.

For further information on
Blackwell Publishing, visit our website:
http://www.blackwellpublishing.com

For my students who have taught me how to read better,
and for my wife, Marcia Jacobson,
my sons, Dave and Jeff Schwarz,
my mother, Florence Schwarz,
and in memory of my father, Joseph Schwarz (1913–2004)

Contents

Acknowledgments

I have been especially fortunate in teaching at Cornell for thirty-six years and having the opportunity to share reading experiences with splendid students within a community of inquiry.

I want to thank Katey Birtcher, Isabelle Liberman, and Rachael Williamson for help with proofreading and Laurie Brown, Michelle Kang, Gillian Klempner, and Sheila Marikar for assisting in the research. My friend Joel Zumoff generously keeps my computer functioning and helped on this project with other technical matters. I have enjoyed working with Blackwell's editors Emma Bennett, and Andrew McNeillie who first proposed my becoming General Editor of the series of which this volume is a part.

I am grateful to the English department staff for creating a supportive work environment: Marianne Marsh, Vicky Brevetti, Robin Doxtater, Darlene Flint, and Heather Gowe. I especially want to express my appreciation for the continuing professionalism and courtesy of Marie Powers of Cornell's Olin Library.

It is hard to overstate my debt to my wife Marcia Jacobson, my best friend and the most perceptive reader I know.

Introduction: Reading the Modern British and Irish Novel 1890–1930

I Approach and Method

Our continuing interest in the modern British and Irish novel reminds us that Modernism is a continuing part of our present, and that consigning writers or artists to historical periods is often a pointless exercise in archeology. Indeed, Modernism originally was not a period preceded by Victorianism or Edwardianism and followed by a period which we now denote as post-Modernism, but an ongoing tradition of experimentation in literature, dance, architecture, music, painting, sculpture, photography, and film. If Modernism is considered the *end* of historical periods, the last gasp of history, what can come next? Because each period thinks of itself as in a state of crisis, Modernism is really not so much a period as a state of mind. To be sure, Modernist narrative is different in degree rather than kind from prior narratives. Its originality derives from building upon and at times transforming interior monologue, stream of consciousness, nineteenth-century journalism, psychoanalysis, and naturalism. Postmodernism's audacious claims of originality and uniqueness not only recall the very claims of Modernism decades ago, but remind us that challenges to unity, fragmentation, radical disjunctions and inconsistency in point of view, multiple perspectives on reality, and moral paralysis reach back to Modernism.

As in all my work from the past three decades, I stress in the following pages that literary works are by humans, about humans, and for humans, and I stress close reading within an historical contextual framework. I am interested in modes of narration and representation. A place is once again being cleared by scholars for literary criticism based on close reading even as it is informed by – but not driven by – theoretical hypothesis. For me literary criticism means an empathetic reading of a text to discover the conscious and unconscious patterns of language that the text conveys to both the reading audience for whom it was written and the contemporary reader. Literary criticism necessarily depends on an awareness of what, in the transaction of reading, a particular reader does to a text. I seek a pluralistic approach which allows for multiple perspectives and a dialogic approach among those perspectives. Such a criticism leaves room for resistant readings – feminist, ethnic, and gay – without allowing the text to be appropriated by theoretical or political agendas. It means teaching our students that reading is an evolving process requiring attention to what the text is saying, to the structure of effects the text generates, and to how authors make conscious and unconscious choices to create their structures of effects.

Novelists begin with their choice of material, often materials drawn from the real world in which they live, even if it is only their own interior reality; they then alter that material as they begin the process of transforming their raw material into fiction. As they do so – as that process takes place – they impose an appropriate form upon their material and decide how they should present it to an audience. Writing is thus how writers read the world; as Stephen Dedalus says in the "Proteus" episode of *Ulysses*, "Signatures of all things I am here to read."

An aesthetics of reading need account for changes in the way we read an author. In a sense, major novels change even though the author writes no more words. The interpretive history of a text is a dialogue among (1) the text as object which critics write about and readers think about; (2) the subjective interests of individual critics and ordinary readers; and (3) the predispositions and assumptions of the culture in which those critics write and readers live.

The literary canon enriches itself because each generation brings something different to major authors and texts. As my teaching has evolved in response to changes in literary and cultural perspectives, the texts that I teach change with them. For example, until 1980 few critics thought about the homoeroticism of the male bonding in "The Secret Sharer"; now it is a foregrounded subject. Thus, in my edition of "The Secret Sharer" in the *Case Studies in Contemporary Criticism* series, every contributor took up the subject of homoeroticism in one way or another. I now see "The Secret Sharer" in the context of other works which focus on seeing and being seen, including James's *The Turn of the Screw* and Mann's *Death in Venice,* and also trace that focus back to the seminal nineteenth-century painter, Manet, and especially his *Déjeuner sur l'herbe.*

The history of modern British and Irish novel criticism is a miniature of the history of Anglo-American criticism in the post-war period. Thus in the criticism of the 1950s and 1960s we see two major aspects of formalism: the New Criticism, a formalism that eschewed biography and reader's response, and emphasized the *isness* of the text; and Aristotelian criticism, a formalism that stressed what we might call the *doesness* of the text – i.e. the structure of effects upon the reader as a result of the creation, consciously or unconsciously, by the author of these effects in the text.

Until recent years, even under the auspices of those practicing the New Criticism and Aristotelian criticism, Anglo-American criticism of English fiction has in part derived from the very tradition of manners and morals that English fiction addresses. Perhaps from an historical perspective this criticism should be seen as a response to British and Irish fiction's interest in content and its moral effects on readers. Thus Anglo-American criticism of British and Irish fiction has tended to focus on the moral context of texts, viewing aesthetic matters as subservient.

We might recall how, in the face of great resistance, the study of English literature in the university emerged in the late nineteenth and early twentieth centuries from the classics and from philology. In the nineteenth century, one read vernacular literature in one's own tongue for pleasure, but did not study it. Even then, if one studied modern literature at all, it was to establish canonical texts. Indeed, as late as the early 1960s, English studies at major universities in Britain and America resisted the acknowledgement of Modernism, a field which began with the writers after Hardy and sometimes with Hardy and Hopkins.

The tradition of close reading fostered by the New Criticism was particularly appropriate to Modernist texts which resisted easy understanding. To be sure, at times the New Criticism – whose philosophical underpinnings included the early critical essays of T. S. Eliot, himself an Anglo-Catholic, and his example of the religious poet and Anglican priest John Donne – may have been appropriated by some as a bulwark for bolstering orthodox religious values, but the emphasis was on powerful close reading of complex texts. Even if the New Critical readings were at times reductive efforts to resolve tension, irony, and ambiguity in overly positivistic and (w)holistic readings – readings in which the teleology of an organic whole mimed the organic "plot" of Christianity stretching from Genesis to Apocalypse – it was more often the case that the New Criticism was a secular and skeptical tool in the service of closely examining the words in a text. For example, in the hands of such practitioners as William Empson, the New Criticism was a method of seeing the need for opening the doors and windows of possibilities. The New Criticism and Aristotelian criticism installed the Kantian category of the aesthetic as central; the aesthetic ideal holds that artistic experience is different in kind from other experiences, and that art is not simply art-as-such, i.e. art as sociology or art as biography, but is unique in itself.

3

Accompanying the rise of English studies was the development of highly sophisticated modes of reading. Thus we can say that the aforementioned Anglo-American critical tradition has yielded an important theory and method. Indeed, did not the modern tradition – the tradition of Joyce, Conrad, James, and Woolf as well as the poets Yeats, Eliot, and Stevens – *depend* upon powerful close formalist reading, based on attention to the text as aesthetic object, to explicate the texts and to make them accessible to college and university students and other serious readers?

Even when Anglo-American criticism through the 1980s is primarily interested in aesthetic issues, that criticism never really abandons humanism. Notwithstanding the modifications of Anglo-American criticism by the theoretical explosion in the last decades of the twentieth century, the lasting concerns of that criticism remain the accuracy, the inclusiveness, and the quality – the maturity and sincerity – of mimesis in the English novel. The special focus of this criticism has been and still is the way that fictional characters live in imagined social communities. Indeed, Anglo-American criticism has usually subscribed to the view that art is about something other than art and that subject matter is important. To be sure, Anglo-American novel criticism takes seriously the importance of form, but its interest in form is inextricably tied to an interest in values. Anglo-American novel criticism believes that the doing – technique, structure, and style – is important *because* it reveals or discusses the meaning inherent in the subject.

The differences that separate various strands of Anglo-American criticism – formalist and historical – prior to the theoretical revolution of the 1970s seem less significant than they once did. Now we are able to see that the New Critics, Aristotelians, *Partisan Review* group, contextualists, and literary historians share a number of important assumptions: authors write to express their ideas and emotions; the way humans live and the values for which they live are of fundamental interest to authors and readers; literature expresses insights about human life and responses to human situations; and that is the main reason why we read, teach, and think about literature. While the emphasis varies from critic to critic, we can identify several concepts that define Anglo-American criticism in general, and we can see that until the theoretical revolution of the 1970s virtually all major critical voices shared similar humanistic assumptions:

1   The form of the novel – style, structure, and narrative technique – expresses its value system. Put another way: form discovers the meaning of content.

2   A work of literature is also a creative gesture of the author and the result of historical context. Understanding the process of imitating the

external world gives us an insight into the artistry and meaning of the work.

3   A novel imitates a world that precedes the text, and the critic should recapture that world primarily by formal analysis of the text, although knowledge of the historical context and author is often important.

4   Humanistic criticism believes that there is an original meaning, a center, which can be approached by, and often almost reached by, perceptive reading. The goal is to discover what authors said to their intended audience *then*, as well as what they say to us now. Acts of interpretation at their best – subtle, lucid, inclusive, perceptive – can bring that goal into sight.

5   Human behavior is central to most works, and should be the major concern of analysis. In particular, these critics are usually interested in how people behave – what they fear, desire, doubt, need. Although modes of characterization differ, the psychology and morality of characters must be understood as if they were real people, for understanding others like ourselves helps us to understand ourselves.

6   The inclusiveness of the novel's vision in terms of depth and range is a measure of the work's quality.

Following Wayne Booth's eloquent insistence on asking "who is speaking to whom" and "for what purpose," scholars of the novel focused in the 1960s and 1970s on the narrator, not only on the role of such figures as Marlow in the turn-of-the-century works such as "Youth," *Heart of Darkness*, and *Lord Jim* and the later *Chance*, as well as the captain narrator's act of telling in "The Secret Sharer" and *The Shadow Line*, but also on the complex omniscient narrators that we find in the texts of Hardy, Forster, Woolf, Joyce, and Lawrence.

The theoretical explosion of the 1980s and 1990s has dramatically reshaped the way we read the modern British and Irish novel. Bakhtin's *The Dialogic Imagination* has given us better tools to discuss pluralistic perspectives in fiction and taught us to be attentive to a novel as a dialogue among perspectives. In the wake of new historicism's return to mimesis and the implications of representation, cultural criticism needs to enter into a dialogue with older forms of contextualism. While trained as a formalist, I have always regarded literary texts as cultural artifacts. In my books such as *Reconfiguring Modernism: Explorations in the Relationship between Modern Art and Modern Literature* (1997) and *The Case for a Humanistic Poetics* (1991), I have advocated a wider cultural criticism that moves beyond micropolitical and macropolitical issues and includes inquiries into such cultural configurations as the relation among Picasso, Joyce, and Wallace Stevens in the genealogy of Modernism

5

and how our understanding of each of them depends on seeing them as a cultural triptych.

We need think about why and how readers choose the critical narratives they do at a given time. I am interested in these choices as interpretive history, as products of socioeconomic forces, and as a history of individual values and temperaments. A dialogue between the neglected underbelly of socioeconomic forces – including micropolitical relations within genders and suppressed classes – and the dominant paradigm of intellectual and social history will necessarily create new, multi-layered cultural and literary history as well as vigorous analyses of what texts represent. For example, when we understand the homoerotic nature of male bonding among the Malay warrior culture, the suicide of Jim in *Lord Jim* becomes not only Jim's abandonment of Jewel but his ritualistic acceptance of punishment for violating a consummated intimacy with Dain Waris.

Rather than a noun that names positions, cultural criticism needs to be thought of as a verb, as a process of inquiring, teaching, and reading. Cultural criticism needs to address the category of the aesthetic and its relationship to the political and the ethical. Now that literary studies has returned since the late 1980s or so to a criticism that focuses on contexts, we need also ask what is the place of the aesthetic in cultural criticism? Why do we find some works beautiful, moving, and pleasing; and why do we respond to the quality and integrity of mimesis – the way the parts of a work are unified – as well as to other formal ingredients of a work, including narrative voice, verbal texture, and characterization? How can we speak of ethical and political value without surrendering the value of the aesthetic? We do not have to subscribe to the view that all art is a separate ontology, its value intrinsic to itself, to ask how we can maintain a place for the aesthetic.

Reading the Modern British and Irish Novel explicitly and implicitly proposes the ingredients for a humanistic cultural criticism that has a place for the aesthetic. A humanistic cultural criticism seeks to define cultural configurations that go beyond positivistic influence studies, and to re-create the economic, social, and political world that the authors inhabit. It tries to define an awareness of the cultural position of the critic and to understand interpretive history as a history of awareness – of aesthetic assumptions, political interests, world views – but also as an idiosyncratic history of individual critics. It seeks a dialogue among various social, economic, and historical factors, between literature and history, between literature and the arts. It tries to operate in a dialogic manner but insists on retaining a place for the aesthetic.

I argue for a cultural criticism which explores similarities that go beyond the borderlines between art forms and between national literatures. At the same time as Modernists were making similar experiments in fiction, Picasso was embarking on Cubism – on scrambling the distinction between foreground and background, on freeing color from the morphology of representation, and on including multiple perspectives on the same subject. Do we not need more courses that juxtapose paintings such as Matisse's 1910 *Dance II* and its sequel *Music* – with their vermilion figures, blue skies, and green hills – not merely to major texts of British and Irish literature but to roughly contemporary texts of other literatures, such as Mann's *Death in Venice* (1912)?

My discussions take account of recent developments in theory and cultural studies, including post-colonial, feminist, gay, and ecological perspectives, and show how reading the modern British and Irish novel has changed in the face of the theoretical explosion since the early 1980s. While still a formalist interested in the inextricable relationship of form and content within an imagined ontology, I stress the historical and theoretical framework a bit more than I once did. In each of my readings, I test some of the claims of recent theory, even while articulating the humanistic poetics that underlie my entire critical project for over three decades.

II Cultural and Historical Contexts: Modernism in Literature and Art

The experiments in technique and theme of Joseph Conrad, James Joyce, Virginia Woolf, D. H. Lawrence, and E. M. Forster – as well as T. S. Eliot, Wallace Stevens, and such European counterparts as Thomas Mann and Franz Kafka – parallel the challenges to mimesis of Henri Matisse, Pablo Picasso, and Paul Klee. Their experiments in color, line, space, and abandonment of representation provided a model for writers who challenged traditional narrative linearity and concepts of lyric. My own story of Modernism is a quarry of memories, recollections, images, and metaphors. This seems appropriate for a tradition that is part elegy, part nostalgia for a time before the fault line between present and past, and part a self-conscious enactment, like Picasso's collages, of fragmentation.

Modernism in painting took diverse paths. Cubism fractured objects into component planes and dramatized diverse perspectives which the perceiver would be able to reconstruct into the object in space as the painter had imagined it. Surrealists, such as Max Ernst and Giorgio De Chirico, sought to tap the irrational world of dreams and the unconscious. Ernst was interested in presenting chance meetings and remote realities in a plane that was, according to conventional expectations, unsuitable to those objects. Theo Van Doesburg in *Art Concrete* called for art that was impersonal in execution and based on scientific or mathematical data. Indeed, Jean Metzinger and Albert Gleizes – notably in his book *Du Cubisme* – related Cubism to Einstein's idea of relativity, a fourth dimension, and Modernist notions of simultaneity of perception. While nineteenth-century realists and naturalists hold nature to be the center of the universe, various symbolists – anti-materialistic, anti-positivistic – rejected rules of reason while exalting feeling, dreams, and mystery. Symbolists followed Schopenhauer, who believed that everything is an infinite succession of transitory phenomena.

Modernism sought new ways of doing what art always does: sharing the immediacy of artistic experience in an effort to connect oneself to the rest of the world. Neither Picasso nor Matisse ever abandoned figure representation. Both held to the belief that art has access to the world; yet their art calls attention to their awareness of the fictionality of art. Art represents – signifies an a priori signified, perhaps a vision of the self or of others and/or of an anterior place and time – but does not copy its subject. Modern art depends on two forms of essentialism. First, often modern art self-consciously and knowingly uses a web of signs – that is, not the artist's original perceptions but a condensation and intensification that transforms what the artist sees into the essential nature of things; that condensation is mediated by conventions and, often, by a sense of audience expectations. Do we not think of Eliot's objective correlative when the art critic John Elderfield discusses Matisse's technique? "The mental image he is painting condenses not the appearance of the subject but the feeling it evokes in him. The painted image that results will therefore correspond to that mental image – will become a transposed, realized form of that mental image – only when it evokes the same emotions that the subject itself did originally."[1] Second, following Romantic antecedents, Modernism often embraced the view that the response to the nature of things needs to be *personal* and *engaged* – a mixture of what the mind perceives and what it creates.

We must not look for reductive consistency in our narrative of Modernism. Modernism depends on the interpretive intelligence of a reader's perspective. We need to look at the assumption that form discovers meaning from a postmodern point of view that is open to destabilizing such an assumption. But we also need to try to understand the world of modern authors and painters by responding to how they intervene, intersect, transform, and qualify the culture in which they are a part, and how they do so with an intense belief in the inextricable relationship between form and content.

As Charles Altieri notes,

> Although the Modernist poets and painters worried a good deal about history as a general phenomenon, for the most part they had little interest in the specific texture of their own historical moment. Theirs was a lonely and, ultimately, self-regarding art, more concerned for the intensity and clarity of its constructed sites than for the social world out of which the sites were made, and to which they had to return for their validation.[2]

Lacking preconceived metaphysics, Modernism understands artistic creation as self-discovery. The playwright David Mamet once remarked, "What you say influences the way you think, the way you act, not the other way around."[3] The very act of writing the word, painting the canvas, carving the stone – all these formal processes shape the way the artists think and act.

Modernism is a response to cultural crisis. By the 1880s we have Nietzsche's *Gay Science* (1882–7) with his contention that God is dead as well as Krafft-Ebing's revolutionary texts on sexuality; we also have the beginnings of modern physics in the work of J. J. Thomson. All challenged absolutist theories of truth. Let us also recall that *Origin of Species* appeared in 1859 and *Essays and Reviews*, which questioned the Bible as revealed history, in 1860. In the period from 1865 to 1870, Karl Marx began to publish *Das Kapital*, Alfred Nobel invented dynamite, while Otto Von Bismarck and Benjamin Disraeli dominated Europe and colonialism expanded its reach.

Modernism is paradoxically both an ideology of *possibility* and *hope* – a positive response to difficult circumstances – and an ideology of *despair* – a response to excessive faith in industrialism, urbanization, so-called technological progress, and the Great War of 1914 to 1918, called for a time the "War to End All Wars." Notwithstanding some notable exceptions, such as Woolf's *To the Lighthouse* and *Between the Acts*, the Great War is the absent signifier in much of the literature and art from 1914 to well into the 1920s. What does Claude Monet's obsession with water lilies in 1917–18 tell us about his historical sense and the position of the artist? Is the presence of the classical in Eliot and Joyce a response to the disorder and chaos of the war? In 1922, the year of *The Waste Land* and *Ulysses*, Jean Cocteau's version of Sophocles' *Antigone* – a play set in the aftermath of war – was put on in Paris with sets by Picasso. Yet *where* is the Great War in either Eliot or Joyce? And what do Stevens, Matisse, and Picasso have to say about the Holocaust? As Paul Fussell writes in *The Great War and Modern Memory*, "It was a hideous embarrassment to the prevailing Meliorist myth which had dominated the public consciousness for a century. It reversed the idea of Progress."[4] Yet it is well to remember that Arnold's "Dover Beach" (1859, 1867) speaks of a world without "certitude, nor peace, nor love, nor light" where "ignorant armies clash by night." In "The Darkling Thrush" (1900), using ironically the traditional Romantic image of the bird's association with poetry, song, and joy (as in Keats's "Ode to a Nightingale," Shelley's "To a Sky-Lark," Hopkins's "The Windhover"), Hardy grimly sees the departing century as a skeleton and imagines the thrush throwing itself upon the gloom. Both Hardy and Arnold anticipate the angst and dubiety of Eliot.

In response to the Great War, Matisse's paintings became more disciplined and less decorative. One might say he responded to despair by finding hope in the formal solutions of his art. Compare the sensuality of *The Red Studio* (1911) with *The Piano Lesson* (1916); as Kenneth Silver writes of the latter, "[Its] narrow horizontal band of arabesques formed by the continuous frieze of the music stand and the balustrade and, at his right, . . . a tiny Matisse bronze of a lounging nude . . . tauntingly suggests the sensual fulfillment and [aesthetic flights]" of Matisse's past works.[5] Yet *The Piano Lesson* owes much to the formal rigor of Cubism; Matisse redid it as the less abstract *The Music Lesson* (1917). Picasso reverted to pre-Cubist themes and representation. Note that Matisse and Picasso exhibited jointly at Galerie Paul Guillaume in 1918, as if, in celebration of the war's end, they would, at least temporarily, suspend their lifelong rivalry.

Modernism, as James Clifford notes, takes "as its problem – and opportunity – the fragmentation and juxtaposition of cultural values."[6] Isn't Modernism a search for informing principles that transcend cultures *as well as* a recognition of both the diversity and continuity of culture? Modernism sought to find an aesthetic order or historic pattern to substitute for the crumbling certainties of the past. Yet at the same time Modernists were aware that the order was elusive – as Eliot put it, fragments to shore against the ruins of their present lives. Certainly *Ulysses*, where Joyce describes a pacifistic, humanistic, urban, family-oriented Jew whose adventures take place within the space of his mind, finds cohesion in both aesthetic order and cultural continuity. Picasso's *Les Demoiselles d'Avignon* – with its ethnographic masks in a European brothel fronted by a still life – affirms a delicate balance between tradition and innovation, between the quest for order and inchoate forces of anarchy and misrule within the work. Yet within each of these seminal texts are strands of irony and disunity, for the fragmentation – the 18 techniques in *Ulysses*, the breakdown of representation and perspective in *Les Demoiselles* – undermine the possibility of a unilateral perspective giving shape and coherence to a single vision.

Modernism goes beyond previous cultures in engaging otherness and questioning Western values. As Clifford notes, in 1900 "'Culture' referred to a single evolutionary process." He articulates an important aspect of Modernism:

> The European bourgeois ideal of autonomous individuality was widely believed to be the natural outcome of a long development, a process that, although threatened by various disruptions, was assumed to be the basic, progressive movement of humanity. By the turn of the century, however, evolutionist confidence began to falter, and a new ethnographic conception of culture became possible. The word began to be used in the plural, suggesting a world of separate, distinctive, and equally meaningful ways of life. The ideal of an autonomous, cultivated subject could appear as a local project, not a *telos* for all humankind.[7]

Modernism contains the aspirations and idealism of nineteenth-century high culture and the prosaic world of nineteenth-century city life; both are colored by an ironic and self-conscious awareness of limitation. Often convictions are framed by or within an ironic stance, an awareness of the difficulty of fulfilling possibility. Prior to Modernist questioning, the possibility of a homogeneous European culture existed. As Elderfield puts it, "history was not always thought to be quite possibly a species of fiction but once comprised a form of order, and might still."[8] In "Tradition and the Individual Talent," Eliot wrote that tradition meant writing with an historical sense that

> compels a man to write not merely with his own generation in his bones, but with a feeling that the whole of the literature of Europe from Homer and within it the literature of his own country has a simultaneous existence and composes a simultaneous order . . . No poet, no artist of any art, has his complete meaning alone. His significance, his appreciation is the appreciation of his relation to the dead poets and artists. You cannot value him alone; you must set him, for contrast and comparison, among the dead. I mean this as a principle of aesthetic, not merely historical, criticism.[9]

Modernism is inclusive, containing both the aestheticism and complexity of high culture, the straightforwardness and earthiness of working-class culture, and an ironic awareness of its own self-consciousness. Just as writers like Thomas Hardy and D. H. Lawrence not only include the working class, agrarian workers, and miners but focus on their lives and aspirations, Modernist painters focus on the vernacular in painting – Cézanne's card players, Degas's laundresses, Picasso's whores, café life, and circus performers. Yet writers such as William Butler Yeats, Joyce, and Lawrence also believed in the power of art and in the artist as visionary prophet. Indeed, Yeats and Lawrence flirted with totalitarianism, and Ezra Pound embraced it. Joyce believed that he – the artist hero – along with his humanistic, pacifistic, family-oriented, secular Jew Bloom, could be the heir to Charles Parnell as the hero that Ireland required. Justifying the Dadaists and his own retreat to Zurich during World War I, Hans Arp wrote, "We were seeking an art based on fundamentals, to cure the madness of the age, and a new order of things that would restore the balance between heaven and hell."[10] Yeats and Joyce derived from an Irish tradition which believed in the power of art; it believed that artists could become possessed by inspirational forces and reveal hidden truths. Phillip Marcus argues, "As seers, the bards had direct access to ideal images. Viewed historically, those images were to be found in the past, closer in time to the Edenic or pre-lapsarian state, and in sacred texts where they had been embodied by bardic predecessors and preserved through a tenaciously conservative tradition."[11]

Modernism is often a dialogue between Platonism and empiricism. In contrast to Eliot's empiricism, one strand of Modernism – what we might call the Platonic strain – believes in the power of art to reveal higher truths, invisible reality. Yeats, a Neoplatonist, felt that Joyce and Pound were seduced and enslaved by whatever happened to enter their minds. For Yeats, whom we now categorize as a Modernist, Modernism often meant values he ostentatiously rejected: positivistic science, Newtonian physics, pragmatism, democracy, and a kind of naturalism he abhorred. Rather naively, Yeats articulated a credo of purity of mind and ascetic contemplation; he mourned the gradual loss since the eighteenth century of an organic community and a systematic world view. He would have agreed with Klee: "Today the reality of visible objects has been revealed and the belief has been expressed that, in relation to the universe, the visible is only an isolated case and that other truths exist and are in the majority."[12]

Modern painting is a journey toward abstraction; yet abstraction expresses meaning, and often – as Kandinsky argued in *Concerning the Spiritual in Art* – transcendental ideas. He believed that contemporary humans had lost their ability to see the spiritual and that *his art* could awaken dormant imaginative, intuitive, and inspirational powers. Abstraction was often part of the Symbolist movement, which sought to go beyond traditional representation to create higher realities and discover cosmic order. As Pepe Karmel writes, "The Symbolists rejected the scientific rationalism of late 19th-century society. Instead they sought new sources of faith, turning to pagan myth, Oriental religion and the childlike, uncritical Christianity of peasants. Or they decided that the real truth of human nature lay in the instinctual drives toward death and reproduction."[13] Kandinsky was influenced by Paul Gauguin's primitivism and mystical imagery and by Matisse's freeing color from naturalism and his outlined forms. Kandinsky was interested in synesthesia, the interrelationship between senses, and wanted to create a total art work, *Gesamtkunstwerk*, integrating painting, theater, music, and poetry. Influenced by Scriabin, he wrote *The Yellow Sound (Der Gelbe Klang)*; he used colored lights: yellow is a "worldly color," while blue signifies spirituality. Like Diaghilev's Russian ballets, Matisse's *Dance* and *Music* are efforts to integrate painting, dance, and music.

One cannot cite an exact moment when color and form begin to share with subject the focus of painting. When we see Vincent Van Gogh's *La Salle de danse à Arles* (1888), we know something has happened and that explosive blocks of color, seething dynamic line, the material and *energy* of paint have changed the very nature of painting. Painting expands infinitely until one subject is paint, whether it is Camille Pissarro's layering or Monet's experiments with light. When reading literature we always recuperate the word into subject. Yet, in modern painting, too, the stress on formal experimentation and stylistic innovation does not overwhelm the centrality of the subject: even such an abstract painter as Klee believed in the centrality of the human subject. Finally, for Klee, "Art does not render the invisible; it renders the visible."[14]

Imagism in its effort to catch the response to experience at an intense moment parallels Impressionism – recall that Monet was already painting his water lilies in 1912 to 1914 – and in its formal rigor, precision, and effort to achieve objectivity parallels Postimpressionism. In his 1913 manifesto, Ezra Pound called for hardness ("Direct treatment of the 'thing,' whether subjective or objective"), exactness ("To use absolutely no word that does not contribute to the presentation"), and cadence ("As regarding rhythm; to compose in sequence of the musical phrase, not in sequence of the metronome").[15] In Pound's two-line poem "In a Station of the Metro," he juxtaposes his response to an experience with an image that renders it: "The apparition of these faces in the crowd / Petals, on a wet, black bough." The poem evaluates and structures the experience as an epiphanic moment of revelation for the speaker. In the characteristic Modernist way, it is a poem about looking. Even if the first time we read from left to right and down the page, we can choose in these short poems – as a kind of exercise in seeing – to let our eye rove on the page to discover other patterns. Our memories of texts, particularly short texts, are rarely in narrative order but usually are partly visual, even if the visual may have the distortions of dreamscapes.

Modernist texts such as *Ulysses*, *The Secret Agent*, *Mrs Dalloway*, *The Waste Land*, and "The Love Song of J. Alfred Prufrock" show the intricate network that holds together the modern city. The city – and the texts about the city – rescues space from neutrality, laying invisible tracks of human connection, even while highlighting terrible moments of marginalization, isolation, and loneliness. The self is cut loose from its spiritual attachments, often from family, and from a common place, such as a village or a piece of land. The Jews – embraced by Joyce, rejected by Eliot and Pound – become an image of the deracinated, rootless self. Eliot's pejorative image of the Jew in *Gerontion* is the obverse of Bloom:

> the jew squats on the window sill, the owner,
> Spawned in some estaminet of Antwerp,
> Blistered in Brussels, patched and peeled in London.

Modernism responded to modern urban culture. As Conrad and Eliot – and Dickens before them – saw, the city can be huge, drab, dirty. When Eliot writes in "The Love Song of J. Alfred Prufrock" of

> half-deserted streets,
> The muttering retreats
> Of restless nights in one-night cheap hotels
> And sawdust restaurants with oyster shells,

he asks us to recompose the city's fragments into our mental neighborhood. The vast interconnections of elaborate canvases with their separate neighborhoods, such as *Moroccans* and *Guernica* – or Eliot's "Prufrock" and *The Waste Land* – as well as novels with one-word titles that imply pulling together vast networks of relationships, such as *Ulysses* and *Nostromo*, may be the result of living in cities or imagining the city as a labyrinth. Such large canvases and texts are pulled together by a willful and often visionary overview. While leaving the city to experience cultural otherness and difference, Matisse, and Gauguin before him, never left its imaginative environs. Underneath Gauguin's Tahitian paintings and Matisse's Moroccan paintings is the wish to resolve the difference, diversity, busyness, and commotion of urban life into a unified and even reductive picture.

III   Modern Art as Quest for Order

Modernism stressed cultural and personal fragmentation and sought techniques to express this idea. Emphasizing how each of us is changing every moment, Henri Bergson wrote in *Creative Evolution*,

> Duration is the continuous progress of the past which gnaws into the future and which swells as it advances . . . The piling up of the past upon the past goes on without relaxation. In reality, the past is preserved by itself, automatically. In its entirety, probably, it follows us at every instant; all that we have felt, thought, and willed from our earliest infancy is there, leaning over the present which is about to join it, pressing against the portals of consciousness that would fain leave it outside.[16]

Bergson continues: "What are we in fact, what is our character, if not the condensation of the history we have lived from our birth?"[17] Note the parallel to Bakhtin's concept that when each of us speaks or writes, our prior systems of language voluntarily and involuntarily manifest themselves in a heteroglossic voice. Given the multiplicity and ever-changing nature of self, each of us has multiple selves and points of view; that shared perception of Modernism is a cause of the dramatized consciousness of James and Conrad, Joyce's diverse techniques in *Ulysses*, and the development of Cubism. Is there not a continuity between Oscar Wilde's concept of lying and Henri Bergson's concept of duration in their mutual effort to transform the tick-tock of passing time – what the Greeks called *chronos* – into significant time or *kairos*? As a way of trying to transcend time Wilde, hounded for his homosexuality, created in *The Picture of Dorian Gray* a mask – an invented lie – of the aesthete and decadent who flouts conventions of society. Indeed, Wilde poignantly did the same in his own life.[18]

Painters, too, search in the forms of art for a coherent identity. In *Notes of A Painter*, a text begun in November 1908, Matisse wrote, "Underlying this succession of moments which constitutes their superficial existence of being and things, and which is continually modifying and transforming them, one can search for a truer, more essential character, which the artist will seize so that he may give reality a more lasting impression."[19] We see the obsessive presence of the past in Matisse's paintings, but in *The Red Studio* – full of references to his prior work – we also see the promise of the future in the plant as well as in the crayons and pencils that will be used to create a work of art. The clock without hands suspends time while paradoxically calling attention to the perpetual presence of time, and expresses an awareness that clock time is an arbitrary measurement imposed by humans. Such self-consciousness about the self as an artist, revealed as self-referentiality, is characteristic of Modernism. It is a feature of Eliot's and Stevens's poetry and is exemplified by the continuity of Marlow and Stephen Dedalus in the works of Conrad and Joyce. Thus in the "Scylla and Charybdis" chapter of *Ulysses*, Joyce calls attention to the presence of Shakespeare the artist in the latter's artistic creations as a way of teaching us how to read Stephen as a surrogate of Joyce in his epic novel.

It was until recently argued that Matisse and Picasso represent diverse streams of Modernism. Never far from the here and now or from bourgeois desires, Matisse wanted, we thought, always to maintain a dialogue with and response to nature, while Picasso sought to show that the imagination could do what it wished when it wished. Yet as the recent Picasso–Matisse exhibition in London, Paris, and New York showed, these distinctions hold no more than those formerly applied to the following pairs of writers: Lawrence and Joyce, Eliot and Stevens, E. M. Forster and Woolf – with the second member of each pair emphasizing the independence of art from representation.

Yet in some ways the Modernists thought of themselves as essentialists and often tried to insulate art from history and even to apotheosize the aesthetic. While aestheticism is an ironic comment on materialism, it is also another form of essentialism. Why did so many Modernists recuse themselves from the Great War and from history itself, while finding refuge in inner systems, fantasy versions of politics, or art as fetish? Modernism's focus on the past can be a way of eschewing present-day politics and history. At times the retreat to art is an escape from history and leads to a kind of historical myopia. In *Death in Venice* Mann analyzes the necessary relationship between the two. Among other things, *Death in Venice, Metamorphosis*, and *The Death of Ivan Ilych* are about the impossibility of escaping history. The effort to eschew history by Matisse, Picasso, Stevens, and Eliot has been ironized by history. That the present is a relentless fury is an important Modernist theme; yet, paradoxically, at times Modernists have a myopic view of the past. Mann dramatizes how Aschenbach idiosyncratically turns myth and history into versions of his own life; Mann weaves a perspective in which Aschenbach, imagining himself to be Socrates, inevitably is caught in the web of his own making. In his understanding of how we myopically turn the subjective into seemingly objective reality, Mann provides a postmodern critique on Modernism. Yet paradoxically – and inevitably – he does the very thing he critiques in Aschenbach; he creates a myth out of his own experience. Indeed, he is an ironic Dedalus, a maker of his own labyrinth.

For the great Modernists, art was a quest; as Jack Flam writes of Matisse and Cézanne, "great painting was not merely a matter of stylization and technique but the result of deeply held convictions about vision in relation to life."[20] While the impulse to make oneself the subject of one's own art includes Rembrandt's self-portraits, the impulse crystallized in the nineteenth century with Courbet's *L'Atelier* (1854–5) – known as the "Real Allegory Determining a Phase of Seven Years of my Artistic Life" – with its intense focus on Courbet at work. In the middle of that painting is a godlike Courbet with a model – if I may quote Julian Barnes, "reinventing the world. And perhaps this helps answer the question of why Courbet is painting a landscape in his studio rather than *en plein air*: Because he is doing more than reproducing the known, established world, he is creating it himself. From now on, the painting says, it is the artist who creates the world rather than God."[21] Does not this description recall Stephen's argument about what the artist does in the "Scylla and Charybdis" section of *Ulysses*, and remind us of how Eliot's artist creates order from cultural and personal fragments?

To suggest his own biographical relationship to *Ulysses*, Joyce has Stephen propose his expressive theory of the relationship between Shakespeare's art and life. What makes Shakespeare a man of genius is that he encompassed in his vision the "all in all in all of us" (IX, 1049–50).[22] Joyce re-creates Shakespeare according to his own experience of him, and thus becomes the father of his own artistic father and the artist whose imagination is so inclusive and vast that it contains the "all in all" of Shakespeare plus the very substantial addition – or, in current terminology, the supplement – of his own imagination. Like Joyce, Shakespeare used the details of everyday life for his subject: "All events brought grist to his mill" (IX, 748). The major creative artist discovers in his actual experience the potential within his imagination: "He found in the world without as actual what was in his world within as possible" (IX, 1041–2). To activate that potential, the artist must have as wide a range of experience as possible; to get beyond the limitations of his own ego in order to achieve the impersonality and objectivity that is necessary for dramatic art, his imagination must have intercourse – and the sexual metaphor is, I think, essential to understanding Joyce's aesthetic – with the world: "His own image to a man with that queer thing genius is the standard of all experience, material and moral" (IX, 432–3).

Joyce, like Mann, is aware of the irony of his youthful artist comparing himself to the master artist or thinker. Joyce's relationship to Stephen in "Scylla and Charybdis" reaches a turning point when he twice penetrates Stephen's mind to show him briefly imposing dramatic form upon his experience by using the traditional typography of plays to organize his monologue (*Ulysses*, IX, 684ff, 893ff). In the second and longer instance, a play that lasts little more than a page, Stephen is the major character speaking to his friends about the same issues he has been discussing throughout the chapter. And the entire chapter puts the argument about the relationship between the author's life and his work in the form of a virtual monodrama. If, according to Stephen's theory, Shakespeare's transparently disguising his identity in his early work foreshadows *A Portrait of the Artist*, the more subtle disguises of biography in *Hamlet* anticipate the technique of *Ulysses*.

Chapter 1

"I Was the World in Which I Walked": The Transformation of the British and Irish Novel, 1890–1930

I Introduction

In the Sculpture Garden of the Museum of Modern Art stands Rodin's large 1897 statue, *Monument to Balzac*. The imposing figure of Balzac is 10 feet tall, and it rests on a 5-foot-high slab. At first, the observer may wonder what this seemingly realistic piece is doing in the citadel of Modernism. But gradually one realizes that the work is a crystallizing image of Modernism, for it depicts the artist as outcast and hero. Towering above onlookers, Balzac is wearing an expression of scornful magisterial dignity. With back stiffly yet regally arched past a 90-degree angle, Balzac looks into the distance and the future as if oblivious and indifferent to the opinions of the Lilliputians observing him from below. The large mustache, massive brows, flowing hair, and enormous ears and nose all emphasize the figure's immense physical stature. As observers we crane our necks to see the features of this commanding figure whose gigantic head is disproportionate to his body. His features are boldly outlined but not precisely modeled. His huge head dominates the massive form; the body enwrapped in a cloak is a taut cylinder; the only visible feature is the feet, which are in motion as if they were going to walk off the slab. Indeed, one foot actually overhangs the slab as if it were about to depart. In the geometric shape of an isosceles triangle, the intimidating figure asserts the dependence of content upon form.

In a number of ways this sculpture, I think, helps us to understand literary Modernism. Rodin has presented the artist as an *Übermensch*, as a physical and moral giant who is indifferent to the opinions of his audience. He depicts Balzac the way Rodin would have liked to see himself: "I think of [Balzac's] intense labor," he wrote, "of the difficulty of his life, of his incessant battles and of his great courage. I would express all that."[1] As Albert E. Elsen remarks, "Rodin has transformed the embattled writer into a godlike visionary who belongs on a pedestal aloof from the crowd."[2] Rodin's presence in the sculpture of Balzac speaks for art as self-expression, and thus declares a new aesthetic that questions the impersonality and objectivity that Balzac sought in his role of moral and social historian of the human comedy. Rodin's Balzac is not someone who serves the community but someone who answers to the demands of his own imagination and psyche; he does not imitate reality, but transforms what he sees into something original. He is more a visionary than a realist. His integrity derives from his genius and his independence. The sculpture shows, too, the inseparable relationship between subject and object – the poised tension between content (Balzac) and form (the original stone) – that is central to Modernism. Finally, Rodin understands that art requires an audience to complete the hermeneutical circle, for he declared that the suggestiveness of his *Balzac* required the viewer to use "the imagination to recompose the work when it is seen from close up."[3]

I would like to take the Rodin statue as a point of departure for speaking of the great change in major British and Irish fiction from the realistic to the expressionist novel, a change that begins roughly in 1895, the year of Thomas Hardy's last novel, *Jude the Obscure*, and reaches a climax with Virginia Woolf's major novels, *Mrs Dalloway* (1925) and *To the Lighthouse* (1927). That some or all of the great British and Irish Modernists – Joseph Conrad, James Joyce, D. H. Lawrence, E. M. Forster, and Woolf – withdraw from their work, eliminate the intrusive author, and move to objectivity and impersonality is still one of the shibboleths of literary history. In this chapter I shall argue that by making themselves their subject they have, in fact, created a more subject-ive, self-expressive novel than their predecessors, and that they *are* present in their works.

Influenced by English Romanticism, developments in modern art, and a changing intellectual milieu that questioned the possibilities of universal values or objective truth, these novelists erased the boundaries between art and life. They no longer believed that they could or should re-create the real world in their art, and they questioned the assumption that verisimilitude was the most important aesthetic value. They realized that each person perceives a different reality and lives in what F. H. Bradley has called a "closed circle."[4] Thus, while mid-Victorian novelists believed in the efficacy of their art,

twentieth-century writers have often despaired at the possibility of communication. They wrote not only to urge their perspectives upon their audience
but to create their own identities and values. On the one hand, artists doubt
that they can change the world but, on the other, they try to convince themselves and their audience that they can.

Twentieth-century British and Irish writers invent ways of seeing the
human psyche in a more subtle and complex manner than prior writers had.
While the Victorian novel focused upon people in their social aspect, Conrad,
Lawrence, Joyce, and Woolf isolate their characters from the social community
by focusing on the perceiving psyche. As J. Hillis Miller has noted, there is
little self-consciousness in most Victorian novels: "the protagonist comes to
know himself and to fulfill himself by way of other people."[5] But the English
novel from 1890 to 1930 made self-consciousness and self-awareness its
subject, and the stream of consciousness within the soliloquy and interior
monologue – both direct and indirect – became more prominent. Since
characters are often versions of the author who either cannot or does not
achieve the traditional distance between author and characters, the experience
and self-consciousness of the characters reflect those of the authors.

In traditional novels we are more conscious of the characters, actions,
themes, and rhetoric and less conscious of what I shall call the author's presence. Patricia Meyer Spacks notes: "Writers before the nineteenth century . . .
often insisted by implication on their *lack* of psychology, defining themselves
in relation to their audiences or in terms of a historical tradition rather than
by personal reactions or feelings."[6] The conventions of editor or omniscient
narrator deserve such a description. In *Moll Flanders* (1722) and *Clarissa*
(1748) the presence of the author is often felt as an editor; in *Tom Jones*
(1749) the author depicts himself as the reader's host. In Victorian fiction
the author becomes an omniscient voice. Yet because modern writers have
written first for themselves, they have been more insistent on affirming
their living presence in their works than on using rhetorical tools to shape
their readers.

II The Modern Novel as Self-Expression

Twentieth-century novels are often songs of myself, and anxious, self-
doubting ones at that. In varying degrees the later Hardy in *Jude the Obscure*,
Conrad, Forster, Woolf, and Joyce take their own imaginations as a major
subject. In a sense their novels are about the process of transforming life
into art. Reading *Emma* (1816) is the discovery of a finished, three-

dimensional, imagined world, while reading the major British and Irish novelists in the period from 1890 to 1930 involves participating in their process of struggling to define their values and their concepts of the novel. It is the difference between a Constable or a Gainsborough and a Matisse or a Picasso. The novel depends on a continuing dialogue between the author's avowed subject and his or her efforts to discover the appropriate form and values for that subject. Writing in "Tea at the Palaz of Hoon" (1921) of how artists finally must discover the world in themselves, Stevens defines the relationship between text and author that informs the writers under discussion:

> I was the world in which I walked, and what I saw
> Or heard or felt came not but from myself;
> And there I found myself more truly and more strange.

The author's struggle with his or her subject becomes a major determinant of novel form. In the 1898–1900 Marlow tales, *The Rainbow* (1915), *Ulysses* (1922), and *Mrs Dalloway* (1925), each author writes to define himself or herself. The writer does not strive for the rhetorical finish of earlier novels but, rather like Rodin in his sculpture, invites the reader to perceive a relationship between the creator and the artistic work, and to experience the dialogue between the creative process and the raw material. While the Victorian novelist believed that he had a coherent self and that his characters could achieve coherence, the Modernist is conscious of disunity in his own life and the world in which he or she lives. The novelist becomes a divided self. He or she is both the creator and seeker, the prophet who would convert others and the agonizing doubter who would convince himself and herself while engaging in introspective self-examination. Even while the writer stands detached, creating characters, we experience his or her urgent effort to create a self. Thus the reader must maintain a double vision. He or she must apprehend the narrative and the process of creating that narrative. In such diverse works as the Marlow tales, *The Rainbow* and *To the Lighthouse*, the process of writing, of defining the subject, of evaluating character, of searching for truth, becomes part of the novel. Yet, as Woolf writes in "Mr Bennett and Mrs Brown" (1924), "where so much strength is spent on finding a way of telling the truth, the truth itself is bound to reach us in rather an exhausted and chaotic condition."[7] "Finding a way" – the quest for values and the quest for aesthetic form – becomes the subject.

Telling becomes a central action in these novels. The reader experiences the author's engagement in defining values as he or she writes. As the search for values often takes precedence over story and as the form of these novels enacts the author's quest, traditional chronology, linear narrative, and ordinary syntax are discarded. Sometimes, as in the Marlow tales, the author's quest for values is transferred to another character whose central activity becomes the search for meaning and for the appropriate language with which to tell the tale. Sometimes a character will become the spokesman for values that the omniscient voice articulates; this is the case in *Jude the Obscure*, *Sons and Lovers* (1913), and *Women in Love* (1920). But this kind of doubling – the protagonist (Jude, Paul, Birkin) and narrative voice saying much the same thing – is not only a function of the author's need to convince himself of the accuracy of his perceptions but of the difficulty of a somewhat confused author's achieving irony toward a version of himself. The structure of a novel is no longer a preconceived pattern in which characters move toward discovering values held by an omniscient voice who is a surrogate for the author. To read the novel is to participate in a process by which the novel-ist uses his characters to propose, test, examine, and discard moral and aesthetic values.

Thus it becomes increasingly difficult for writers to remove themselves from the text. In fact, the major modern British and Irish authors remain in their work in much the same way as some Renaissance painters who placed an image of themselves in a corner of their canvas watching the main spectacle. The stream of consciousness, which has been thought of as a movement toward objectivity, is actually often a disguise for authorial presence rather than a means for the author to absent himself. For example, do we not feel that Joyce is selecting and arranging the stream of consciousness, including mythic parallels and image patterns that help give the stream its meaning and significance? We know a great deal more about Joyce from *A Portrait of the Artist as a Young Man* (1916) and *Ulysses* than we know about Austen from *Emma* and *Pride and Prejudice* (1813), or about Fielding from *Tom Jones*, notwithstanding his host-narrator. Austen or even Fielding would hardly have asserted, as Conrad did in 1912:

> A novelist lives in his work. He stands there, the only reality in an invented world, among imaginary things, happenings, and people. Writing about them, he is only writing about himself. But the disclosure is not complete. He remains, to a certain extent, a figure behind the veil; a suspected rather than a seen presence – a movement and a voice behind the draperies of fiction.[8]

While there was always an autobiographical strain in the English novel (*Tristram Shandy* [1767], *The Mill on the Floss* [1860], *David Copperfield* [1850]), this was surely a minor motif in the history of the genre. *Jude the*

Obscure, *Sons and Lovers*, and *A Portrait of the Artist* thinly disguise the presence of the authors in their work. The quest of Stephen for artistic values, for self-recognition, and for the approval of others is Joyce's quest. The *agon* is the author's quest to understand himself. Hardy becomes a spokesman for *Jude* because he sees Jude as a version of himself – the outsider aspiring to be recognized by a more educated elite society. In *Sons and Lovers* the omniscient narrator of part I gives way in part II to a spokesman for Paul's perspective. He strains to justify Paul's (Lawrence's surrogate) role in his relationship with Miriam (Lawrence's lover, Jessie Chambers). Our reading of Lawrence's dramatic scenes often belies the interpretation imposed by his narrative voice. For example, the voice does not recognize that Paul suffers from the very problems of frigidity and repression of which he accuses Miriam. Nor does he understand that he turns away from Miriam at the very time that she begins to respond sexually to Paul or that Paul discards Clara because his relationship with her threatens to succeed. Paul's oedipal relationship with his mother requires that he find fault with Clara as soon as he consummates that relationship.

Within a culture once there is no longer agreement about social, political, and personal values, an author cannot depend upon the reader to recognize the ironic disjunction between what a character thinks and what the author wants the reader to think. The omniscient narrator may be thorough and careful in establishing his or her point of view, but he or she has no special status. The novelist does not believe that any single perspective holds the entire truth. As we read modern novels told by an omniscient speaker, we realize that the novelist's commentary has imposed a perspective upon events, even while implying, through the dramatic actions and sometimes his pluralistic values, the possibility of another perspective. This is true not only for *Jude the Obscure* and *Sons and Lovers*, in each of which the omniscient narrator becomes more and more an empathetic spokesman and apologist for the major character, but even for *The Rainbow* and *Ulysses*. Thus the technical convention of omniscience survives, but not the concept of a shared value system that originally gave rise to the convention.

The recognition that self-expression and subjectivity are at the heart of the transformation of the English novel was long inhibited by the acceptance in fiction criticism of the New Critical credo that the best literature depends on the author's separating his or her personal life from the imagined world of the novels or, at the very least, on his or her repressing those aspects of experience that do not have "universal" interest. If we are to come to terms with the expressive aspect of modern fiction, we must develop an appropriate aesthetic. For example, can we separate the prophetic voice of *The Rainbow* from Lawrence's personal quest for self-realization or his quest for the appropriate

23

grammar of passion with which to render sexual relationships, if we recall his writing, "Now you will find [Frieda] and me in the novel, I think, and the work is of both of us"?[9] Nor can we ignore the parallels between Marlow's search for values and Conrad's.

Wayne Booth's *The Rhetoric of Fiction* (1961) still stands as the indispensable study of rhetoric and voice in fiction. Booth's reluctance to appreciate the ambiguous rhetoric of modern literature has often been criticized. But has anyone gone beyond his work and developed a rhetoric to describe the authorial presence within a novel that may be either narrator or character or both? Nevertheless, Booth's concept of implied author, while valuable, does not seem quite satisfactory to define the mask that the author wears within his or her works. This presence is somewhat different in each of an author's novels because its personality and character are functions of the words chosen and the events and characters described. Booth's implied author may be somewhat workable for a Fielding or Austen novel, where the narrative voice is an artifice controlled and manipulated by an objective author in full command of his or her rhetorical devices. But it does not do justice to the strong, subjective authorial presence within much modern fiction. To approach the modern writers under discussion, we must reconcile fiction as rhetoric and as self-contained ontology with fiction as self-expression. For there are frequent moments in twentieth-century fiction when the subject is the author's quest to define himself or herself. In much of the work of Conrad, Joyce, Woolf, Forster, and Lawrence, the speaker is a thinly disguised version of the writer's actual self who is actively seeking moral and aesthetic values; this authorial self, or presence, is a dynamic evolving identity that is an intrinsic – not an implied – part of the novel's form. The presence that the novelist projects reflects the particular circumstances of the novelist's life when he or she wrote the novel and the *Zeitgeist* in which the novel was written. While we should begin with what a book is and what a book does, we should not ignore what the author does, particularly in novels where the subject is the author's self. The best way to locate this presence within the text is to know beforehand something about the historical figure. In other words, the text more readily yields its presence to those who know about an author's other works, life, and historical context.

As readers we respond to an imitation of the real creator of the text. The actual author is in the imagined world as a distortion – at times, a simplification, an obfuscation, an idealization, a clarification – of the creating psyche. In earlier periods the words of a novel signify a human presence within the text; that presence may be urging the reader to a particular attitude, but in modern fiction the presence also is usually involved in affirming his or her identity and values. The reader, knowing that the presence mimes the historical figure who wrote the book, imagines that figure as a reality. As Spacks notes, "if poets create themselves as figures in their poems, readers choose, consciously or unconsciously, to accept such figures as more or less appropriate to reality."[10]

Since novels are written by people, it seems the antithesis of a humanistic approach to settle for a formalism – whether it be New Criticism or more recent varieties – that excludes authors from the text. The process of locating a human being within the text recognizes that reading is not merely a verbal game but a shared experience between writer and reader. It is another way of saying that we wish words to signify something beyond themselves. Because we desire coherence and meaning, we seek a tangible identity within the imagined world and respond to the energy of the author's creative imagination. We demand of words that they form connections to human experience, even though we make fewer demands of lines and shapes or musical notes. (Painting and sculpture, of course, have had a tradition of mimesis while music has not.)

The author's presence in the text usually serves the rhetorical purpose of reinforcing the meaning conveyed by the other elements: structure, narrator, language, characterization, and setting. But at times the presence is subversive in that it undermines the meaning that the author intended. In many modern novels that voice is divided into two or more aspects, each of which projects a different identity. Sometimes we can speak of a dominant and a secondary voice or, as in *The Nigger of the "Narcissus"* (1897), of a tension between competing voices. Conrad's effort to overcome writer's block by means of mastering the raw material of his narrative – the sea experience of his earlier life – is as much the subject of the novel as the journey of the *Narcissus*. For Conrad the sea voyage – with its clearly defined beginning and ending, its movement through time toward a destination, its separation from other experiences, and the explicit requirements that must be fulfilled by the crewmen and officers – provided the necessary model for completing a work. Since he had actually sailed on a ship named the *Narcissus* in 1884, he could draw upon romantic memories of an ordered and accomplished voyage at a time when his creative impulses were stifled by doubts. Thus the voyage of the *Narcissus* provided Conrad with an imaginative escape from his writing frustrations. *The Nigger of the "Narcissus"* also reflects a reductive dichotomy within Conrad's psyche between the evil land, where he was terribly frustrated as he launched his new career, and the sea, where, as he remembered it, he had been fairly tested and had ultimately succeeded. This dichotomy explains the schism between the first-person speaker who is a part of the crew and the third-person speaker who strives to play the role of the traditional omniscient speaker.

Ulysses is Joyce's attempt to resolve the Stephen and Bloom within his psyche, and that effort is writ large on every page. Among other things, *Ulysses* is a search for values, a dialogue within Joyce's psyche among the intellectualism and abstraction of Stephen, the humanity and empiricism of Bloom, and the sensuality and spontaneity of Molly. The novel works its way through a panorama of values in modern life. It tests and discards patriotism, nationalism, piety, Platonism, and aestheticism, and affirms the family paradigm, affection, consideration, tolerance, and love. Beginning with "Wandering Rocks," *Ulysses* examines not only ways of living but ways of telling. Joyce parodies romantic fiction in "Nausicaa," examines whether fiction can be patterned on musical composition in "The Sirens," explores the possibilities of the scientific temperament in "Ithaca," and tests the mock epic in "Cyclops." "Eumaeus," narrated by Joyce's omniscient narrator in the style in which Bloom would have told it, is Joyce's love song for Bloom in the form of an affectionate parody and the author's sequel to the end of "Hades," when Bloom affirms the value of life. In "Ithaca" not only Bloom's humanity but the possibility of significant action in the form of personal relationships emerges despite the mechanical nature of the scientific catechism, a style that enacts the indifference and coldness of the community to individuals. Thus *Ulysses* is Joyce's odyssey for moral values and aesthetic form. It is not only Bloom but Joyce who survives and triumphs over what he calls in "Aeolus" the "grossbooted draymen" of the modern city. This kind of pastiche of former styles in the service of a quest for personal values is also very much a part of modern painting and sculpture. It is in this sense, in this profoundly humanistic sense, that modern painting is about painting and modern literature is about writing.

III   Parallels Between Modern Literature and Modern Art

Virginia Woolf wrote that "on or about December 10, 1910 human character changed," because the first Postimpressionist exhibition organized by Roger Fry and called "Manet and the Post-Impressionists" ran in London from November 8, 1910, to January 15, 1911.[11] According to Samuel Hynes, she "chose that occasion as an appropriate symbol of the way European ideas forced themselves upon the insular English consciousness during the Edwardian years and so joined England to the Continent."[12] The Postimpressionists provide an example of the abandonment of realism and the movement of the artist to center stage. The Postimpressionists had discarded representation for form. For example, in his famous *Card Players*, Paul Cézanne is less an observer of peasant life than a composer of formal harmony and disparate pictorial planes, while in his works Paul Signac is concerned with the possibilities of objectively capturing light. These painters demonstrated that artists could create their own order in a chaotic world. Thus they intentionally neglect some details, while they simplify, distort, exaggerate, and stress others to express their emotions, solve problems of pictorial space, and create effects. In a sense, the artist's temperament and perspective become the subject in the work of Van Gogh, André Derain, Matisse, and Picasso. We recall Van Gogh's insistence that "what is eternally alive is in the first place the painter and in the second place the picture."[13] It is quite possible that the abrupt cutting of figures, the elimination of traditional perspective, the foreshortening of images influenced the tendency of Woolf, Lawrence, Forster, and Joyce (who, of course, saw similar paintings in Paris) to move beyond realism to more expressive forms of art. Can we read *Ulysses* or *The Secret Agent* (1907) without realizing that something has happened to the visual imagination of nineteenth-century novels and that even Dickens did not continually create the kinds of illuminating distortions, cartoons, and grotesques that populate these modern urban novels? Novelists no longer wrote what they saw, but what they knew.

The 1978 London exhibition entitled *Great Victorian Pictures* made clear, I think, the revolutionary character of Fry's exhibition. Victorian painting often told a story, either of history or of contemporary life. As Rosemary Treble wrote in the introduction to the catalogue for that exhibition: "The constant refrain in all the writing of the period and the touchstone of every judgment was whether the work attained 'truth' generally to nature and therefore, by implication, to God's creation, whether its sentiment was appropriate and whether it was morally healthy and therefore fit for consumption."[14] And the values by which Victorian fiction writers were evaluated were not too different. A painting like William Powell Frith's *The Railroad Station* (1862) was considered a national epic because it included every class. William Edward Frost's allegorical women were thought to be uplifting, although to us they seem self-absorbed and repressed. The avant-garde in England, beginning with the Pre-Raphaelite brotherhood and including Burne-Jones's precious symbolism, hardly affected the supremacy of conventional painting. To be sure, the works of James Whistler and Walter Sickert were exceptions. But the fact remains that, until Fry's painting exhibition, fiction usually conformed to the existing theories of art, and those theories (most notably orthodox realism, often in the service of Victorian pieties) with few exceptions tended to serve conventional morality.

The English novel after Hardy was deeply affected by Russian art in a number of ways. In the Edwardian years the Russian influence challenged

British insularity. Fyodor Dostoyevsky, although patronized by Conrad, now became popular, and the exuberant and flamboyant Russian Ballet appeared in 1911. In the pre-war years, Russian music, dance, and painting made their mark on London. (Russians were included in the second show of Postimpressionism.) In general, Russian art, in contrast to British art, depended more upon energy than craft, more upon fantasy than realism, more upon the artist's vision than subjectivity, more upon flux than stasis, more upon experimentation than tradition, more upon mysticism than reason, and more upon the spiritual and psychological than the moral. As Woolf understood, these qualities inevitably questioned the conventions of the British novel: "The novels of Dostoevsky are seething whirlpools, gyrating sandstorms, waterspouts which hiss and boil and suck us in. They are composed purely and wholly of the stuff of the soul."[15] In the essay "Modern Fiction" in the same volume Woolf wrote: "If we want understanding of the soul and heart where else [but in Russian fiction] shall we find it of comparable profundity?"[16] The violence of Dostoyevsky's emotions influenced not only Conrad in *Under Western Eyes* (1911), but, in more subtle ways, Woolf, Lawrence, and Forster.[17] Indeed, Lawrence consciously imports the Russian element into his imagined world in the person of the Slavic Lydia Lensky, who is the mysterious, libidinous, passionate soulmate for Tom Brangwen, Lawrence's *Übermensch* of the passions, and the grandmother of Ursula, the novel's heroine, who, like Lawrence, must come to terms with twentieth-century life. Indeed, Lawrence used the Dostoyevskian strain – the inchoate, urgent, uncontrolled "stuff of the soul" – to fertilize the English novel of manners.

The novel also changed because artists increasingly felt that the modern world required different kinds of art. The search for innovation in form and technique is inseparable from the search for values in a world where the British empire had lost its sense of invulnerability, the political leadership had suffered a crisis of confidence, and industrialization had created worker unrest. We see the effects of the first two in *A Passage to India* (1924) and *Mrs Dalloway*, and of the third in the character of Verloc in *The Secret Agent*. The urbanization of England undermined the sense of continuity that had prevailed in the country since Elizabethan times, a continuity that even the revolution of 1640 did not entirely disrupt. This continuity derived from land passed down from generation to generation, from the rhythms of rural culture, from monarchical succession, from the strong sense of English family, and from the relatively stable role played by the clergy, the aristocracy, and Parliament. George Dangerfield has described how England had become by 1914 "a liberal democracy whose parliament had practically ceased to function, whose Government was futile, and whose Opposition had said enough to put lesser men in the dock for treason."[18] Modern writers are conscious of writing in a period of crisis and transition; certainly this sense of crisis gives *Nostromo* (1904), *The Rainbow*, and *Ulysses* much of their intensity. It may be that the boldness and scope of these novels are a response to the ennui, cynicism, and solipsism of the *fin de siècle*, a response all the more violent because their writers felt threatened by these negative attitudes. The great Modernists – Joyce, Lawrence, Conrad, Forster, Hardy, Woolf – have a clear and ordered sense of a past from which they felt permanently separated. Conrad realizes that traditional personal values are threatened by compulsive materialism, often in the guise of politics. For Hardy and Lawrence a pastoral vision of agrarian England is an alternative to present mechanism and utilitarianism. *Jude the Obscure* and *Howards End* (1910) are elegies for this rural civilization. For Joyce, like T. S. Eliot, it is the European cultural tradition that has been debased by the meanness of the present. Joyce, Conrad, Woolf, and Forster long for a tradition of social customs and personal relationships that has become obsolete under the pressure of urbanization and materialism.

Noel Annan has written of the change in England between 1880 and 1910, a change that affected the subject matter of the novel:

> The restraints of religion and thrift and accepted class distinctions started to crumble and English society to rock under the flood of money. The class war, not merely between labour and owners, but between all social strata of the middle and upper classes began in earnest . . . A new bitterness entered politics, a new rancour in foreign relations and a materialism of wealthy snobbery and aggressive philistinism arose far exceeding anything hitherto seen in England.[19]

Although often bourgeois in their impulses and unscathed by these factors, novelists began to write more frequently about class struggle (*Jude the Obscure*), the ethics and effects of imperialism (*Heart of Darkness* and *A Passage to India*), the implications of politics on private lives (*The Secret Agent*), and the corrupting influence of industry and commerce (*Nostromo*).

If we compare *Mrs Dalloway* with the novels of Austen, we see how the sensibilities of Woolf's major characters have been deeply influenced by wars, empire, and commerce (although these play less of a role in the rather anachronistic life of Mrs Dalloway than in the lives of Peter Walsh and Septimus Smith). The lack of community values is enacted in the fragmented form, in the lack of meaningful purpose in politically influential figures (Richard Dalloway, Lady Bruton), and finally in the crystallizing image of Septimus Smith, who, as he walks the streets of London, seems to epitomize the failure of Londoners to discover purpose or coherence in their city. The confrontation of traditional English values with those of other cultures is central to

A Passage to India, Heart of Darkness (1899), and *Women in Love* (especially in the Bohemian and European sections). Yet even as novelists write about different value systems, they explore the importance of those systems for their own lives. They do not, like eighteenth-century novelists, simply measure the strange cultures against established values. The structure becomes a process, a process that mimes the author's quest for values. Thus even in *A Passage to India* – which we think of as an heir to the Victorian novel – the oscillation among Muslim, Hindu, and English and the shifts in the third-person narrator's distance between the personal perspective and the cosmic perspective reflect Forster's search. As Wilfred Stone has written, Forster's novels are "dramatic installments in the story of his struggle for selfhood . . . They tell of a man coming out in the world, painfully emerging from an encysted state of loneliness, fear, and insecurity."[20] The same, I am arguing, could be said of Woolf, Joyce, Lawrence, and Conrad.

Comparing H. G. Wells, Arnold Bennett, and John Galsworthy with their major predecessors, Woolf wrote:

> *Tristram Shandy* or *Pride and Prejudice* is complete in itself; it is self-contained; it leaves one with no desire to do anything, except indeed to read the book again, and to understand it better. The difference perhaps is that both Sterne and Jane Austen were interested in things in themselves; in character in itself; in the book in itself. Therefore everything was inside the book, nothing outside. But the Edwardians were never interested in character in itself; or in the book in itself. They were interested in something outside. Their books, then, were incomplete as books, and required that the reader should finish them, actively and practically, for himself.[21]

But I think the major British and Irish twentieth-century figures under discussion, including Woolf herself, were interested in both "something inside" and "something outside." For these writers no longer accepted the traditional Christian beliefs that divine providence expresses itself in earthly matters or that this life is a necessary prelude to eternity. And the world outside could no longer be limited and contained by authors whose own moral vision was tentative, incomplete, and lacking in conviction. We should not be surprised that the movement of *Nostromo*, *Women in Love*, or *Ulysses* enacts kinds of uneasiness and turbulence that are absent in, say, an Austen novel. Because the writer is striving to discover his or her moral and aesthetic values, this uneasiness and turbulence at times reflect unresolved social issues, characters whose motives the novelist does not understand, and inchoate form.

The social and historical milieu in which an artist writes determines the artistic problems that he or she must solve. Thus Conrad, Lawrence, Joyce, Forster, and Woolf had to discover an appropriate form with which to show (if I may boldly list the striking characteristics of the period) that motives could not be fully understood, that the world was not created and shaped by divine providence, that chance might determine human destiny, that human desires and aspirations were often not likely to be fulfilled, that social institutions were ineffectual, and that materialism and industrialization were destroying the fabric of life. Consequently, these authors invented plots that at times reflect disorder, flux, discontinuity, fragmentations, and disruption without themselves having those qualities; they needed to use the *Odyssey*, *Hamlet*, the Bible, and, in *Ulysses*, even such Jewish legends as "The Last of the Just" to give shape to seemingly random events. They had to invent means not only for rendering the inner life but for showing the unacknowledged private self that played such a large role in shaping behavior. Thus Conrad shows that Jim is the victim of compulsions, obsessions, and fixations that he cannot understand. These writers needed innovative syntax and language to reveal the secret recesses of each psyche and the impact made upon it by experience, especially the kind of ordinary daily experience that was once thought to be insignificant. The unpunctuated, effervescent stream of consciousness of Molly fertilizes the presentation of both Stephen and Bloom by emphasizing – in form and content – fecundity, sexuality, spontaneity, passion, and indifference to history and morality.

IV   The Order of Art Replaces the Order of Life

Let us think for a moment of some major Victorian novels – say *Bleak House* (1853), *Vanity Fair* (1848), or *Middlemarch* (1872). Victorian fiction depends on the mastery of space and time in an unfolding narrative. It seeks to create an imagined world that both mirrors and exaggerates the external world. Its use of an omniscient, ubiquitous narrator implies the pre-eminence of the individual perceiver. Now let us think of *The Secret Agent* (like *Bleak House*, a novel of London), *Ulysses* (like *Vanity Fair*, a satirical examination of relatively recent times), and *The Rainbow* (like *Middlemarch*, a panoramic novel about provincial life). Do not these examples of modern British and Irish fiction undermine the idea that space and time can be mastered by anyone, including the author? Like the subject matter, the setting resists the traditional patterns. The setting itself recoils from idealization, control, and order and expresses the turmoil and anxiety within each author's psyche. (By becoming foreground rather than background, setting plays a similar role in the Post-impressionist works of Van Gogh, Matisse, and Picasso.) The setting – the physical conditions under which the imagined world functions – becomes not only background but a moral labyrinth which the characters are unable to negotiate and which not only shapes their destiny but often subsumes them. Hardy's Wessex, Forster's India, Joyce's Dublin, and Conrad's London are manifestations of an amoral cosmos that pre-empts the characters' moral choices. By forging a web of social circumstances that encloses and limits characters, these settings displace the traditional role of individual will in shaping the lives of characters. Yet even as these settings often become coterminous with destiny and fate, they may also be a symptom or cause of a bankrupt social system, or a metaphor for the narrator's and the characters' own moral confusion.

In the nineteenth-century novel, characters are defined in terms of their moral choices in social situations. In *Vanity Fair* Becky Sharp consciously chooses to seek wealth and status, although we do not watch the processes of her mind; in *Bleak House* Esther Summerson's loyalty, sympathy, and integrity result mostly from conscious decisions. But Woolf, Joyce, Lawrence, Forster, and, quite frequently, Conrad perceive their characters in terms of the honesty and integrity of perceptions rather than in terms of the moral consequences of their behavior. What characters *are* is more important than what they do. The integrity and purity of their souls are standards by which they are primarily judged. *Is-ness* (the quality and intensity of the soul and heart) replaces *does-ness* (the effects of behavior) as the norm for characters. Thus we value Bloom and Mrs Ramsay for their uniqueness rather than their effectiveness. And this corresponds to the shift in emphasis in the art of the novel from traditional effects upon audience to self-dramatizing narrators in search of values and feelings.

The writers we are discussing saw that people no longer lived together bound by common values and social purposes. Each person is his or her own secular sect, and the interaction of these sects creates a social Babel. The order of art becomes a counterbalance to the disorder of life, and the novel mimes a momentary unity in the novelist's mind rather than in the external world. Thus in Woolf and Joyce, a novel's lack of form may nevertheless seem to have a coherence that the subject of the novel lacks because the texture is reflexive and self-referential. Indeed, at times the writers under discussion try to replace, as Malcolm Bradbury puts it, "the linear logic of story, psycholog-ical process, or history" with the "logic of metaphor, form, or symbol."[22] But do we not see that this effort has a compulsive quality, and that Woolf and Joyce are as much committed to transforming their lives into art as to creating a symbolic alternative to realistic fiction?

In *The Form of Victorian Fiction*, J. Hillis Miller remarks that, for Victorian novelists, "the writing of fiction was an indirect way for them to reenter the social world from which they had been excluded or which they were afraid to enter directly."[23] By contrast, the great Modernists wrote fiction to define themselves outside the social world and to confirm their special status as artists. They did not want to re-enter the social world but rather to leave it for islands (actual and imaginary) where life was more honest and true to the promptings of their hearts; these islands were often their novels. They could look at a society from which they felt excluded and criticize its values. Woolf's moments of enlightenment, Joyce's epiphanies, and Lawrence's states of passionate intensity emphasize the individual's life as separate from the community. Novels move not to a comprehensive vision of society but to unity within a character's imagination and perception. In *Heart of Darkness* and *Lord Jim* (1900) Marlow's experience and insight not only are his own, but leave him, like the Ancient Mariner, separate from his fellows. If in Victorian fiction the narrator is, as in *Our Mutual Friend* (1865) or *Vanity Fair*, a detached outsider observing characters who often function successfully within the community, in modern British and Irish fiction, such as *Ulysses* and *Women in Love*, the narrator and the protagonists are both separate from the community, and the community itself is corrupt and morally bankrupt. Woolf saw the problem. On the one hand, she knew that her novels give credence to various kinds of personal Crusoeism and raise the hope of solutions separate from the traditional community. But, on the other hand, she also understood the dangers of her fiction becoming self-indulgent and narcissistic: "I suppose the danger is the damned egotistical self . . . Is one pliant and rich enough to provide a wall for the book from oneself without its becoming . . . narrowing and restricting?"[24]

In *To the Lighthouse* the completion of Lily Briscoe's painting might serve as a metaphor for the hermetic nature of one strand of Modernism. She has her vision and completes her painting, but she turns her back on the opportunity for community in the form of marriage to Mr Ramsay. Her art is at the expense of social life:

> Here she was again, she thought, stepping back to look at it, drawn out of gossip, out of living, out of community with people into the presence of this formidable ancient enemy of hers – this other thing, this truth, this reality, which suddenly laid hands on her, emerged stark at the back of appearance and commanded her attention.[25]

And Mrs Ramsay's victories are more aesthetic than moral; thinking of Mrs Ramsay, Lily realizes that her friend "[makes] of the moment something permanent (as in another sphere Lily herself tried to make of the moment something permanent) – this was of the nature of revelation. In the midst of chaos there was shape: this eternal passing and flowing (she looked at the clouds going and the leaves shaking) was struck into stability."[26] Life *struck into stability* is what happens when pattern is imposed on life by art, but it is also a foreshadowing of death. Lily is a version of her creator, and her struggle with her painting mimes that of her author with the subject. We realize that Woolf's quest for values in the "eternal passing and flowing" continues through the novel.

V   Conclusion

Let us conclude with some final observations about Modernism's focus on the consciousness of both the creator and his or her subjects. Even novels with an epic scope – *Ulysses, Nostromo, The Rainbow* – discover meaning in the isolated perceiving consciousness of such characters as Bloom, Mrs Gould, and Ursula. Although these novels present an anatomy of social problems in the tradition of *Tom Jones* and *Bleak House*, they do not propose political and social solutions but personal ones – family ties (*Nostromo*); passion (*The Rainbow* and *Women in Love*); kindness, tolerance, and affection (*Ulysses*). Indeed, we should understand that the epic and romance strands in Conrad, Lawrence, Joyce, and Forster are part of the search for values of desperate men who seek to find in older traditions a continuity that evades the confusions of modern life. There is a reflexive quality in *Nostromo, Ulysses,* and *The Rainbow*, a self-consciousness, a personal urgency, lacking in the eighteenth- and nineteenth-century novel. In *Nostromo* we sense Conrad's awareness that he has very little to offer as an alternative to social and political chaos, an awareness that derives from his feeling that all social systems are "hollow at the core." As he searches for values in Costaguana, he proposes every major figure as heroic and every political program as redemptive only to undermine them systematically and finally to discard them. Furthermore, in *Nostromo* and *Lord Jim* he charts the failure of modern humanity both by the realistic standards of the nineteenth century and by the older standards of romance, epic, and legend. At the very center of *Lord Jim*, Conrad proposes Stein as an oracular figure before finally revealing him as uncertain and far from articulate in the gloom created by descending night. *Ulysses* and *The Rainbow*, in their reliance on Homer and the Bible for shape and significance, express their authors' nostalgia and enthusiasm for the simpler shapes of human experience and the narratives that rendered that experience. Perhaps this nostalgic enthusiasm is a reaction to the authors' own rather unheroic lives, which were punctuated by disappointment and frustration. What they sought was to retrieve their own feelings and attitudes, but, more than that, to convince themselves and their audiences that their feelings and attitudes typified those of others and had the kind of universality which realism had provided for the Victorians. To be sure, Joyce and Lawrence understood the need to invent a syntax and diction to render the flux of perceptual and sensory experience, the life of the subconscious, and the impulses of the unconscious life. But that experience, that life, and those impulses were also their own. When we respond to the presence of the author, when we feel his or her urgent pulsation within the novel, the focus of fiction is no more "narrow and restricting" than that of any other kind of mimesis.

The 1980 Picasso exhibition at the Museum of Modern Art made it clear that, as Hilton Kramer puts it, "any criticism that refuses to acknowledge the esthetic reality of this autobiographical element in Picasso is doomed to be incomplete."[27] What distinguishes the movement in modern painting and sculpture from Impressionism onward through abstract expressionism, including Postimpressionism, Cubism, and Fauvism, is its expressionist quality, its insistence on the validity of what the artist sees and feels, and this movement has its parallel in literature. The pressures of society had driven the artist from the world to the word. In painting, as the Picasso exhibition reminded us, the shift toward the more abstract, the spatial, and the chromatic was not so much a movement to objectivity as research into the possibilities of art's subjects, forms, and effects in response to different conditions of life. Could we have *Guernica* without the enormity of modern warfare? Similarly, modern fiction's innovations are an effort to breathe new life into a world that seemed to have become inert and superfluous. Or, as Woolf puts it:

> The idea has come to me that what I want now to do is to saturate every atom. I mean to eliminate all waste, deadness, superfluity: to give the moment whole; whatever it includes. Say that the moment is a combination of thought; sensation; the voice of the sea. Waste, deadness, come from the inclusion of things that don't belong to the moment; this appalling narrative business of the realist: getting on from lunch to dinner: it is false, unreal, merely conventional. Why admit anything to literature that is not poetry – by which I mean saturated?[28]

In "An Ordinary Evening in New Haven" (1949) Stevens (another great Modernist who made his life the subject of his art) writes of the relationship between the artist and his art in terms that I have been describing:

> The poem is the cry of its occasion,
> Part of the res itself and not about it.
> The poet speaks the poem as it is,
> Not as it was . . .
>
> . . . He speaks
> By sight and insight as they are. There is no
> Tomorrow for him . . .
>
> In the end, in the whole psychology, the self
> The town, the weather, in a casual litter,
> Together, said words of the world are the life of the world.[29]

The great British and Irish Modernists, I think, have also said in their fiction that their words are their life; as Lawrence puts it, "I must write to live." We respond to those words and the presence behind them because their words are also the life of *our* world.[30] They have transformed the novel from a realistic social document into a "cry of its occasion" and affirmed that the act of telling is their paramount concern as artists.

Chapter 2

Hardy's *Jude the Obscure*: The Beginnings of the Modern Psychological Novel

By 1895, the year of the publication of Thomas Hardy's last novel, *Jude the Obscure*, he felt like Matthew Arnold in "Stanzas from the Grande Chartreuse," "Wandering between two worlds, one dead, / The other powerless to be born." Hardy had written a series of novels – including *Far from the Madding Crowd* (1874), *The Return of the Native* (1878), *The Mayor of Casterbridge* (1886), and *The Woodlanders* (1887) – that had brought him fame as well as, in the case of *Tess of the d'Urbervilles* (1891), considerable criticism. Providing a fictional history of Dorset, he created an imaginary world which he called Wessex and traced how social and economic forces and the intellectual crosswinds of the nineteenth century affected rural culture. In *Tess of the d'Urbervilles*, and even more so in *Jude the Obscure*, humans are restless, isolated, and frustrated as they lose their physical and moral roots. One of the impressions that remains with readers is of Tess and Jude walking aimlessly through Wessex country, even while they believe they have embarked on a significant journey.

Hardy is the first English novelist who wholeheartedly rejects the conventional Christian myth of a benevolent universe. Within his imagined world, he shows the irrelevance of that myth and shows how his characters are educated by their experience to adopt an alternative perspective. Hardy creates a malevolent world in which characters live not in light which is good, but in moral darkness which is bad. In an 1890 journal entry, he writes, "I have been looking for God for 50 years, and I think if he had existed I should have discovered him. As an external personality, of course – the only true meaning of the world."[1] Hardy's creation of a blighted star is his response to the premise that God's creation is a holy plan. When Hardy uses that phrase in the third chapter of *Tess of the d'Urbervilles*, he is specifically responding to Wordsworth, who, in line 22 of "Lines Written in Early Spring," speaks of "Nature's holy plan."[2] In Hardy's world, things turn out badly. A combination of what he calls in "Hap," "crass casualty" or fate, social forms (marriage laws, economic inequality), and human behavior (obsessions, fixations, dimly acknowledged needs) undermines human aspirations. Hardy is also responding to those Romantics and Victorians who, as M. H. Abrams has remarked, fuse "history, politics, and philosophy, and religion into one grand design by asserting Providence – or some form of natural teleology – to operate in the seeming chaos of human history so as to effect from present evil a greater good."[3] Hardy's novels collectively are in part a response to the biblical myth of benevolent creation directed by a just and beneficent God. We need think of Hardy not only as a Victorian realist, but also in the tradition of Blake, Lawrence, and Faulkner – other great mythologizers who create their own world complete with its own rules and traditions. Hardy presents a detailed and realistic depiction of Wessex, but places it within a dark framework that questions the central postulates of Christian cosmology, namely that humans can achieve personal salvation under the auspices of a just and merciful God thanks to the intervention of his martyred son, Jesus Christ. After *Far from the Madding Crowd*, Hardy's prophecy of disaster radically contrasts with the biblical prophecy of the Second Coming of the Messiah. Fulfillment in the biblical myth depends upon the release of the eternal soul at death, the intervention of Christ, his return to earth, and the Last Judgment. While Hardy liked to think of himself as meliorist, he creates a grim cosmos where death is nullification of life, where moral improvement is rare and ineffectual, and spiritual life is a fiction.

If, as we shall argue, *The Rainbow* is Lawrence's Bible, Hardy's vision in his Wessex novels is of a Bible manqué. Like Kafka and Lawrence, Hardy intensifies some aspects of his imagined world and distorts others to such an extent that he presents an alternative cosmology with its own mode of operation. His cosmos is not organized in a benevolent pattern, moving toward fulfillment of a divine plan in which the Apocalypse will bring the heavenly kingdom to deserving souls, but is, to use Conrad's term, a "remorseless process."[4] Beginnings and endings rhyme in Hardy's plan, but in a way which often makes it seem as if humans were the butt of a cosmic joke. The human condition is inseparable from the process which shapes that condition; neither social forces nor a hypothetical moral or spiritual revolution will enable humans to affect that process, or their position within it.

In Hardy's later novels, the human psyche becomes the principal means through which the malevolent process works. Increasingly, Hardy exposes the folly of thinking that rational decisions and conscious motives direct human behavior, and writes about psychic needs, compulsions, and obsessions, although not with the Freudian vocabulary we now employ. Anticipating Lawrence, Hardy stresses how unconscious, often libidinous needs direct human behavior, particularly psychosexual life. Anticipating Conrad, he understands that an atavistic self lurks within each of us. While he prepares the way for Conrad and Lawrence, he also marks a turning away from the traditional resolution of Victorian novels. Not only in literary history but in Hardy's career, what we call the beginning is often the end. For once Hardy completed the groundwork for the modern British novel, he abandoned fiction altogether.

In many ways, but especially in the complexity of its psychology, *Jude the Obscure* is the first modern English novel. Hardy realizes that social laws and conventions are not necessarily part of progress and rejects the post-Darwinian view that England is evolving into a higher form of social organization. He understands how reactionary marriage laws, the exclusion from universities of women as well as those who are not born to social privilege, and the generic treatment of women are symptoms of a dysfunctional social system. For example, when Sue disappears from the training school, the matron is horrified not so much because Sue may have drowned as because she would cause a scandal at the college.

As the word "obscure" in the title indicates, Hardy realizes that our psyche is not controlled by rational decisions and he understands that we are often obscure to ourselves. Hardy understands that we don't have coherent selves. He is a Modernist in his awareness of how sexual problems can divide a couple. His pervasive gloom anticipates the dark angst of Conrad and Kafka. That gloom derives in part from a rejection of the Romantic view of nature and from an awareness that human instincts are not necessarily benign and, in the form of sexual urges, can get humans into trouble. Hardy is a Modernist in his use of the theme of the double; when humans don't have a vertical dimension descending from God, they tend to apotheosize one another – as Sue and (especially) Jude do to one another – only to have that idealized view inevitably disconfirmed by subsequent perceptions.

Hardy's open form – his refusal to resolve issues in a characteristic happy ending – anticipates the ambiguous endings of twentieth-century fiction. He is a Modernist in his use of illuminating distortion. He often deliberately undermines traditional realism with exaggeration, hyperbole, symbolic moments, and even allegorical figures. Finally, he transforms the omniscient narrator into a complex figure – alternately a spokesman, a harsh critic, an apologist for his protagonist as well as a mythologizer, a social historian, and a gloomy prophet. Responding to the rich polyphonic voice in its various and often contradictory roles becomes part of our reading experience.

Hardy is not a deft stylist savoring every word within a crafted prose that approaches the density of poetry in the tradition of James, Conrad, Joyce, and

Woolf. Often at his best as a story teller, his unit is a set of paragraphs comprising a crystallizing anecdote rather than a sentence. He retains vestiges of the traditional Victorian novel in his omniscient voice, characterization, and structure, even while making new departures in psychology, voice, and form. If, on the first reading of a Hardy novel, the reader has a sense that he or she has anticipated and almost experienced actions that occur for the first time, that is because Hardy has created an imagined world where actions seem inevitable. Hardy's prophetic (and proleptic) openings, in which every detail seems to foreshadow major themes, in conjunction with conclusions that confirm these openings, are in large part responsible for this sense of inevitability. The openings take us into a world where, because external circumstances connive with hidden flaws, human aspirations are blunted, and well-meaning protagonists rapidly discover that things will most likely turn out badly.

By "fulfilling" the promise of the beginnings, the endings imply that the world in which humans live is closed and almost invulnerable to essential change. That the title of the last phase of *Tess of the d'Urbervilles* is "Fulfillment" implies something important about Hardy's world view and aesthetic. By fulfillment, Hardy means the inevitable bringing to fruition of the pattern that derives from the interaction of the central character's psyche with the world in which he or she is placed. After *Far from the Madding Crowd*, when the reader reaches the ending of a Hardy novel, it is as if a prophecy has been fulfilled. Hardy's endings perpetuate conditions that have prevailed before the narrator has begun his telling and will prevail after the narrative is finished.

The narrative voice is crucial to our understanding of *Jude the Obscure*. As Ian Gregor has remarked,

> Both Hardy and Lawrence have produced a fiction in which the presence of the author is an important element in our experience, but it is not a presence like that, say, of Fielding or George Eliot, where we feel the author filtering the book through to us, but rather where the author is participant, undergoing the experience of the book with the characters.[5]

While I am not sure whether any narrator is ever a mere filter, completely devoid of the author's personal urgency, certainly in Hardy and Lawrence we are acutely aware of the personal engagement of the author in the narrator and of the narrator's empathetic involvement in the psychic and moral life of major characters. Hardy's self-dramatizing narrator is a skeptical, gloomy, fatalistic presence, defined by his pessimistic philosophy and bitterly ironic stories of human failure and human foible, as well as gloomy "forebodings" of "ominous" – to cite recurring phrases – events with dire consequences and grim mediations as the events unfold. Characteristically, observing how Sue and Phillotson behave after introducing them, the narrator remarks: "The ironical clinch to his sorrow was given by the thought that the intimacy between his cousin and the schoolmaster had been brought about entirely by himself" (II.v.89).[6]

Hardy's narrator stresses Jude's history as a representative late nineteenth-century drama of a man's abortive attempt to improve his socioeconomic position in a world resistant to such aspirations. Thus while Jude, upon arriving in Christminster (Hardy's version of Oxford), is lost in dreams of a fulfilling future, the narrator emphasizes how the present is ineluctably weaving a pattern that makes this imagined future impossible. Commenting on Jude's satisfaction at finally having contact with the students at Christminster, the narrator bitterly recalls:

> Yet he was as far from them as if he had been at the antipodes. Of course he was. He was a young workman in a white blouse, and with stone-dust in the creases of his clothes; and in passing him they did not even see him, or hear him, rather saw through him as though a pane of glass at their familiars beyond. Whatever they were to him, he to them was not on the spot at all; and yet he had fancied he would be close to their lives by coming there. (II.ii.70)

To those persons whose fellowship Jude desperately seeks, he is, as a stone-mason in dusty working clothes, transparent, a non-person to the students. He has cast into stone the word "THITHER" to define his aspiration to reach Christminster, but to the reader the word defines his destination: death.

The focus of the narrator's consciousness is the emotional and psychological responses of Jude, although he does try to understand what he – like Jude – finds as the baffling complexity of Sue Bridehead. That the narrator's early comments are heavily weighted with foreknowledge of Jude's destiny gives the plot a sense of inevitability. The narrator's emotional and intellectual attitudes are approximately those that Jude would have held had he survived to tell the story, although the narrator's knowledge of how the world works is more worldly, more cynical, and more dismal.

Rereading *Jude*, we see aspects of a dark fairy tale. Arabella's last name, "Donn," emphasizes the finality of their moments of sexual play; Jude's last name of "Fawley" emphasizes how her seduction puts him on an inevitable downward path from which he never escapes. Sue Bridehead's surname combines maidenhead, to emphasize her frigidity, with her resistance to conventional marriage or even cohabitation. To a first-time reader, the narrator's gloom and bitterness in the first chapters may seem disproportionate to the events described. But that is because Jude's completed life dominates the narrator's consciousness. Unlike Hardy's prior narrators, he has neither the mood nor the inclination for nostalgic views of former cultures, pastoral settings, and anecdotes about rural folk.

The first four chapters of *Jude the Obscure* are among the great openings in the English novel. In these chapters Hardy dramatizes a young boy's discovery of the moral and physical geography of the amoral, indifferent, if not hostile cosmos. Hardy's purpose is to show that Jude's experience is universal rather than particular to him. He educates the reader to see that the world in which Jude and Sue live does not permit positive fulfillment. While hopes, dreams, and emotional needs are not fulfilled, what is fulfilled is every character's foreboding of evil.

Implicit in the attitudes of the narrative voice is that life is barely better than the nullification of life; if death is not to be actively sought, it can be accepted with equanimity in a world hostile to human aspirations. The narrator's comments on Jude's "weakness" of not being able to "bear to hurt anything" are bitterly ironic: "This weakness of character, as it may be called, suggested that he was the sort of man who was born to ache a good deal before the fall of the curtain upon his unnecessary life should signify that all was well with him again" (I.ii.15). When, as a boy, Jude is punished for failing to chase birds out of Farmer Troutham's field and reflects on his boyhood disgrace, he momentarily adopts the narrator's mature perspective:

> Events did not rhyme quite as he thought. Nature's logic was too horrid for him to care for. That mercy towards one set of creatures was cruelty towards another sickened his sense of harmony. As you got older, and felt yourself to be at the center of your time, and not at a point in its circumference, as you had felt when you were little, you were seized with a sort of shuddering, he perceived. All around you there seemed to be something glaring, garish, rattling, and the noises and glares hit upon the little cells called your life, and shook it, and warped it. (I.ii.17)

The shift to the second person in the above passage conflates Jude's and the narrator's voices and thus implies that the view of life as a hostile force, a mechanistic juggernaut attacking the vitality of a helpless cell, is the mature narrator's as well as young Jude's. We hear a resonance of the late nineteenth- and early twentieth-century debate between mechanists and vitalists, between life as something that can be understood as a mechanical process and life as something derived mysteriously from God's will. Reluctantly perhaps, Hardy sides with the former.

In the above passage, Jude, in a moment of rare insight, has prematurely discovered the capriciousness of nature's logic. His melancholy is no mere childish moment, but encapsulates the narrator's mature wisdom, which shapes the entire telling and to which the latter had presumably been brought by adult experience. Jude seems to have prematurely reached an end. He anticipates not only his final death wish, but the vision that caused Father Time to end his own life and that of his siblings. Yet, finally, the biological, physiological self beneath Jude's gloomy consciousness recoils from this insight: "Then, like the natural boy, he forgot his despondency, and sprang up" (I.ii.17). The boy's initial response is validated as Jude's aspirations are continually blunted by a combination of his psychic needs, a hostile social and economic structure, and the remorseless cosmology in which things inevitably turn out badly. While Jude's dreams are filled with scholarship and religion, his instincts respond to the tawdry sensuality of Arabella and his psyche to the sadomasochism of Sue.

Phillotson, Jude's first teacher at Marygreen, who himself sets out for Christminster with great hopes, is as much Jude's double as Sue is. Phillotson anticipates Jude in the way he ambitiously formulates imprecise and ephemeral plans which he has little hope of fulfilling. Phillotson is a prototype of Jude as a hopeful, aspiring man trying to improve himself, who, when faced with unanticipated difficulty in mastering a hoped-for skill – such as playing a piano or getting an education – subsequently becomes disillusioned. He shares not only Jude's enthusiasm for learning, but also his inconsistency and masochism. Jude regards him as a paradigm; when he meets Phillotson in Christminster, he tells his former schoolmaster that the latter's aspirations "to be a university man and enter the Church" (II.iv.83) had been an inspiration to him.

In the first chapter Phillotson is leaving Marygreen, as Jude will some years later, for the purpose of getting a university education so he can be ordained. When Jude subsequently fictionalizes Christminster as the new Jerusalem, it is in part because the one person who treats him like a human being has gone there. A lonely and isolated orphan, his efforts to recreate Phillotson as a father-figure reflect his isolation and loneliness. But, anticipating Jude, Phillotson cannot fulfill his dreams and remains essentially the man he was in Marygreen.

Jude the Obscure is something of a "road" tale, a picaresque story manqué about a man's futile movement from place to place in a quest for fulfillment. One correlative to Jude's desire to be upwardly mobile in status is his bent for travel. Hardy's novels show that one may move from place to place, but one never leaves oneself behind. They debunk the Protestant myth of self-improvement that pervades English fiction from Defoe onwards. Hardy's endings confirm rather than transfigure what precedes and reject the notion that experience brings wisdom and maturity. Within a Hardy novel, linear physical movement with a purpose – whether it be Clym's movement to Paris in *Return of the Native*, Tess's search for her relatives, or Jude's first journey to Christminster and his subsequent movements through Wessex – is ironic. Indeed the linear movement of Hardy's narratives – whether from episode to episode or even from the beginning to the end – confirms that the characters are rarely changed by their experience.

In *Jude the Obscure*, Hardy does not restrict himself to traditional realism. Indeed, one aspect of Modernism not only in literature – Kafka, Mann, James, Faulkner, Joyce – but in painting – Picasso, Matisse, Miro – is to introduce aspects of fantasy and fable into otherwise realistic narratives as if to call attention to the fictionality of the art. An allegorical character, Father Time is not only an objectification of Jude's present superego as well as of his earlier despondent understanding of what life offers, but an extension, or at least a reductive version, of the narrator's own attitudes. Like Father Time, the narrator is the victim of his own insight and hyper-acuity and, most of all, of the morbid patterns of human life that his mind contains. To the narrator, the son of Jude and Arabella – the sensuous yet insidious woman who has entrapped him and seeks to divert him from his aspirations – is an abstraction, a symbolic figure. The narrator wishes to convince the reader that Father Time is a representative of a new generation that is developing as humanity progresses to greater consciousness of its plight, and as human vitality seems to be increasingly threatened by industrialism and other forms of modern life.

The narrator ascribes to Father Time a vision that approximates his own: "A ground swell from ancient years of night seemed now and then to lift the child in this morning-life, when his face took a back view over some great Atlantic of Time, and appeared not to care about what it saw" (V.iii.217). Using Father Time as a symbol – a rhetorical, illuminating distortion – to reinforce his perspective, the narrator imputes the omniscience to Father Time that he claims for himself, and implies that Father Time has the ability to hold the entire pattern of the past within his mind as a shaping aspect of his perception of the present. The narrator is empathetic to the awesome burden that the child's insight places upon him: "He then seemed to be doubly awake, like an enslaved and dwarfed Divinity, sitting passive and regarding his companions as if he saw their whole rounded lives rather than their immediate figures" (V.iii.217). Aware of how the curse of knowledge separates himself and the child from those who do not fully understand the desperate plight of humankind, and particularly those condemned by social circumstances to poverty, the narrator is empathetically aware of how Father Time's perspicuity corrupts his chances for happiness:

It could have been seen that the boy's ideas of life were different from those of the local boys. Children begin with detail, and learn up to the general; they begin with the contiguous, and gradually comprehend the universal. The boy seemed to have begun with the generals of life, and never to have concerned himself with the particulars. To him the houses, the willows, the obscure fields beyond, were apparently regarded not as brick residences, pollards, meadows, but as human dwellings in the abstract, vegetation, and the wide dark world. (V.iii.218)

Father Time has the vision of doom that Jude was able to partially reject when as a young boy he was chastised by Farmer Troutham, but his instinctive renunciation of life anticipates Jude's final echo of Job: "*Let the day perish wherein I was born, and the night in which it was said, There is a man child conceived*" (VI.xi.318). The narrator presents Father Time as a pathetic victim, the grotesque result of social law and human frailty:

On that little shape converged all the inauspiciousness and shadow which had darkened the first union of Jude, and all the accidents, mistakes, fears, errors of the last. He was their nodal point, their focus, their expression in a single term. For the rashness of those parents he had groaned, for their ill-assortment he had quaked, and for the misfortunes of these he had died. (VI.ii.265)

In terms of the novel's form, Hardy creates Father Time as the symbol of the narrator's – and Jude's – morbid wisdom that death alone can make things well for an "unnecessary life."

Let us consider Sue Bridehead. If Arabella represents the sensual side of Jude's divided self, Sue represents his intellectual and spiritual side. In the postscript to the 1912 edition, Hardy does not reject the view of a critic that Sue is an example of "the woman of the feminist movement – the slight, pale, 'bachelor' girl – the intellectualized, emancipated bundle of nerves that modern conditions were producing, mainly in cities as yet" (p. 8). She is related to the so-called New Woman, who is critical of marriage as economically and sexually degrading (with males holding unlimited conjugal privileges) and favors a free monogamous union of committed equals. To Jude, she is an oddity, a woman who in his view speaks in a "philosophical" way, but whose sexuality is a puzzle (III.iv.117). After recounting how she broke a former suitor's heart and how she is still a virgin, she tells Jude, "People say I must be cold-natured – sexless – on account of it. But I won't have it! Some of the most passionately erotic poets have been the most self-contained in their daily lives" (III.iv.119). We sometimes feel that Sue, as in the above speech, causes Jude great grief by over-talking every aspect of her feelings, in part because we respond to Sue as a function of Jude's and the narrator's perspectives; after the above speech, the narrator, barely containing his own anger and frustration, remarks: "He felt that she was treating him cruelly, though he could not quite say in what way" (III.iv.118).

Because Hardy's narrator has great difficulty understanding this character – a character based in part on Hardy's cousin Tryphena Sparks, with whom he once had an unsatisfactory intimate relationship, and in part on Florence Henniker, a woman who captivated him in the 1890s – it is hardly surprising that she is an elusive figure for readers. On one hand, we see her as a victim of social codes that prevent women from realizing their potential and impose marriage expectations without allowing for convenient divorces if the convention of marriage does not work. But on the other, she is an emotional sadomasochist whose peculiar nature causes great harm to her cousin and sometime lover Jude. There is a schism between the sophistication of her feminist views and the density of her feelings. Knowing Jude loves her, Sue asks him to give her away to another man since Jude, as she writes him, is "the only married relation" whom she has (III.vii.136).

On the occasion when she walks Jude down the aisle of the very church where she will marry Phillotson that very day, the narrator justifiably and bitterly calls her "an epicure of emotions" (III.vii.138). Empathetic to Jude, the narrator – as if he were outraged and stunned – recounts Sue's perverse behavior as she leads him to the church: "By the irony of fate, and the curious trick in Sue's nature of tempting Providence at critical times, she took his arm as they walked through the muddy street – a thing she had never done before in her life – and on turning the corner they found themselves close to a grey Perpendicular church – the church of St Thomas" (III.vii.137). As they enter, the narrator stresses not merely Sue's ambivalence but an insouciant emotional immaturity that inflicts great harm: "Sue still held Jude's arm, almost as if she loved him. Cruelly sweet, indeed, she had been to him that morning" (III.vii.138).

Isn't Sue actually acting out her anger for what she believes is Jude's inaccessibility, since he is not divorced from the marriage partner of his foolish youthful sensuality? A Dostoyevskian character, a doppelganger whose every word has the effect of resonating within Jude's own tortured psyche, Sue plays mercilessly upon his feelings as if she were punishing him for being married to Arabella and degrading him for it: "My curiosity to hunt up new sensations always leads me into these scrapes. Forgive me! . . . You will, won't you, Jude?" (III.vii.138). Sue, the reader understands, is immersed in her narcissism. Contemplating giving her away during the service, and shaped by the preceding scene, Jude first seeks refuge in generalization, before he adopts the narrator's outrage in a way that anticipates his later cynicism:

> Women were different from men in such matters. Was it that they were, instead of more sensitive, as reputed, more callous and less romantic or were they more heroic? Or was Sue simply so perverse that she wilfully gave herself and him pain for the odd and mournful luxury of practising long-suffering in her own person, and of being touched with tender pity for him at having made him practise it? . . . Possibly she would go on inflicting such pains again and again, and grieving for the sufferer again and again in all her colossal inconsistency. (III.vii.139–140)

Phillotson, of course, is also continually punished by her behavior; after she has taken Jude to church and then meets Phillotson, her betrothed, she exclaims to the latter: "We have been doing such a funny thing! . . . We've been to the church, rehearsing as it were" (III.vii.138). As if to stress Sue's savoring every peculiarity of her eccentric behavior, the narrator adds that she "requested her lover [Jude] not to be a long time" before "she departed with the schoolmaster" (III.vii.139).

Put another way and using a distinction that Elizabeth Langland has borrowed from Bakhtin, Sue "embodies the internally persuasive voice," while Jude clings to "authoritative discourse," that is, he often responds to situations in terms of social codes.[7] Thus, according to Langland, "Jude's susceptibility to the chivalric code of helpless women and protective and honorable men allows Arabella to use her claims of pregnancy to trap him into marriage."[8]

Later Sue leaves Phillotson for Jude – thanks in part to Phillotson's generosity, for which she not only expresses gratitude in her usual over-verbal and ambivalent way but repeats those feelings to Jude upon her arrival in Melchester: "I never was so near being in love with him as when he made such thoughtful arrangements for my being comfortable on my journey, and offering to provide money. Yet I was not. If I loved him ever so little as a wife, I'd go back to him even now" (IV.v.190). That she is reluctant to commit to a sexual relationship deeply disturbs Jude. She seems affected by Phillotson's generosity but also by her own psychological reluctance to let go, and she finds refuge in elaborate explanations and her own rigid perspective: "I quite realized that, as a woman with man, it was a risk to come. But as *me* with *you*, I resolved to trust you to set my wishes above your gratification. Don't discuss it further, dear Jude!" (IV.v.190). As resistant readers, we see that Sue is desperate for control, invents her own version of conventions, and is afraid of sensuality and passion. Jude is becoming more perspicacious: "I have some-time thought, since your marrying Phillotson because of a stupid scandal, that under the affectation of independent views you are as enslaved to the social code as any woman I know" (IV.v.191). And she does not deny this, but admits to her own narcissism in leading on Phillotson, even while we under-stand that what she says is also applicable to her relationship to Jude: "But sometimes a woman's *love of being loved* gets the better of her conscience, and though she is agonized at the thought of treating a man cruelly, she encourages him to love her while she doesn't love him at all" (IV.v.191).

While Jude may not see how much Sue is jealous of his having spent a night with Arabella recently, and perhaps fears being measured against a woman with whose sexuality she compares herself unfavorably, he realizes that while she articulates rebellion against convention, she is the slave of convention. Although he lacks a Modernist vocabulary, he intuitively feels the schism between the passionate values she articulates and the tepid and evanescent woman who has come to him and has forbidden that he have sex with her: "It is more than this earthly wretch called Me deserves – you spirit, you dis-embodied creature, you poor, dear, sweet tantalizing phantom – hardly flesh at all; so that when I put my arms around you I almost expect them to pass through you as through air!" (IV.v.194). Yet part of her appeal to him is that she is not Arabella; she is talkative, ratiocinative, intelligent, and he can idealize her as his secret sharer. Indeed, one pattern of the novel is his mythi-cizing her as a soulmate, even while the reader – and often the narrator – can see that she is quite different. Indeed, after she escapes from the training school and comes to his flat, and finally falls asleep, "[H]e stood with his back to the fire regarding her, and saw in her almost a divinity" (III.iii.116). And she does the same with him, in part because, like him, she lacks not only a supportive family but same-sex friendships.

With a sexual woman's intuition, Arabella says to Cartlett, whom she has married in Australia: "I am inclined to think that she don't care for him quite so much as he does for her" (V.v.230). Yet the narrator is at times reluctant to focus on the dysfunctionality of Sue and Jude's relationship as when, a few paragraphs before Arabella's above comment, he remarks: "That complete mutual understanding, in which every glance and movement was as effectual as speech for conveying intelligence between them, made them almost the two parts of a single whole" (V.v.229). While Hardy is puzzled by Sue's behavior, he does understand that, while Jude often looks to authority for standards of behavior, Sue follows her own lights. As Langland puts it, "Jude's return to Christminster spells a rejection of Sue and an embrace of the patriarchal discourse that originally attracted him . . . By returning to Christminster, Jude privileges a hierarchic order in opposition to his more egalitarian relationship with Sue."[9]

Hardy turned away from the traditional, benevolent resolution of the English novel from *Tom Jones* and *Emma* to *Bleak House*, where marriage often takes the reader to a comfortable stopping point. Hardy is questioning the institution of marriage at a time when marriage and divorce were foregrounded topics in England, in part due to Parnell's adultery with the wife of Captain O'Shea and the production of Ibsen's plays, but also due to elaborate discussions of marriage in the *Fortnightly Review*. Remarriage and death become synonymous for Sue and Jude when they each remarry their former partners, she Phillotson and he Arabella. That Jude remarries Arabella in an alcoholic stupor shows that he has not grown sufficiently to avoid compulsively repeating the past. While his intellectual positions remain enlightened and reflect what he has learned, his character and behavior do not reflect personal growth. Whether he was intoxicated or not, his remarrying Arabella is a manifestation of his own propensity for self-destructive and masochistic behavior and is hardly less pathological than Sue's conduct. He cannot leave Arabella because he has lost the will to live. Jude intuitively understands the parallelism of his and Sue's fate and the mutual disintegration of their mental and moral energy. Widow Edlin's remark, "Weddings be funerals," applies to both of them (VI.ix.314). Fanatically and obsessively, they both embrace their own destruction. Jude's quoting Job (who unlike Jude eventually rallied from despair) is a symptom of ineffectual self-pity. His willingness to die and his abandonment of living by his principles are the poignant fulfillment of "nature's logic."

The novel's iterative structure – the remarriages, the return to Marygreen, the final interview between Gillingham and Phillotson, and the presence of the charlatan Vilbert at the end – mimes the inability of humans to improve their socioeconomic condition or to change their destiny or psyche. Jude and Sue reiterate the perverse errors of the past in their remarriages to those who are completely wrong for them. These remarriages underline the progressive diminution of human stature in Hardy's novels. Arabella's and Vilbert's survival, while better people are driven to neurotic and compulsive remarriage, madness, and death, reinforces our impression of human devolution. Perhaps Hardy stopped writing novels because of his frustration with trying to find an equilibrium between men and women.[10]

Returning to Arnold, with whom I began this chapter, we realize that he found solace in myths created from the cultural tradition in which he believed; one thinks of the Scholar Gypsy, Thyrsis, Wordsworth, and Goethe, all functioning as sustaining images within his poetry. But, unlike Arnold, Hardy could no longer find objective correlatives to dramatize the process of discovering values. In formal terms, after struggling with transforming his most autobiographical hero, Jude, into a representative victim of social and cosmological forces, and often finding that both Sue and Jude are quirky and idiosyncratic figures who defy generalization, Hardy turned to allegory in the form of Father Time and in doing so parted company with the realistic novel. And if that was not reason enough to give his full attention to poetry, perhaps another clue is in Father Time's fate, a fate which embodies Hardy's excruciating pain caused by his burden of knowledge and perspicacity.

Chapter 3

Conrad's *Heart of Darkness*: "We Live, as We Dream – Alone"

I Beginnings

Conrad's first two novels, *Almayer's Folly* (1895) and *An Outcast of the Islands* (1896), reflect his state of mind and reveal his values. In these early novels, narrated by a conventional omniscient narrator, Conrad (1857–1924) tests and refines themes and techniques that he will use in his subsequent fiction. In a way that will become characteristic of Conrad's early works, he uses fictional material from his own adventures as his source material. He not only draws upon his experience when he sailed as mate with the *Vidar* (1887–8), but bases the title character of his first novel on a man he actually knew. While these two novels seem to be about remote events, they actually dramatize his central concerns.

Sambir, the setting for *Almayer's Folly* and *An Outcast of the Islands*, is the first of Conrad's distorted and intensified settings. Like the Congo in *Heart of Darkness* (1899) and Patusan in *Lord Jim*, Sambir becomes a metaphor for actions that occur there. It is also a projection of Conrad's state of mind as it appears in his letters of 1894 through 1896: exhaustion and ennui alternate with spasmodic energy. Conrad's narrator is in the process of creating a myth out of Sambir, but the process is never quite completed. Like Hardy's Egdon Heath, Sambir is an inchoate form that can be controlled neither by physical endeavors nor by the imagination. The demonic energy that seethes within the forests is a catalyst for the perverse sexuality of the novel's white people and their subsequent moral deterioration. With its "mud soft and black, hiding fever, rottenness, and evil under its level and glazed surface," Sambir refutes the romantic myth that beyond civilization lie idyllic cultures in a state

51

of innocence. Sambir's river, the Pantai, is a prototype for the Congo; the atavistic influence it casts upon white men, drawing out long-repressed and atrophied libidinous energies, anticipates the Congo's effect on Kurtz. Sambir's primordial jungle comments critically on the illusion shared by Dain and Nina, as well as by Willems and Aissa, that passionate love can transform the world. Sambir's tropical setting seems to be dominated by the processes of death and destruction, and the jungle's uncontrollable fecundity expresses itself in devolution rather than evolution. The dominance of the Pantai and the forest implies that Conrad's cosmos is as indifferent to human aspirations as the cosmos of his contemporary, Hardy, whose *Jude the Obscure* was also published in 1895.

Before he created Marlow as his narrator, Conrad had difficulty controlling the personal turmoil that we see in his letters of the 1894 to 1896 period. He feels isolated in a meaningless universe; he is cynical about human motives and purposes on this earth; he senses that he is an artistic failure; he doubts his ability to communicate even while expressing his desperate need to be understood. If his speaker's commentary is not always appropriate to the dramatic action that evokes it, it is because Conrad is using his speaker to explore his own bafflement in a universe he regards as amoral, indifferent, and at times hostile.

In these first two novels, when Conrad uses the narrator as a surrogate for himself to place an episode in an intellectual and moral context, Conrad is often testing and probing to discover what the episode means to him. He subsequently learns to capitalize on his reluctance to be dogmatic; he dramatizes Marlow's process of moral discovery and shows how Marlow continually formulates, discards, and redefines his beliefs through experience. But because in 1894 and 1895 Conrad had difficulty embracing a consistent set of values, his narrator's commentary does not always move toward a consistent philosophic position, but rather may posit contradictory perspectives. Quite frequently, the omniscient voice of his first two novels, *Almayer's Folly* and *An Outcast of the Islands*, explores characters and action from the perspective of a man committed to family ties, the work ethic, sexual constraint, individual responsibility, and racial understanding. Yet these basic humanistic values are often at odds with the artistic tentativeness and moral confusion that derive from Conrad's own uncertainty and anxiety. The unresolved tension between, on the one hand, Conrad's personal concerns and, on the other, his attempt to objectify moral issues is revealed in conflicts between the values expressed by the narrator and the implications of his plot and setting.

Conrad's early artistic code, the original afterword to *The Nigger of the "Narcissus"* (1897), is remarkable for its emphasis on creating a community of readers. Seen in the context of his own fear of loneliness and of not communicating, it reflects his decision that fiction will not only enable him to arrest the flux and turmoil within himself but also relieve him of his sense of isolation. He defines art as "a single-minded attempt to render the highest kind of justice to the visible universe, by bringing to light the truth, manifold and one, underlying its every aspect" (p. vii).[1] The artist's mission is to reveal the experience that unites us all and, in particular, to make the reader aware of the common humanity each of us shares with the rest of humankind. Conrad hopes for a community of responsive temperaments to verify the effectiveness of *his* creation; this hope may be behind the intensity of the famous but elusive assertion, "My task which I am trying to achieve is, by the power of the written word, to make you hear, to make you feel – it is, before all, to make you *see*" (p. viii).

Conrad's 1914 preface to the American edition of *The Nigger of the "Narcissus"* makes clear that he meant the tale's focus to be on the crew's response to Wait, the black malingerer who in fact thinks he is feigning illness and ends up duping not only the crew but himself: "In the book [Wait] is nothing; he is merely the centre of the ship's collective psychology and the pivot of the action" (p. ix). Sentimentalism is the peculiar form of egotism that preys upon the crew's response to Donkin's poverty at the outset and that causes the men to sacrifice their integrity in a desperate and pathetic effort to forestall Wait's inevitable death. Neither Wait nor Donkin has an identity independent of that conferred by the crew's sentimentalism; they flourish *because* the crew responds to them.

Wait is in a parasitic relationship with the crew: "Each, going out, seemed to leave behind a little of his own vitality, surrender some of his own strength, renew the assurance of life – the indestructible thing!" (pp. 147–8). Once the crew responds to Donkin with a "wave of sentimental pity," "the development of the destitute Donkin aroused interest" (pp. 12–13). When he responds to Wait and Donkin against his better judgment, the sailor-speaker embodies Conrad's own fear of sentimentalism. After he had completed *The Nigger of the "Narcissus"* but before it had begun to appear in the *New Review*, Conrad wrote: "I feel horribly sentimental . . . I want to rush into print whereby my sentimentalism, my incorrect attitude to life . . . shall be disclosed to the public gaze."[2] Just as the eternal truths of Singleton and Allistoun triumph over the "temporary formulas" of Donkin and the crew's misguided sentimentalism, the fiction writer must eschew fashionable aesthetic philosophies: "Realism, Romanticism, Naturalism, even the unofficial Sentimentalism . . . all these gods must . . . abandon him . . . to the stammerings of his conscience and to the outspoken consciousness of the difficulties of his work," Conrad wrote in his 1897 preface (pp. x–xi).

The speaker-crew member, and possibly Conrad too, wants to believe that the crew's experience with Wait represents a confrontation with death. If the speaker were to lower the rhetorical ante, he would be left with his nominalistic adventure tale, which clearly reveals his own mediocre behavior. Sympathy with Wait almost causes the men, including the speaker-crew member, to refuse duty. Thus their catatonic fear of death, evoked by the presence of Wait, displaces the captain as master. Although the men detest Wait as a possible malingerer, they irrationally equate preserving him with forestalling their own deaths.

Writing *The Nigger of the "Narcissus"* enabled Conrad to discover that the voyage experiences of his sea career could free him from the debilitating restraints of shore life and be an ordering principle for his new career as a writer. Like the passing of a period in a man's life, a ship's docking – the end of its voyage – is a kind of prolepsis of the ship's final demise. But when Conrad presents his narrative to his readers, the created world and the self embodied in that world achieve a kind of immortality that defies temporally defined endings.

II   The Marlow Tales

Conrad was concerned with the dilemma of transforming the "freedom" of living in a purposeless world from a condition into a value. And Marlow enabled him to examine this dilemma in "Youth" (1898), *Heart of Darkness*, and *Lord Jim* (1900). Writing enabled Conrad to define his values and his character. He uses his narrators and dramatic personae to objectify his feelings and values. Marlow is a surrogate through whom Conrad works out his own epistemological problems, psychic turmoil, and moral confusion; his search for values echoes Conrad's. Thus he is a means by which Conrad orders his world. He is defining not only the form of the story but the relation between Conrad's past and present selves. The younger Marlow was explicitly committed to the same conventional values of the British Merchant Marine to which Conrad had devoted his early adulthood, but the mature Marlow has had experiences that have caused him to re-evaluate completely his moral beliefs. That Marlow is a vessel for some of Conrad's doubts and anxieties and for defining the problems that made his own life difficult is clear not only from his 1890 Congo diary and the 1890 correspondence with Mme Poradowska, but even more so from the letters of the 1897 to 1899 period.

The meaning of several other novels, most notably *The Nigger of the "Narcissus"* and *The Rescue* (1919), depends on our understanding the way that Conrad's emotional life becomes embodied in the text. In *Nostromo* (1904), the suicidal despair of Decoud reflects a mood that Conrad had known many times in his novel-writing years. Even such an objective work as "The Secret Sharer" (1910) becomes more meaningful once we recognize that it has an autobiographical element. At the outset of his voyage, the captain not only relives emotions Conrad once felt during his first command but reflects the uncertainty and anxiety that Conrad experienced in the period when he wrote it.

"Youth," the first short story after *Tales of Unrest* (1898) was completed, addresses the dour view of European life presented there. Marlow is the heir of the white men of such early Conrad stories as "The Lagoon" (1896) and "Karain: A Memory" (1891) – those sensitive, if disillusioned, men who neither live passionately like the natives nor believe in any sustaining ideals. "Youth" is about Marlow's efforts to create a significant yesterday so that his life will not seem a meaningless concatenation of durational events. Marlow's narrative reflects his need to "arrest" time and pre-empt the future. Somewhere past the middle of his life, Marlow attempts to discover a symbolic meaning in the past voyage of the *Judea*. He wishes to believe that his first journey to the East was one of "those voyages that seem ordered for the illustration of life, that might stand for a symbol of existence" (pp. 3–4). As he recalls his great adventure, he discovers that, in spite of the voyage's failure, it not only contains great significance for him but enables him to recapture on occasion his feeling of youthful energy. Conrad takes a good-natured, ironical view of the supposedly mature Marlow's attempts to expose his own youthful illusions. While he purports to take an objective and detached view of a meaningful experience of his youth, the mature Marlow is ironically revealed as a romantic sentimentalist, and sentimentalism, as we have seen, is something Conrad critiques. Conrad shows us that reality is partly subjective and that our illusions and oversimplifications are as real to us as so-called objective facts.

III Marlow's Role in *Heart of Darkness*

The primary subject of *Heart of Darkness* is Marlow, but the presence of Conrad is deeply engraved on every scene. Marlow's effort to come to terms with the Congo experience, and especially with Kurtz, is the crucial activity that engaged Conrad's imagination. Marlow's consciousness is the arena of the tale, and the interaction between his verbal behavior – his effort to find the appropriate words – and his memory is as much the action as his Congo journey. Both the epistemological quest for a context or perspective from which to interpret the experience and the semiological quest to discover the signs and symbols that make the experience intelligible are central to the tale.

The Congo experience has plunged Marlow into doubt and confusion. Sitting "apart, indistinct, and silent" in his ascetic Buddha pose, he is deliberately trying to separate himself from the cynicism and hypocrisy that he associates with Europeans. As in "Youth," while Marlow is telling the story he arrests the future, places his back against the present, and becomes part of the created world of his own imagination. The tale he tells becomes not only a version of but an epistemological quest into "the culminating point of my experience" (p. 116). The experience proves recalcitrant to Marlow's efforts to understand it. His probing mind cannot impose an interpretation on Kurtz: "The thing was to know what he belonged to, how many powers of darkness claimed him for their own. That was the reflection that made you creepy all over. It was impossible – it was not good for one either – trying to imagine" (p. 116). Part of Marlow's hostility to his audience derives from his own frustrated desire to discover the language that will make his experience comprehensible to himself. His is the voice of a man desperately trying to create meaning; unlike Kurtz, who "could get himself to believe anything," Marlow has trouble convincing himself that there is the possibility of belief.

Marlow's narration is a quest to explain the darkness that still haunts his imagination. Ernst Cassirer, in *The Logic of the Humanities*, provides a helpful gloss:

> The possibility and necessity of . . . a "breaking free" of the limitations of individuality emerges nowhere so clearly and indubitably as in the phenomenon of speech. The spoken word never originates in the mere sound or utterance. For a word is an intended meaning. It is construed within the organic whole of a "communication," and communication "exists" only when the word passes from one person to another.[3]

Marlow's experience in the Congo invalidated his belief that civilization equaled progress. While Kurtz, the man who seemed to embody all the accomplishments of civilization, reverted to savagery, the cannibals showed some semblance of the "restraint" that makes civilization possible. Kurtz was a poet, painter, musician, journalist, potential political leader, a "universal genius" of Europe, a man who "had come out equipped with moral ideas of some sort," and yet once he traveled to a place where the earliest beginnings of the world still survived, the wilderness awakened "brutal instincts" and "monstrous passions."

Marlow's journey from Europe to the Congo helped prepare him to sympathize with Kurtz. From the outset he was offended by the standards and perspectives of the European imperialists, and gradually he began to sympathize with the natives against the predatory colonialists. As an idle passenger on a boat taking him to the Congo, he caught glimpses of the inanity which he later encountered as an involved participant. Even then, he saw the fatuity of the "civilized" French man-of-war's shelling the bush: "Pop, would go one of the six-inch guns; a small flame would dart and vanish, a little white smoke would disappear, a tiny projectile would give a feeble screech – and nothing happened" (p. 62).

Soon, more than Marlow's Calvinistic belief in the redemptive powers of purposeful labor was offended. He viewed the company's outer station from an ironic standpoint, noticing the neglected machinery, lying like an animal's "carcass"; the "objectless blastings"; and the native workers, their rags resembling tails, chained together as if they were a team of mules. He mocked the folly of those who put out fires with buckets that have holes in the bottom and who considered diseased and starving men "enemies" and "criminals." His original epistemological stance, dependent not upon a naive, idealized conception of the trading company's commercial ventures but simply upon his belief that European civilization represents a tradition of humane values, was shaken. He began to realize that this version of civilization is not an "emissary of light" but an instance of exploitative imperialism at its worst. After arriving at the central station, Marlow's quest soon focused on discovering an alternative to the amoral pragmatism and cynicism illustrated by the manager and his uncle. The manager's only objection to Kurtz's abominations was that the results were unsatisfactory.

Marlow describes his quest to meet Kurtz in romance terms, suggesting ironically his kinship with folk and legendary heroes who also search for miracles and magicians to solve their problems and relieve their anxieties. Standing in the blood of his helmsman, Marlow could only think that Kurtz was dead, and that he would never be able to speak to Kurtz. It was as if he were frustrated in a journey to consult an oracle. After discovering that Kurtz had "taken a high seat among the devils of the land," he did not renounce his existential commitment to Kurtz as "the nightmare of my choice"; Kurtz still seemed preferable to the hypocrisy and malignity of the Europeans who have deprived language of its meaning, civilization of its ideals, and life of its purpose. Marlow, formerly a representative of European civilization, desperately identified with a man he knew to be ostracized by that civilization. Ironically, Marlow turned only to a different form of greed and egotism; Kurtz's atavistic impulses – modeled on the Belgian King Leopold's predatory imperialism – have a magnitude and purity that contrast with the pettiness and niggling greed of the imperialists.

We do not know how perceptive Marlow was when he met Kurtz, but he *now* knows that Kurtz was without the restraint that even the helmsman and other cannibals had: "Mr Kurtz lacked restraint in the gratification of his various lusts ... there was something wanting in him – some small matter which, when the pressing need arose, could not be found under his magnificent eloquence" (p. 131). Earlier in his narration, Marlow seems to be preparing to excuse Kurtz; he asserts that the "idea" behind an action can be redemptive for the committed individual. However, his narrative discredits this view that the ultimate test of an action is the sincerity of the concept that motivates it. Originally, Kurtz had "set up and [bowed] down before" a benevolent idea, but when the wilderness had "sealed his soul to its own by the inconceivable ceremonies of some devilish initiation," Kurtz's idea became its own solipsistic parody: "My Intended, my ivory, my station, my river, my – " (pp. 115–16).

Marlow invests Kurtz with values that fulfill his own need to embody the threat of the jungle in one tangible creature. If Kurtz is considered the center of the "heart of darkness," the business of following Kurtz and winning the "struggle" enabled Marlow to believe that he had conquered a symbol of the atavistic, debilitating effects of the jungle. This belief is central to his interpretation of the journey's significance. For Marlow, capturing Kurtz after he escapes symbolizes a personal victory over darkness. Increasingly, Kurtz had been attracted to the jungle by the urge to go ashore for "a howl and a dance." Having given in to his primitive urges he appropriately crawled away on all fours. Marlow recalls how he too was tempted by savage impulses and confused his heartbeat with the beat of the natives' drums. Uncharacteristically, he thought of giving Kurtz a "drubbing." He was "strangely cocksure of himself" and enjoyed stalking his prey. His assertion that "he left the track" indicates that he, too, was in danger now that he was alone in the jungle; he thought that he might never get back. But when Marlow confronted Kurtz, he recalls, "I seemed to come to my senses, I saw the danger in its right proportion" (p. 143). To Marlow, the confrontation represents coming to terms with the dark potential within himself against the background of primitive and unspeakable rites. But he did not surrender to the appeal of the wilderness precisely because he had internalized the restraints imposed by civilization.

IV   Toward a Pluralistic Reading of *Heart of Darkness*

Let me suggest lines of inquiry to pursue in our reading and teaching of *Heart of Darkness*. Of course, we should regard the questions that follow as only instances of the multiple possibilities of a pluralistic approach. Let us think of these questions as concentric circles of inquiry, circles that vary in their relevance from reader to reader, from passage to passage, and, for us rereaders, from one of our readings to another. My questions stress the inseparability of ethical, aesthetic, political, and contextual issues, and the order of the questions is not meant to indicate their relative importance.

1 How is *Heart of Darkness* a personal story written out of moral urgency, which reflects Conrad's Congo experience and his own epistemological and psychological inquiry at a time of personal crisis in 1898? How can we use the Congo diary and Conrad's letters to relate his life and work? How (as we have discussed earlier) is Marlow a surrogate for Conrad? If we see Marlow as a fictional surrogate for Conrad, how does such an approach relate to the fiction-making and masks of the late 1890s and the first decade of the twentieth century, as instanced in Wilde's *The Decay of Lying*, Yeats's poems, and Joyce's use of Stephen Dedalus in *A Portrait of the Artist as a Young Man* and *Ulysses*?

2 How is *Heart of Darkness* a voyage of Marlow's self-discovery? Do we need to stress how that self-discovery takes place in a political frame and is a political reawakening? Conrad's narrative enacts the *value* that the Africans and Europeans share a common humanity: the English too were once natives conquered by the Romans and England too was once one of the dark places of the earth. Moreover, Europeans not only require laws and rules to restrain their atavistic impulses, but they become more monstrous than those they profess to civilize. Finally, terms like "savage" and "barbarian" are arbitrary designations by imperialists who in fact deserve these epithets more than the natives.

3 How is *Heart of Darkness* a political novel concerned with the Belgian King Leopold II's rapacious exploitation of the Congo? While the megalomaniacal Leopold ruled the Congo Free State from 1885 to 1908, the native population was cut in half by his predatory practices. His regime ravaged the land, destroyed the food supplies, precipitating famine, forced people to labor in terrible conditions with little or no pay, and demanded unreasonable production quotas of rubber and ivory. To break the will of the natives, Leopold's army and minions either took their native colonial subjects hostage or killed and tortured them. The Europeans also introduced new diseases into the Congolese population.[4]

Thus in *Heart of Darkness*, we need ask, what attitudes do imperialists take to the natives and why? How is it, as Marxists would contend, a story about the "commodity fetishism" of later capitalism? Is it, as Chinua Achebe has claimed, a racist drama whose images reinforce white stereotypes about the dichotomy of black and white?[5] Is *Heart of Darkness* an imperialistic romance about the conquest of Africa? Or is it more accurate to stress how it is an ironic inversion, a bathetic reification, of such a genre? Are black and white and light and dark always equated with the polarity of civilization and savagery, good and evil, corrupt and innocent, or is the dialectic of images more subtle than that?

Conrad plays on the clichés and shibboleths of his era, when Africa was the "dark continent" – the place of mystery and secrets – and the primitive continent where passions and emotions dominated reason and intellect. He asks us to consider whether we can cross cultural boundaries without transgressing them. Perhaps we then need to ask: in situating himself as a critical and ironic respondent to imperialistic exploitation, is Marlow able to separate himself from colonial domination? And can we as Westerners teach a story like *Heart of Darkness* in a non-Western setting without reinscribing ourselves as colonialists? When we teach *Heart of Darkness*, are we in the same position as Western museums displaying non-Western art; that is, are we invading a different culture with our texts about colonialism? Whether in Ireland, Malaysia, or Africa, Western colonialism for the most part despoiled the people and the land it touched.

But let us remember that *Heart of Darkness* speaks with passion about the issues of colonialism and empire. If we can understand the *agon* as an enactment of how the natives' energy and instincts have been corrupted by materialistic, overly rational imperialists, we can see that the charge of racism is itself reductive.

Heart of Darkness debunks the concept of the white man's burden and shows how the concept of empire is a sham. Conrad chooses to show Kurtz's "Exterminate all the brutes" as a stunning abandonment of the moral pretensions on which imperialism is based. Kurtz's radical transformation exposes his reductive perspective and that of Marlow, King Leopold of Belgium, other Europeans – indeed, all of us who would seek to adopt a stance whereby one culture views another from a stance of superiority. For his era Conrad was avant-garde in acknowledging that at times Africans were more controlled and ethically advanced than Westerners; he, like Gauguin, knew that their cultural practices and their art – chants, dance, drumming – were alien to Western concepts of display, that their art was religious in function, linking daily experience to abstract beliefs, and that their art was used performatively in funerals, weddings, and initiation rites.

4 How are the disrupted narrative, the circumlocutory syntax, and the alternation between impressionistic and graphic language indicative of Modernism? Should we also think of *Heart of Darkness* as part of the awareness of modern artists that multiple perspectives are necessary? After all, in 1895,

Conrad wrote, "Another man's truth is a dismal lie to me."[6] We need to stress how *Heart of Darkness* takes issue with Victorian assumptions about univocal truth and a divinely ordered world. Conrad's use of the dramatized consciousness of Marlow reflects his awareness that "we live, as we dream – alone," and the concomitant awareness (seen in the development of Cubism and Joyce's ventriloquy in *Ulysses*) that one perspective is not enough.

Picasso's and Braque's Cubist experiments demonstrate how they, too, are trying to achieve multiple perspectives. Moreover, just as the Fauvists and Cubists were freeing traditional ideas of representation from the morphology of color, Conrad was freeing black and white from the traditional morphology that those colors evoked. Conrad is also freeing his language from the morphology of representation – as in his use of adjectives for purely affective rather than descriptive reasons. Conrad's use of allegorized rather than nominalistic adjectives, such as "subtle" and "unspeakable," invites both the frame narrator and Conrad's imagined audience to respond in terms of their own experiences and to validate in their responses that they, too, dream alone. When creating his Congo, Conrad knew Gauguin's 1893 Tahitian journal *Noa Noa* and was influenced by that and perhaps by Gauguin's paintings. Gauguin anticipated Picasso and other Modernists in seeing not only the elemental and magical aspects of primitive lives but also the passion, simplicity, and naturalness of those lives.

A crucial link between Gauguin and Conrad is that *Heart of Darkness* also contains a painting, namely Kurtz's painting of his Intended, which Marlow finds with Kurtz and expects to give back to the Intended: "I had taken him for a painter who wrote for the papers, or else for a journalist who could paint" (pp. 153–4). He had first seen the Intended's portrait at the Central Station: "Then I noticed a small sketch in oils, on a panel, representing a woman, draped and blindfolded, carrying a lighted torch. The background was somber – almost black. The movement of the woman was stately, and the effect of the torchlight on the face was sinister" (p. 79). In its late Victorian – perhaps Pre-Raphaelite – mode of painting, the portrait idealizes and allegorizes her: "She struck me as beautiful – I mean she had a beautiful expression. I know that the sunlight can be made to lie, too, yet one felt that no manipulation of light and pose could have conveyed the delicate shade of truthfulness upon those features. She seemed ready to listen without mental reservation, without suspicion, without a thought for herself" (pp. 154–5).

Heart of Darkness creates a dialectic between the European ethos and the African one, between the assumptions of an art that emphasizes truth to nature and one that renders diverse perspectives, interiority of subject, and the painter's imagination. The grotesque images are almost Surrealistic: the visual depiction of the native women, the jungle, and Kurtz's comment on the aesthetic assumptions of the staid and conventional portrait of the Intended, just as Kurtz's moral devolution ("Exterminate all the brutes") and reversion to savagery comments on the conventional moral assumptions of so-called civilization.

The idealized portrait of the Intended influences Marlow's behavior in the final scene. What is striking is the difference between the conventional and stereotypical late Victorian portrait and the modernity and metaphoricity of Marlow's visual imagination. But can we be sure that Marlow can be trusted as a perceiver here? By depicting the women in his narrative in graphic visual terms, as if the women were paintings on which to gaze – from the Manet-like depiction of the knitting women in Brussels ("Two women, one fat and the other slim, sat on straw-bottomed chairs, knitting black wool" [p. 55]) to the Savage Mistress to the allegorized Pre-Raphaelite Intended – isn't Marlow revealing something about himself? Isn't he too a kind of painter? His visual memory of Kurtz is the kind of illuminating distortion that we associate with Modernism: "He looked at least seven feet long. His covering had fallen off, and his body emerged from it pitiful and appalling as from a winding sheet. I could see the cage of his ribs all astir, the bones of his arm waving" (p. 134).

The figure of Kurtz occupies the entire canvas. Conrad anticipates the Surrealistic distortions of Ernst and Dali and the powerful images of *Guernica*. Conveying the elaborate ritual patterns of his story, the image of Kurtz might be an African statue embodying spiritual insight and demonic transcendence. More important, Conrad's visual images are free from the mid-nineteenth-century's realistic expectations and give the experience the form and perspective – even the lines and color – of Postimpressionism.

Marlow's images reflect the movement in late nineteenth- and early twentieth-century painting away from realism to illuminating distortion, to the grotesque, and to the abstract. His experience in the Congo is, among other things, about the challenge to his visual expectations. Notice the *metaphoricity* with which Marlow's imagination transforms what he sees: "I came upon a boiler wallowing in the grass, then found a path leading up the hill. It turned aside for the boulders, and also for an undersized railway truck lying there on its back with its wheels in the air. One was off. The thing looked as dead as the carcass of some animal" (p. 63). Or, note how the Postimpressionist perspective – with its stress on light and shadow – of Marlow's response to the natives mixes foreground and background and focuses on sharply drawn physical shapes: "Black shapes crouched, lay, sat between the trees leaning against the trunks, clinging to the earth, half coming out, half effaced within the dim light, in all the attitudes of pain, abandonment, and despair" (p. 66). Like Gauguin's Tahitian paintings, these passages reveal as much as they conceal and depend on the perceiver's gaze to recompose them into significance.

What Cleo McNelly wrote of Conrad is also true of Gauguin: "For Conrad (and for Baudelaire and Lévi-Strauss as well) home represents civilisation, but also order, constraint, sterility, pain and ennui, while native culture . . . represents nature, chaos, fecundity, power and joy."[7] It is the complex view of native life that gives both *Noa Noa* – "Noa Noa" means fragrance – and the far richer narrative of Conrad much of their power. As Edward Said has noted in *Culture and Imperialism*: "Never the wholly incorporated and fully acculturated Englishman, Conrad therefore preserved an ironic distance in each of his works."[8] *Noa Noa* and Gauguin's Tahitian paintings resist the imperialistic discourse that stresses the superiority of the white man, but they do not propose their alternative – Tahitian paradise – as simply as it had once been thought. Yet by recognizing an alternative to materialism and acquisitiveness, by responding to passion, romance (or his version of it), intuition, imagination, and, yes, the essence or *fragrance* of experience, Gauguin does imply ways of resisting imperialism and finding interior and later external space for native cultures. And Conrad goes a step further, for *Heart of Darkness* speaks directly to the issues of colonialism and empire, to the corrupting influence of European culture on African customs and civilization.

I want to take partial issue with Said's view that "Marlow and Kurtz are also creatures of their time and cannot take the next step, which would be to recognize what they saw, disabling and disparagingly, as a non-European 'darkness' was in fact a non-European world *resisting* imperialism so as one day to regain sovereignty and independence, and not, as Conrad reductively says, to reestablish the darkness."[9] Whether in Malaysia or Africa, for Conrad Western colonialism in the name of civilization despoils the people and the land it touches. As Marlow puts it, "We were wanderers on prehistoric earth, on an earth that wore the aspect of an unknown planet. We could have fancied ourselves the first of men taking possession of an accursed inheritance, to be subdued at the cost of profound anguish and of excessive toil" (p. 95). Yet Conrad understands that the natives are part of a common humanity: "They howled and leaped, and spun, and made horrid faces; but what thrilled you was just the thought of their humanity – like yours – the thought of your remote kinship with this wild and passionate uproar . . . The mind of man is capable of anything – because everything is in it, all the past as well as all the future" (p. 96).

Conrad wants to propose the possibility of human continuity, even as he suggests that perhaps civilization corrupts native energy. It is the narrator, not Marlow, who speaks of "The dreams of men, the seed of commonwealths, the germs of empires" (p. 47). Marlow speaks about European newspaper articles that made ethical claims for the trade mission, articles that spoke of "weaning those ignorant millions from their horrid ways" (p. 59). In *Heart of Darkness*, Western man is imaged as the idiosyncratic Brussels doctor who measures crania, the cynical manager and his more cynical uncle, the chief accountant of the outer station, and, of course, Kurtz. Isn't imperialism figured as the pail with the hole in the bottom with which one of the white men at the central station tries to put out fires? Supposed emissaries of light, like Kurtz, become exploiting imperialists.

Our multicultural perspective need mention Conrad's use of Asian and Eastern contexts to comment on European behavior. A traveler who becomes transformed into a scathing critic of Western pretensions, Marlow is aligned by Conrad with the East: "He had sunken cheeks, a yellow complexion, a straight back, an ascetic aspect, and, with his arms dropped, the palms of hands outwards, resembled an idol" (p. 46). A moment later the first narrator remarks on Marlow's lotus posture and contemplative demeanor: "[L]ifting one arm from the elbow, the palm of the hand outwards, so that, with his legs folded before him, he had the pose of a Buddha preaching in European clothes and without a lotus flower" (p. 50). Marlow had returned from "six years in the East," the time presumably when *Lord Jim* took place. His familiarity with the East extends to Noh plays and puppet theater: the place-names in Africa, given by Europeans, "seemed to belong to some sordid farce acted in front of a sinister back-cloth" (p. 61); perhaps such names as "Central Station" and "Inner Station" speak to the Japanese propensity to allegorize experience.

5 How does *Heart of Darkness* relate to the intellectual history of Modernism? How is Kurtz indicative of the Nietzschean will-to-power that was a major strand of the intellectual fabric of imperialism and fascism? How does Conrad's text relate to his contemporary Freud's probing of the unconscious? How does *Heart of Darkness* speak to the breakdown of moral certainty, the sense that each of us lives in a closed circle, and the consequent fear of solipsism? Conrad feared that each of us is locked in his or her own perceptions, and despaired in his letters that even language will not help us reach out to others. Thus, Marlow's fear that "we live, as we dream – alone" is also an idea that recurs throughout the period of early Modernism, a period in which humans felt, to quote F. H. Bradley, that "my experience is a closed circle; a circle closed on the outside . . . In brief . . . the whole world for each is peculiar and private to that soul."[10] That the frame narrator can tell the story shows that Marlow has communicated with someone and offers a partial antidote to the terrifying fear of isolation and silence that haunted Conrad.

6   How is *Heart of Darkness* a comment on the idea of social Darwinism that humankind was evolving into something better and better? *Heart of Darkness* refutes the position that history was evolving historically upward. Recall Conrad's famous letter about the world as a knitting machine, where the ironic trope of the world as a machine is a rebuttal to Christianity: "It knits us in and it knits us out. It has knitted time, space, pain, death, corruption, despair and all the illusions – and nothing matters. I'll admit however that to look at the remorseless process is sometimes amusing."[11]

7   How would a pluralistic approach address the meaning of "The horror! The horror!" as a part of an evolving *agon* that generates a structure of affects? Let us look at "The horror! The horror!" in the context of what precedes. That Kurtz has achieved a "moral victory" may very well be a necessary illusion for Marlow. But did Kurtz pronounce a verdict on his reversion to primitivism and achieve the "supreme moment of complete knowledge" (p. 149)? Or is this what Marlow desperately wants to believe? How credible is Marlow's interpretation that "The horror! The horror!," coming from a man who "could get himself to believe anything," is "an affirmation, a moral victory paid for by innumerable defeats, by abominable terrors, by abominable satisfactions" (p. 151)? When Kurtz had enigmatically muttered, "Live rightly, die, die . . . ," Marlow had wondered "Was he rehearsing some speech in his sleep, or was it a fragment of a phrase from some newspaper article?" (p. 148). Marlow had just remarked that Kurtz's voice "survived his strength to hide in the magnificent folds of eloquence the barren darkness of his heart" (p. 147). If Kurtz had, as Marlow contends, kicked himself loose of the earth, how can Kurtz pronounce a verdict on his ignominious return to civilization or an exclamation elicited from a vision of his own imminent death? For the reader – the reader responding to the inextricable relationship between the ethical and the aesthetic in Conrad's text – Kurtz remains a symbol of the way the human ego can expand infinitely, to the point where it tries to will its own apotheosis.

8   In what ways does *Heart of Darkness* reveal overt and covert sexist attitudes? Is *Heart of Darkness* a sexist document? Patrick Brantlinger writes, "The voices that come from the heart of darkness are almost exclusively white and male, as usual in imperialist texts."[12] In a situation where opportunities for heterosexuality are limited, what does *Heart of Darkness* say about male bonding among the whites and about miscegenation? Are we offended that one of Kurtz's supposedly "abominable practices" is the taking of a savage mistress? If we understand Marlow's patronizing attitude toward women as naive and simple, can we not use the text to show the difference between authorial

and resistant readings, between the way texts are read when they are written and the way they are read now? Does the lie to the Intended reveal Marlow's sexism? Is Conrad aware of Marlow's sexual stereotyping, even if Conrad means the lie to the Intended to be a crucial moment of self-definition for Marlow? We need to examine the assumptions about women that dominate this final episode, and to align them with the passage in which he tells us that the women are always "out of touch with truth." But, of course, the tale dramatizes that all of us live in a world of our own, and none of us is in a position to patronize the other, be it natives, women, or others who go to the Congo armed with ideals.

For a reader today, *Heart of Darkness* raises important questions because at first it seems to present women from a perspective that is reductive and even sexist and racist. We need to understand that the views expressed by Marlow are not Conrad's, and indeed are a dramatization of a perspective that Conrad uses ironically. Yet it is important to acknowledge that he does not adequately separate himself from Marlow's view of women, a view that assumes that women are more sentimental, myopic, and domestic than their male peers. Marlow seems to believe that it is the male role to protect the women from the more searing truths and to help them live in their illusions.

9   How is *Heart of Darkness* a heteroglossic text embodying diverse modes of discourse? Marlow's recurring nightmare begins not only to compete with his effort to use language discursively and mimetically, but to establish a separate, more powerful telling. The narrative includes the semiotics of a primitive culture: the non-verbal gestures of the savage mistress and the Intended; the beating of the drums; the shrill cry of the sorrowful savages; and the development of Kurtz into Marlow's own symbol of moral darkness and atavistic reversion. This more inclusive tale, not so much told as performed by Marlow as he strains for the signs and symbols that will make his experience intelligible, transcends his more conventional discourse. Conrad shows that these instinctive and passionate outbursts, taking the form of gestures, chants, and litany, represent a tradition, a core of experience, that so-called civilized humankind has debased.

V   Conclusion

Finally, why do we continue to read Conrad? Does the concept of canon have value? Is it not the urgent questions – and, yes, relevance to us – that *Heart of*

Darkness elicits that give it value today? We need a criticism that, as Martha Nussbaum has put it,

> talks of human lives and choices as if they matter to us all ... [Literature] ... speaks about us, about our lives and choices and emotions, about our social existence and the totality of our connections. As Aristotle observed, it is deep and conducive to our inquiry about how to live, because it does not simply (as history does) record that this event happened; it searches for patterns of possibility – of choice, and circumstance, and the interaction between choice and circumstance – that turn up in human lives with such a persistence that they must be regarded as *our* possibilities.[13]

A study of Modernist culture and the colonial Congo, Conrad's *Heart of Darkness* also speaks to our culture and raises urgent issues for us. Is that not why we read it, even as we consign some former canonical texts to the margins? Because it is an urgent political drama, because it raises questions of racial and sexual identity, and because it is a wonderful story that probes our identity with our human antecedents, *Heart of Darkness* lives for us as surely as Kurtz lives for Marlow, and Marlow lives for the narrator.

What does Marlow's reading of Kurtz teach us about our reading of texts and lives? As an allegory of reading, *Heart of Darkness* resists easy simplifications and one-dimensional readings, resists attempts to explain in either/or terms. Even as it remains a text that raises questions about the possibility of meaning, it suggests the plenitude of meaning. Just as Marlow gradually moves from seeing a drama of values to living a drama of character, so as readers do we. Like him, we make the journey from spectator to participant. Are we not trying to make sense of Marlow as he is trying to make sense of Kurtz? And are we not also trying to make sense of the frame narrator who is trying to make sense of Marlow making sense of Kurtz? Does not the tale's emphasis on choosing a sign for our systems of meaning call attention to the arbitrary nature of choosing a framing sign and make us aware of the need for multiple perspectives? Do we not learn how one invests with value something not seen or known in preference to the ugly reality that confronts us? Is not Conrad's ironic parable about belief itself, including the Christian belief in whose name much of imperialism was carried on?

Thus, in essence, the tale urges us toward a pluralistic perspective. Finally, one-dimensional readings bend to the need for a pluralistic reading that takes account of Marlow's disillusionment and his magnetic attraction to Kurtz as the nightmare of his choice. For Conrad has turned a story about a present journey to Africa into a journey through Europe's past as well as into each human being's primitive psyche. As a teacher, I find that our students and non-academic readers remind us that narrative, story, and response in human and ethical terms triumph over excessively ideological readings. For, finally, does not all our reading, including our reading of "bits of absurd sentences" (p. 46) – to use Marlow's words to describe what he hears from the manager and the manager's uncle and tries to *read* in terms of his own experience – need to be understood in terms of our most fundamental text: the story of our lives?

Chapter 4

Conrad's *Lord Jim*: Reading Texts, Reading Lives

I Introduction

I shall argue that the experience of reading *Lord Jim* (1900) enacts a dialogue between two major ideologies of reading – deconstruction, in its diverse forms, and what I call humanistic formalism. While engaging us in both approaches, I believe *Lord Jim* privileges the reading of humanistic formalism, which urges, so far as it is possible, an absolute judgment on Jim's behavior and an organic and coherent text, over the deconstructive or resistant reading which raises questions about the possibility of formal unity, explanations of behavior, and standards of judgment. Ultimately, *Lord Jim* affirms the possibility of significance and values, and refuses to endorse the relativity of Marlow or the solipsism of Stein.

In *Lord Jim*, Conrad uses an omniscient narrator to establish – by careful reference to Jim's prior cowardly behavior – normative judgments in the early chapters only to undermine them with the introduction of Marlow. The novel's carefully crafted tripartite structure and dense verbal texture reveal Marlow's obsessive psychic investment in Jim as well as his own moral short-comings and show why, in spite of himself, he identifies with Jim as a double. We must read Conrad slowly for every word is weighted with resonance – as opposed to, say, Hardy, where the reading unit is more likely to be the paragraph if not a complete narrative incident.

Since J. Hillis Miller has been among the most influential of the decon-structionists working in prose fiction, I would like to take a moment to look at his argument about *Lord Jim*. In his chapter on *Lord Jim* in *Fiction and Repetition*, Hillis Miller has proposed that the repetition – the structural and thematic doubling that dominates the language and form of *Lord Jim* – implies that Jim's behavior cannot be explained. By contrast, I shall contend that Jim's behavior can be judged. *Lord Jim* proposes – and Conrad expects the reader to perceive – a hierarchy of explanations. But to see the hierarchy, one has to understand that the omniscient narrator proposes an absolute judgment, just as surely as Marlow proposes a relative one based on his complex and often sympathetic understanding of Jim. When Miller contends that *Lord Jim* lacks the reliable narrator of Victorian fiction, he is, I think, misreading the first four chapters. Miller argues that *Lord Jim* "reveals itself to be a work which raises questions rather than answering them . . . The indeterminacy lies in the multiplicity of possible incompatible explanations given by the novel and the lack of evidence justifying a choice of one over the others."[1] By contrast, I shall be arguing that *Lord Jim* in its complex and eccentric way answers the questions it raises.

Our first critical task is to recall that *Lord Jim* has three separate tellings: first, the omniscient narrator's presentation of Jim in the first four chapters; on occasion this voice returns to remind us of his presence; second, Marlow's long monologue from chapters 5 through 35; and third, Marlow's response to Jim's demise on Patusan, which takes the form of an epistle received by one of the listeners to his monologue.

To understand why Conrad thinks each of us is locked into her or his own perceptions and that all values are ultimately illusions, perhaps we should further examine Conrad's ironic image of the cosmos as created by an indifferent knitting machine – an image he proposed in the aforementioned 1897 letter to his optimistic socialist friend Cunninghame Graham:

There is a, – let us say, – a machine. It evolved itself (I am severely scientific) out of a chaos of scraps of iron and behold! – it knits. I am horrified at the horrible work and stand appalled. I feel it ought to embroider, – but it goes on knitting. You come and say: "This is all right: it's only a question of the right kind of oil. Let us use this, – for instance, – celestial oil and the machine shall embroider a most beautiful design in purple and gold." Will it? Alas, no! You cannot by any special lubrication make embroidery with a knitting machine. And the most withering thought is that the infamous thing has made itself: made itself without thought, without conscience, without foresight, without eyes, without heart . . .

It knits us in and it knits us out. It has knitted time, space, pain, death, corruption, despair and all the illusions, – and nothing matters. I'll admit however that to look at the remorseless process is sometimes amusing.[2]

Conrad uses this elaborate ironic trope to speak to the late Victorian belief that the industrial revolution is part of an upwardly evolving teleology; this belief is really a kind of social Darwinism. According to Conrad, humankind would like to believe in a providentially ordered world vertically descending from a benevolent God – that is, to believe in an embroidered world. But we actually inhabit a temporally defined horizontal dimension within an amoral, indifferent universe – or what Conrad calls "the remorseless process."

In *Lord Jim*, in particular, Conrad dramatizes that humans always judge one another in terms of their own psychic and moral needs at the time that they are making judgments. Put another way, we recall that Conrad believes that "another man's truth is a dismal lie to me."[3] But – and here I shall iterate a major point in my opening chapter, but one for which *Lord Jim* is a paradigmatic example in the Conrad oeuvre – notwithstanding the fallibility of all judgments, we must strive to make objective judgments and to sustain values and ideals, even if we know that we will always fall short of them. Thus when Conrad writes that all is illusion, he means that all we can do is make working arrangements with the cosmos, and that there are no absolute values derived from an external source. But he does not mean that all values are equal. Similarly, merely because we cannot discover an absolute, final, original reading, it does not follow that all readings are equal. Rather, as readers, even while acknowledging that our readings are a function of our limitations, we must strive to establish judgments and values within complex texts. By affirming the value of the search for meaning in the lives of his characters within his imagined world, Conrad is rhetorically enacting the value of this search in reading texts.

The process of reading *Lord Jim* involves the reader in the remorseless process of responding to different judgments of Jim's behavior. First, there is the judgment of the omniscient narrator that precedes not only our meeting Marlow, but our learning what happens on the *Patna*. Does the reader ever forget the original rigorous judgment established by the omniscient narrator in the first three chapters, a judgment that is based on adherence to absolute standards? Does not that judgment accompany the reader as he wends his way through Marlow's narrative of his own efforts to find some terms with which to understand Jim's terrible failure on the *Patna*, when Jim, along with the rest of the white officers, abandons the native crew and passengers? And, of course, the reader must sort out the significance of Stein's oracular but hazy pronouncements. No sooner do we hear Marlow's judgment delivered in his long monologue after knowing that Jim has succeeded on Patusan, and, at least in Marlow's eyes, justified Marlow's confidence in him, than we are confronted with Marlow's final, inconclusive judgment after Jim has failed; this judgment is halfway between the rigorous one of the absolute narrator and the empathetic one that had informed Marlow's telling.

Let me conclude my introduction by outlining the program for the rest of my discussion of *Lord Jim*. In my next four sections I shall focus respectively on the function of the omniscient narrator in the novel's opening chapters;

on Marlow's complex response to Jim; on the role of Stein, that odd figure who inhabits the middle of the novel; and on the implications of the ending for shaping our final response to the novel. Finally, in the last section I shall offer suggestions for reading *Lord Jim* that have implications for reading other novels.

II The Function of the Omniscient Narrator

Prior to Marlow's first words in chapter 5, the omniscient narrator in the opening chapters judges Jim by fixed standards and shows him wanting. Without any ambiguity, Conrad uses this narrator to show us that Jim's jump from the *Patna* is a characteristic one rather than – as Jim would like to believe and as Marlow is at times tempted to accept – a gratuitous action that just happened to an unfortunate young man.

Lost in his fantasies of heroism, Jim fails to respond to an emergency on the training ship. Because he has not internalized the proper responses, when he is faced with an actual chance to take part in a rescue he becomes physically and morally paralyzed: "He stood still. It seemed to him he was whirled around" (p. 5).[4]

But he rationalizes that he had not really failed: "The gale had ministered to a heroism as spurious as its own pretence of terror . . . [A] lower achievement had served the turn. He had enlarged his knowledge more than those who had done the work. When all men flinched, then – he felt sure – he alone would know how to deal with the spurious menace of wind and seas" (p. 7). The strength and resilience of Jim's imagination enable him to forget his failure, and to transfer – in the phrases "the pretence of terror" and "the spurious menace" – the *pretence* of his courage and the *spurious* quality of his fantasies to the physical events that revealed his pretence. We should note that, at this point before he succumbs to the temptation of the exhortation to "Jump," Jim is a kind of magician with language – a poet – who can arbitrarily rearrange words as he sees fit.

Jim's second failure is when, while serving as first mate, he loses his nerve. The omniscient narrator tells us that until then Jim had never been tested by "those events of the sea that show in the light of day the inner worth of a man, the edge of his temper, and the fiber of his stuff; that reveal the quality of his resistance and the secret truth of his pretences, not only to others, but also to himself" (p. 7). Notice how the narrator ironically applies to Jim the term "pretence" – the very word Jim had used to describe the gale on the training ship. When the storm strikes, Jim is disabled: "[He] spent many days stretched on his back, dazed, battered, hopeless, and tormented as if at the bottom of an abyss of unrest . . . He lay there battened down in the midst of a small devastation, and felt secretly glad he had not to go on deck . . . [He felt] a despairing desire to escape at any cost" (p. 8). The "abyss of unrest" looks forward to the abyss or "everlasting deep hole" into which Jim jumps, while the word "secretly" not only scathingly echoes and exposes the secret truth of Jim's pretences, but reinforces our sense of the immense schism between the man Jim would be and the man he is (p. 68). With bitter irony and without any interrupting transition, the omniscient narrator concludes the above paragraph: "Then fine weather returned, and [Jim] thought no more about it" (p. 8). In the "despairing desire to escape at any cost," do we not sense a foreshadowing of Jim's suicide at the novel's end? Like Jukes in Conrad's 1902 novella "Typhoon," Jim's imaginative ability to think of *what might possibly happen* leads him through corridors of terrible fantasies and finally to a nervous exhaustion indistinguishable from catatonia. That Conrad himself, the seaman who would be an author, feared that what the omniscient narrator calls "Imagination, the enemy of men, the father of all terror" would prey upon his own capacity for action is evident in a number of his texts, from "Typhoon" and *Lord Jim* to "The Secret Sharer" and *The Shadow-Line* (p. 8).

Conrad's narrative coding continues to create a concatenation of episodes that judges Jim's moral dereliction and psychological incapacity. Each episode iterates the prior one's indictment, even while it adds another piece of evidence to the charge that Jim has not internalized the fixed moral standards of the merchant marine – the code stipulating honor, fidelity, courage, and a highly developed sense of responsibility – on which civilized life in the colonies depends. Thus Jim, after he recovers from his leg injury, takes a post on a boat with those who eschew the "home service" of the merchant marine for easier employment:

> They loved short passages, good deck-chairs, large native crews, and the distinction of being white . . . They talked everlastingly of turns of luck . . . and in all they said – in their actions, in their looks, in their persons – could be detected the soft spot, the place of decay, the determination to lounge safely through existence. (p. 9)

As in the above passage, it is characteristic of Conrad to introduce parallel phrases with recurring words; within a sentence these phrases often increase in intensity as they move to an explosive conclusion; thus in the first of the above sentences, Conrad's appositional phrases move from rather neutral description to the morally intense and scathing indictment (in the climactic phrase "the distinction of being white") of those who believe they are privileged on racial grounds. While Jim assumes that he will not be tarnished by the company of the kind of men who choose to work on boats like the *Patna*, the ironic narrator places Jim among these men with soft spots and places of decay. Conrad's adjectives here do not so much describe an internal condition as participate in a structure of effects to give the reader a sense of Jim's moral flaw. We cannot visualize a soft spot or a place of decay any more than we can see an *"invisible* halt" in Jim's gait.

The fourth episode or vignette that inexorably illustrates that, contrary to Jim's contention, his jump was a characteristic rather than a gratuitous action, is his behavior on board the *Patna*; as on the training ship, his mind is wooed from his duty to the "human cargo" of pilgrims by fantasies of accomplishment: "[H]is thoughts would be full of valorous deeds: he loved these dreams and the success of his imaginary achievements. They were the best part of his life, its secret truth, its hidden reality" (p. 13). That the words "achievement" and "secret" echo prior passages documenting his flawed nature shows how Jim is iterating his past as he will throughout his life. Repeating the term "secret" – which has, as Stephen Marcus has shown in *The Other Victorians*, a sexual connotation (as in *My Secret Life*) – underlines how Jim has separated himself from reality and has paradoxically created *in his actions* – as opposed to his dreams – a narcissistic self (a self in hiding) that has no social role to play. Conrad thus gives the nuance of narcissism to Jim's self-indulgent fantasies. Living in the world of his fictions rather than in the world of actual duties and responsibilities, Jim is a hopelessly divided self unfit for his tasks.

Cumulatively, these four vignettes stand as an absolute judgment of Jim, a judgment based on applying the rigorous standards of the merchant marine which, Conrad believed, were the essential underpinnings to life at sea and to colonial life in primitive areas. Even as Marlow becomes an apologist for Jim, even as he uses Jim's case to look into his own case and the moral nature of all men, these vignettes retain their validity and accompany our reading, just as surely as Jim's past experience accompanies him after he abandons ship and wanders from place to place trying to catch up with his irrevocably lost self.

Conrad uses the omniscient narrator to establish that, contrary to Jim's argument to Marlow, Jim's jump was not something that could have happened to anyone but was, rather, the inevitable result of a character flaw. The omniscient narrator conducts his trial – performs Jim's trial for the reader – before the actual trial at which Marlow meets Jim. By beginning the novel with an omniscient voice which clinically and ironically shows that Jim's jump is characteristic of a morally flawed person, Conrad gives the reader a standard

– a moral barometer – from which he or she cannot escape. Just as Jim feels imprisoned by a "serried circle of facts" after he has jumped and must explain what happened to the human community and, in particular, to a tribunal of his peers, Conrad has created in the remarkable opening chapters a narrative code which uses "a serried circle of facts" to indict Jim and imprison him. Conrad thus prevents the reader from fully joining Marlow's subsequent apologia for Jim. Moreover, by scrupulously alerting the reader to Jim's process of rationalization and self-delusion, Conrad rhetorically prepares the reader to judge Marlow's myopia when he, Marlow, begins to rationalize both his own responses to Jim and, increasingly, his own behavior.

III Marlow's All-Too-Human Judgment

Originally, Marlow wanted to judge Jim by absolute standards. Marlow would have liked to read Jim as if he, Marlow, were the omniscient narrator, and, indeed, for a brief moment, Conrad teases us into thinking that we have been listening to Marlow – or at least an omniscient double of Marlow – all along. In the first moments of his monologue about Jim, Marlow aligns Jim with beetles, criminals, alloyed metal, and "to men with soft spots, with hard spots, with hidden plague spots" as if he were going to continue the narrator's indictment (p. 21).

But the self-dramatizing Marlow soon reveals that he is vulnerable to those who, like Jim, claim extenuating circumstances because Marlow does not sufficiently believe in himself to uphold absolute values. He cannot, as Stein will advise, shut his eyes and see himself as a fine fellow, a saint. He must face the ambiguity of living in a relative world which lacks anterior concepts of order. Because of his own needs, he begins to read Jim as Jim would like him to. In Marlow's evolving sympathy with Jim as "one of us," in his taking up a position as Jim's apologist, in his gnawing and disturbing suspicion that he may not be able to claim a superior moral position because anyone might do what Jim did, Marlow begins to abandon the credo of the merchant marine and British imperialism and increasingly allows Jim to become a standard by which he, Marlow, measures himself. But the omniscient narrator has taught us not to be a Jim-reader of Jim; when Marlow becomes a Jim-reader of Jim, we back off from accepting Marlow's authority as a reader of himself. In Marlow's world, once he loses his beliefs in fixed standards, there are no sources or origins and everything exists – as Conrad's text, where every episode replicates another, indicates – as a variation of the other; such infinite variation makes judgments difficult.

As Marlow becomes an apologist for Jim, the reader is expected to adopt a stance of judgment toward Marlow – is expected to see that he, too, is a fallible human being who is different in degree but not in kind from Jim. On three occasions Conrad undercuts Marlow's pretensions to moral authority:

1 first, when during Jim's trial, Marlow offers Jim Brierly's plan to evade the trial and escape the rituals of civilized judgment (p. 93);
2 second, when Marlow goes to Stein because he wishes to "dispose" of Jim, in part to avoid his bizarre fear of having Jim – in the role of a common vagrant – confront him in London;
3 and, finally, when during his visit to Patusan, Marlow loses control in his interview with Jewel for no reason other than his own need to assure himself that he is better than Jim at a time when Marlow's ability to make moral distinctions is threatened: "I felt the sort of rage one feels during a hard tussle . . . 'You want to know [why the world does not want him]?' I asked in a fury. 'Yes!' she cried. 'Because he is not good enough,' I said brutally" (p. 194). Marlow's self-indulgent indiscretion – what purpose is served by telling Jewel that Jim is not good enough? – strikingly contrasts with the climax of *Heart of Darkness*. There, we recall, when an embittered and disillusioned Marlow returns to Europe, he is, although he hates a lie, willing to lie to the Intended and to let her think that Kurtz's last words were her name in order that she have the sustaining illusion of Kurtz's undying devotion.

The novel questions the possibility of absolute standards in other ways. That Brierly, the precociously successful young captain who seems to have achieved everything that Jim dreams of, and who seems to be the very man most suitable to judge Jim, kills himself after serving on the tribunal at Jim's trial, structurally illustrates the impossibility of one man's judging another. Who could have had better personal and professional credentials to judge Jim than Brierly, whose career trajectory was the exact opposite of Jim's? Yet looking into Jim's case, Brierly begins to look into his own and begins to believe that what one person does any person can do. Does not Brierly's radical empathy become a warning to the reader of what could happen to Marlow if he allows the distance between himself and Jim to close? Recalling "The Secret Sharer," where the captain irrationally identifies with the escaped murderer Leggatt, with whom he has very little in common and whose values are diametrically opposed to his own, we realize Conrad's own anxiety about failing to fulfill his commitments at sea and perhaps on land.

Isn't Conrad using Brierly's strong misreading of Jim's life to issue a rhetorical warning to the reader to strive for distance and judgment and to avoid the radical empathy that leads to flagrant misreading? Within the text, we are being told to attend to the rhetoric of the text and not to create our own text. To recall my subtitle for this chapter: "Reading Texts, Reading Lives."

Throughout the novel, the omniscient narrator's judgment coexists with Marlow's inevitably human, somewhat sentimental, and finally flawed perspective.[5] Even when we as readers participate in Marlow's search for explanations, even when we are moved by his efforts to make sense of Jim's behavior and his, Marlow's, own life, the original, objective judgment of Jim remains engraved on our minds. While Marlow's judgment is wavering, relative, and unsure of its ground, the omniscient narrator's judgment is absolute, and refers to anterior standards. To read *Lord Jim* properly, one must hold in mind these contradictory perspectives.

Do not the absolute judgment of the omniscient narrator and the relative, human judgment of Marlow revolve around one another as we read *Lord Jim*? As humans with our doubts and anxieties, with the memories of our failures, and fears about our shortcomings, we are prone to the kind of humane, and, yes, on occasion, sentimental sympathy and radical empathy with which Marlow responds to Jim. In current terms, it is tempting to say that these judgments deconstruct one another so that neither becomes privileged. Indeed, Marlow's reading of Jim can be taken as a model for intratextual reading based on contiguous relations within a text, while the omniscient narrator's reading depends on a belief in anterior standards. The paradox is that here it is the humanistic reading that is deconstructing the novel's – and the reader's – quest for unity.

But while Marlow enacts the moment of irreconcilable impasse or *aporia* of Modernism, Conrad, I am arguing, does not. For, as we have seen, Conrad's omniscient voice stands in judgment of Jim's behavior and of Marlow's understandable efforts as one of us – lonely, doubting humans in a confusing world that Conrad thought of as a "remorseless process" – to explain Jim's behavior. Conrad expects the reader to understand that Marlow's confidence in absolute values has been undermined by his own experience, and that we readers must, like judges, sift through the data as objectively as possible, even while recognizing that, like Brierly and Marlow, we are all prone to skewed judgments based on our own needs. But while the novel tempts us to be a Jim-reader of Jim, or a Brierly-reader or a Stein-reader, and even more urgently to be a Marlow-reader – who at times is a Jim-reader, a Brierly-reader, and a Stein-reader – it finally insists on our being an omniscient reader and as unforgiving and unyielding in our judgments as the omniscient narrator.

The taut organic unity of the novel, in which every part echoes every other part and in which every word rings with resonance, is the significant form for establishing a world dense with meaning and judgment. It is the form – including the relationship between the romantic second part in unexplored Malay islands and the realistic first part within the colonized East where western maritime values have gained a foothold, between the part dominated by the *Patna* and the part dominated by Patusan – that enables Conrad to reclaim the subject, center the meaning, and reject *aporia*. Does not even such a small matter as the name "Patusan" being an anagram of the letters of *Patna* plus "us" remind the reader of the community commitment which Jim lacked on board the ship? Does not the novel's doubling call attention to the almost reflexive nature and organic form of Conrad's fictive world?

IV The Function of Stein

The oracular Stein makes a claim for omniscience – or, rather, Marlow, in search of a conclusive or ultimate meaning, seeks to apotheosize Stein. By placing Stein in the center of the novel, by endowing his life with heroic proportions which make him an image of what Jim would like to be, by giving him a history which in many ways echoes that of Jim (excluding, of course, jumping ship), and, finally, by giving him the ambiguous speech of an oracle figure, Conrad arouses the reader's expectations that Stein may solve the novel's moral issues.

Let us look briefly at Stein's argument. He proposes that one must existentially commit oneself to one's ideals as a means of dealing with the "destructive element." Shouldn't we think of that element as the necessary result of an indifferent, amoral cosmos that Conrad conceived in terms of a machine that insists on knitting rather than embroidering? Because Jim has not internalized his dreams, because they do not support his ego-ideals, he cannot, according to Stein's compelling but finally unsatisfactory oversimplifications, sustain his dreams. Humans have a need to fulfil anterior ideals and at the same time have baser impulses which may result in cowardice and mediocrity. But if one shuts one's eyes to reality and embraces one's dreams, then one has a chance of sustaining oneself in the destructive element or remorseless process:

> [Man] wants to be a saint, and he wants to be a devil – and every time he shuts his eyes – he sees himself as a very fine fellow – so fine as he can never be . . . In a dream . . . and because you not always can keep your eyes shut there comes the real trouble – the heart pain – the world pain. I tell you, my friend, it is not good for you to find you cannot make your dream come true, for the reason that you not strong enough are, or not clever enough. *Ja!* . . . And all the time you are such a fine fellow, too! (p. 130)

In an ironic reversal of Jim's jump which occurs when Jim abandons his dreams and sees that he will certainly drown, dreaming – closing one's eyes and living one's dreams and illusions – is equated by Stein with falling into the sea:

> A man that is born falls into a dream like a man who falls into the sea. If he tries to climb out into the air as inexperienced people endeavor to do, he drowns – *nicht war?* . . . No! I tell you! The way is to the destructive element submit yourself, and with the exertions of your hands and feet in the water make the deep, deep sea keep you up. (p. 130)

Climbing into the air is a metaphor for failing to keep oneself afloat in one's dreams; if one does climb into the air, then one opens one's eyes to one's own limitations and sees the world as it is – as a destructive element. The way to survive, according to Stein, is "To follow the dream, and again to follow the dream – and so – *ewig – usque ad finem*" – which translates as "perpetually until the end" or "all the way to the end" (p. 131). When Jim opens his eyes on the *Patna* to the real danger, he abandons his dream of heroism and the merchant marine credo that insists that he stick to the ship under all circumstances. When he lets the scoundrel Gentleman Brown insinuate a kinship with him, he abandons his position as the political and ethical leader of the Patusan community. In both cases, his self-image is not strong enough to stand up to his collision with circumstances in the not-I world that represent the destructive element or remorseless process.

Something more of an 1890s figure than is usually noticed, Stein understands the nature of masks and fictions; he knows the value of adhering existentially to one's dream or values as a way of making sense of a meaningless world. But has it sufficiently been stressed how Stein is preaching a form of solipsism and that he says nothing at all about the failure of Jim to sustain traditional community values? Many critics have mistakenly privileged Stein's remarks because they have failed to notice that Conrad no sooner raises expectations that Stein might be a Wisdom Figure than he deflates those expectations. For one thing, what Stein says in his broken English is rather ambiguous. For another, no sooner does he deliver his advice than his pretensions to sphinx-like wisdom are undermined; Marlow notices that Stein loses his poise and confidence: "The hand that had been pointing at my breast [like a pistol] fell . . . The light had destroyed the assurance which had inspired him in the distant shadows" (p. 130). And, finally, that Stein is depicted by Marlow in the novel's last paragraph as aging and ineffectual shows us that he not only has not found any absolute knowledge, but may not even retain faith in the credo that he has articulated in the above passage. The Stein episode teaches the reader that there can be no one center of meaning in texts or in life. Just as neither Stein nor Jim can be the key to meaning for Marlow, so Marlow cannot be the source of meaning for his listeners; and, for us readers, no one character or scene can be privileged over the others.

Of course, discrediting Stein as a Prospero figure does not invalidate the human search for meaning; nor does the absence of ultimate meaning suggest that there cannot be hierarchies of relative meaning. The reader is expected to understand Stein's advice as another working arrangement that individual humans make with the cosmos. Even Marlow does not arrive at formulations that would replace Stein's, for ultimately Conrad does not believe in one-dimensional explanations of behavior or philosophic formulations that can be imposed on every situation.

V The Ending of *Lord Jim*

Jim's betrayal of his followers in Patusan derives from his inability to believe in his own triumph – or, put another way, to read the text he himself wrote about the hero that makes good on his second chance. He alone does not believe in his triumph and believes that his accomplishments are apocryphal. Doesn't he say at the height of his triumph: "If you ask them who is brave – who is true – who is just – who is it they would trust with their lives? – they would say, Tuan Jim. And yet they can never know the *real, real, truth*" (p. 185; emphasis mine)? Because Jim does not believe in his own redemption, words cannot be part of what Marlow calls "the sheltering conception of light and order which is our refuge" – a conception that, as Marlow puts it, protects us from "a view of the world that seemed to wear a vast and dismal aspect of disorder" (p. 190); do we not hear in these words an echo of Stein's destructive element? Once Jim responded to the word "Jump" on board the *Patna*, he had leapt into an abyss where belief in the innocence of language as an ordering principle in a fundamentally hostile world is no longer possible. Like a voice from within insidiously suggesting to Jim that he *belongs* to him as part of his imprisoning fate, Gentleman Brown convinces him that they are moral and emotional brothers and that Jim must provide him a safe departure. But Brown and his murderous band betray Jim's trust and slay Jim's followers. In Marlow's words, "[Jim] had retreated from one world, for a small matter of an impulsive jump, and now the other, the work of his own hands, had fallen in ruins upon his own head" (p. 248).

In the imagined world of *Lord Jim*, Conrad gives voice and speaking precedence over writing. For Marlow, who has used spoken language to summon almost magically what is past and to put his back to the future, who has used telling to re-create himself, the written word is a kind of deferral of the immediacy of spoken language and an indication that he is giving up his inquiry into himself. Thus the written language of the epistolary section becomes itself a metaphor for the moral weariness and resignation he feels and a recognition of mortality and defeat. Now Marlow too seems to have lost faith in language. His valedictory passage defers meaning and leaves him without that presence or epistemological counter which Jim had provided for Marlow's quest for moral and spiritual meaning:

> And that's the end. He passes away under a cloud, inscrutable at heart, forgotten, unforgiven, and excessively romantic ... For it may very well be that in the short moment of his last proud and unflinching glance, he had beheld the face of that opportunity which, like an Eastern bride, had come veiled to his side.
>
> But we can see him, an obscure conqueror of fame, tearing himself out of the arms of a jealous love at the sign, at the call of his exalted egoism. He goes away from a living woman to celebrate his pitiless wedding with a shadowy ideal of conduct. Is he satisfied – quite, now, I wonder? We ought to know. He is one of us – and have I not stood up once, like an evoked ghost, to answer for his eternal constancy? Was I so very wrong after all? Now he is no more, there are days when the reality of his existence comes to me with an immense, with an overwhelming force; and yet upon my honour there are moments, too, when he passes from my eyes like a disembodied spirit astray amongst the passions of his earth, ready to surrender himself faithfully to the claim of his own world of shades. (p. 253)

Does Marlow forgive him? Note how Marlow sometimes forgets Jim, while in *Heart of Darkness* he never could forget Kurtz, who haunts his memory. When he describes Jim in such terms as "under a cloud, inscrutable at heart, forgotten, unforgiven and excessively romantic," Marlow is describing his *response* to Jim, rather than Jim. (As readers of *Heart of Darkness* recall, this is not unusual in Conrad, where such adjectives as "abominable" or "unbounded" are used more to create a structure of effects for the reader than to describe an objective situation within the imagined world.) But these non-referential adjectives enact the way that, since the omniscient narrator turned over the narration to Marlow, he has moved from reflection to self-immersion. Perhaps Marlow's final judgment (especially "unforgiven") is a step toward reasserting the rigorous code from which he had departed. While he withholds judgment – "I affirm nothing" – does he not send his packet to a listener whose views are close not only to those of the omniscient voice, but also to those Marlow had held when he first met Jim (p. 206)? For the privileged recipient is chosen because he believed in the imperialistic dream that the white Europeans are emissaries of enlightenment, "in whose name are established the order, the morality of an ethical progress" (p. 206).

Surely, we readers moving outside the linguistic circle of Marlow and Stein understand that the cloud, like the invisible halt of Jim's gait and his spot of decay, is a metaphor for Jim's moral blemish; we cannot see Jim clearly because, for Marlow, his morally ambiguous behavior places him in the shadows of Marlow's imagination. And do not the above adjectives call attention finally to Jim's moral emptiness and raise questions about whether he is still worth the effort? Marlow understands that Jim is still wooed by his fantasies; Jim leaves behind the reality of the woman who loves him, and to whom he has human ties, for a romantic ideal of honor. Isn't Marlow's final stance, as much as Stein's aging, a reassertion of the impossibility of permanently suspending time and of creating an imaginative world? But this impossibility paradoxically gives the omniscient narrator's positivistic judgments validity.

Poignantly, in his allowing Doramin to shoot him, Jim chooses the masculine world of physical action, represented by the pistol (recall how he had entered Patusan "with an unloaded revolver in his lap"), over the alternative, more feminine world of values represented by the talismanic friendship ring given to him by Stein – the ring that he gave to his messenger, "Tamb Itam, to give to Dain Waris as a sign that his messenger's words should be trusted" (p. 149). But as we have seen, words for Jim are a deflated currency in which he has little confidence.

Just as his achievements in the native black world can never be as real to Jim as the failures in the white home world, feminine values – those of romantic love and personal ties – cannot be as real to him as the world of male heroism. He can love Jewel in his romance world of "knight and maiden," but not in the real world of partial failures and relative successes (p. 189). By choosing to face the male pistol, Jim, in fact, ironically closes the eternal circle implied by the feminine ring. After Doramin shoots Jim:

> People remarked that the ring which [Doramin] had dropped on his lap fell and rolled against the foot of the white man, and that poor Jim glanced down at the talisman that had opened for him the door of fame, love, and success within the wall of forests fringed with white foam, within the coast that under the western sun looks very like the stronghold of the night. (pp. 252–3)

Is not Jim's suicide – along with Jim's jump from the *Patna* and his trusting Gentleman Brown – a third betrayal? Do not the moral absolutism and breakdown of distance that propel him to suicide repeat Brierly's suicide? In Conrad's moral universe a man's character is his fate and Jim has not fundamentally changed. But this does not invalidate meaning. Indeed, what happens is that Jim accepts the verdict of the omniscient narrator, the verdict that had judged Jim's jump from the *Patna* not as a gratuitous act but as part of a concatenation of events that revealed his flawed character. More than Marlow, Jim had continued to judge himself according to absolute standards from which he had departed – the very standards articulated by the omniscient narrator at the beginning of the novel. Doesn't Jim's internalizing of these judgments make the circular ring an appropriate image for the form of the novel? In retrieving the original standards by which he had failed, Jim most certainly weds himself to what Marlow calls "a shadowy ideal of conduct" (p. 253). But that shadowy ideal is in fact the credo of the novel that is articulated by the omniscient narrator in the opening chapters.

In the ending, then, we see not an abandonment of values but a reassertion of the original values articulated by the omniscient narrator. To be sure, individual voices – whether Stein's, Brierly's, or Marlow's – are unable to establish authority. In Marlow's and the novel's last paragraph, Stein is reduced to speaking vacuously of "preparing to leave" and seems to lack both the imaginative and rhetorical energy of his prior appearance. Marlow no longer imposes his all-too-human order on his experiences (p. 258). Jim dies "with his hand over his lips," an emblem – or a statue – of his estrangement from language. In subsequent works, Conrad himself will no longer rely on Marlow as a surrogate for his epistemological quests; he moves on to other voices and techniques, returning in *Chance* (1912) to a Marlow who resembles the earlier one more in name than in intellect and who lacks the ability to make subtle moral discriminations. But the words of the novel and, in particular, of the omniscient narrator survive to communicate their judgments to the reader.

VI Suggestions for Reading *Lord Jim*

Like any complex work, *Lord Jim* teaches us how to read itself. We should think of our experience – our process – of reading it as the reader's odyssey. We should be aware of what the novel does to us as we read it and how its disrupted chronology and multiple modes of narration establish an unusually complex relationship between text and reader. In my view the principal interest of *Lord Jim*'s chronological disruptions, its multiple perspectives, its structural doubling, and its stylistic idiosyncrasies is in how they shape a reading of the novel. Just as Marlow is engaged in a moral odyssey as he repeats the journeys of Jim's physical odyssey, so, too, does the reader take part in an odyssey of judgment in which he or she is presented with an abundance of evidence and opinions.

The reader must establish a perspective for both Marlow and Jim that survives and transcends the novel's plethora of judgments, its wealth of detail, and its protean transformations of characters. At times, Conrad's use of adjectives – in, for example, the passage we examined from the ending – is a kind of subjective correlative for which the reader must fill in the space between signifier and signified; this activity on the reader's part provides a linguistic model for the necessary corrective judgment that the reader must provide for the novel's ethical issues. In Conrad, style is inseparable from what it *does* to the events and characters it describes and what it *does* to the reader as he or she negotiates the journey through the novel to the final destination, the novel's end. Since Conrad's focus always returns to the characters and their meaning, we should assume that the effects of his language upon the reader – what we might think of as the *does-ness* of the text as opposed to the *is-ness* – were never far from his mind.

The odyssean reader must wend his or her way through a variety of experiences, but these experiences can best be understood in terms of *Lord Jim*'s major formal principle. This formal principle urges the reader to see *Lord Jim* as a completely organic and integrated novel in which one can conceive in every part some aspect of the meaning and harmony of the whole. In his book *Gödel, Escher, Bach* Douglas Hofstadter describes the graph of a mathematical function INT[eger] (x), every section of which is a replica of the whole.[6] Since every individual part of each section is also a replica of the whole, the graph consists of an infinite number of copies of itself. Thus INT[eger] (x) becomes an apt metaphor for a humanistic reading of *Lord Jim*, because it expresses the humanistic idea that within the specific narrative about a few characters can be perceived universal truths or at least important evidence of what a culture values. Another model for organic unity is the genetic code which determines the macrostructure of an organism, but which is contained in every separate part of the organism.

Opposed to this totalizing perspective is the formal principle that insists that, as Geoffrey H. Hartman puts it, "literary language displays a polysemy, or an excess of the signifier over the signified."[7] While, for the most part, *Lord Jim* insists that its readers interpret every detail in terms of larger patterns, one must acknowledge a secondary and subordinate story of reading *Lord Jim*. At times, the novel's focus on isolated moments of life and ingenious linguistic pyrotechnics may temporarily deflect the reader from stories of reading that propose organic unity. At some points in our reading experience, the text seems to be questioning the reader's quest for meaning with troubling data, as in the passage where Stein's oracular stature is undermined or when Marlow loses control. On occasion, focusing on the quirky and idiosyncratic aspects in human behavior, *Lord Jim* does immerse the reader in the nominalistic world of the lives of a few characters; furthermore, by presenting Jim through Marlow's explanatory and apologetic lens, Conrad does raise the possibility that some of the novel's implications cannot be resolved.

Throughout *Lord Jim*, Conrad is aware that the possibility of meaninglessness is inseparable from the probability of significance. By constantly proposing, testing, and discarding multiple explanations for Jim's behavior and by presenting Marlow as an evolving, self-dramatizing character, Conrad urges us toward such a complex response. He wants us to read profanely and to experience the agony of Jim's demise through Marlow's puzzled eyes; he wants us to entertain the possibility that *Lord Jim* is not merely inconclusive, but that it is skeptical about discovering significance from the plethora of details within his novel – and, by implication, as skeptical of our own efforts to come to terms with crucial events in our own lives.

But ultimately the narrative form of *Lord Jim* privileges the original judgment – the prologue narrated by an omniscient voice preceding Conrad's elaborate orchestration of the multiple but limited and self-interested perspectives of the novel. And Conrad re-integrates those moments of seeming *aporia* into his pattern of moral significance. By doing so, he establishes a hierarchy of meanings in which the relative, marginal, or deconstructive reading is subordinated to the novel's moral judgment as revealed by the novel's organic form.

The dialectic between the two modes of reading – the formally coherent humanistic one and the skeptical deconstructive one – is crucial not only to the experience of reading *Lord Jim* but to reading many modern (and postmodern) novels. While nineteenth-century novels are more likely to use the omniscient speaker and to propose a unified artistic and moral vision, modern novels as diverse as *Ulysses* and Eco's *The Name of the Rose* characteristically carry the seeds of their own self-doubt about the possibility of meaning and coherence. For the sake of intellectual housekeeping, it would be neater either to give the two modes of reading *Lord Jim* – the one that insists on moving from immersion to interpretive reflection and to acts of construing, the other that stresses immersion in the text for its own sake – equal importance, or to claim that the linguistic reading deconstructs the humanistic one. But it is more accurate to say that for the most part *Lord Jim* invites the first mode of reading, the traditional humanistic mode of reading that stresses unity of form and content, rather than the latter, deconstructionist mode of reading which questions meaning, coherence, and significance. Put another way, in *Lord Jim* the humanistic reading is dominant and the deconstructive

Chapter 5

Lawrence's *Sons and Lovers*: Speaking of Paul Morel: Voice, Unity, and Meaning

I   Introduction

Each novel generates its own aesthetic. Paradoxically, part of our aesthetic pleasure and part of our empathetic pain in reading *Sons and Lovers* (1913), Lawrence's autobiographical novel, is watching how Lawrence uses his omniscient narrator simultaneously to probe his past experience and to shape the novel's form. The resistant reader realizes that Lawrence's omniscient narrator does not see the implications of the behavior of Paul Morel – the novel's protagonist and Lawrence surrogate – toward his lovers, Miriam and Clara. Moreover, the omniscient narrator does not understand how Paul Morel's behavior is shaped by his oedipal love relationship with his mother.

Beginning with the earliest reviews of *Sons and Lovers*, Lawrence has been indicted for his "inability to efface himself" and for giving us a "narrative [that] reads like an autobiography."[1] Later, Mark Schorer's provocative remarks about the confusion between Lawrence's "intention and performance" sharply focused critical attention upon the crucial relationship between voice and form in *Sons and Lovers*. Schorer argued that *Sons and Lovers* should be considered a "technical failure" whose "artistic coherence" has been destroyed by its inconsistencies. Specifically, he observed "the contradiction between Lawrence's explicit characterizations of the mother and father and his tonal evaluations of them"; he also remarked upon the novel's efforts both to "condemn" and "justify" the mother and both to expose and rationalize Paul's failures.[2]

Schorer's complaint about the novel's aesthetic unity reflects both his discomfort with a novel that implies conflicting and contradictory values, and his belief that if a reader has to engage in judging the reliability and perspicacity of a technically omniscient third-person speaker, the integrity of the novel is necessarily disturbed. In this chapter I shall argue that: (1) the discrepancies between the narrator's interpretations and ours create a tension that becomes an intrinsic part of the novel's form; (2) the fluctuating and complex relationship between Lawrence's narrator and Lawrence's major characters enables the reader to participate in the agonizing but wonderfully exciting aesthetic process by which an author tries to give shape and unity to his recent past; and (3) the failure of Lawrence to sort out the blame, to neatly "master" his materials, is a major reason for the novel's subtlety and complexity.

Louis L. Martz has convincingly refuted Schorer. Arguing for the efficacy of Lawrence's technique in chapters VII ("Lad-and-Girl Love") through XI ("The Test on Miriam"), he writes:

> The point of view adopted is that of Paul; but since confusion, self-deception, and desperate self-justification are essential to that point of view, we can never tell, from the stream of consciousness alone, where the real truth lies. But we can tell it from the action; we can tell it by seeking out the portrait of Miriam that lies beneath the overpainted commentary of the Paul-narrator. This technique of painting and overpainting produces a strange and unique tension in this part of the novel.[3]

Though Martz's fine essay considerably furthers the discussion of the aesthetic unity of *Sons and Lovers*, I should like to take issue with him on several counts:

1   I do not believe Lawrence "resumes" "the method of the objective narrator" in chapters XII ("Passion") through XV ("Derelict"), and I do not perceive a tonal change in the narrator's voice in these later chapters of part two (Martz, "Portrait of Miriam," p. 364).
2   I do not agree that the narrator in part one is "working with firm control, [setting] forth the facts objectively" (ibid., p. 344).
3   I think Martz's insistence on seeing a "growth in [Paul's] self-knowledge" deflects him into a reading of the ending that blurs the negative implications of the final paragraphs (ibid., p. 367).
4   I feel that his term "overpainting" ignores the temporal nature of the reader's perception of a work of fiction. Although a reader's impressions are continually qualified or even displaced by subsequent narrative commentary or dramatized scenes, two contrasting impressions do not really exist in the reader's mind simultaneously like a negative that has been double-exposed.

Lawrence's struggle to come to terms with his own experience is revealed in the novel's conflict between narrative incident and narrator commentary. This conflict reflects Lawrence's continuing re-evaluation of his experience as he rewrote *Sons and Lovers*, at a time when he was torn between the desire to be true to the sacred memory of his mother and the desire to respond to the views of his first lover, Jessie Chambers, and later of Frieda Weekley Richtofen, the woman with whom he had an affair and then married in 1914 after her divorce from one of his former Nottingham University professors. To come to terms with his autobiographical material, Lawrence tries to divide himself into two separate characters: Paul and the narrator. Paul, a former self and the embodiment of his past, is a subjective creation; Lawrence immerses Paul in a narrative that mimes crucial events of his own life, but does not ask Paul to judge himself scrupulously. That task is left to the narrator, the embodiment of the present self who is supposed to be an objective figure charged with evaluating and measuring Lawrence's former self and tracing his linear development. But this dichotomy breaks down as Lawrence's objective self becomes empathetic to his former self, Paul Morel. Because Lawrence is not emotionally removed from the narrated experience, his superego has not grown sufficiently beyond the experience to evaluate and control his own mother-love. In a December 1910 letter written while his mother was dying, Lawrence had said of the relationship with his mother: "We have loved each other, almost with a husband and wife love, as well as filial and maternal."[4] That his narrator's consciousness is incompletely developed and very much in the process of becoming is appropriate for a novel in which the protagonist's aesthetic rejects "the stiffness of shape" for the "shimmeriness" inside (p. 152).

The narrator is an apologist for Mrs Morel and an adversary of Miriam. He takes distinctly different stances toward similar behavior in the two women. If it is proper for Paul to resist having his "soul" possessed by Miriam, why is the narrator rather tolerant of Mrs Morel's "root[ing]" her life in Paul and becoming "the pivot and pole of his life, from which he could not escape" (pp. 141, 222)? Anxious to justify Mrs Morel's behavior, the narrator provides half-convincing excuses which he desperately wishes to believe. Mrs Morel had to suffer the disgrace of poverty, while her sisters helped support her first son; her own father had been a Puritan who had browbeaten her mother (so, presumably, Mrs Morel is excused for being on the offensive in her marriage); she had already been disappointed by one weak-willed man, John Fields.

The narrator perceives Mrs Morel's insistent claims upon Paul within individual scenes, but he is unwilling to recognize the significance of the evolving pattern. Paul is aware of how Mrs Morel has substituted her sons for her husband, but Paul refuses to acknowledge how individual organic moments with his mother, in which they share attitudes, ideas, and epiphanies of nature's beauty, add up to a perverse pattern. Nor does he acknowledge that Mrs Morel's smothering and stifling maternity is often conscious, volitional, and willful. In the final scene in part one, the narrator refuses to recognize the implications of what is occurring when Mrs Morel transfers her affections from the recently deceased William to Paul while the latter is suffering from pneumonia. The narrator empathizes with both Paul and his mother and renders the scene without irony or detachment:

"I' s'll die, mother!" he cried, heaving for breath on the pillow.
She lifted him up, crying in a small voice:
"Oh, my son – my son!"
That brought him to. He realised her. His whole will rose up and arrested him. He put his head on her breast, and took ease of her for love . . .
The two knitted together in perfect intimacy. Mrs Morel's life now rooted itself in Paul. (p. 141)

Their mutual passion is restorative for both of them. But this apparently perfect moment of intimacy forges a fateful link that severely impedes Paul's sexual and emotional growth. Subsequent events make clear to the reader that it is Mrs Morel's complicity in the oedipal love – her willingness to fuse herself to him – that blights Paul's maturation. But does the narrator acknowledge that this fusion of two lives – a concept which Lawrence unfavorably contrasts in "The Study of Thomas Hardy" with the "Two-in-one," the ideal heterosexual relationship in which each member has independence – is potentially destructive? If there seems to be a hint of ambivalence in the words "rooted" and "knitted," this is extinguished by the insistence that the new relationship is restorative for both of them. As he recalls this scene, Lawrence's speaker cherishes rather than criticizes the intimacy between his younger self and his mother.

Yet Lawrence undoubtedly meant to create a speaker who, while sympathetic toward Paul, could detach himself enough from Paul's oedipal love to be able to show the reader more about the protagonist than Paul knew about himself. In the novel's first part, Lawrence tries with some success to establish a discrepancy between the narrator's perspective and Paul's and thus demonstrates that Lawrence wishes to separate himself from Paul. But the autobiographical material of *Sons and Lovers* resisted the convention of omniscient narration in which Lawrence conceived it. When he has his narrator represent the evolution of Paul's responses to nature and sex, when the narrator seeks to translate the silence of Paul's unconscious into non-discursive rhythms and images, we see that Lawrence is fully empathetic toward Paul, and the narrative distance breaks down completely. The objective voice, the evaluative superego with his gently ironic view of Lawrence's younger self, is displaced by the urgent voice of the *vates* seeking to transport the reader into a sensual, vitalistic rapport with the young man who is finally discovering his long-repressed passionate self.[5] For example, notice the texture of the passage in which Lawrence renders Paul's and Clara's most successful sexual consummation, the one that takes place in the fields along the canal:

> All the while the peewits were screaming in the field. When he came to, he wondered what was near his eyes, curving and strong with life in the dark, and what voice it was speaking. Then he realised it was the grass, and the peewit was calling. The warmth was Clara's breathing heaving. He lifted his head and looked into her eyes. They were dark and shining and strange, life wild at the source staring into his life, stranger to him, yet meeting him; and he put his face down on her throat afraid. What was she? A strong, strange, wild life, that breathed with his in the darkness through this hour. It was all so much bigger than themselves that he was hushed. They had met, and included in their meeting the thrust of the manifold grass stems, the cry of the peewit, the wheel of the stars. (p. 353)

In such sexual and passionate moments, Lawrence is intruding into the silence of unconscious physiological experience and inviting the reader to participate directly in the sensual life of his characters. His metaphors seek to transform the space in which the sexual act or passionate moment occurs into a place where the texture of life is sensuous, physical, instinctive, and biological and where cognitive life is absent. Such metaphors, rather than creating objective correlatives, are lyrical explosions whose rhythms and images are supposed to engage immediately the reader's libidinous self without the intervening cognitive process by which a reader usually transforms a narrative episode into signification. A sentence such as "They had met, and included in their meeting the thrust of the manifold grass stems, the cry of the peewit, the wheel of the stars" implies that during the sexual act the power of the participants' libidinous energy displaces the diurnal world in which they dwell and makes their world coterminous and spatially equivalent with the cosmos; in a word, microcosm becomes macrocosm. When it works, as I believe it does here, Lawrence's style becomes his argument. Sexual intercourse enables the participants to become part of the natural world and the energy that breathes through it; in Blakean terms, it restores, if only temporarily, the lapsed soul to Beulah.

II Mrs Morel and Paul's Oedipal Problem

While acknowledging the complexity of part two, Martz calls part one "[a] triumph of narration in the Old Victorian style" of objective omniscient narration (Martz, "Portrait of Miriam," p. 345). But the fluctuating perspective of the first chapters is rather more complex than he allows. Desiring to render Mr Morel with objectivity and to acknowledge his vitality, the narrator depicts him making his fuses, fixing his breakfast, and, especially, relishing his masculine holidays. The narrator does show how Mrs Morel isolates Morel from his own children, and even briefly adopts a perspective sympathetic to Morel when analyzing the deterioration of the marriage. On rare occasions, the narrator depicts the frustrations of *both* ill-matched partners. When Morel cuts William's hair, the narrator catches the pathology of his wife's rage: "I could kill you, I could!" (p. 15). Yet his sympathy is with Mrs Morel. Basically, the narrator empathizes with her desire for a sanctuary from "poverty," "ugliness," and "meanness," and he fails to stress – as the reader soon learns from dramatized scenes – that her dissatisfaction with her lot makes impossible a viable relationship with her husband (p. 5). Mrs Morel's "air of authority" and "rare warmth" give her primacy within her home and within the lives of her children. While acknowledging her inability to accept her husband, the narrator minimizes the way her willful desire to establish to her children that she is better than her husband pre-empts his position in the family. As she gradually establishes her dominant position, she assumes the role of father.

The first chapter establishes the pattern of the novel. Mrs Morel evaluates her husband and his companions according to arbitrary social and economic standards. She has a compulsion to improve herself and her family. In a perverse way that neither she nor the narrator understands, she equates material and social progress with blessedness. Trying in turn to shape Mr Morel, William, and Paul, she creates for each of them expectations that they cannot meet. Mr Morel's *manners* distress her, but her continual search for a surrogate husband begins when she learns that he does not take pride in his economic independence. That he actually pays his mother's rent disturbs her as much as or more than that he has lied. Just like her father she is proud of her "integrity," but integrity in a husband means something rather narrow to her: the ability to pay one's bills and to provide for one's wife. She would not deign to take in mending like the other Bottoms' wives. Mr Morel's drinking is to her, above all, indicative of his economic and social irresponsibility, which undermines her efforts to consider herself better than her neighbors. If ever Mrs Morel indicts herself as niggling and petty, it is when she recalls:

"[Mr Morel] had bought no engagement ring at all, and she preferred William, who was not mean, if he were foolish" (p. 115).

As Mrs Morel begins to allow William to play the role of surrogate husband, she unconsciously seeks to reduce her husband to a child; we recall how she mocks his efforts to run away after he had stealthily taken sixpence from her pocketbook. Meanwhile, as if she were a feudal "queen" she accepts "tribute" from William, who "gave all his money to his mother" (p. 52). William is subconsciously compelled to choose for a sexual partner someone who is the complete opposite of his mother–lover, whom he has unconsciously dedicated himself to serving chivalrously. Mrs Morel needs to control, dominate, and subdue; yet one part of her despises her husband because he allows himself to be emasculated: "She sat trembling slightly, but her heart brimming with contempt. What would she do if he went to some other pit, obtained work, and got in with another woman? But she knew him too well – he couldn't. She was dead sure of him" (p. 43).

Unconsciously at first, but later quite intentionally, Mrs Morel transfers her libidinous self – the night-time self that in spite of her rationality and pragmatism responds to the sensuality of flowers and moonlight – to her children because she finds her husband's social, public self wanting. The first chapter shows how she struggles between, on the one hand, the external norms that she has inherited from the Coppard tradition, and, on the other, her sensual and passionate potential. No matter how she would deny her biological self and renounce Morel, her libido expresses itself in her physical response to her husband and her narcissistic experience with flowers. As her orgasmic moment with the symbolically virginal lilies indicates (she "melts out" of herself into "a kind of swoon"), by the time chapter I ends Mrs Morel is no longer completely dependent upon her husband to fulfill her sexual needs (p. 24). (Whatever Lawrence's intention, I think that the scenes in which Mrs Morel, Paul, Miriam, and even Clara have passionate intercourse with flowers must be regarded in part as a function of their sexual frustrations.)

If part one did have an objective narrator, would he not stress how Paul's class snobbery, self-righteousness, and ambition are shaped by the force of his mother's will? Mrs Morel is obsessed with her sons' social and economic success because of her husband's failure to give her the vicarious recognition and economic status that she craves:

She felt . . . that where [Paul] determined to go he would get . . . Now she had two sons in the world. She could think of two places, great centres of industry, and feel that she had put a man into each of them, that these men would work out what *she* wanted; they were derived from her, they were of her, and their works also would be hers. (p. 101; emphasis Lawrence's)

The narrator accepts Paul's view that his mother's "hardness" and defensive behavior are rather understandable in light of the disappointments she has endured. Explaining how she copes with her anxiety about sending a 14-year-old boy to work at a factory, where his health suffers from "darkness" and "lack of air," the narrator asserts: "But she herself had had to put up with so much that she expected her children to take the same odds. They must go through with what came" (pp. 108–9). Mrs Morel is often the ultimate materialist. She is aggressive and even hostile to those with whom she enters an economic relationship; one need only recall the waitress at Nottingham, the man who drives the carriage to the cottage that the family has rented, or even the man from whom she buys a decorated dish. While Paul's response to the mine is aesthetic, imaginative, and organic, hers is primarily economic. When Paul notices the beauty of the pits, she can only think of the economic significance, notwithstanding her earlier observation that "the world is a wonderful place" (p. 123).

Once William indicates the extent of his attachment to Gyp, Paul begins to replace him as Mrs Morel's surrogate husband. When Mr Morel breaks his leg, "in her heart of hearts, where the love should have burned, there was a blank" (p. 86). Even though she continues to have intermittent if infrequent feelings of affection for her husband, her attitude at this time gives special urgency to the imploring question that she asks Paul: "What do you want to be?"(p. 88). At the age of 14, he accepts without protest her charge that he make his way in the world, although the thought of taking a job seems like "bondage" to him and "[kills] all joy and even life" (p. 89). But in her determination that he succeed, Mrs Morel is oblivious to his needs. Significantly, her concern for Paul's success in the outer world corresponds to her gradual realization that William is betraying her trust and her love. The emphasis on Paul in chapter V ("Paul Launches into Life") alternates with brief but significant vignettes about William. Before Mrs Morel sets off to Nottingham with Paul, "gay, like a sweetheart," she has begun to suspect that William, who sent her money only twice from London, is not fulfilling the acknowledged role of provider and the suppressed role of gallant knight that would make him a substitute for Morel (p. 92).

Although at first Mrs Morel seems physically and psychically weakened after William's death, she recuperates when Paul's illness gives her an opportunity to transfer her affections to the next son. As William's relationship with Gyp had developed in intensity and as William had ceased to pay her economic homage, she already had begun turning toward Paul: "Mrs Morel clung now to Paul . . . [S]till he stuck to his painting and still he stuck to his mother. Everything he did was for her. She waited for his coming home in the evening, and then she unburdened herself of all she had pondered, or of all that had occurred to her during the day . . . The two shared lives" (p. 114). Perhaps in the choice of verbs ("clung," "stuck," "unburdened"), we can feel something of Lawrence's resentment as his narrator recalls how Paul was asked to play a role of surrogate husband that deprived him of much of his adolescence. Since Mrs Morel teaches her children by example to be dissatisfied with spouse and home, William's disastrous choice of someone completely unsuited to him and the very antithesis of the people he has known, as well as Paul's dissatisfaction with the women in his life, can be in part attributed to Mrs Morel's influence. How devastating is the effect on the young adolescent of his mother's speaking of the family parlor as "a beastly cold, sunless hole" (p. 98)! Rather grossly and insensitively, Mrs Morel specifically calls William's failure to Paul's attention: "But they're all alike. They're large in promises, but it's precious fulfillment you get . . . They don't care about helping you, once they've gone" (p. 99).

Just like the mother in Lawrence's 1926 story "The Rocking-Horse Winner," Mrs Morel's economic discontent wrenches family relationships. Yet we see little to indicate that the Morels are ever so destitute that it interferes with their basic comfort. Mrs Morel attributes almost magical significance to money. As in the later story, money becomes a virtual substitute for sperm. Money is the means by which Mrs Morel accepts sexual fealty. Her resentment both of Gyp and of her husband's male camaraderie and the concomitant drinking involves not only anger that money is being wasted, but sexual jealousy. Until William's affair with Gyp, she takes special pride in his salary. Money is a sanctioned sexual tribute that her sons may deliver without guilt on the part of giver or recipient. The narrator's voice has a touch of wonder and awe as he recounts how William becomes ill because he has delivered both his money and his actual sperm to Gyp. It is worth recalling that to a considerable extent William is based on the actual history of Lawrence's brother Ernest. But within the fictive world, William's sudden pneumonia and subsequent death have the parabolic, non-mimetic quality of Paul's death in "The Rocking-Horse Winner," as if he were being punished for some mysterious transgression involving the mother.

Beginning with chapter IV ("The Young Life of Paul"), the structure of each chapter affirms the extent of Paul's bondage to his mother and the claustrophobic effect of these ties upon his emotional development. Characteristically, a chapter raises the hope of experience which will move Paul outward. But, gradually, Mrs Morel's influence restricts and confines the possibility of new relationships and important self-discovery. Each movement outward is arrested by Paul's obsession with his mother. For example, chapter VII, "Lad-and-Girl Love," begins with the promise of exorcising the intense but destructive passion between mother and son with which part one ended. Paul and Miriam are both excessively self-conscious but they gradually establish a rapport. Throughout the chapter, Mrs Morel's disapproval intervenes to block the natural development of Paul's relationship with Miriam. This chapter's conclusion shows why "their intimacy was so abstract" and why he "suppressed into a shame" his sexual desire; his mother's rebuke for returning late punctuates a chapter in which his loyalty to his mother comes between Miriam and himself (p. 178). At crucial moments, when he is tormented by his passion for his mother and tortured by his inability to respond sexually to Miriam or his mother, his repressed libidinous urges find an outlet in antagonism to Miriam: "He hated her, for she seemed in some way to make him despise himself . . . He loved to think of his mother, and the other jolly people" (p. 179). Of course, his mother is, with rare exception, a humorless figure.

In the next chapter, "Strife in Love," the narrator shifts his focus on Miriam and Paul to show briefly how the mother's influence continues. When Paul wins the painting contest, her joy has a self-indulgent aspect as she takes these victories as self-vindication: "Paul was going to distinguish himself . . . She was to see herself fulfilled. Not for nothing had been her struggle" (p. 183). The extent to which Mrs Morel's perspective, which to the reader seems limited and self-serving, is given legitimacy and implicit endorsement by the narrator can be seen when the narrator anticipates Mrs Morel's thought that Miriam "wants to absorb him" with the comment that "[Miriam] loved him absorbedly" (pp. 189, 193). Paul's reasons for hating Miriam are illogical, implausible, and revealing: "If Miriam caused his mother suffering then he hated her – and he easily hated her. Why did she make him feel as if he were uncertain of himself, insecure, and an indefinite thing . . . ?" (p. 193). Later in the chapter, after he seems to have found an outlet for his libido in adolescent sex play with Beatrice, Mrs Morel rebukes him for failing to care for the bread while Miriam was there. His response is to remind her of his age: "You're old, mother, and we're young" (p. 212). This is the catalyst for a quarrel which ends in Mrs Morel's conclusive triumph over Miriam in the form of Paul's and his mother's passionate, incestuous embrace.

The narrator continually insists upon distinctions between Miriam and Paul, and between Miriam and Mrs Morel, while the narrative shows that in many ways the Leivers family mirrors the Morels. If Miriam is a "maiden in bondage, her spirit dreaming in a land far away and magical," Paul is a lad in bondage to his mother (p. 145). Considering the altercations and antipathy that divide the Morel family, it is astonishing that Paul criticizes the "jangle and discord in the Leivers family" (p. 147). That Paul is immediately attracted to the rather supercilious and patronizing Leivers family at all shows how he has been educated by Mrs Morel's social pretensions: "Ordinary folk seem shallow to [the Leivers], trivial and inconsiderable. And so they were unaccustomed, painfully uncouth in the simplest social intercourse, suffering, and yet insolent in their superiority" (p. 147). His attraction to someone whom he later suspects of wishing to dominate him and who imagines herself a "princess turned into a swine-girl" shows that he responds to those qualities that suggest his mother (p. 142). That Miriam feels a need to "swathe" and "stifle" her 4-year-old brother recalls vividly how Mrs Morel passionately encloses her sons. The narrator gives a motive for Mrs Morel's jealousy by implying, without ever providing real dramatic corroboration, that Miriam wishes to mother Paul: "If she could be mistress of him in his weakness, take care of him, if he could depend on her, if she could, as it were, have him in her arms, how she would love him!" (p. 143). As Paul becomes dependent on Miriam for aesthetic stimulation and for bringing out his spiritual aspect, he almost gives her the status of his mother and creates competition between the two women within his psyche.

Do we not need to remember that there are also substantial differences between the Leivers and Paul's own family? He is first attracted to Mrs Leivers because she – unlike his mother – responds to the significance of an experience in terms other than economic. In contrast to his mother's expedience and pragmatism, the Leivers perceive spiritually and think abstractly. Their effect on him is different: "They kindled him and made him glow to his work, whereas his mother's influence was to make him quietly determined, patient, dogged, unwearied" (p. 149).

Within the narrative, it often seems that Miriam represents the "shimmeriness" which is "the real living," while it is the mother who is the "shape" which "is a dead crust" (p. 152). If Paul talks about "shimmeriness," he does so in "abstract" speeches, while it is Miriam's "dark eyes alight like water that shakes with a stream of gold in the dark" (p. 152). When she yearns for him, he desires to kiss her in "abstract purity" and then he criticizes her for not "[realizing] the male he was" (pp. 188–9). In "Strife in Love," while he is watching his mother's bread and teaching Miriam French, Miriam is described in terms that suggest the bride in the Song of Songs ("She was coloured like a pomegranate for richness") and only awaits Paul's sexual response to arouse her: "Her dark eyes were naked with their love, afraid, and yearning" (p. 208). But it is Paul who cannot respond: "He knew, before he could kiss her, he must drive something out of himself" (p. 208). As Paul stomps to the oven, Lawrence's narrator cannot but reveal how Paul has affected his vulnerable but complaisant friend: "Even the way he crouched before the oven hurt her. There seemed to be something cruel in it, something cruel in the swift way he pitched the bread out of the tins" (p. 208). Rather than allowing Miriam to complement his experience and *enjoy* her difference, he uses his mother's qualities as norms to *judge* the difference he discovers in Miriam: "Her intensity which would leave no emotion on a normal plane, irritated the youth into a frenzy . . . He was used to his mother's reserve. And on such occasions, he was thankful in heart and soul that he had his mother, so *sane* and *wholesome*" (p. 153; emphasis mine).

The narrator's distinction between Miriam's desire to shape Paul and his mother's need to will his future often seems a distinction without a difference. Like Mrs Morel, Miriam "gave him all her love and her faith" and wishes to "guard" the best of him from the pollution of the outside world (p. 249). Deliberately mocking both Miriam's view of her sexual role and the hyperbolic conventions of Platonic love to which (according to him) she subscribes, the narrator remarks: "Nay, the sky did not cherish the stars more surely and eternally than she would guard the good in the soul of Paul Morel" (p. 249). Using ironic religious language, the narrator presents Miriam's self-sacrifice as perverse: "Miriam [is] tortured . . . [because] he [is] utterly unfaithful to her" (pp. 250–1). But Mrs Morel is also a worshipper who denies herself so that her idealized son – her godhead – might flourish. She is tortured by his need for a sexual partner. And she, too, transfers her sublimated passion into religious paroxysms; she "prayed and prayed for him, that he might not be wasted" (p. 258). Even more than Miriam's prayers, hers derive from her compulsion to shape his life to her model, and to live through his achievements. Mrs Morel's prayer is the expression of her will and hence, according to the values that pervade Lawrence's work, mechanistic and contrary to organic being. The reader understands that prayer is a socially sanctioned means by which she can direct her son's life. Intellectually, Paul knows "that one should feel inside oneself for right and wrong, and should have the patience to gradually realise one's God" (p. 256). But because he has "realised" his mother, his god – the individuating principle that makes each person be himself or herself and enables each person to tap his or her latent potential – eludes him. The narrative dramatizes the tension between extrinsic standards inculcated by his mother and his inherent need to fulfill himself.

III Loving Miriam: Paul at War with Himself

Our basic premise has been that Paul's inadequacies are unconsciously ignored and underplayed by the narrator, but that the dramatic events render a more complex vision of the human relationships that form the subject of *Sons and Lovers*. The preterite does not guarantee objectivity. That Lawrence was still coming to terms with the experience that forms the novel's raw material undoubtedly deflected him from objective analysis. The tension between the narrator's myth-making and the greater objectivity of much of the dramatic action may be part of the hold that the novel exercises upon its readers. We, as readers, participate in Lawrence's continuous and often ineffectual struggles with his mother's influence and his oedipal love. The concatenation of individual moments gives a different perspective to the scenes in which Paul and Miriam struggle with their inhibitions and psychic problems. The narrator's persistent efforts to attribute to Miriam insidious emotions that are not demonstrated within the dramatic action finally raise doubts about the quality of the narrator's analyses.

An example of how the narrative renders the complexities of the issues despite the narrator's insistent defense of Paul occurs in the early pages of "Defeat of Miriam," a chapter that might just as appropriately be entitled "Defeat of Paul." After he makes his commitment to his mother not to marry while she lives, the degeneration of his relationship with Miriam accelerates. Although the narrator begins by rendering Paul's narcissistic reactions, he finally turns to Miriam's confused response to Paul's announcement that he cannot love her physically:

[Paul] hated her bitterly at that moment because he made her suffer. Love her! She knew he loved her. He really belonged to her. This about not loving her, physically, bodily was a mere perversity on his part, because she knew she loved him. He was stupid like a child. He belonged to her. His soul wanted her . . . She guessed somebody had been influencing him. She felt upon him the hardness, the foreignness of another influence. (p. 222)

Although the narrator starts by attributing to Miriam both an attitude of condescension and a sense of ownership, this distorted view gives way to a more sympathetic understanding of her plight. The preceding and subsequent events make clear that: (1) Paul's "hatred" derives not from making her suffer, but from his obligations to "another influence," Mrs Morel; (2) his arrested sexual development does make him behave "like a child."

Lawrence's use of omniscience to render a spurious version of Miriam's thinking is an example of what we might call the aesthetics of distortion. A significant breakdown in narrative distance occurs when the narrator accepts Paul's interpretation of Miriam's response to his terminating of their relationship ("The Test on Miriam"). She protests that Paul has always been fighting to free himself. Neither Paul nor the narrator realizes that her response is defensive, deriving from her "self-mistrust." Seeking a reason to make her the scapegoat, Paul becomes enraged that "She had hidden all her condemnation from him, had flattered him, and despised him" (p. 297). Intellectually, the narrator knows that Paul's indignation is inappropriate and hyperbolic, but he cannot bring himself to condemn Paul. In consecutive paragraphs, he renders Paul's consciousness with gentle irony and Miriam's with bitter, scathing irony. Paul's adolescent and exaggerated response is presented in a series of short, almost choppy, declarative sentences to parody logical thought; the quality of his clichéd thinking is self-indicting. Yet, despite his guise of critically observing Paul, the narrator's presentation of Miriam's thoughts seem to confirm Paul's belief that he is the wronged party in the relationship:

> He sat in silence. He was full of a feeling that she had deceived him. She had despised him when he thought she worshipped him. She had let him say wrong things, and had not contradicted him. She had let him fight alone. But it stuck in his throat that she had despised him whilst he thought she worshipped him . . . All these years she had treated him as if he were a hero, and thought of him secretly as an infant, a foolish child. Then why had she left the foolish child to his folly? His heart was hard against her. (p. 298)

But both this passage and the one that immediately follows are inconsistent with the Miriam whom we know. Can we really believe that her mind has worked in Machiavellian ways to entrap subtly a man whom she regards as a "foolish child" and as a "baby"?

> Why this bondage for her? . . . Why was she fastened to him? . . . She would obey him in his trifling commands. But once he was obeyed, then she had him in her power, she knew, to lead him where she would. She was sure of herself. Only, this new influence! And, he was not a man! He was a baby that cries for the newest toy. And all the attachment of his soul would not keep him. Very well, he would have to go. But he would come back when he had tired of his new sensation. (pp. 298–9)

According to the narrator, Miriam deliberately manipulates her "bondage" into "conquest" by seeming to obey while actually taking the lead. After experimenting with other relationships, Paul will return to her because he is a captive of her will, an instrument to fulfill her narcissistic needs, and a child who needs a tolerant mother figure. (Such a view of Miriam gives validity to the indignation that the narrator shares with Paul.)

The reader knows that Miriam does not think in these terms and realizes that the narrator is attributing these motives to her as a means of exonerating Paul, who has been increasingly exploiting her. Her love for nature, her idealism, and her spiritual quest make it clear that even if she were to lack vitality and passion (as Paul and the narrator incorrectly assume), she surely is not lacking in integrity and dignity. The Miriam of the novel may temporarily oversimplify her relationship to Paul as a "battle" from the beginning, but she is not a Machiavelli of sexual politics capable of loving the man she despises. If she is bitter, sufficient reasons are found in the narrative. Paul cannot commit himself to her, while she can to him. Despite her self-mistrust and masochism, her bondage is the pathetic one of the woman who loves not wisely but too well. The above passages also inadvertently reveal how the Jessie–Miriam relationship in its non-sexuality helped compensate for the childhood of which Lawrence had been partially deprived by his mother's demands. That Miriam, the narrator, and even Paul use the child metaphor for Paul indicates that Lawrence suspected that his oedipal relationship had arrested his sexual and emotional development.

The narrator's insistence that Paul's infatuation with his mother is a representative rather than an idiosyncratic one and that it typifies the "tragedy of thousands of young men in England" derives from Lawrence's need to believe this. But the novel presents little evidence that others share Paul's particular problems. Morel, Baxter, and Arthur may have various forms of emotional difficulties, but they seem to function sexually. William's problem is not that he is diffident and shy, but that he becomes entrapped by a naive pursuit of what he has been taught by his mother to consider the Better Life. No, the polemic derives from Lawrence's need to generalize his surrogate's sexual difficulties with Miriam.[6]

In the crucial opening paragraph of "The Test on Miriam," Paul wills himself to try to "get things right" sexually and marry Miriam. (At this point, the intellectual, logical, and almost mechanical process by which he arrives at a decision mimics his mother's process of thinking.) Again we see that the test on Miriam is really the test of Paul's ability to break loose from his mother. In *Fantasia of the Unconscious* (1922), Lawrence might be addressing Paul's problem when he writes:

> Every frenzied individual is told to find fulfillment in love. So he tries. Whereas, there is no fulfillment in love. Half of our fulfillment comes *through* love, through strong, sensual love. But the central fulfillment, for a man, is that he possess his own soul in strength within him, deep and alone. The deep, rich aloneness, reached and perfected through love and the passing beyond any further *quest* of love.[7] (emphases Lawrence's)

Paul cannot find joy and fulfillment in an adult relationship because he is possessed by his mother.[8] The obtrusive ironic images – the four dead birds, and the remains of the cherries on which they had fed (the ripened cherries had at first seemed proleptic of the young couple's sexual maturity) – suggest that the retrospective narrator takes a morbid view of the sexual consummation and regards it as merely another mutual act of desperation to blur Paul's and Miriam's fundamental incompatibility. Although he uses these fictive devices to suggest that Paul is the victim of Miriam's frigidity, the narrator acknowledges that Paul found the coition reasonably satisfying: "[H]e felt as if nothing mattered, as if his living were smeared away into the beyond, near and quite loveable. This strange, gentle reaching out to death was new to him" (p. 287). If he achieves inner peace in the sexual act, surely Miriam is partly responsible. Intercourse divests him of the values his mother has rooted in him, neutralizes temporarily the urgency and intensity that she has given his life and career, and enables him to experience nature's rhythms and energy. Saying that he feels "so strange and still," he explains to Miriam: "To be rid of our individuality, which is our will, which is our effort – to live effortless, a kind of curious sleep – that is very beautiful, I think; that is our after-life – our immortality" (pp. 287–8). Moreover, Paul discovers the stillness and inaction of death and the unknown, aspects of existence that Mrs Morel has increasingly denied, but that his father instinctively knows.

That his mother refuses to accept death reveals her fundamental incompatibility with nature. She had tried to reincarnate William by shifting her love to Paul. Later, she willfully refuses to accept the natural cycle of life after she almost perversely holds to life after illness has reduced her body to a virtual skeleton. Because of his joyous sexual release, Paul does escape from his mother for a moment. His desire to eschew effort and will derives from the pressure of Mrs Morel's compelling demands upon him. Temporarily, the sex act nullifies his mother's hold on him and makes her values irrelevant. But precisely because of this, he cannot admit that his sexual relationship with Miriam is satisfactory. Technical omniscience gives Lawrence the sanction to plead his case. Considering what Paul seems to have achieved, the narrator's criticism of Miriam's giving herself as a "sacrifice in which she felt something of horrors" should be taken as an example of Lawrence's need to believe that Miriam is incapable of passion (p. 286). In view of her prolonged virginity, her prior repression and self-denigration, we should hardly be surprised if she experiences a moment of awkwardness and self-doubt.

Their sexual consummation is the prelude to the demise of their personal relationship, and Lawrence's speaker must shift the onus to Miriam. Can one really trust his version of their meeting at Miriam's grandmother's house?

Paul's perspective is a subjective one that reflects his own problems, and his interpretation of her gestures and gazes is moot:

> [H]er hands lifted in a little pleading movement, and he looked at her face, and stopped. Her big brown eyes were watching him, still and resigned and loving; she lay as if she had given herself up to *sacrifice*; there was her body for him; but the look at the back of her eyes, like a creature awaiting immolation, arrested him, and all his blood fell back. (pp. 289–90; emphasis mine)

That years of sexual restraint have marked their relationship is reflected by her slight sign of physical reluctance, but this does not necessarily indicate Miriam's disinclination for sex. Although she says that she wants him, the narrator insists that she regards her sexual participation as "sacrificial." Since the religious terminology is within Paul's mind (he has just said to her: "Your face is bright . . . like a transfiguration"), perhaps the terms "sacrifice" and "immolation" should be ascribed to his imagination (p. 289). Paul's need to criticize her at this point is intensified by his having just compared her with his mother: "He thought she gave a feeling of home almost like his mother" (p. 289). The domestic arrangements within the cottage create a situation in which Miriam displaces his mother as the one responsible for caring for him.

Sex as a ritual between master and victim answers both their impulses. If Miriam's understanding of her sexual role involves sacrifice and submission, Paul does not discourage her from this. He associates sex with death, because he feels guilty for betraying his mother: "As he rode home he felt that he was finally initiated. He was a youth no longer. But why had he the dull pain in his soul? Why did the thought of death, the after-life, seem so sweet and consoling?" (p. 290). That Paul thinks of the word "initiation" in association with "pain" and "death" is revealing because it shows that he regards sex as a ritual to be passed through at a cost to oneself – indeed, as a sacrifice. If Paul and Miriam do not achieve a mutual orgasm, is it not in part because his subconscious will not allow him to replace his mother as his primary passion? Since a fulfilling sexual relationship would give a benediction to his friendship with Miriam, Paul has to find fault with it. The narrator tries to muster evidence to support the view that the alleged sexual failure is Miriam's responsibility when he has her cite the lesson she has learned from her mother: "There is one thing in marriage that is always dreadful, but you have to bear it" (p. 291). But Miriam disavows this rubric and is ready to respond to Paul's tenderness and understanding were Paul able to manifest these qualities. The reader knows that Paul must severely criticize Miriam now that he has been sleeping with her, because he already belongs to his mother.

IV Loving Clara: Paul's Temporary Escape

No sooner does Paul begin his sexual relationship with Miriam than his sub-conscious requires that he discard her and turn his thoughts to Clara. The narrator is not ironic about Paul's rapid reversal of field: "But insidiously, without knowing it, the warmth he felt for Clara drew him away from Miriam, for whom he felt responsible, and to whom he felt he belonged" (p. 292). As he turns from Miriam to Clara, his anxiety and tension ease. Interestingly, when Paul announces that he is breaking off with Miriam, the narrator stresses natural and vital aspects of her appearance that Paul has been ignoring: "She has made herself look so beautiful and fresh for him. She seemed to blossom for him alone" (p. 295). Just as the narrator is on occasion grudgingly fair to Mr Morel – Paul's father – in part one, so in part two he will reluctantly give Miriam her due. But the parallel is instructive precisely because the narrator purports to *value* Miriam – with whom Paul is in love – while he is obviously hostile to Paul's father.

Martz argues that narrative objectivity is resumed in chapter XII and speaks of Paul's "remarkable self-understanding" in chapter XIII. But neither Paul nor the retrospective narrator understands (1) why Paul is attracted to Clara, and then needs to reject her and to reconcile her to Dawes; (2) why he is tempted to revive his relationship with Miriam; and (3) why he is unable to posit a direction for himself after his mother's death. Martz oversimplifies the effect on Paul of his affair with Clara. If it really has a "clarifying, purgatorial" effect, why is Paul as self-conscious, self-doubting, and fretful as he has always been (Martz, "Portrait of Miriam," p. 365)?

Although Clara has helped Paul to discover that sex can be vital and healthy, has it really enabled "them to find a truth" beyond sex (ibid.)? His behavior with Clara is hardly more logical than it is with Miriam. His interpretation of Clara's attitudes and motives is not substantiated by her behavior and conver-sations, and his criticism of her after their sexual relationship develops derives from his psychic need to separate himself from her, a need that is intensified by his mother's failing health. In chapters XII through XV, as in chapters VII through XI, and to a lesser extent in the first six chapters, the narrator engages in myth-making, exoneration of his protagonist, and hypothetical theories of conduct that seem inadequate to the phenomena that he presents.

Paul does find limited sexual fulfillment with Clara. In a setting that looks backward to a prehistoric time before humans inhabited the earth ("The cliff of red earth sloped swiftly down, through trees and bushes, to the river that glimmered and was dark between the foliage"), he has sex without real emo-tional involvement (p. 308). As the sexual relationship continues and as an emotional tie begins to evolve, he feels that Clara, too, wishes to possess him. Once Mrs Morel understands that Clara is not a real threat ("It would be hard for any woman to keep him. Her heart glowed; then she was sorry for Clara") she is soon "at her ease" (pp. 321–2). Yet the Puritanical Coppard value system has been inculcated in Paul, and he recognizes Clara as a lesser woman than Miriam "if it came to goodness" (p. 326). When the narrator renders Clara's alleged sense of guilt ("After all, she was a married woman, and she had no right even to what he gave her"), we cannot but feel he is really revealing his and Paul's discomfort over sleeping with a somewhat older woman who is married to a man not dissimilar to Mr Morel (p. 352). When Paul arouses Clara as his father had his mother and displaces Baxter, a man who resembles his father in age, manner, and behavior, he slips into the dialect of his father. Paul ritualistically restores Clara to her proper mate as if to compensate for his disloyalty to his father. The very title of the chapter most concerned with Paul's and Clara's sexual relationship, "Baxter Dawes," may be indicative of Lawrence's unconscious need to pacify his memories of his disloyalty to his father even as he tells the tale.[9]

That the narrator's conception of the ideal sexual relationship involves the very self-sacrifice on the part of the woman that he had condemned in Miriam reveals not only his inconsistency, but the residue of his oedipal love: "[Clara] took him simply because his need was bigger either than her or him, and her soul was still within her. She did this for him in his need, even if he left her, for she loved him" (p. 353). Because of his non-involvement with Clara's soul, because he regards her as a sexual object – and as an older woman with whom, unlike his mother, he can legitimately have sex – he can remain comfortably separate from her once the sex act is complete. The narrator accepts Paul's distinctions between sex with Clara and with Miriam, even though the differences are not nearly as clear as both Paul and the narrator make them. The sexual act is an "initiation" and "satisfaction" for each, because it transports them from their conscious selves into a timeless world where the processes of the intellect are suspended: "To know their own nothingness, to know the tremendous living flood which carried them always, gave them rest within themselves . . . There was a verification which they had together. Nothing could nullify it, nothing could take it away: It was almost their belief in life" (p. 354). But is this so different from Paul's original response to sex with Miriam (pp. 287–8)?

Paul becomes dissatisfied with Clara because she, too, cannot fulfill his need for impersonal sex (does he not really mean anonymous sex?). And she is much less satisfactory than Miriam at directing his passive energies – something that his mother has taught him both to expect and require from his women. According to the narrator's argument, Clara needs to arrest the sexual moment because she herself is incompletely developed as a person. While

Paul needs to keep his sexual life "impersonal," Clara wants to "hold him" and possess him (p. 354). Yet, paradoxically, he also wants someone to "keep his soul steady" (p. 355). Neither Paul nor the narrator realizes that it is Miriam who would have come closer to Paul's emotional and sexual needs if Paul had been tender and responsive to her.

Paul, however, is uncomfortable *because* of the success of the sex with Clara: "She made him feel imprisoned when she was there, as if he could not get a free deep breath, as if there were something on top of him" (p. 359). Paul cannot accept sexual satisfaction, and needs to discover the ways in which Clara is not quite as sufficient as their joyous coition might indicate: "[T]he baptism of fire . . . was not Clara. It was something that happened because of her, but it was not her" (p. 354). If "baptism of fire" means the capacity to bring about sexual ecstasy and passionate fulfillment, how could any person be any more than a coequal partner? Does not Paul's expectation that Clara should be the autonomous means by which he achieves fulfillment show simultaneously how he places impossible demands upon his partners and how he sees himself as a rather passive participant to whom things are supposed to happen? Clara offers him passion, but he now must define her according to the very standards by which he had once found Miriam appealing but which he had rejected when he discredited her. Rather suddenly, the quest for the Good and Beautiful, the quest that was the catalyst for the evolution of the non-sexual relationship with Miriam, again becomes important: "Here's the seacoast morning, big and permanent and beautiful; there is she fretting, always unsatisfied, and temporary as a bubble of foam. What does [Clara] mean to me, after all? She represents something, like a bubble of foam represents the sea. But what is *she*? It's not her I care for" (p. 358; emphasis Lawrence's). Apparently, Clara is as wanting in soul and substance as Miriam had been in passion. His fear that Clara will "absorb" him hardly seems appropriate since his kisses seem "detached, hard, and elemental" and since Clara's "mission" is described by the narrator as "separate" from his (pp. 358, 361).

According to the narrator's myth, the passionate relationship with Clara enables Paul to grow and mature because his soul has been fertilized. But what about Clara? The narrator, Paul's surrogate, convinces himself that Paul has been the agent of Clara's revitalization: "It was almost as if she had gained *herself* and stood now distinct and complete. She had received her confirmation . . . [S]he *knew* now, she was sure of herself. And the same could almost be said of him" (p. 361; emphases Lawrence's). Once Clara realizes that she cannot meet his impossible expectations and that Paul will not accept her as she is, she wants to sacrifice herself to her former husband: "She wanted to humble herself to him, to kneel before him. She wanted now to be self-sacrificial" (p. 384). If Paul's psychic games and subsequent rejection of her cause the experienced and considerably more self-sufficient Clara to lose her sexual pride (for, no matter what the narrator says, "sacrifice" implies not only self-abnegation but submission), it is not surprising that the inexperienced adolescent Miriam had temporarily lost her sexual identity and had begun to worship perversely the young man who could not make love to her.

V   The Significance of the Ending

Paul and the narrator envision a linear pattern that dramatizes the development of Paul's consciousness, but the novel itself weaves an enclosing pattern that qualifies, if it does not parody, the final affirmation. The triumph of the mother within the novel is such that even Paul's turning away from death and acceptance of himself as a spark in the void are really an acceptance of his mother's notion that one can shape one's life by the sheer force of one's will: "But no, he would not give in. Turning sharply, he walked towards the city's gold phosphorescence. His fists were shut, his mouth set fast. He would not take that direction, to the darkness, to follow her. He walked towards the faintly humming, glowing town, quickly" (p. 420). As he walks toward the city where his mother had dreamed of his economic and social triumph, his expression (fists shut, mouth set fast) mirrors hers as she had approached death: "Her mouth gradually shut hard in a line. She was holding herself rigid . . . He never forgot that hard, utterly lonely and stubborn clenching of her mouth, which persisted for weeks" (pp. 385–6). Grotesquely, Mrs Morel's will continues to dominate Paul after her death. In turning from darkness, he turns to another kind of darkness because he has not yet exorcised the ghost of his destructive oedipal relationship. Thus the "drift towards death," the description Lawrence used to describe Paul's plight in the famous letter to Garnett, is an apt description of Paul's final state within the novel.[10]

The reader perceives that the narrator who renders the final scene as an affirmation is not yet free of the autobiographical sources. While Paul can withdraw from the Clara–Baxter–Paul triangle, he can never withdraw from the enclosing circle of his mother's influence:

> Sometimes he hated [Mrs Morel] and pulled at her bondage. His life wanted to free itself of her. It was like a circle where life turned back on itself, and got no farther. She bore him, loved him, and his love turned back into her, so that he could not be free to go forward with his own life, really love another woman. (p. 345)

That, after Mrs Morel's death removes the incest taboo, Paul perceives her in strikingly sexual terms shows her continuing hold on him: "She lay like a maiden asleep . . . She lay like a girl asleep and dreaming of her love . . . He bent and kissed her passionately. But there was coldness against his mouth" (p. 399). When Paul whimpers "mother" at the end of the novel, he completes the formal circle; he has finally and conclusively responded to Mrs Morel's desperate cry with which part one ended: "Oh, my son – my son!" (pp. 420, 141).[11]

Sons and Lovers mimes Lawrence's psyche rather than his intent.[12] The unsuccessful struggle of the omniscient narrator to achieve objectivity is as much the text's *agon* as the tale of Paul's abortive quest for psychosexual maturity. Reading *Sons and Lovers*, one also experiences the author's creative problems. That the retrospective narrator is hardly more perceptive than the protagonist, that the narrator is an insistent, urgent, and empathetic apologist for Paul, reveals the hold Lawrence's mother had upon his psyche. *Sons and Lovers* stares down the convention that technical distance and authorial omniscience imply objectivity or truth. It invites us to consider how obsessions and psychic needs penetrate a work of art, and transform and distort the intended form into something more complex, more disturbing, and more compelling.

Chapter 6

Lawrence's *The Rainbow*: Family Chronicle, Sexual Fulfillment, and the Quest for Form and Values

Now you will find [Frieda] and me in the novel, I think, and the work is of both of us. (April 22, 1914)[1]

I Introduction

A major subject of much modern literature is the author's quest for self-definition. In particular, the search for moral and aesthetic values is central to the novels of Joyce, Proust, Woolf, Conrad, and Lawrence. Yet we have neglected how novels reveal their authors because much modern criticism has been uncomfortable with the expressive qualities of texts. Certainly, the New Criticism insisted that texts be examined as self-referential ontologies which are distinct from their authors' lives. Unwilling to commit the intentional fallacy, Anglo-American formalism ceded discussion of the author to biographers, psychoanalytic critics, and, more recently, theorists and critics focusing on such issues as gender and power relationships. Yet because the quest for values – and the form and language by which these values are expressed – is a central subject in much modern fiction, it must be discussed as a formal component within the text, separate and distinct from the narrator or implied author. To neglect the dialogue between the creative process and the subject matter of the story is to ignore a fundamental part of the novel's imagined world. Lawrence's struggle with his subject (his relationship with Frieda) is a major aspect of *The Rainbow* (1915), just as *Sons and Lovers* dramatizes his struggle to come to terms with his relationship with Jessie Chambers and his mother. Moreover, the author's quest for self-understanding is central to other late nineteenth- and early twentieth-century British and Irish novelists: Conrad in the Marlow tales, Joyce in *A Portrait of the Artist* and *Ulysses*, and Woolf in *Mrs Dalloway* and *To the Lighthouse*.

With his propensity for hyperbole and iteration as well as his defiance of traditional literary forms, Lawrence defined himself as the bull in the china shop of the English novel and the English Christian tradition. As Lawrence's New New Testament arguing that Christianity's sexual prohibitions are in error, *The Rainbow* frames in a biblical context a family chronicle reaching from before the mid-nineteenth century to the first decade of the twentieth.

Well before *Lady Chatterley's Lover* (1928), Lawrence made a claim for being the spokesman for the body's pleasures. Is there any other male writer who examined woman's sexuality with such empathy? Breaking down gender stereotypes, Lawrence understood not only the intense and often unconscious sexual passion driving the behavior of men and women, but also the continuum between friendship and sexuality, between homosocial and homosexual behavior.

Lawrence's quest within *The Rainbow* for values and for an appropriate form is as important to the experience of reading the novel as his polemic. He wanted to write about the passions of men and women in a new way. He also wanted to re-create himself and to urge his readers to re-create themselves. He felt that the novel is particularly suited in its spaciousness for proposing, testing, and discarding formulations as its author seeks truth. *The Rainbow*'s unfolding process presents a history of his struggle for fulfillment. Each phase of the Brangwens' history dramatizes a crucial episode in Lawrence's development. We must read *The Rainbow* with a pluralistic perspective that takes account of its prophetic and polemical impulses, but does not grant them an authority over the text. The reader must be attentive to the novel's oscillation between, on the one hand, its prophetic and mythic impulses and, on the other, its dramatization of Lawrence's own process of discovery. I shall argue that (1) *The Rainbow* dramatizes Lawrence's quest for the kind of fiction that is appropriate both for passionate sexual relationships between men and women and for the struggle within each man between, to use his terms, mind-consciousness and blood-consciousness; (2) *The Rainbow* enacts Lawrence's quest for self-realization. In one sense, each generation represents aspects of his psyche and is a means by which he uses the novel to discover his own individuality.

As with *Sons and Lovers*, the telling of *The Rainbow* is as crucial an *agon* as the tale. Although the Ursula section was written first and the opening last, the book still roughly mimes the history of Lawrence's self-development. In the traditional novel narrated by an omniscient voice, one expects the voice to embody the values to which the characters evolve. But in *The Rainbow*, the narrator's values evolve and grow just like his characters, and the standards by which he evaluates behavior become more subtle and more intricate as the novel progresses. What is good for Tom and Lydia would not necessarily be sufficient for Ursula, or even Anna and Will. Each generation must go beyond its predecessor to sustain itself; Lawrence seeks to discover new standards as the family chronicle moves forward toward the time when he wrote the novel, in the second decade of the twentieth century.

Lawrence sought to dramatize the importance of sexuality, but he also sought to discover an aesthetic that would embody his ideas. Proposing a Newer Testament to replace the extant one is part of the dialectical struggle that is at the center of his creative life. In life and in art, he believed, the best we can do is open up infinite possibilities. The climactic rainbow is not only for Ursula and for England, but represents an *enactment* of the aesthetic success achieved by writing the novel; Lawrence walks through the final arch to create anew in *Women in Love* (1920). Like Ursula, his surrogate, he had to overcome dubiety and anxiety before he could go forward; hadn't he written in January 1915: "My soul lay in the tomb – not dead, but with a flat stone over it, a corpse, become corpse-cold. . . . I don't feel so hopeless now I am risen . . . We should all rise again from this grave . . . I know we shall all come through, rise again and walk healed and whole and new in a big inheritance, here on earth" (January 30, 1915; Huxley, *Letters*, p. 222)? This pattern – a downward movement followed by an upward one – anticipates the closing scene when Ursula overcomes despair by rediscovering not only her biological self, but her potential to be alive passionately and sensually.

Lawrence wrote his novel to announce a credo to replace the Christian mythology and value system that dominated English life for several centuries. He conceived himself as prophet, seer, visionary, shaman, and Divine Messenger. Reduced to its simplest terms, his message is that humankind must rediscover the lost, instinctive, biological, passionate self that has become sacrificed to democracy, imperialism, industrialism, and urbanization. Lawrence adopts biblical tales, images, syntax, and diction for the purpose of expounding a doctrine that undermines the traditional reading of the Bible. Yet he uses the biblical material to confer the stature of a Holy Book upon his novel, which argues for the centrality not of God but of the relationship between man and woman.

Given Lawrence's evangelical background, it was essential to his psyche that he come to terms with rather than reject the Bible. For him, the Bible itself was the prototypical novel because of its prophetic message. It has as its acknowledged purpose to announce God's law, and to show by its dramatic incidents how people should and should not behave.[2] Influenced undoubtedly by Frazer's *The Golden Bough* and the turn-of-the-century's interest in ethnology, Lawrence understood that the Bible embodied the ethical archetypes of European civilization. As with Hardy, the shape and intensity of Lawrence's unorthodox beliefs are only possible because he had once been a believer. *The Rainbow* reflects the needs of Lawrence's Puritan conscience (which he owed to his mother's fastidious piety) to atone for the sacrilege of allowing his imagination to supplant faith and reason. He sought to create myths that would be more true to his generation than the ones it inherited.

The Rainbow is Lawrence's quest to rediscover humankind's instinctive, libidinous, biological potential, which he believed lay underneath the trappings of the social self that civilization has produced and required to play acceptable roles. While each novel contains its own genesis with its own physical and moral geography, few novels take us into such an extraordinary world as *The Rainbow* does. What Lawrence must do in his early chapters is nothing less than re-educate the reader to a new grammar of motives where the value of a character's behavior is understood according to the degree to which it is true to its inner essence. Readers of *The Rainbow* are often baffled by what happens because the terms with which Lawrence describes behavior are so strange. Often they read the novel in an undergraduate course as part of a series of English novels in which manners and morals are stressed. Just as the episodes of Genesis provide us with the standards – the grammar of motives – to measure the rest of the Old Testament, the purpose of *The Rainbow*'s early chapters is to provide a grammar of passions so that in later chapters we will understand and recognize the deeper self beneath the mental processes of the conscious self.

Lawrence argues that passionate sexual relationships are not only beyond our understanding, but beyond our conscious control. That in *The Rainbow* he meant to propose a strikingly different kind of novel is clear from his oft-quoted letter about characterization: "I don't so much care about what the woman *feels* – in the ordinary usage of the word. That presumes an *ego* to feel with. I only care about what the woman *is* – what she *Is* – inhumanely, physiologically, materially" (June 5, 1914; Huxley, *Letters*, p. 200). But as he writes the novel, the characterization becomes increasingly complex until he does show us something of Ursula's feelings *and* ego.

The Rainbow shows how a writer's exploration of the potential of a genre can itself become part of his subject. Writing of an early draft of the then nameless book, Lawrence remarked: "It is all crude as yet. . . . most cumbersome and foundering . . . so new, so really a stratum deeper than I think anybody has ever gone in a novel" (March 11, 1913; Huxley, *Letters*, p. 113). He wished to write about "*the* problem of today, the establishment of a new relation, or the readjustment of the old one, between men and women" (April 17, 1913; Huxley, *Letters*, p. 120). Lawrence deliberately tries to reinvent the genre to address the passions of men and women. He writes of the unconscious life that he believed had escaped articulation by his predecessors and eschews, for the most part, the world of manners and morals that had provided the principal subject of the English novel. His prophetic voice displaces the ironic gentility of the traditional omniscient narrator of Victorian fiction. Nor does Lawrence adhere to the linear chronology of the realistic novel; he ignores references to the characters' ages and dates, and moves backward and forward when he chooses. Highlighting certain episodes and details while overlooking others aligns him not only with biblical tradition but also with Cubism and Postimpressionism, both of which had immense influence in England from the time of the major London exhibitions in the period 1910–12.

The structure and aesthetic of *The Rainbow* reflect Lawrence's evolving relationship with Frieda, who, in fact, gave the novel its title.[3] *The Rainbow* is part of his effort to destroy the old within him and to build a new self based on, but not limited by, his passionate marriage. Writing the novel became inextricably related to loving Frieda: "I am going through a transition stage myself . . . But I must write to live . . . It is not so easy for one to be married. In marriage one must become something else. And I am changing, one way or the other"(January 29, 1914; Huxley, *Letters*, p. 180). For all the certainty of the prophetic voice, his love for Frieda created new anxiety and uncertainty: "I seem to spend half my days having revulsions and convulsions from myself" (April 3, 1914; Huxley, *Letters*, p. 188). The concept of the novel as process and movement – so central to Lawrence's aesthetic – derives from his personal needs. In the famous letter to Garnett in which he rejected the old concept of character, he commented scathingly on novelists using a "moral scheme into which all the characters fit"; he wrote of *The Rainbow* (which, in this letter, he still called by the earlier title *The Wedding Ring*): "Don't look for the development of the novel to follow the lines of certain characters: the characters fall into the form of some other rhythmic form" (June 5, 1914; Huxley, *Letters*, pp. 200–1).

Thus *The Rainbow* is a personal novel, even at those moments when it is most prophetic. The novel dramatizes Lawrence's quest for the myth of the passionate Elect. It is also an outlet for his frustrated messianic impulses, impulses that neither his wife nor friends took very seriously. Emile Delavenay speaks of Lawrence's "constant search for disciples, which goes with the sense of a divine mission, of being predestined to make some revelation to mankind."[4]

No less than his Romantic predecessors – Blake, Shelley, and Wordsworth – Lawrence sought refuge from the stress of life in the comfort of his fictions. The opening pages of *The Rainbow* express his fantasy of men who live purposeful, proud, sexually fulfilled lives and who are not inhibited by artificial social restraints. Each Brangwen generation corresponds (1) to an historical period; (2) to stages of growth in the passionate Elect; (3) to an historical phase of England's development: from rural (Tom and Lydia) to village (Will and Anna) to urban, industrial society (Ursula); and (4) to important phases of Lawrence's relationship with Frieda. The process of myth-making, the reaching out for biblical archetypes, is part of Lawrence's effort to cleanse and to refresh himself. For him, each generation of Brangwens represents a partial recovery of freshness – a phase of growth that occurs both in his recollection of his past history and again in the very act of writing.

In the very first pages, the anonymous pre-verbal Brangwens represent the reaffirmation of the primitive instinctive origins of humankind. They dominate the space they inhabit as if they were twenty times or fifty times the size of normal people. They are giants of the earth bestriding their land like Colossi (p. 2).[5] For Lawrence this generation represents mythic forebears whose example still has meaning for modern humanity. Even as the opening renders the energy within nature and the men who are inseparable from nature, it announces the hyperbole, myth, and process that are central to the novel's aesthetic. After the canal and the railroad are introduced, the familial, agrarian life is no longer possible. Thus within Lawrence's myth of the giants of the earth, the Nephilim version of the creation myth, he also proposes a fortunate fall. The women are not content to live in "the drowse of blood intimacy" (p. 2). They feel that their world is anachronistic once industrialism touches it. They begin a quest for a richer life, for a life that contains an awareness of oneself and the world beyond the farm.

Lawrence is ambivalent toward the women's quest for knowledge and their turning away from a way of life where language and the life of the mind are secondary. Part of him wishes to return to the innocence of prehistory. But, as the novel evolves, he acknowledges that this old existence may obliterate distinctions among people, prevent the growth of the individual, and limit people's possibilities to contribute to the community. On the one hand, a nostalgic Lawrence eulogizes a world that had never really been and longs for what that past represents. On the other hand, Lawrence the contentious polemicist wishes to change the world through his fiction, and assumes the prophetic mantle to speak for the religion of the body.

II Tom and Lydia

Although Lydia, the experienced foreign woman, bears the first name of Lawrence's mother, she is a version of Frieda. Tom, the man aroused to his sexual and instinctual potential, is Lawrence's fantasy version of himself as a deeply passionate, intellectually unsophisticated figure. Tom and Lydia's instinctive relationship corresponds to Lawrence's sense of the early stage of his relationship with Frieda. Their climactic consummation is a paradigm for the surrender of ego and rebirth that Lawrence sought. Tom's hesitant steps outward to acknowledge and fulfill his deepest needs, followed by his subsequent immersion in a passionate, sensual embrace, represent the kind of unconscious life flow that people must rediscover. *Sons and Lovers* left Lawrence with some residual effects from his mother-love and the frigid relationship with Jessie Chambers. Tom, I believe, represents another attempt to get things right sexually. (Nor should we forget, if we understand the personal nature of this novel, that variations on Lawrence's own oedipal problems are central to Anna's relationship with her stepfather and Ursula's with her father.)

Tom and Lydia provide the first principle of Lawrence's grammar of passion. Lawrence uses the relationship between Tom and Lydia to show that *passionate* attraction takes place beneath the conscious level and disarms the intellect and the will. Lydia is roused to life despite her intention to withdraw from passionate attachments after the death of her husband. In Lawrence's Bible, passionate sexual attraction is akin to discovering Christ. On the basis of the most superficial acquaintance, of a few scant words between them, Tom feels Lydia's influence upon him: "There was an inner reality, a logic of the soul, which connected her with him" (p. 36). Tom is "nothingness" until he is completed and fulfilled by Lydia's acknowledgment. Stressing the impersonal physiological nature of this attraction, Lawrence uses pronouns which are adrift from their antecedents to describe the scenes of passionate interaction. Thus when Tom comes to announce his intention, she responds to his eyes: "The expression of his eyes changed, become less impersonal, as if he were looking almost at her, for the truth of her. Steady and intent and eternal they were, as if they would never change. They seemed to fix and to resolve her. She quivered, feeling herself created, will-less, lapsing into him, into a common will with him" (p. 40).

The scene is a deliberate parody of the traditional Victorian courtship scene where a man asks for the hand of the woman. Not only is the father absent, and the woman a widow with child; not only has the man's announcement preceded any social relationship; but the amenities and conventions of English proper behavior are flouted at every turn. Lawrence's audience would have hardly expected the following dialogue in a relationship that took place in the 1860s:

> "You want me?" she said . . .
>
> "Yes," he said . . .
>
> "No," she said, not of herself. "No, I don't know." (p. 40)

Nor did such a dialogue conform to the conventions of 1915. Such a scene could serve as Lawrence's epigraph, if not epitaph, to the novel of manners and morals that continued to be England's dominant genre, despite the recent work of Joyce, an exiled Irishman, and Conrad, a Polish *emigré*.

As we read *The Rainbow* we experience Lawrence's search for the appropriate language with which to convey unconscious, physiological states. When the voice speaks in biblical diction, he provides a benediction for his characters; echoing Genesis to describe Tom's and Lydia's first passionate kiss, he implies that a new beginning is something that is continually possible for every individual soul: "[Tom] returned gradually, but newly created, as after a gestation, a new birth, in the womb of darkness . . . And the dawn blazed in them, their new life came to pass, it was beyond all conceiving good, it was so good that it was almost a passing-away, a trespass" (p. 41).

Lawrence goes beyond *Sons and Lovers* in the use of nature imagery to confer value on his characters' sexual responses and to make human sexuality a microcosm of the natural cycle of the cosmos. In a realistic novel, the following sentence, describing Lydia's response to Tom, would not mean much: "But she would wake in the morning one day and feel her blood running, feel herself lying open like a flower unsheathed in the sun, insistent and potent with demand" (p. 50). The gathering sexual energy of such words as "running," "lying," "open," "unsheathed," "insistent," "potent," and "demand" charges the sentence with implication and power independent of its syntactical meaning. Furthermore, "blood," "flower," and "sun" place the urgent sexuality in the context of nature's rhythms. The sentence's one metaphor, "open like a flower," suggests that the opening of the woman for sex is akin to the receptiveness of the flower to the fertilizing bee. Beginning with the first use of "feel," moving to "blood," and continuing through "potent" and "demand," the heavily stressed prose (suggestive of Hopkins's poetry) gathers to a crescendo the sentence's power and urgency. As if to mime the arousing of her unconscious self, "running" carries Lydia's awakened instincts through to "potent" and "demand." The onomatopoeia of "running" stands in a phonic tension with the slow, stately power of "potent with demand." Within the sentence the sexual act is encapsulated. Not only does the male sperm "run" to the awaiting female, but the male, who feels incomplete, turns to what Lawrence regards as the stronger physicality of the female. And this is exactly what happens in the action of the novel.

While the quoted sentence describes Lydia's passionate awakening, the sentence also anticipates the sexual act which her arousal from sleep makes possible. Once Lydia becomes awakened to her instincts and passion, she stands in readiness for the male. Lydia's awakening becomes a standard, albeit not the only one, by which Lawrence measures the more complex psyches of Anna and Ursula. Lydia is representative of immersion in sexuality and family, immersion that becomes increasingly difficult as England moves from agrarian to industrial society. The purity and simplicity of analogies with nature in the above passage disappear from the novel when the sexuality of later generations is described. Yet even Lydia's life is a quantum jump in complexity from the anonymity of the opening pages. Each of the four phases of Brangwen life takes Lawrence more time to describe because changing external conditions introduce new complexities into people's quest to realize their being.

A major difficulty in Lawrence's quest for form is that he wished to dramatize the continuing flux of passions as that flux sought what he called, somewhat paradoxically, an "external stillness that lies under all movement, under all life, like a source, incorruptible and inexhaustible."[6] He found this stillness in myth. *The Rainbow* depends on a tension between the movement of the narrative and the stasis of myth, which by its nature implies iteration of human experience. In the climax of the story of each generation, myth displaces process. The result is more like an elaborate rococo painting than a linear episode.

In the climax of the Tom and Lydia section, Lawrence proposes a parallel to the apocalyptic wedding in Revelation; Lydia as the Holy City comes down from heaven as a bride adorned for her husband, Tom, who has heretofore held something of himself back and not fully accepted her otherness. Tom and Lydia surrender their egos and give themselves over to their passionate embrace, but something seems to be missing. Their victory comes at the expense of separateness and individuality. Part of the problem is the religious context: "[H]e relinquished himself . . . losing himself to find her, to find himself in her" (p. 90). The very terms of the victory make us aware of the limitations of the biblical parallel. While the Bible moves toward apocalypse and the suspension of time, the displacement of *chronos* (chronological time measured by the tick-tock of the clock) by *kairos* (significant time), the regenerate soul never comes to rest. It is always seeking but never finding *kairos* except during the sex act.[7] By definition, apocalypse implies that all become one in the kingdom of heaven, and distinctions will no longer be possible. But Tom and Lydia must return to the everyday temporal world.

Thus while they are born into another life, there is something unsatisfactory about their kind of union. On one hand, it provides a shelter for the children, or at least for Anna, in whom the Brangwens' passionate heritage mysteriously resides, although she was not born a Brangwen. But, on the other hand, the children of blood intimacy do not develop their full potential, as if there was something stifling to the growth of the soul in the marriage of Tom and Lydia. Their sexual passion creates a "richness" of physiological energy at the expense of mental activity and awareness of the world (p. 100). Anna finally lapses into such physiological richness and Ursula is tempted by it when she is pregnant. While one part of Lawrence longed for this, another knew that such a life placed a constraint upon further development.

Lawrence is ambivalent toward Tom's and Lydia's victory, because their embrace *excludes* that aspect of him that must participate in the world of community and utterance. He moves on to the next generation in part because once he establishes the quality of Tom's and Lydia's passionate embrace, he is no longer interested in Tom and can no longer identify with him. Tom, who once had the need to explore new and strange experiences, lapses into the blood intimacy of his forebears. Gradually, almost reluctantly, the voice acknowledges that Tom's achievement comes at the cost of giving up his quest into the unknown. Lawrence needs to extricate himself from his immersion in Tom because he is no longer an appropriate model for Lawrence's own quest to resolve blood-consciousness and mind-consciousness. Tom has been the means of dramatizing one aspect of Lawrence to the exclusion of others.

But Lawrence resists easy answers in defining his grammar of passions, and that resistance, that refusal to allow his myth to triumph over his own insights, is part of the novel's aesthetic, its meaning, and, ultimately, its greatness. Competing for his attention with the prophetic impulse is the nominalistic impulse, which insists on making distinctions and undermining the simplifications of polemics.

Lydia articulates Lawrence's basic premise in the novel: "Between two people, the love itself is the important thing, and that is neither you nor him. It is a third thing you must create" (p. 172). But neither the novel's opening dumb-show nor the story of Tom and Lydia speaks to the problem between Anna and Will. In his impulse to lose himself either in sexuality or in religious mystery, Will is trying to go back to a simpler world. His effort to reconcile his aesthetic impulse with "passionate embrace" mimes Lawrence's. Except when they come together in passion, Anna and Will must inevitably remain separate; nor do they have, like Tom and Lydia, the teeming richness of the farm to sustain them.

III Anna and Will

The Anna and Will section corresponds to the passionate struggle that raged between Lawrence and Frieda while he wrote the novel. In the Anna–Will relationship, Lawrence explores the second principle of the grammar of passions: each person must bring an independent existence to marriage. The sheaf-gathering scene defines the essential problem between Anna and Will. Like Hardy, who uses the May-dance in *Tess*, Lawrence knew that, within rural life, vestiges of primitive rites survived in England. He implies that the way forward may be to reach back to our anthropological origins when humankind was one with nature. Anna is defined in terms of extended space and of nature ("[S]he called . . . from afar . . . like a bird unseen in the night" [p. 119]), but Will is restricted by something within him that keeps him from fully participating in the pagan sexual dance. Will cannot lapse out of consciousness; his name defines the quality that holds him back: will. By will, Lawrence means an active need to assert one's consciousness upon the world, a need he recognized in himself.

The chapter entitled "Anna Victrix" defines the problem of man and woman after they have awakened to self-consciousness and are no longer in rhythm with nature in a pastoral world. Now that he has introduced new social and economic conditions, Lawrence must redefine the terms with which to describe physiological, passionate needs. Lawrence opens "Anna Victrix" with a passage suggesting that Anna's and Will's marriage resembles both the expulsion from Paradise and the family of Noah after the old world has been destroyed (p. 140). But since Anna and Will do not fulfill the Brangwen promise, Lawrence does not perceive these parallels in terms of a consistent biblical pattern and he discards them. Because their separation from the rest of the world mimes the dislocation caused by his own relationship to Frieda, there are passages in which the language strains to the point of breaking down. We feel his excruciating pain embodied in the narrative voice's account of the difficulties between Anna and Will.

Will has the potential either to become alive passionately or to lapse into a kind of passionate anomie, when, despite his sexual satisfaction with Anna, he does not fulfill himself and his passionate energy becomes corrupted. Deprived of his male pride and lacking an independent identity, Will's destructive passion is not so dissimilar from Uncle Tom's or from Gerald's in *Women in Love*. For a time the couple succeeds in creating a timeless world within the diurnal one. As if to stress the parallel between generations, Lawrence echoes the earlier biblical language ("They were unalterably glad"). But the struggle between them is different and more complex. Will must come to terms with an industrial world that Tom and Lydia are virtually able to shut out. Will's dark intensity is a function of his need to believe in something more than the relationship between man and woman. He believes in the miracle of Cana and "loved the Church" (p. 168); in defense, Anna, "almost against herself, clung to the worship of the human knowledge" (p. 169). They never discover an equilibrium in which their separate selves enrich one another to form a union, a third entity stronger than the other two. Rather, each often becomes the other's emotional antithesis. As the passionate needs of one define contrary impulses in the other, the tension creates a destructive emotional friction that is never quite resolved.

Thus "Anna Victrix" is an ironic title. By winning, Anna loses. Anna is indifferent to the outside world, but, like Lawrence, she needs to find a balance between mind-consciousness and blood-consciousness. Just like Lawrence, Will requires his life in the world beyond his relationship; like Frieda, Anna is oblivious to these needs, and thus must share with Will the blame for the couple's problems. Anna needs to defeat Will in body and spirit. She defeats him by despising his job, depriving him of his spiritual life, and taking away his pride. Will may be more the quintessential sensual man than any other male figure, but he also objectifies Lawrence's fear that sexual passion will deprive him of his creativity. By abandoning his wood-carving of Adam and Eve, Will submits to the routine of the everyday world. In an ironic echo of the sheaf-gathering scene, during her pregnancy Anna dances alone in her search for the something that her life lacks: at an unconscious level, she is trying to "annul" Will by means of the primitive and atavistic dance. Anna's victory is not only Will's defeat, but ultimately her own.

Reading *The Rainbow*, like reading many of the great innovative twentieth-century works such as *Ulysses*, *The Waste Land*, and *Absalom, Absalom*, means discovering the secret of what at first seems a partially closed semantic system. At times the correspondence of words to things and feelings is elusive. The text resists becoming part of the world of shared discourse and remains a lyrical overflow outside of recognized semantic codes. Yet even these passages have their own semantic logic. Take the one in "Anna Victrix" in which two consecutive paragraphs beginning "And ever and again" render Anna's and Will's perception of each other in rapidly changing images (p. 167). The essence of the passage is its movement. Lawrence is straining to invent the appropriate language to convey the passionate yet unconscious struggle between himself and Frieda. As important as the individual images is the process of metamorphosis, the rapid change in the vehicles or images of the metaphors. These images convey the struggle between Lawrence and Frieda that was the catalyst for these scenes. That Lawrence does not quite succeed in detaching himself from the struggle, does not move from immersion to reflection, becomes part of the reading experience for the reader who knows something about Lawrence's life.

Corresponding to the medieval period, the period between an agrarian and an industrial society, the period in which villages and crafts dominate life in England, the Anna–Will section is the one in which religion is explored in its most personal form. Lawrence's evangelical conscience required that he explore the church as a putative source of values. At the center of the novel is the very short chapter entitled "Cathedral." The cathedral, like the novel itself, is an artifice that reconciles opposing dualities. But, to use Lawrence's terms, the cathedral, like Raphael's paintings, arrests motion, while Lawrence's form, like the painting of Botticelli, is in motion.[8] In "Cathedral," Lawrence shows the constraints that Christianity has placed upon people's efforts to realize fully their potential. Lawrence stresses how the church denies process and movement and reduces everything to oneness. The Romanesque arch is a false rainbow because it reduces the variety of life to itself, something that Lawrence believed Christianity does by imposing arbitrary shibboleths ("Only the poor will get to heaven"; "The meek shall inherit the earth").

The cathedral represents an historical phase that humans must put behind them if they are to continue the journey to fulfillment. Moreover, its geometric *resolution* is reductive. In Laurentian terms, the arch denies the "Two-in-one" and represents nullifying fusion, rather than union between two strong, contending souls that are independent in themselves. Like the blood intimacy of the early Brangwens, it is another form of the dominance of what Lawrence called the Will-to-Inertia.[9] For Anna, as for Lawrence, God is something within and beyond one's self, but not within the church. We may regard Anna as a Moses figure who has viewed the Promised Land, but will not enter it. Before Anna lapses into child-bearing she carries on the Brangwen promise by refusing to submit her individuality to the church. Anna resists submission to "the neutrality, the perfect, swooning consummation, the time-less ecstasy" of the Romanesque arches (p. 199). When she responds to the separateness of the gargoyles, she is compared to Eve. She seduces Will to a knowledge that he would deny; for him the church can no longer be a "world within a world" (p. 202). Her resistance is described in terms of a bird taking flight, a striking image because it suggests the natural world that, Lawrence felt, was absent from the cathedral and that has been shut out by the artificial rainbow (p. 200). Her desire to rise anticipates that of Ursula in the section when the latter assumes the mantle of Christ; her refusal to be fixed anticip-ates Ursula's refusal to submit to Skrebensky. The bird has freedom of move-ment in contrast to the church's insistence on one direction. Anna's victory over Will's desire to use the church as a spiritual womb to which they both

As Ursula imagines Christ speaking for the Law of the Body in the diction of the Bible, Lawrence's voice subsumes Ursula's. In the climax of his quest for a new credo, Lawrence insists that as Christ's return must be in the body, so must people be reborn in the body: "The Resurrection is to life, not to death. Shall I not see those who have risen again walk here among men perfect in body and spirit, whole and glad in the flesh, living in the flesh, loving in the flesh, begetting children in the flesh arrived at last to wholeness . . . ?" (p. 280). This is the moment when Lawrence, at the center of the novel, ascends his rhetorical Pisgah and looks to the future. As he speaks with urgency and intensity, we realize that the prophetic voice is a major character in the novel – that he is not only the teller but an essential character in the tale. Thus "The Widening Circle," the chapter in which the above passage appears (and the first of two with that title), describes not only Ursula's expanding range of experience, but that of Lawrence's dramatized voice. That voice has progressed from rendering the impersonal and anonymous life in the opening to creating an individualized life where personal values and attitudes are important. Just as the Brangwens lose their anonymity and their individual quests become significant, so Lawrence affirms through his intrusive, prophetic, idiosyncratic voice the value of a self-aware, unique personality. This is a value that was unknown to the early Brangwens, but is crucial to Ursula as she seeks her own identity even while responding to the demands of her body.

That her first love affair with Skrebensky is prolonged, unsatisfactory, and inhibiting reflects Lawrence's own view of his relationship with Jessie. At 21, Ursula has experienced the kind of philosophical and psychological development Lawrence had achieved in his late twenties when he was creating her. He takes pleasure in Ursula's unconventional attitudes toward Christianity and in her flouting of traditional standards as, for example, when she argues for making love in a cathedral. Her feelings of superiority and iconoclasm are Lawrence's as he sought to define a new aristocracy of the passionate Elect. Election should be understood not only in terms of evangelical theory that there are men and Men, damned souls and saved souls, but also in terms of Lawrence's snobbery and iconoclasm. The Brangwens, like Lawrence, have a pathological fear of being undifferentiated from the mass of people.

Yet if Lawrence is Ursula, he is also Skrebensky. Skrebensky embodies Lawrence's own fear that he will not be able to fulfill Frieda. Skrebensky is unformed and lacks the potential for growth and fulfillment. In their first love-making under the moon, he needs to "enclose" and "overcome her" (p. 320). He lacks the passionate energy that she requires: "What was this nothingness she felt? The nothingness was Skrebensky" (p. 320). Whereas Will has a problem of unconsciously restraining and thus corrupting his passionate potential, Skrebensky is inherently defective. While Will struggles toward a kind of limited fulfillment, Skrebensky becomes a factotum for the social system, a soldier who mindlessly fights for the nation's political goals. We might note that the males decline from generation to generation, while the women move forward in their balance between blood-consciousness and mind-consciousness – although Anna's painful triumph at times seems a necessary step sideways.

Ursula's oscillation between the demands of the conscious self and the passionate self continues in an upward spiral to the novel's final pages as she moves toward the unreachable goal of what Lawrence calls "full achievement" of herself (*Phoenix*, p. 403). (It is Lawrence's version of Zeno's paradox that this goal recedes as it is approached, for there are always further levels of self-realization beyond the one that has been reached.) We recall her mother's desire to take flight in order to escape Will's confinement in the cathedral. But Skrebensky holds Ursula back. Because Skrebensky exists "in her own desire only," she did not "live completely" (p. 331). Ursula's first love baptizes her into "shame" (the title of the ensuing chapter), just as Lawrence believed Jessie had taught him the meaning of shame.

Like her Brangwen forebears, Ursula is at ease in nature and open to experience. But at this point she does not have the independence that she will later have and desperately searches for someone to complete her. Yet her failure with Skrebensky, like Lawrence's own with Jessie Chambers, intensifies her quest. She turns her passion to a beautiful and proud young teacher, Winifred Inger. At first, Winifred seems to Ursula an example of one who has combined the best of female and male: "She was proud and free as man, yet exquisite as a woman" (p. 336). But after a brief affair, lesbian love proves a dead end. (Lawrence, who would endorse Birkin's bisexuality in *Women in Love*, has a different standard for women, whose bisexuality he condemns.) While Ursula is associated with lions and later horses, Winifred is associated with moist clay and prehistoric lizards: "[Ursula] saw gross, ugly movements in her mistress, she saw a clayey, inert, unquickened flesh, that reminded her of the great prehistoric lizards" (p. 350). Lawrence is not above name-calling to denigrate characters who are unsuitable for his major figures. Winifred and Uncle Tom are arbitrarily aligned with the corruption of Wiggiston, although Lawrence does not *dramatize* why. It is as if he needed to turn against part of his creation and to expel it from the heightened, passionate world he has created for the Elect: "[Uncle Tom's and Winifred's] marshy, bitter-sweet corruption came sick and unwholesome in Ursula's nostrils. Anything to get out of the foetid air. She would leave them both forever, leave forever their strange, soft, half-corrupt element. Anything to get away" (p. 350). Within the Brangwen strain and Lawrence's psyche is a struggle between the living, represented by Ursula, and the dead, represented by Uncle Tom. That the Brangwens have a corrupt line creates within the novel a viable threat to Ursula's and Lawrence's own quests.

V The Significance of the Ending

At the close, Lawrence and Ursula are inseparable. When she agrees to marry Skrebensky and have his baby, her capitulation to what Lawrence regards as obsolete conventions and traditions mimes his own fear that he, too, might lack the strength to break free. But the horses represent the atavistic energy that he felt he needed to write *The Rainbow*. The painful activity of writing is mirrored by Ursula's terrible confrontation with an unacknowledged energy that must be expressed in spite of her conscious self. Just as she must return from experiencing the "hard, urgent, massive fire" of the horses to "the ordered world of man," so must Lawrence (pp. 487–8). After she decides not to marry Skrebensky, her declaration prior to the final vision is also Lawrence's:

> I have no father nor mother nor lover, I have no allocated place in the world of things, I do not belong to Beldover nor to Nottingham nor to England nor to this world, they none of them exist. I am trammelled and entangled in them, but they are all unreal. I must break out of it, like a nut from its shell which is an unreality. (p. 492)

Very much like the dark night of the soul in traditional Christianity, this denial is a necessary prologue to her final vision. One must experience the Everlasting No on the road to the Everlasting Yea. Ursula is enacting the crucial prophetic passage where Lawrence has assumed the voice of Christ and imagined his own resurrection: "[Ursula] slept in the confidence of her new reality. She slept breathing with her soul the new air of a new world . . . When she woke at last it seemed as if a new day had come on the earth. How long, how long had she fought through the dust and obscurity, for this new dawn" (p. 492). The "new dawn" and "new day" confirm the novel's insistence that the possibility of transfiguration is always present.

The final vision is not only Ursula's but Lawrence's. It is the moment to which the narrative and the narrator have moved. The novel has redefined God to be something remote, whose presence pervades nature but is indifferent to the individual human quest. Ursula thinks: "What ever God was, He was, and there was no need for her to trouble about Him" (p. 324).

Yet God also becomes the name of each individual's fullest potential, the aspect of life that is immune to Dr Frankstone's mechanism ("I don't see why we should attribute some special mystery to life" [p. 440]). Thus Ursula is recognizing the god within her when she understands that "Self was a oneness with the infinite. To be oneself was a supreme, gleaming triumph of infinity" (p. 441). Such an insight is an essential prelude to the ending. Although Genesis is her favorite book, and her grandfather's death in a flood established him as a Noah figure, she mocks God's command to Noah: "Be ye fruitful and multiply and replenish the earth" (p. 323). Ursula must discover what Lawrence sees as the meaning of that myth – as a figuration of death followed by rebirth, despair by hope – if she is to carry out the Brangwen promise. Her vision of the rainbow is the fulfillment of God's covenant that he will never destroy the things of the earth:

> And the rainbow stood on the earth. She knew that the sordid people who crept hard-scaled and separate on the face of the world's corruption were living still, that the rainbow was arched in their blood and would quiver to life in their spirit, that they would cast off their horny covering of disintegration, that new, clean, naked bodies would issue to a new germination, to a new growth, rising to the light and the wind and the clean rain of heaven. She saw in the rainbow the earth's new architecture, the old, brittle corruption of houses and factories swept away, the world built up in a living fabric of Truth, fitting to the over-arching heaven. (p. 495)

Here the narrator and Lawrence are like a suspended series of intersecting circles. Ursula's vision is the fulfillment for Lawrence of the urgent quest that produced both "The Study of Thomas Hardy" and *The Rainbow*; it signifies the continuing possibility of transfiguration for all humankind. Lawrence takes the worst case – the men of Wiggiston – and imagines them bursting forth, like the red poppy in "Study of Thomas Hardy," with new life.[10] Lawrence's novel is the equivalent to Ursula's final vision, the rainbow that follows the terrible task of creation. If we recall his denial of life after death, we see that heaven means, paradoxically, a transformed life on earth where people will be alive passionately. Each must discover the God within herself or himself, or in different terms, rewrite the Bible for herself or himself.

However, the ending presents some difficulties. *The Rainbow* announces itself as an alternative to the novel of manners and morals. In a letter to Lady Ottoline Morrell, Lawrence wrote of his utopian ideal: "I want you to form the nucleus of a new community which shall start a new life amongst us – a life in which the only riches is integrity of character. So that each one may fulfill his own nature and desires to the utmost, but wherein . . . the ultimate satisfaction and joy is the completeness of us all as one" (February 1, 1915; Huxley, *Letters*, p. 224). At the end of *The Rainbow* Ursula has cleansed herself of inhibiting manners and morals, but she has not formed any attachments on which the kind of community Lawrence desired could be based. What precedes in the text belies the final vision. Furthermore, the vision is an epiphany for Lawrence and Ursula of the possibility of transfiguration, but it does not dramatize a future. His novel does not prepare his readers for a new community and offers no more than the vaguest hope that such a community can occur within England. And *Women in Love*, by showing the world in disintegration, takes back the hope of a transfigured community that is offered by the ending of *The Rainbow*.

Like Hardy, Lawrence proposes a cosmology other than the traditional Christian one that dominates the English novel. Lawrence appropriates the Christian myth stretching from Eden to the apocalypse to define his passionate Bible. But does that myth also appropriate Lawrence's plot? What distinguishes Hardy is the fulfillment of a malevolent pattern. As if Lawrence could not sustain the implication of his insights, he imposes an apocalyptic ending on his material. His ending undercuts and disregards the novel's dramatization of the pervasive growth of a destructive strand of human life, represented by Skrebensky, Winifred, Uncle Tom, and Dr Frankstone. Lawrence's prophecy and his testimony are at odds. One cannot quite believe in the utopian simplification of Ursula's transforming vision because it is contradicted by the cumulative power of Lawrence's dramatic evidence. Within the novel, her triumph is hers alone. Lawrence's myth contradicts the novel's unfolding process. Moreover, by relying on the Judaic–Christian mythology for his epiphanies, Lawrence inadvertently restores some credibility to the very system that he is criticizing as anachronistic.

The movement of *The Rainbow* reflects Lawrence's efforts to clarify his own ideas and feelings, and to search for the appropriate aesthetic. Reading Lawrence, we must be attentive to the authorial presence embodied within the text. Knowing something about his life and beliefs is essential. While *The Rainbow* nominally has an omniscient voice, we gradually realize that Lawrence's self-dramatizing voice reveals his values, emotions, idiosyncrasies, and conflicts. Straining the convention of omniscient narration to its breaking point, he desperately tries to create a prophetic form out of his personal needs.

When we read *The Rainbow*, we participate in Lawrence's struggle to define his values and his concept of the novel. He writes of his own passions and experiences even when he assigns them to invented characters. We respond to the process by which his subject is converted into art. Like Rodin in his sculptures, Lawrence never detaches himself from the medium in which he is

Chapter 7

Joyce's *Dubliners*:
Moral Paralysis in Dublin

I Introduction: The Unity of *Dubliners*

While writing *Dubliners*, Joyce had many audiences in mind: Dublin's drows-
ing citizens whose consciences and consciousness needed arousing; the Catholic
hierarchy; the Irish artistic and intellectual elite, including Yeats; the British
public; readers of English and perhaps, in translation, of other European
languages; and possibly a prospective publisher for his stories. In 1904 Joyce
published early versions of several stories in *Dubliners* ("The Sisters," "Eveline,"
and "After the Race"); the novella "The Dead," the final piece to be written,
was completed in 1907. In the first three stories – "The Sisters," "An
Encounter," and "Araby" – Joyce uses the young boy to demonstrate the
values of a representative pre-adolescent in Dublin and to show the way that
Catholicism and British domination of Ireland shape the boy's epistemology
and language, even as the speaker performs for us the consequences of that
upbringing.

Joyce deeply resented that England had let a patronizing Anglo-Irish
Protestant oligarchy dominate Ireland, and knew that colonial powers –
whatever their stated intention about bringing progress and enlightenment to
the colonized people – dedicated their energies to maintaining power. Indeed,
Ireland's population had been halved by famine in the nineteenth century.
And Joyce knew how the Irish sought refuge from imperialism in the Catholic
church. As Mary Gordon writes, "But if the relationship with Mother England
was fragile and vexed . . . there was the Rock of Peter upon which the church
stood . . . [W]hatever the winds blowing across the Irish Sea, the breath of the
Holy Spirit could be felt every time a nun or a priest opened his or her mouth."[1]

Not only the Irish and English, but the reader, too, is the object of Joyce's
artistry, the figure whose lapsed soul must be restored and who must rediscover

her or his humanity so that Dublin can become healthy and whole. Joyce wants to teach imperfect Irish readers to make sense of Dublin by showing them what it really is. What Giuseppe Mazzotta has written about Dante's *Divine Comedy* is just as true of *Dubliners*: it "dramatizes in a fundamental way the activity of interpretation – it recounts the effort of the poet–exegete to read the book of the world."[2] Joyce is reading the book of Dublin for us. Like Dante, we are pilgrim-spectators, and Joyce is Virgil showing us the inferno of contemporary Dublin. The reader, accompanied by the narrator-guide, sees the landscape of Dublin and is urged to think of the possibility for renewal. The reader in his or her sense-making must establish not only hierarchies among his or her critical approaches, but also hierarchies among the details. Our reading iterates the characters' efforts to make sense of the world, but our reading must go beyond their sense-making. *Dubliners* teaches the reader that he must abandon Dublin-think and Dublin-speak if he is to find meaning. Because the reader's sense-making involves fulfilled expectations and understood patterns, his activity is at odds with the frustrated quests of most of the figures in *Dubliners*. But because the speaker's telling reveals that he is only at a resting place and that he has the resources of language and imagination to resume the struggle to discover meaning in his quest, the reader may have more in common with the speaker in "Araby" than with the other protagonists and narrators.

In *Dubliners* we see the totality of Dublin life and the evolving patterns that hold Joyce's visions of the city together even when aspects of that pattern are located in different stories. We see stories in a spatial configuration as if they were stars in a constellation held together by what might be called the magnetism of significance. We should think of *Dubliners* as an evolving series of stories, a kaleidoscope in which each story takes a turn as the centerpiece in the pattern. The episodes cohere into what may be called a mindscape of Dublin and enact the repetitious cycle of blunted aspiration and frustration, of crass materialism, of sexual repression, of drunkenness, of moral idiocy. *Dubliners* is a cityscape, a representation of Dublin; as such it looks forward to, and becomes part of, Joyce's later depictions of Dublin's characters in *Ulysses* and *Finnegans Wake*.

The first three stories of Dubliners might be called "A Portrait of the Artist as a Very Young Man"; they speak of the transformation of consciousness that Joyce experienced as he became disillusioned with what he felt was Catholicism's rigorous, repressive, and hypocritical attitudes toward sexuality. Indeed, these first three stories are part of a fictional sequence, including *A Portrait of the Artist* and *Ulysses*, about a young man growing up in Dublin.

II "Araby" as Paradigmatic *Dubliners* Text

With the goal of suggesting how we might read each individual story of *Dubliners*, I shall look closely at "Araby," perhaps the most subtle of the stories preceding "The Dead." That "Araby" is the third of a series of stories in which boys wander through Dublin looking for meaning, and in which sexuality seems debased and corrupt, creates a context for our response. Yet the stylistic signature of the speaker is different from the first-person speaker's alienated detachment from his subject in "The Sisters" – where spaces between anecdotes enact his anesthetized condition – and the relatively straightforward account of "An Encounter," where the speaker's obsession with the homo-sexual flagellant is in stark contrast with the speaker's circuitous distancing of "The Sisters."

Unlike the other characters in the first three stories, the boy in "Araby" is a magician with words. Yet his speech, like the pervert's in "An Encounter," finally "circles round and round in the same orbit" as if he cannot leave the church's epistemology. Just as he is constrained by his English and Catholic masters in action, he iterates his past experience. He flagellates himself as (to recall a key phrase from "An Encounter") a "rough and unruly" boy who has, as he puts it in his reminiscence, been "driven and derided" by vanity. He "whips" himself for having a "sweetheart." Indeed, at the end of "Araby" isn't he accusing himself of simony, the worldly traffic in spiritual things of which the priest in "The Sisters" was supposedly guilty?

The engaged first-person speakers of the first three stories create an identification, an empathy, that makes the ironic detachment of the following stories – "Eveline," "After the Race," "Two Gallants" – all the more striking. We may link the young boy's sexual repression with the frustrated and guilty sexuality of the title character of the subsequent story, "Eveline." Eveline is a version of the aged spinster in "The Sisters." She is a warning not only of what Mangan's sister might become but also of what the boy might become should he not have the imaginative resources to create his own world. "Eveline," a more flagrant and indeed pathological story of reflexive self-imprisonment, retells "Araby" in the third person.

Not only is the speaker much older than the speaker of "Araby," but she also lacks the latter's imaginative power – a power that has the potential to transform the drab world of Dublin. The final image of her leaning on the rail is a metonym for imprisonment by the Catholic epistemology and by Irish traditions and conventions, both of which define pleasure and self-gratification as sinful – a definition of sin that creates damaged psyches, which feed on repression, sublimation, and projection. In the face of the systems of cognition embedded in her psyche, Eveline becomes catatonic when she has a chance for escape from Ireland: "She set her white face to him passive, like a helpless animal. Her eyes gave him no sign of love or farewell or recognition." At this crucial moment she recoils to religion ("her lips moved in silent prayer"); we recall her promise to her dead mother ("she prayed to God to direct her, to show her what was her duty"). Her unintelligible Celtic speech – "Derevaun Seraun! Derevaun Seraun!" – reminds us that even as early as 1904 Joyce was skeptical of Yeats and the Irish Renaissance and that he felt Ireland's future lay with the European community. Didn't Joyce have Stephen say in the opening chapter of *Ulysses*: "I am the servant of two masters . . . an English and an Italian . . . And a third there is that wants me for odd jobs"?

If we see "Araby" as belonging to a sequence of stories that thematizes the moral paralysis of Dublin; as a product of the socioeconomic reasons for that paralysis; as the third story of the sexual initiation of a young boy in a series beginning with "The Sisters" and "An Encounter"; as an earlier version of Joyce's *A Portrait of the Artist as a Young Man*; as a confession that carries heavy autobiographical freight; as a polemic urging us to see what happens when we are limited and defined by systems of perceptions not our own; as an elegy for boyhood; as a satire on the inhibiting and debilitating effects of a Catholic education; as an artistically organized structure of linguistic effects; as a dramatic monologue; and as an instance of early Modernism in several ways (including its turn-of-the-century fascination with masks, its biographical relationship to the author, and its demands upon the reader to weave the meaning of the text) – if we see "Araby" in all these ways, then we begin to define what kind of story we are dealing with.

When reading "Araby," each of us becomes a member of a number of different audiences:

1 The 1895 audience to whom Joyce imagines that the adolescent speaker is narrating his story – a story based on the young Joyce's visit to an actual bazaar in 1894. This narrative audience, whom the speaker addresses, is an implied audience within an imagined world who know the customs, politics, routines of Dublin, and even the popular culture of Dublin, including its songs and folk legends.
2 The 1904 historical audience that the author had in mind as he wrote the story.
3 The early twenty-first-century contemporary audience. Those of us who read and teach Joyce are often conditioned by the interpretive history of "Araby" and our varying knowledge of Joyce's life and text.

A pluralistic interpretation of Joyce's "Araby" might address the following interrelated questions.

1   What is the point of view? Who is speaking to whom and for what purpose? Who is telling the story, and on what occasion? What is the speaker's relation to Joyce? What does Joyce expect of the reader? My own reading of "Araby" argues for a triple perspective. An indeterminate time has passed between the boy's original experience and the slightly older boy's retrospective first-person telling of that experience. Joyce expects us to share his ironic perspective toward a retrospective teller who is myopic and limited in his understanding, embedded in the ecclesiastical language he would disavow, and, as a very young artist, infatuated with what he believes is poetic and literary language. The young speaker's interior verbal world – excessive, colorful, elegant – contrasts poignantly with his inability to *speak* to Mangan's sister. Indeed, does not the *lack* of dialogue between the speaker and Mangan's sister poignantly comment on the rest of his world, which seems full of talk – the talk of priests, his uncle and aunt, his friends – that does not speak to his soul? For the boy, as for Wallace Stevens in "An Ordinary Evening in New Haven," "the words of the world are the life of the world."

2   To what genre does "Araby" belong? What kind of text are we reading? As discourse, "Araby" needs to be generically defined in terms both of the dramatic monologue and of what has been called the mask lyric. As a story, it needs to be seen as having aspects in miniature of confession, kunstlerroman, and bildungsroman. It also may be seen in terms of Joyce's generic distinction between lyrical, dramatic, and epical form as presented in *A Portrait of the Artist*:

[A]rt necessarily divides itself into three forms progressing from one to the next. These forms are: the lyrical form, the form wherein the artist presents his image in immediate relation to himself; the epical form, the form wherein he presents his image in mediate relation to himself and to others; the dramatic form, the form wherein he presents his image in immediate relation to others . . . The lyrical form is in fact the simplest verbal vesture of an instant of emotion . . . He who utters it is more conscious of the instant of emotion than of himself as feeling emotion. The simplest epical form is seen emerging out of lyrical literature when the artist prolongs and broods upon himself as the center of an epical event and this form progresses till the center of emotional gravity is equidistant from the artist himself and from others. The narrative is no longer purely personal. The personality of the artist passes into the narrative itself, flowing round and round the persons and the action like a vital sea . . . The dramatic form is reached when the vitality which has flowed and eddied around

133

each person fills every person with such vital force that he or she assumes a proper and intangible esthetic life. The personality of the artist, at first a cry or a cadence or a mood and then a fluid and lambent narrative, finally refines itself out of existence, impersonalizes itself, so to speak. The esthetic image in the dramatic form is life purified in and reprojected from the human imagination.[3]

3   What does "Araby" reveal as an *expression* of Joyce's life? In what way does Richard Ellmann's monumental biography *James Joyce* become part of our intertextual response to the story?

4   How is "Araby" a socioeconomic text produced by Ireland's historical circumstances – in Joyce's view, by Ireland's twin servitude to the Catholic church and England? How is "Araby" a satire on Catholicism, which – along with England – is the social and political antagonist of the story? Isn't Joyce using the boy to demonstrate the values of a representative pre-adolescent in Dublin and showing what forces – notably Catholicism and British domination of Ireland – shape the boy's epistemology and language, even as the speaker performs for us the consequences of that upbringing?

5   How is "Araby" a study of sexual repression? Can it be discussed in psychoanalytic terms?

6   How is "Araby" a chapter in the evolving collection called *Dubliners*? How do we link the speaker to the younger first-person narrators of the two prior stories, "The Sisters" and "An Encounter"? Because of the continuity among the three stories, does he not become a shadowy portrait of the artist as a *very* young man? In that vein, how are these three stories part of a fictional sequence, including *A Portrait of the Artist* and *Ulysses*, about a young man's growing up in Dublin? How do we link his sexual repression with the frustrated and guilty sexuality of the title character of the subsequent story, "Eveline"?

7   How is "Araby" part of Joyce's cityscape – his representation of Dublin – and how does that look forward to, and become part of, his later depictions of Dublin's character in *Ulysses* and *Finnegans Wake*?

8   How is "Araby" a 1904 text that depends on historical and literary allusions which have to be recuperated by historical scholarship? As a 1904 text, "Araby" is an historically determined production written by a specific author at a particular time. Joyce had no one "horizon of expectation," but, as we have noted, he had several audiences in mind at the same time. One critical task is to reconstruct audience response when the story originally appeared and to understand the distinction between the response then and a contemporary response

9   How does "Araby" enact a dialectical linguistic drama in which realistic, descriptive language rendering the pedestrian world of Dublin struggles with

the language of the romance world? Within the boy's mind the language of sexual desire, religious education (especially the ritual of confession), Irish songs, and literary naturalism struggle not only with one another, but also with his own desire and efforts as a putative artist to invent stylized and mannered forms to render his past experience. The boy's romance language – the language borrowed from his reading rather than his experience – is transformed and undermined by the pedestrian world of Dublin and the obsessive hold of the church.[4]

10   How does "Araby" fulfill the conventions of the modern short story – including endings that are the fulfillment of prior hints, dense verbal textures in which the linguistic subject reinforces the theme and action, as well as the compression of story time (several weeks) into a few pages to be read within a 20-minute reading? How does "Araby" look back to the naturalism and realism of nineteenth-century fiction?

11   How is "Araby" a story of what happens to the ideal reader – although we realize an ideal reader is a fiction – as he moves from the beginning to the end, making sense of the story as he responds to the structure of effects that results from the voice, organization, conventions, and linguistic patterns?

12   In what way is the text an experience, like other experiences, which resists full understanding, but iterates the boy's quest for understanding – a quest which is the subject of the boy's adventure and of his retelling? As readers, we find what we look for: our readings may be creative, open, and part of our realization of the world; or they may be narrow, stilted, unimaginative, and controlled *completely* by the text. The adolescent speaker's reductive reading of his experience teaches us what happens when we read in either extreme way.

13   Finally, as reader, critic, and teacher should I not try to explain how and why I am touched at every stage of my life by the story of a young boy whose quest for love and language mirrors, parodies, and tropes aspects of my own quest? Should I not share my personal experience of reading "Araby," my original identification as an adolescent with the boy's love of language and pre-pubescent sexual anxiety, my visits to Dublin, and my 36 years of pleasure in teaching and speaking about the story?

III   Reading "Araby"

A fundamental tenet of my approach throughout this study is that texts teach us how to read them. Depending on our earlier reading experience and other interests, they teach us somewhat differently. But the nuances of dialogue and description, the ordering of events, the way the work opens and closes, the modes of characterization, the choice of narrator, the relationship of the narrator to the author, his characters, and the audience create the readers' responses.

Let us turn to the elusive beginning of "Araby": "North Richmond Street, being blind, was a quiet street except at the hour when the Christian Brothers' School set the boys free. An uninhabited house of two stories stood at the blind end, detached from its neighbours in a square ground. The other houses conscious of decent lives within them, gazed at one another with brown imperturbable faces."

This first paragraph (1) provides a physical correlative to moral paralysis stifling Dublin; (2) enacts the speaker's desire to postpone and defer the difficult telling of an embarrassing story about pre-pubescent sexuality and subsequent guilt; (3) enacts his adolescent and imaginative tendency to ascribe power to external things and to be intimidated by his environment. The houses are anthropomorphized ("conscious of decent lives," "gazed") and the school "set[s] the boys free." At the same time, the speaker's act of using words is a creative experience that reflects the anterior reality prior to this experience of telling. Because we write and speak to others, because our acts of speech and of writing are basic to our lives, we take words as *real*. We live within the world of novels in a different way than we listen to music or see paintings because words themselves evoke the illusion of life. Words in literature are not merely marks, traces, indeterminate signifiers. Isn't the self-conscious dramatized voice of Conrad and James an effort to exploit speech and create a form that recognizes telling as action? Isn't the ventriloquy of styles in *Ulysses* a recognition that unitary stories of reading are incomplete? "Araby" is an example of such a controlled, self-dramatizing perspective. As readers, we impose formal coherence on our experiences – whether aesthetic, religious, political, or social – even as we understand that they are fictions evoking reality in a metaphorical or "as if" sense. They discover for us – even as we discover in them – an order that we need and that our lives lack. We leap to discover teleological organizing principles, even as we step back and doubt these principles.

In reductive terms, "Araby" is a dialogue between two perspectives, the realist and romance, and two kinds of language – the literal and the metaphorical – as well as between reason and passion and between the vertical, value-oriented life and the horizontal, time-oriented life. Joyce chooses words which imbue the story's plot with a subtext or supratext. The opening paragraphs contain language – "blind," "musty," "littered," "useless," "enclosed" – which for the rereader becomes associated with the culture which is stifling the boy's growth. The "brown imperturbable faces," living "decent lives," represent the coarse, materialistic, paralyzed life of Dublin; in Yeats's words, these are the faces of those who "fumble in a greasy till" ("September 1913"). The boy's sexual and romance fantasies are a response to this life, and the words he uses as he retrospectively recalls what has happened align themselves as an alternative, not merely in their sensuous, mysterious connotation but in their circumlocutory syntax, incantational intonation, and performative quality: "The career of our play brought us through the dark muddy lanes behind the houses where we ran the gauntlet of the rough tribes from the cottages to the back doors of the dark dripping gardens where odours arose from the ashpits to the odorous stables where a coachman smoothed and combed the horse or shook music from the buckled harness." The speaker revels in sounds, smells, touches, and disrupts the expected patterns of syntax to savor and linger over the words which evoke them.

The speaker's (and reader's) discovery of "I" – the tentative discovery of "I" – with which he begins the last three longish paragraphs of "Araby," struggles with the earlier paragraphs in which "I" was submerged and distanced. Who would guess from the story's first paragraph, or even the second or third paragraph, how the teller's secret feelings will emerge as the central focus? The telling itself mimes the speaker's tendency to submerge his sexuality and often his real feelings: "North Richmond Street being blind" is the language of an official tour guide. "The former tenant of our home" submerges the apparent orphan state of the boy – the felt loss of his parents whether from death, desertion, or consignment of him to relatives – and seems to begin a paragraph focusing on the loss of a tenant. Isn't the next paragraph also dominated by his belonging to the enclave defined by his aunt and uncle and his playmate? Gradually the speaker reveals that Mangan's sister – whose name he cannot articulate even now – is the focus of his attention: "I imagined that I bore my chalice safely through a throng of foes. Her name sprang to my lips at moments in strange prayers and praises which I myself did not understand. My eyes were often full of tears (I could not tell why)." As he recalls these events, he transforms them into sensuous, romantic images; yet he cannot escape the religious epistemology in which he was educated, even as he seeks to find refuge in the medieval romance of Walter Scott's novels. Moreover, savoring words and creating excessive sentences that do not quite work, he is Joyce's ironic portrait of the artist as a very young man: "I did not know whether I would ever speak to her or not or, if I spoke to her, how I could tell her of my confused adoration. But my body was like a harp and her words and gestures were like fingers running upon the wires."

Rather than sing of his love in terms of his personal feelings, the boy ironically chants the religious language that has been written on his consciousness and conscience. Mangan's sister is enclosed by the silver bracelet and spikes of the railing, images of the enclosure of Irish culture – particularly the church. Note how light creates a halo over her bowed head, as if to make her an ironic version of a saintly virgin: "The light from the lamp opposite our door caught the white curve of her neck, lit up her hair that rested there, and falling, lit up the hand upon the railing." Her bondage metonymically extends to him: "When she spoke she turned a silver bracelet round and round her wrist . . . She held one of the spikes, bowing her head towards me." In anticipation of the ending, his excessive and hyperbolic language is disproportionate to the data: "What innumerable follies laid waste my working and sleeping thoughts . . . I wished to annihilate the tedious intervening day." Yet the trip to the bazaar confirms the tedium he desperately needs to annihilate.

At the close, the speaker of "Araby" bitterly recalls his own experience and iterates his self-disgust for deviating from his religious training. But Joyce asks the readers to see that the narrator's self-damnation is ironically poignant and self-defeating – and finally an indictment if not a damnation of a culture that represses sexuality and feeling. Aren't we overwhelmed by the poignant, self-castigating voice of the conclusion of "Araby": "Gazing up into the darkness I saw myself as a creature driven and derided by vanity; and my eyes burned with anguish and anger." Isn't he left to stare into darkness for new words? Indeed, do we not realize that the church had already taken possession of his words when he compares the "darkness" and "silence" to a "church after a service" or compares the coins on a tray at the bazaar to "money on a salver."

Because of his ecclesiastical education, the speaker reads *in the darkness* – the darkness of his own mind – that he is guilty of one of the seven deadly sins, namely vanity or pride. In this case, aren't vanity and pride really kinds of shame? As Mary Gordon remarks, "One of the most ancient and thriving products of Irish industry . . . is shame," and it is the church that produces that product.[5] It is those words or ghosts, and the images they summon, that physically affect him – to paraphrase, "burn his eyes"; for to him they have the reality of physical things. Just as the Catholic code imprisoned Mangan's sister, the words and the images they evoke torture him. Even as we intrude a trace of skeptical reading that casts a shadow of doubt over whether the speaker means his self-condemnation, we are moved by the boy's pain. His traumatic response to disappointment takes the form of using the very linguistic system that he had sought to disavow. Ultimately isn't his response an enactment of the terrible force of language, of teaching, transformed into obsession? Isn't he as paralyzed as the dying priest in "The Sisters"?

Because of its name, "Araby," the boy associates the bazaar with English enchantment and romance. But the English woman at the bazaar who speaks "out of a sense of duty" and asks him whether he wishes to buy anything is deflecting his dreams and evoking his internalized fears that, by abandoning his work for his quest for love, he is sinning. The darkness and silence in the above-quoted closing sentence of the story are the closed text – the text written on him by convention and Catholicism – and the erasure of his feelings. The phallic jars remind us of the sexuality that he is missing and "her wares" remind us how sex has become a commodity in the modern world. "Araby" recalls for us how the English Modernists (Forster, Conrad, Lawrence) turn faraway places (India, Italy, Malaysia, Mexico, and New Mexico) into libidinous, sexual ones. In a sense "Araby" is about the detumescence of adolescent sexual expectations – expectations associated by the boy with otherness of place ("The Arab's Farewell to his Steed," "Café Chantant").

In "Araby," sexuality – repressed by Catholicism – has expanded infinitely in the guise of romance and the bazaar to challenge the limits and confines of the rest of his world. Under the power of childhood sexual obsession – the speaker's "image" of Mangan's sister and the quest to fulfill his mission – he cannot "read" his experience as we must do to understand the story. Our synchronic reading sees that he has become, without reading it, a poignant Dante – Dante on a quest for his Beatrice – or a priest obsessively serving the blessed Virgin.

The boy's metaphors for the quest and for the fair have died and become transformed into a bleak memory of experience; his words refer not to the train-ride but to the fair, and finally to the catatonic state of mind in which the boy is left. The "magical" name "Araby" is demystified, deprived of its metaphorical potential by his experience; retelling, he stresses the "deserted train," the "intolerable delay," the "ruinous" – not ruined – "houses," the "bare carriage." Apparently, cultural mediocrity can even rob one of the magic of words. Does this not provide us with a poignant allegory for unsatisfactory reading of texts – and lives?

The phrase "I never said such a thing" from the dialogue that the boy overhears at the bazaar could be taken as the epigraph for the story, for the phrase stands for what the boy cannot say about his psychosexuality. "Thing" becomes a metonymic substitution for sexuality – for after all, isn't sexuality the subject not only of the conversation among the English at the bazaar, but of the boy's entire discourse? Thus, in another result of their imperialistic triumph in Ireland, the English have appropriated sexuality by cheapening the word-world in which sexuality exists for the boy.

Let us think of the boy's telling as an imaginative structure built up to counteract a literal, physical structure, a house that stands in the blind street and that is filled with musty, stifling air creating an enclosed, claustrophobic space: the lights go out in the final scene and the house is left in darkness. As a physical structure the house – standing with the other drab, dusty, musty houses on a blind street – is a metaphor for Dublin; put another way, each story of *Dubliners* is a room in a house called Dublin. Until the end when the boy is overwhelmed by guilt and frustration, he is telling or building his own alternative "house" in the interior world of his mind to stand in contrast to the paralysis of Dublin.

The clash of voices and styles is inherent in "Araby." The boy's disillusionment relates to the English accents at the bazaar and to the demystification of sex into stale, vapid flirtation. His romance style, his affected literary style, his genuine love of the sounds and textures of words, the ecclesiastical style inculcated at the Christian Brothers' School, and his desire as a young artist to see his experience in universal and metaphoric terms, struggle with one another as he seeks his voice. His choice of language often clashes with the lower middle-class English speech, the half-attentive, intoxicated speech of his uncle, the popular songs and poems (including those derived from his uncle's pub culture), as well as the conventional responses of his aunt (both of which are aspects of the "adult" world) and the naturalistic style where metaphors are deprived of their meanings – that is, the style with which the story opens and which reasserts itself as he experiences the blighted expectation of his quest. In addition to the dialogue of styles, past and present inform one another, clash, modify one another and yet cannot be separated. Just as his former self sought to fulfill his mission and return with a present to the girl, the speaker at an indeterminate distance of time seeks to define for himself what happened to him – and he fails, even while Joyce succeeds in rendering that failure.

IV "The Dead"

"The Dead," the longest and concluding story of *Dubliners*, dramatizes a dialogue between Gabriel's consciousness and unconsciousness, or, in Freudian terms, among his sexual desire (id) and his sense of responsibility (superego) and ego. In the first section below I will briefly discuss the relation between Joyce's psyche and Gabriel's before examining, in the following section, Gabriel's paralytic self-consciousness in detail. In the third section, I shall place Gabriel's psyche in a cultural and historical context. Finally, I shall pull together biographical, formal, and cultural aspects in a sustained reading of the conclusion of "The Dead."

A Joyce and Gabriel

A psychological criticism needs to consider issues that undermine traditional shibboleths about the separation of life and text. Joyce used his life as a source and believed that the universal genius (himself) "found," as Stephen says of Shakespeare in the "Scylla and Charybdis" section of *Ulysses*, "in the world without as actual what was in his world within as possible." Joyce created characters who were metaphors for himself, who were the means by which he explored and defined his identity. Joyce's fiction draws upon the actual, the life he lived; yet influenced by Wilde's *The Decay of Lying*, he creates masks for what he feared to become. Isn't Gabriel a metaphor for one facet of Joyce, just as Stephen Dedalus and Bloom are metaphors for other facets?

Wearing glasses, hair parted in the middle, Gabriel resembles Joyce. And his appearance, like his character, is a version of what Joyce feared becoming: bourgeois, conventional, a writer of reviews who supported himself teaching. Ellmann has reminded us of other important ways in which Gabriel resembles Joyce:

> In Gretta's old sweetheart, in Gabriel's letter, in the book reviews and the discussion of them, as well as in the physical image of Gabriel with hair parted in the middle and rimmed glasses, Joyce drew directly upon his own life . . . Gabriel's quarrels with his mother also suggest [James Joyce's father] John Joyce's quarrels with his mother, who never accepted her son's marriage to a woman of lower station.[6]

There is no doubt that Gabriel saw Gretta, as Joyce saw Nora Barnacle, as an alternative to the petty, insular Dublin social rituals.

We should think of Gabriel as a function of Joyce's self-critique. Gabriel is middle-class, conventional, neurotic, married to a woman of greater passion than himself, a writer of minor reviews for a conservative newspaper, the *Daily Express*, which was opposed to Irish independence, and a secondary schoolteacher. He represented a life that Joyce in 1907 could see himself leading had he not left Ireland or had he failed as a writer and had to return there. Another way of putting this is to say that Gabriel was that bourgeois nightmare which in part took Joyce away from Ireland.

One might even say that Gabriel has the same kind of alternating sympathy and irony toward himself as Joyce did to himself. Like Stephen Dedalus and Joyce, Gabriel tries unsuccessfully to maintain a stance of iconoclastic aloofness. He expresses Joyce's fear of betrayal – sexual, political, and personal. Joyce's tone toward Gabriel oscillates among sympathy, empathy, and grimly ironic disdain. Joyce is bitter toward a culture which, in his view, creates the kind of sexually dysfunctional adults that we see in *Dubliners*; from the acorn of the boy in "Araby" grows the tree of James Duffy in "A Painful Case." *Dubliners* thinly disguises Joyce's anger at a culture he feels is paralyzed by

Catholic dogma, British exploitation, its own propensity for self-delusion, alcoholism, and Irish hyperbole and blarney. Indeed, "The Dead" enacts some of Joyce's own discomfort with Yeats and the Irish Renaissance – including a need to separate himself from Yeats as an artistic father figure – and what he felt was a misplaced effort to align Ireland with Celtic culture and away from Western culture.

Our reading will depend on whether we see "The Dead" as the last of a sequence of stories about the "moral history" of Ireland, written in what Joyce calls "a style of scrupulous meanness" (*Dubliners*, p. 269), or as an independent story of Gabriel's self-delusion and troubled relationship with Gretta. To a reader of the preceding stories of *Dubliners*, Gabriel is the result of cultural contexts that have been developed carefully to show the moral sterility of contemporary Dublin. He is a somewhat more benign and pitiful figure because we see him in the context of the claustrophobic world in which he was raised, and because we understand that the young boy in the first three stories – "The Sisters," "An Encounter," and "Araby" – is a metonymy for both Joyce and Gabriel as very young men.

B Gabriel's paralytic self-consciousness

At the opening of "The Dead," we watch Gabriel from an ironic distance as he behaves clumsily toward Lily and we respond with a complex set of emotions – sympathy, judgment, impatience – to his failure to connect fully with other people. As he oscillates uncomfortably between self-diminishment and self-aggrandizement, as we realize that his social clumsiness relates to an emptiness within, does not our ironic distance narrow? Can we look at this paralytically self-conscious man from a steep and icy peak? Gabriel's own narrative of failure begins with Lily's retort:

> He was still discomposed by the girl's bitter and sudden retort . . . He was undecided about the lines from Robert Browning for he feared they would be above the heads of his hearers . . . He *would* only make himself ridiculous by quoting poetry to them which they could not understand. They *would* think that he was airing his superior education. He would fail with them just as he had failed with the girl in the pantry. He had taken up a wrong tone. His whole speech was a mistake from first to last, an utter failure. (p. 24; emphasis mine)[7]

Gabriel's sense of superior education, debilitating self-consciousness, and emotional dwarfism not only reflects his creator, but speaks to a characteristic paralytic self-consciousness of Modernism. More than that, it reflects Joyce's fear that education isolates us from our focus; it may even speak to a cliché accepted by some that too much education anesthetizes us to feelings.

When we reread the passage quoted above and see the words "discomposed," "undecided," "feared," "make himself ridiculous," we see Gabriel as if he were a part of a narrative code that prepares us for his later failure – or his perceptions of that failure. Gradually we realize that he is almost pathologically tense and nervous; twice our attention is called to his trembling fingers and his nervous laughter; his anxiety and desire to escape seem disproportionate unless he suffers from claustrophobia.

Pompous, pedantic, and patronizing, Gabriel vacillates between self-diminishment and self-aggrandizement, between seeing himself as a Lilliputian and a Brobdingnagian. As the above paragraph indicates, when Lily distances his efforts to charm and to be fatherly with what he takes as a rebuke, he responds with characteristic lack of proportion. When threatened, he characteristically finds refuge in self-importance and, in this case, begins to look at his speech. While thinking of his audience, he searches for a psychic oasis in which he can slake the thirst of his insecurities:

> It had cast a gloom over him which he tried to dispel . . . He was undecided about the lines from Robert Browning for he feared they would be above the heads of his hearers. Some quotation that they could recognise from Shakespeare or from the Melodies would be better. The indelicate clacking of the men's heels and the shuffling of their soles reminded him that their grade of culture differed from his. (p. 24)

While Gabriel seems to be an established teacher and enthusiastic bibliophile, he lacks a coherent self. He takes his identity from his social position; his dandified appearance – "patent-leather shoes," waistcoat to cover his "plump body," "glossy black hair . . . parted in the middle and brushed in a long curve behind his ears," "gilt rims of glasses," "goloshes" – reinforces this. While he seems to see himself as the center of the party and to feed on the attention he receives, he continually allows minor events to marginalize him and deprive him of his feelings of self-worth. In truth, his need to control is equal to his need to be loved. His fixation on the health of his intimates demonstrates his need to improve and correct and ultimately live through others; he insists that his wife wear galoshes, has his son wearing shades at night and lifting dumb-bells, and has his daughter eating "stirabout." Gabriel loves by *controlling*.

Because of his pomposity and patronizing manner, Gabriel is reduced to a bundle of quirks and tics. We see a man stripped of his pretensions as the evening progresses. He "laugh[s] nervously" when Gretta gently rebukes him

143

for his smothering solicitude (p. 25). Gabriel mistakes solicitude for love. Thinking of his speech after Lily's rebuke, he not only reduces Lily to "the girl in the pantry," but shows that his purported self-esteem is a sham.

Among other things, the psychological aspect of "The Dead" needs to be understood in terms of economic issues and class distinctions that shape Gabriel's psychic responses. While the aunts dress plainly and live in a rental house, their students are from the "better-class families." He is conscious that Gretta is a country girl from Connacht and that he has married beneath him. He feels that the relatives and guests come from a "grade of culture beneath him." From this we infer that by going to a university and becoming a teacher, Gabriel has raised himself and is extremely proud of this. Note how uncomfortable Mary Jane, his cousin (and perhaps a little younger than he), is with herself.

The reason for the annual party is that it is a way for his aunts, Julia and Kate, and their niece, Mary Jane, to advertise their music school. Indeed, the protagonist of *Ulysses*, Leopold Bloom, advertising salesman, might have proposed the occasion. In the absence of social security and sufficient old age pensions, the music lesson business provides a means of support for the women. If their economic provision disappeared, hyperconscientious Gabriel, as the oldest surviving male relative, would feel that he was responsible for their support. That is why he thinks of himself as a pennyboy for his aunt. A pennyboy is both a boy who runs errands for a penny and the monkey that shakes a cup for an organ grinder – a street or arcade figure – who was what we now call a street musician. Gabriel has a desperate need to be needed, and we realize that *he* is a family caretaker; he has been reduced to that role and *relishes* that role. Like Lily and her father, he performs tasks for his aunts' party. Kate says to Gretta: "I always feel easier in my mind when he's here" (p. 26).

In a sense, Gabriel's orphaned cousin Mary Jane is the delegated provider for the family in that she has taken on the task of supporting the aunts and, not so incidentally, herself. For Mary Jane gives the piano lessons on which the older women live. We need to be aware of the position of the women; Lily and, presumably, Gretta and Gabriel's servant girl do not go to school. Gretta apparently does not work. Perhaps the party is short of women because, except for pupils and an independent woman like Miss Ivors, single women are less likely, in contrast to men like Freddy Malins and Mr Browne, to go to such parties alone, in part because, as the rest of *Dubliners* shows, many women have caretaker roles of one kind or another. We recall other women in prior stories of *Dubliners* – Eveline in the story of that name, Maria in "Clay," and the sisters in the opening story of that name – who seemed to sacrifice their own lives for relatives.

Ironically, once Gabriel carves the goose and sits down to eat, he does not converse. Rereading, we realize that until the conversation in the hotel with Gretta – a conversation in which he reveals his awkwardness in achieving intimacy – he has not really listened and responded or expressed his feelings in conversation. He is a man of words without the ability to communicate; he is frustrated in expressing himself. If he had self-knowledge, he would say with Eliot's Prufrock: "It is impossible to say just what I mean!" ("The Love Song of J. Alfred Prufrock").

His language reveals a pedestrian mind, full of banalities. Indeed, he lives in clichés: "Here I am as right as the mail" is how he announces his arrival, or when he declares of galoshes: "everyone wears them on the continent" (p. 26). The quintessence of his self-created identity is his public after-dinner speech:

Let us toast them all three together. Let us drink to their health, wealth, long life, happiness and prosperity and may they long continue to hold the proud and self-won position which they hold in their profession and the position of honour and affection which they hold in our hearts. (pp. 107–8)

The chorus led by Mr Browne stands and sings "For they are jolly gay fellows / Which nobody can deny / Unless he tells a lie," and, we realize, telling a lie is what Gabriel has been doing, since he does not believe what he says at all.

Gabriel allows himself to become a function of the perceptions of others, to be drained of his self-hood and deprived of his ego. Lacking a coherent identity, Gabriel can, chameleon-like (like Conrad's Kurtz), get himself to believe in anything because finally he believes in nothing. (And this crisis of belief – when Christianity no longer provides emotional bulwarks – is a subject of Modernism and a cause, too.) Gabriel's crisis of identity recalls that of Eliot's Prufrock and the captain-narrator in Conrad's "The Secret Sharer," other characters in modern literature who are defined by anxious, self-doubting thoughts about how others regard them. Conrad's captain himself is a stranger and outsider and begins to become depersonalized by the appearance of Leggatt, whom he regards as a second self, until he cannot distinguish between self and other. Like Prufrock and Conrad's captain, Gabriel is fixated on the approval of others. As with those characters, the integrity of Gabriel's personality is threatened by a disbelief in the authenticity of self. As the existential psychologist R. D. Laing puts it in *The Divided Self*:

If one experiences the other as a free agent, one is open to the possibility of experiencing oneself as an *object* of his experience and thereby of feeling one's own subjectivity drained away. One is threatened with the possibility of

> becoming no more than a thing in the world of the other, without any life for oneself, without any being for oneself. One may find oneself enlivened and the sense of one's own being enhanced by the other, or one may experience the other as deadening and impoverishing.[8]

Are not the terms of the Modernist crisis directly related to Laing's description of schizoid conditions? Modernist authors fear that we will become what others in our culture expect us to be; even if we strive for our own way, we may return to the beaten path of acculturation, the verbal symptom of which may be cliché. What is Gabriel's failure? In part, it is simply a sense that he is not good enough, the self-accusation that permeates the fiction of the era from Hardy's Jude and Sue in *Jude the Obscure* to Conrad's Jim in *Lord Jim* to Woolf's Lily Briscoe in *To the Lighthouse*. Like those characters, Gabriel is paralytically self-conscious. Isn't part of him always standing to one side watching his behavior? He thinks he is being watched and talked about more than he is. He has trouble reaching a decision. He is at once a self-absorbed narcissist and someone who thinks he is always the object of the gazes of others. Gabriel is a divided self, regarding his sexuality as something that belongs to another. Confused about the difference between love and lust, he rebukes himself for feeling lust when he is sexually aroused.

Like Eliot's Prufrock or Gerontion, Gabriel embodies the world about which he complains:

> [W]e are living in a sceptical and, if I may use the phrase, a thought-tormented age: and sometimes I fear that this new generation, educated or hypereducated as it is, will lack those qualities of humanity, of hospitality, of kindly humor which belonged to an older day . . . I must confess . . . that we were living in a less spacious age. Those days might, without exaggeration, be called spacious days: and if they are gone beyond recall let us hope, at least, that in gatherings such as this we shall still speak of them with pride and affection, still cherish in our hearts the memory of those dead and gone great ones whose fame the world will not willingly let die. (p. 43)

His fastidiousness, pretension, and pomposity are mirrored in his circumlocutory speech, including the use of the first-person pronoun – "If I may use," "I fear," "I must confess" – to make minute, hesitant, and verbose distinctions. Gabriel finds refuge in his own fantasies. As with Prufrock, his separation from instinctive behavior renders the comparison between past figures and himself as ironic. Gabriel's ego is not adequately negotiating between the demands of his superego and his id. His ego is embedded in a welter of temporary refuges and disguises, and his speech puts him in the same new generation he so critically patronizes. He cannot have a conversation without replaying it in his mind; it is as if his ego were separated from his libido and his passions. He is the living embodiment of mind-consciousness – of creeping mentalism – that Joyce's contemporary and sometime rival D. H. Lawrence spent his life fighting.

Gabriel's entire public speech is a disguised autobiography in which he unwittingly becomes the object of his own text: "[W]e could not find the heart to go on bravely with our work among the living. We have all of us living duties and living affections which claim, and rightly claim, our strenuous endeavours" (p. 44). Do we not as rereaders feel the presence of the dead in his repetition of "living" three times in two lines? Unwittingly, Gabriel's genre is elegy. To a rereader his speech, full of clichés and bromides, resonates with irony at his expense. He is caught in a verbal labyrinth of his own making. Put another way, his words are a mirror of his own psyche, and he has not been able to move beyond himself.

Gabriel has problems with women: Lily, his mother, Miss Ivors, and, of course, Gretta. Both Gretta and Miss Ivors are more comfortable with themselves than Gabriel is and more integrated than he is; they have a healthy self-regard and positive egotism. But Gabriel is made uncomfortable by their very coherence. Women become mirrors in which he sees himself; they penetrate his fantasy of self-importance, and intrude *other*, difference, libido, shadows. When he thinks of Miss Ivors as one of the "*serious and hypereducated generation*"(p. 35; Joyce's emphasis), we realize that it is the epithet "serious" he had used for his mother (his aunts "seemed a little proud of their serious and matronly sister" [p. 30]): "A shadow passed over his face as he remembered [his mother's] sullen opposition to his marriage" (p. 30). These recurring shadows and shades are the visual metaphors both for inevitable death and for the obsessions, memories, and fixations that enclose him in a coffin of his own making – a coffin in which he, like the monks, rests.

Gabriel finds refuge in manners, fastidious behavior, small social distinctions, and a nostalgic and idealized view of the past, and some of this comes from his memory of his mother. He has something of an oedipal complex. His eye is drawn to a family photograph containing his mother, a photograph in which "she held an open book on her knees and was pointing out something in it to Constantine who, dressed in a man-o'-war suit, lay at her feet. It was she who had chosen the names for her sons for she was very sensible of the dignity of family life" (p. 30). He has been acculturated by his mother's snobbery. He is haunted by her picture in the family photograph – as Stephen Dedalus will be haunted by the ghost of his mother and Bloom by the ghost of his father. He worries about his mother's dismissal of Gretta as "country cute"

(p. 30); isn't Gabriel, like his mother, "very sensible of the dignity of family life" (p. 30)? He knows Gretta's standards of value are not those of his family, but he was drawn to her as a younger man, when he loved passionately enough to overcome his mother's objection. When Miss Ivors scolds him and tells him that "I'm ashamed of you," it is as if she were his mother scolding him. Mother and mother church may have a role in his harsh judgment of his own sexual arousal; for after Gretta rejects his advances, he thinks of "his own clownish lusts" and alludes to the Cain story: "[H]e turned his back more to the light lest she might see the *shame* that burned upon his forehead" (p. 56; emphasis mine).

Gabriel is haunted by memories of the past. Isn't his speech finally an elegy for himself? The narrator's irony at his expense includes his pompous, self-serving speech, in which he uses the rhetoric of revenge to get back at Miss Ivors. Gabriel savors small pretensions and lives in a simplified world he has created – a world with, on the one hand, rigid assumptions about marriage and courtship, and, on the other, fears about how Gretta regards him despite his self-importance. He has wrapped himself in an envelope of defensiveness and allusion. Note his snobbery when she tells him about Michael: "*What* was he?" he asks (p. 56; emphasis mine).

Gabriel needs to be the center of attention, the object of the gazes of others. He is *realized* by the knowledge that he is part of the perception of others, and seeks fulfillment and completion in the opinion of others. Yet, paradoxically, he is uncomfortable with himself and dislikes being the focus; as if he were claustrophobic, he longs to be outside, elsewhere, and beyond:

> How cool it must be outside! How pleasant it would be to walk out alone, first along by the river and then through the park! The snow would be lying on the branches of the trees and forming a bright cap on the top of the Wellington Monument. How much more pleasant it would be there than at the supper-table! (p. 34)

Because he is uncomfortable he continually imagines another world – a kind of psychic utopia – outside. For he desperately needs to be elsewhere. Insecure and anxious, he creates a reductive version of another place, a kind of imaginative journey away from the pain he feels. When he is anxious he engages in repression and transference; he feels others looking at him. Directly before his speech, he nervously sees others looking at him:

> People, perhaps, were standing in the snow on the quay outside, gazing up at the lighted windows and listening to the waltz music. The air was pure there.

In the distance lay the park where the trees were weighted with snow. The Wellington Monument wore a gleaming cap of snow that flashed westward over the white field of Fifteen Acres. (p. 42)

We should notice how, in anticipation of the performative ending, Joyce shows that for Gabriel the snow becomes an image of escape and distance, while the west is associated with the primitive and spontaneous.

C "Distant music": Gabriel's psyche amidst cultural and historical contexts

Gabriel always sees himself as *other*. We must also understand that he has aspects of paranoia – the domestic kind that haunts all of our insecurities – in his sense that he is always being watched, weighed, regarded, put to a test, and found wanting. Sometimes the division between his public presence and his private, insecure self is so great that he perceives as if he were traumatized or at least depressed. He is reactive rather than active and occasionally behaves as if he were anesthetized. Of course, we understand that the one who is always watching Gabriel *is* Gabriel. In the tiny world of his aunts' party, he is the dominant male who knows how to carve a goose, cope with a drunk guest, and give a speech. But he is as fragmented as his hodgepodge of knowledge. He needs to differentiate himself from others and to patronize others.

Gabriel suffers from hyperacuity of perception, and the narrator uses modes of hyperacuity to invite the reader to measure him. Ironically, Gabriel sees himself as if he were a painting, an object, or a text requiring another to bring him to life. We might recall Jacques Lacan's insight about the painter's gaze:

The painter gives something to the person who must stand in front of his painting which, in part, at least, of the painting, might be summed up thus – *You want to see? Well, take a look at this!* He gives something for the eye to feed on, but he invites the person to whom this picture is presented to lay down his gaze there as one lays down one's weapons. This is the pacifying, Apollonian effect of painting. Something is given not so much to the gaze as to the eye, something that involves the abandonment, the *laying down*, of the gaze.[9]

Indeed, Gabriel has the same kind of alternating sympathy and irony toward himself, whom he often views as strangely detached, the object of his own gaze, a kind of painting he regards in the same way he gazes at his wife on the stairs. His watching her laughing at him for making her wear galoshes anticipates the later view of her as a painting: his "admiring and happy eyes had been wandering from her dress to her face and hair" (p. 25).

The Lacanian perspective, like the Freudian and Laingian perspectives, is important, in part because it stresses the need to be aware of the place of women in the text. We realize that Lacan's words apply to the way Gabriel watches himself, and that it is this division between himself as subject and as object which is at the heart of his problem. As Garry Leonard writes:

> In the most fundamental sense, Lacan divides the subject in two. The speaking subject he calls *je* or "I." The object-like stable sense of subjectivity, what we might call an ideal sense of identity, Lacan designates as the *moi* or me . . . The *je* tries to bring about, through other subjects, the messages that the *moi* requires in order to believe in its existence . . . One cannot become aware of the perpetual failure of language to join the *moi* and *je* into a unified whole without also becoming aware of the fact that masculine subjectivity is a cultural construct that only appears to exist between the two.[10]

But isn't the disjunction between the *moi* and *je* a cultural construct for both genders and thus also true of the feminine subjectivity of Miss Ivors, Lily, and Gretta? Who has self-awareness in "The Dead," except perhaps Gabriel, who oscillates between too much and too little?

When Gabriel sees Gretta as a painting, he is a captive of his visual imagination, which is ironic because he wears spectacles and has difficulty seeing:

> He stood still in the gloom of the hall, trying to catch the air that the voice was singing and gazing up at his wife. There was grace and mystery in her attitude as if she were a symbol of something. He asked himself what is a woman standing on the stairs in the shadow, listening to distant music, a symbol of. If he were a painter he would paint her in that attitude. Her blue felt hat would show off the bronze of her hair against the darkness and the dark panels of her skirt would show off the light ones. *Distant Music* he would call the picture if he were a painter. (p. 48)

Earlier, Gabriel notices the paintings over the piano of the death scenes in *Romeo and Juliet* and of the murdered princes; the reader realizes how these grim death scenes are not Irish pictures that Miss Ivors – or followers of the Celtic Renaissance – would approve of. It is indicative of Gabriel's attachment to Western Europe that he travels to the continent, cites the continental precedent for galoshes, thinks of Browning and Shakespeare, and alludes to Paris and the Golden Apple. When Gabriel declares to Miss Ivors that he is sick of his own country, we may think of Stephen telling Bloom in the "Eumaeus" section of *Illysses*, "Since we can't change the country, let's change the subject." That the west of Ireland is associated with the primitive and sexual recalls the association of sexuality with primitivism – with the Orient or with the South Sea Islands – in the paintings of Gauguin and Matisse or the writings of Stevenson and Conrad.

In turn-of-the-century Modernist texts, dance becomes an image of the Dionysian and libidinous. We might think of Aschenbach's dream of a Dionysian, orgiastic dance featuring a version of his beloved Tadzio in Mann's *Death in Venice* (1912). Dance became a sanctioned expression of the libido; it enabled participants to express sexuality in forms ranging from passion to flirtation within permissible boundaries. Diaghilev was in Paris, and Isadora Duncan performed in 1909. One might say that Gabriel does a pirouette around an arabesque of uncertainty. After Gretta falls asleep at the hotel, he thinks of how the "riot of emotions" – his sexual desire – had derived "[f]rom his aunts' supper, from his own foolish speech, from the wine and dancing, the merrymaking when saying good-night in the hall, the pleasure of the walk along the river in the snow" (p. 58). The place of dance – waltzes, quadrilles, and lancers – in this 1907 text is significant if we think of Matisse's great painting *Dance* (1910) and its sequel *Music* (1911), which showed the importance of dance and music to turn-of-the-century culture. Does not the dispute between Miss Ivors and Gabriel while they are dancing recall the broken circle of Matisse's *Dance*, where we realize that the individual dancers are dancing partly alone, some clockwise and some counterclockwise, in their own private space?

Under the influence of Walter Pater, music was thought by many turn-of-the century artists to be the highest form of art and the one toward which other arts should strive, but music is diluted in "The Dead" by Mary Jane's Academy piano piece, which can only be followed by Mary Jane and Aunt Kate. Except for Bartell D'Arcy's singing, it seems agreed upon among the characters that the best music is in the past, a theme reinforced by much of *Dubliners*, especially "A Mother." Indeed, we might think of the anesthetized, isolated musicians of Matisse's *Music*. Among other things, we might note that "The Dead" is about the inability of the other arts to revivify Gabriel's life; neither music, nor dance, nor painting does the trick.

A psychological criticism may also address how characters iterate and depart from mythic prototypes. (Joyce would have known Frazer's *The Golden Bough*.) What Eliot wrote of *Ulysses* is also applicable to "The Dead"; Joyce's references to myth, Eliot contended, are "a way of controlling, of ordering, of giving shape and significance to the immense panorama of futility and anarchy which is contemporary history."[11] The allusive technique of "The Dead" anticipates *Ulysses*. After calling his Aunt Kate, Aunt Julia, and Mary Jane "The Three Graces," Gabriel says, "I will not attempt to play to-night the part that Paris played on another occasion. I will not attempt to choose between them" (p. 44). Reading, we realize that it is not Gabriel but Gretta who is the Paris figure choosing between men – and, at least in Gabriel's mind, it is he who has not been chosen.

Indeed, Paris does not award the Golden Apple among the Three Graces, but among Athena, Aphrodite, and Hera. (The Three Graces were Aylaia [splendor], Euphrosyne [mirth], and Thalia [good cheer].) The judgment of Paris inspired the *Iliad* and the *Odyssey*, but what will Gabriel inspire? He is mocked by his own allusions, which weave a circumference of irony around him. Isn't there a bathetic irony in his comparing himself with Paris and his aunts and cousin with the Three Graces? Moreover, Paris's abduction of Helen began the Trojan War, and Gabriel is a kind of mock Paris who took Gretta from the west of Ireland. Gabriel aesthetizes his experience as if he were locked into a set of perceptions from which he can't escape; he perceives in set scenes. Similarly, the narrator creates a perceptual epistemology that emphasizes the breakdown of narrative and the development of Gabriel's sense of self. The dinner is described as if it were a still life, and may have been influenced by Joyce's awareness of that form in Postimpressionistic paintings that he saw in Paris, including those of Cézanne:

A fat brown goose lay at one end of the table and at the other end, on a bed of creased paper strewn with sprigs of parsley, lay a great ham, stripped of its outer skin and peppered over with crust crumbs, a neat paper frill round its shin and beside this was a round of spiced beef. Between these rival ends ran parallel lines of side-dishes: two little minsters of jelly, red and yellow; a shallow dish full of blocks of blancmange and red jam, a large green leaf-shaped dish with a stalk-shaped handle, on which lay bunches of purple raisins and peeled almonds, a companion dish on which lay a solid rectangle of Smyrna figs, a dish of custard topped with grated nutmeg, a small bowl full of chocolates and sweets wrapped in gold and silver papers and a glass vase in which stood some tall celery stalks. In the centre of the table there stood, as sentries to a fruit-stand which upheld a pyramid of oranges and American apples, two squat old-fashioned decanters of cut glass, one containing port and the other dark sherry. On the closed square piano a pudding in a huge yellow dish lay in waiting and behind it were three squads of bottles of stout and ale and minerals, drawn up according to the colours of their uniforms, the first two black, with brown and red labels, the third and smallest squad white, with transverse green sashes. (p. 38)

The striking juxtaposition of this unfolding presentation of plenty – superficial plenty – coming within the context of spiritual and physical want, not only in "The Dead" but in preceding stories like "A Painful Case," "Ivy Day in the Committee Room," "A Mother," and "Grace," emphasizes the limits of life in Dublin. It is as if Joyce were stressing the voyeuristic at the expense of intimacy and using the visual, as opposed to the touch of physical intimacy, to show how Gabriel has displaced his feelings onto a world of material stuff. Seen from this perspective, is not the tale's last paragraph a conclusion to a narrative of landscapes and a hint that Gabriel still has a way to go before he becomes a flexible, responsive adult like Leopold Bloom in *Ulysses*?

A psychological criticism notices patterns of language beneath the surface and understands the verbal play as if the text were a patient recalling more than she or he realizes. Joyce deftly creates a verbal texture that immerses the reader's mind in death and mortality until the reader is shaped to see an inevitability about death; it is almost as if the verbal texture were subliminally supporting the plot. Within the text there are continual references to death: Gabriel speaks of how his wife "takes three mortal hours to dress herself" and the aunts respond that "she must be perished alive" (pp. 22–3). The monks "slept in their coffins"; the "subject" of the monks "had grown lugubrious" and "was buried in a silence" (p. 42). Later we are told that Mrs Malins "will get her death of cold" (p. 45). The pictures on the wall above the piano of the murdered princes and of the balcony scene in *Romeo and Juliet* suggest death as well as the frustration of love and hope. Words like "gloom" and "shadows" almost become ghosts invisibly stalking the text. When Gabriel gazes at his wife listening to Bartell D'Arcy's singing, he is in "the gloom of the hall" and we recall the gloom he felt after Lily's retort, a gloom that left him wanting to be outside the room in which the waltzing was taking place.

In a sense, Joyce invites the reader to join him as one of those who are emotionally and spiritually alive, and one way that the reader feels enlivened is by seeing more perspicaciously than the characters in the tale entitled "The Dead." Rereading, we realize that Joyce creates a word-world in which phrases that are applied to other people actually define Gabriel. Thus, it is not only Julia but Gabriel, too, "who did not know where she was or where she was going" (p. 24). When Gabriel refuses to acknowledge that he should be ashamed of himself for writing for the *Daily Express*, the very iteration of "ashamed" three times in the context of his conversation creates an association in our minds between him and shame, an association which is fulfilled when we are later told: "A shameful consciousness of his own person assailed him" (p. 56). Note, too, the passivity of his stance in his sense of being assailed; it is as if things happen to him that he can't control, as when he feels at the moment when he expected to triumph in his affection for Gretta "some impalpable and vindictive being was coming against him" (p. 57). While Gabriel's paralytic self-consciousness is a poignant echo of Hamlet, another figure caught up in a rotting, alcoholic culture and drawn to his mother, Michael Furey is posing perhaps as the ghost of Hamlet's father.

D Gabriel's transformation

While Gabriel's irony fails when he learns of Michael and his passionate love for Gretta, Joyce's narrator's irony does not. Can we be sure that Gretta is any more reliable than Gabriel? Ironically, she has taken seriously Gabriel's advice in his speech to "cherish in our hearts the memory of those dead" which "the world will not willingly let die" (p. 43). Perhaps in her imagination she creates the passionate, heroic lover. This is the kind of legend that has informed the whole story. And Gabriel, as Vincent P. Pecora has written, then reinvents himself as a heroic figure with abundant generosity:

> To avoid being further humiliated by others, Gabriel must of course humiliate himself. In the name of Michael Furey, his legendary hero and personal saint, Gabriel sacrifices himself to the past, and to the dead, more profoundly than any of his compatriots does. Moreover, he appears completely assured of the sincerity of his gesture. That is, Gabriel has reproduced in himself, like his vision of Michael Furey, the most fundamental structuring device for heroism, generosity, self-knowledge, and spiritual transcendence in his culture: the story of Christ . . . If Gabriel fools himself, if in the very process that we accept as self-discovery he only reimplicates himself blindly in the cultural conditions he longs to transcend, then we may simply be doing the same thing, in our reading, in our lives.[12]

That Gretta's memories of Michael are evoked by associations and provoked by a song, "The Lass of Aughrim," recalls Freud's idea of free association as well as Proust's. It is necessary to know that Gretta is responding to a song which tells of a seduced and abandoned young woman standing in the rain – with her baby in her arms – who is rejected in an attempt to see her former lover; the lover asks her a series of questions but does not let the young woman in to see him. For Gabriel, Gretta's associations become ironically Gabriel's reality; this is part of the vulnerability of his insecurity. Joyce shows how the interior space of the mind can become hell to those who lack religious faith; indeed, raised as an orthodox Catholic and a former novitiate, Joyce disbelieves as only a former believer can.

Gabriel's hell is his obsessions, fixations, memories, insecurities, and dimly acknowledged needs. But throughout he is aware of aging and mortality. He knows his wife's face is "no longer the face for which Michael Furey had braved death" (p. 58). As much as the dead, his memories and insecurities are the shades and shadows which resist him. Indeed, in speaking so much of death and the dead, Gabriel creates a subtext that undermines the conclusion's positive implications and makes us aware of how he is reformulating and recirculating the elegiac and nostalgic mode that stresses the past.

That Gabriel cannot respond to Gretta as a sexual equal, that he is awkward and displaces his desire and cannot separate lust from passion, is Joyce's way of castigating the Catholic church for producing dysfunctional Irish males. (In Joyce's rural Ireland, as opposed to Dublin, both men and women seem to be less deflected from desire by the church: think of Gretta and Michael, the woman who seduced Davin in *A Portrait of an Artist*, and, of course, Nora.) Because of his Irish Catholic upbringing, Joyce implies, Gabriel cannot speak the language of desire: "To take her as she was would be brutal. No, he must see some ardour in her eyes first. He longed to be master of her strange mood . . . He longed to cry to her from his soul, to crush her body against his, to overmaster her" (p. 54). Yet Gabriel's need to master and control is an extension of his own problems as well as an instance of his culturally produced responses. Indeed, lacking a coherent self, Gabriel is a weather vane, affected by both cultural practices and the most recent conversations. Because of his awkwardness in sexual and passionate matters, he seeks refuge in Elizabethan language: "Gabriel, feeling now how vain it would be to try to lead her whither he had purposed" (p. 56).

Yet one should also think about Gretta's behavior and motives. Why does she not realize that her words will hurt Gabriel and that this hyperconscious, insecure, anxious, and guilt-ridden man – her husband – will be upset and troubled? Is she not somewhat insensitive and inconsiderate to her husband? Should she not know that Gabriel, educated in a Catholic epistemology that regards premarital sex as a sin, will respond almost as if he were a victim of adultery? Even if she had been passionately in love, even if (which is hardly supported by the text) she and Michael had been lovers, does that discredit their marriage? His response to her revelation shows the degree to which he has suffered acculturation and recalls – in a kind of pentimento (where images of an earlier and painted-over version peek through the painting that we are examining) that makes us aware of how the boy in the early stories is the spiritual father of the man Gabriel – the final retrospective comment of the boy in "Araby" who thinks he has sinned because of his puppy love: "Gazing up into the darkness I saw myself as a creature driven and derided by vanity; and my eyes burned with anguish and anger" (*Dubliners*, p. 35). Isn't it part of Gabriel's immaturity that he regards this relationship that took place before he met Gretta as a rejection? Joyce's criticism is directed at an Irish moral education, which includes a Catholic epistemology that teaches that the bride must be an innocent and a virgin. Part of the story's irony is that Gabriel, who would reject Irish superstition and be more enlightened, is locked into the system of values that he would reject.

Poignantly, Gabriel does not believe in his own intellect or passion. It is in the last section that he descends into hell. While the box-like hotel room recalls a coffin, the Charon-like clerk who takes them to their room upstairs as if he were rowing them across the river Lethe recalls other journeys to hell and death, including Mann's *Death in Venice*, and anticipates the "Hades" section in *Ulysses*. Florence Walzl notes, "The box-like hotel room, the removal of a candle, the darkness, the chill, and the bed on which Gretta lies, all build the impression of a vault where the dead rest frozen on their biers."[13] That Gabriel has no coherent identity is underlined when he imagines himself approaching the region of the dead: "His own identity was fading out into a grey impalpable world: the solid world itself which these dead had one time reared and lived in was dissolving and dwindling" (p. 59). In the face of disappointment, he, like snow, melts, and his ego dissolves. Note how he intuits something threatening when Gretta refers to "The Lass of Aughrim," the song to which she has been listening: "As he passed in the way of the cheval-glass he caught sight of himself in full length, his broad, well-filled shirt-front, the face whose expression always puzzled him when he saw it in a mirror and his glimmering gilt-rimmed eyeglasses" (p. 55). His gaze reflexively catches himself, as it does so often throughout the text. He is both subject and object in the mirror; we recall Wilde's *The Picture of Dorian Gray*, which Joyce surely would have had in mind, where Dorian's superego is transferred to the portrait that ages as a reflection of his dissipated lifestyle, even while he apparently retains his youthful appearance.

After Gretta tells Gabriel about the boy of her past, he thinks that he has been rejected:

Gabriel felt humiliated by the failure of his irony and by the evocation of this figure from the dead, a boy in the gasworks. While he had been full of memories of their secret life together, full of tenderness and joy and desire, she had been comparing him in her mind with another. A shameful consciousness of his own person assailed him. He saw himself as a ludicrous figure, acting as a pennyboy for his aunts, a nervous well-meaning sentimentalist, orating to vulgarians and idealising his own clownish lusts, the pitiable fatuous fellow he had caught a glimpse of in the mirror. Instinctively he turned his back more to the light lest she might see the shame that burned upon his forehead. (p. 56; to the 1914 reader, the term "secret life" was a term that implied one's sexual life)

When we look at this passage we should respond pluralistically to Gabriel's psychological drama in terms of other characters, of Joyce's doubts and fears, and of his narrator's elegizing a culture that now lacks coherence. We should see, too, Gabriel as an instance of *fin de siècle* intellectual isolation, which looks forward to that theme in *Portrait* and in *Ulysses*.

The man of words is deprived of words. Finally he realizes that he had always spoken in clichés and abstractions, and that he speaks in words that are culturally inscribed. After he hears of Gretta's love for Michael – and the emperor's new clothes are once again stripped from his vulnerable vanity – he thinks of how he will be speaking at Aunt Julia's funeral:

> Soon, perhaps, he would be sitting in that same drawing-room, dressed in black, his silk hat on his knees. The blinds would be drawn down and Aunt Kate would be sitting beside him, crying and blowing her nose and telling him how Julia had died. He would cast about in his mind for some words that might console her, and would find only lame and useless ones. Yes, yes: that would happen very soon. (p. 58)

Again he imagines himself playing a part. Readers of *Ulysses* will recall how "yes," iterated by Bloom and affirmed by Molly, is a crucial word linking the two estranged lovers throughout June 16, 1904. In the above passage, Joyce might have expected Irish readers to hear the echo of a line from the song "Arrayed for the Bridal": "May life to her prove full of sunshine and love, full of love, yes! yes! yes!!"

As we read we respond in multiple ways, including our awareness of how each of these aspects alternately becomes more dominant and then recedes in the face of the claims of the others. Does not the ending of "The Dead" make this clear? For as the last protagonist in a series of stories about moral paralysis in Ireland, Gabriel's paralytic self-consciousness and his inability to connect with Gretta give him significance as a representative of the failure of will, breakdown of family, and sexual inadequacy that, along with (and perhaps as a result of) Catholicism and English imperialism (personified by the statue of the British hero Wellington) are paralyzing Ireland. But as a particularized figure who has realized his limitations as a lover and a man and feels generosity to his wife, Gabriel is interesting and significant because he has the potential for growth and transformation. Thus his transformation at the end of "The Dead" is a personal one – one that does not free the rest of Dublin's residents from moral and spiritual paralysis but is a moment of hope rendered as a performance in which the reader participates:

> Generous tears filled Gabriel's eyes. He had never felt like that himself towards any woman but he knew that such a feeling must be love. The tears gathered more thickly in his eyes and in the partial darkness he imagined he saw the form

of a young man standing under a dripping tree. Other forms were near. His soul had approached that region where dwell the vast hosts of the dead. He was conscious of, but could not apprehend, their wayward and flickering existence. His own identity was fading out into a grey impalpable world; the solid world itself which these dead had one time reared and lived in was dissolving and dwindling.

A few light taps upon the pane made him turn to the window. It had begun to snow again. He watched sleepily the flakes, silver and dark, falling obliquely against the lamplight. The time had come for him to set out on his journey westward. Yes, the newspapers were right; snow was general all over Ireland. It was falling on every part of the dark central plain, on the treeless hills, falling softly upon the Bog of Allen and, farther westward, softly falling into the dark mutinous Shannon waves. It was falling, too, upon every part of the lonely churchyard on the hill where Michael Furey lay buried. It lay thickly drifted on the crooked crosses and headstones, on the spears of the little gate, on the barren thorns. His soul swooned slowly as he heard the snow falling faintly through the universe and faintly falling, like the descent of their last end, upon all the living and the dead. (p. 59)

What is performed is the suspension of rational and linear thought. While, as we know from John Huston's wonderful film of "The Dead," the passage can be visualized, does it not enact a state of being that finally transcends the visual, a state when the soul, as Yeats puts it in "Sailing to Byzantium," "clap[s] its hands and sing[s]"? For loving Gretta, for understanding that passion is itself a value, this is Gabriel's reward ("Better pass boldly into that other world, in the full glory of some passion, than fade and wither dismally with age"), just as the vision of Rudy is Bloom's reward.

Discursively, the last sentence makes little sense. One cannot hear snow falling through the universe and the antecedent of "their" is indeterminate (snowflakes? all the dead? Gretta and Michael? Gretta, Michael, and himself? all the past and future dead?). Gabriel's move outside the enclosure of his ego is enabled/performed by the phonics and reversals of the passage, particularly the last sentence. The passage's meaning derives from its place in a process; it contrasts with the mimesis of the preceding pages of the story and with Gabriel's paralytic self-consciousness, rationality, and literalism.

The ending is discourse not story; yet as discourse it shows us what Gabriel needs but lacks: song, lyricism, metaphoricity, escape from time into non-rational, passionate states of being, a loosening of the bonds of self-consciousness. The dissolution of his ego is for him a positive move because he can surrender to the lyrical moment, to a time when the soul claps hands and sings. In a sense, at this moment he joins the dance of life, or thinks he does.[14] It is a moment of rare serenity – visual, tonal, emotional serenity – a moment which resists (perhaps resents?) the critic's rational efforts to order it because it is allegorical and asyntactical. Even while acknowledging the brilliance of Huston's visualization, do we not feel that it encroaches on our interior experience, on our private admiration of the scene and reduces our rich, polyauditory response to Gabriel's interior life and Joyce's rendering of it to a sequence of visual images? Isn't that often the problem when we see our intimate reading experience transformed into a film?

What is absent is as important as what is present in responding to character. The snow imagery focuses our attention on a world outside Gabriel – a natural world where generations live and die and survive their sense of self-importance. We recall that snow has the potential to become ice (death) and water (life). Obviously, as ice it also suggests the emotional sterility of a world reduced to social gestures, empty talk, and loveless relationships – a world where a tiny pathetic "I" cannot connect to others to form a loving, passionate, tender couple; a world that does not even give Gabriel the feeling he so desperately needs, that of being part of a social mosaic. We can never be sure whether Gretta is waiting for Gabriel in the way that Molly is waiting for Bloom, because we see less of Gabriel's dignity and integrity than we see of Bloom's and more of Gabriel's selfishness and narrow-mindedness. Perhaps we do not quite sympathize with Gabriel's sense of isolation and disappointment as we do with Bloom's because of the latter's generous concern for others – such as Paddy Dignam's family and Mrs Purefoy.

Note how fiction's realistic code reasserts itself when basic emotions of love and death are the subject. We respond powerfully to descriptions of Gabriel's transformation and use psychological grammar to understand that transformation, including his realization that conscience and self-consciousness are not the full parameters of living, that the love shared by Michael and Gretta contained passion, intensity, and intimacy that go beyond concern with whether or not Gretta wears galoshes. We might therefore speak of the precedence of subjects and note how our aesthetic sense itself is more likely to be pushed aside and relegated to the back burner when we are engaged by issues that matter to our human feelings – notably, issues of the human psyche. And we might say that most of us will be engaged mainly by the representation of emotions that interest us. Indeed, in speaking of the precedence and hierarchy of subjects that engage us, should we not acknowledge that a culture's ever-changing preferences, together with its continuing interest in certain themes and problems such as adult sexual love, help create and recreate its literary canon?

Chapter 8

Joyce's *Ulysses*: The Odyssey of Leopold Bloom and Stephen Dedalus on June 16, 1904

I Introduction: "O Rocks . . . Tell us in Plain Words"

Now that a century has passed since June 16, 1904 – the date the events of *Ulysses* occurred – we need ask why we are interested in the details, even in the minutiae, of the lives of the novel's three central figures on that day. Or, put another way, how, without discernible action to justify a novel of its inordinate length, which covers less than 24 hours in one day, does Joyce arouse and maintain our interest in the arrogant, paralytically self-conscious, putative author, Stephen Dedalus; the compassionate, gentle, and generous Irish Jew, Bloom; and his lusty, intuitive, and adulterous wife Molly? What is it about these characters' thoughts and feelings, memories and desires, hopes and fears, fixations and obsessions that fascinates us? The very question in part provides the answer – namely that it is less the events of the day than the characters' interior lives that are Joyce's concerns. No different than ourselves, these characters live in a complex modern world and have little opportunity for the traditional grand actions of earlier epics suggested by the book's title.

In *Ulysses* – published in 1922, the same year as Eliot's *The Waste Land* – Joyce transforms the ordinary events of one day, June 16, 1904, in the lives of his three major characters – Stephen Dedalus, Leopold Bloom, Molly Bloom – into significant form. Joyce read Homer's *Odyssey* as a family drama in contrast to the bellicose and xenophobic *Iliad*; what was central, Joyce thought, was Telemachus' search for his father and Ulysses' quest to return home to his wife. In Joyce's twentieth-century retelling, Stephen is Telemachus, Bloom is Ulysses, and Molly is Penelope. In stressing Bloom's commitment to home and family, Joyce thought he was returning to the original spirit of the *Odyssey*, which he saw as contrasting with the *Iliad*'s focus on war.

The crucial events are often based on details of Joyce's own life. In June 1904, Joyce met his future wife Nora Barnacle – on June 10 in all probability – and on about June 20, following a drunken spree in Dublin, he was taken home by Alfred Hunter, a man who may have been both Jewish and an unfaithful husband. Hunter became the source for Bloom, the humanistic Jewish hero of *Ulysses*, from whom Stephen learns about family, courage, caring, and life. When writing *Ulysses*, Joyce's imagination assigned both dates to June 16, 1904, the day Joyceans celebrate as Bloomsday.

Why *Ulysses*? Why do we care about one day, June 16, 1904, in the life of a 38-year-old advertising salesman who is barely a Jew, his lusty and frustrated wife, and a 22-year-old depressive recovering Catholic who would like to be recognized as a major writer although he hasn't written more than a "capful of odes"? Why do we put up with a novel which includes not only a plethora of arcane references and allusions, but often nearly impenetrable phrases if not whole sentences? Why do we regard *Ulysses* as the centerpiece of Modernism?

We need to remember that we read novels because novels are by humans, about humans, and for humans. Specifically, we respond to *Ulysses* because Joyce creates compelling characters; we are empathetic with Stephen Dedalus, the marginalized artist, and his counterpart, Leopold Bloom, the man of enterprise and a flaneur; because we have an interest in the sexuality and concomitant dysfunctionality of the Bloom marriage; because June 16, 1904, resembles the diurnal activities of our days, albeit our obsessions, frustrations, fixations, and ambitions may be different from Stephen's, Bloom's, and Molly's; and because *Ulysses* gives significance to the small tribulations and triumphs of modern life that recall our own lives.

Joyce's representation of human behavior depends on his management of his narrative economy in such a way that he engages us in a process of reading that gives pedestrian events significance and makes us feel that they matter. He does this in part by placing these events in a larger context evoked by patterns of allusion to prior eras, including, notably, the Homeric period, the biblical periods – the material of both the Old (the Hebrew Bible) and New Testament (the Christian Bible) – and the plays of the Elizabethan world of Shakespeare, as well as the imagined worlds evoked by Dante, Milton, Swift, and the contemporary world evoked by Yeats, Wilde, and others.

We read *Ulysses*, too, for several other important reasons. The novel shows us the inner workings of the modern city; it enacts the effects of colonialism on the colonized. In the multi-perspectivism of the ventriloquistic narrator, *Ulysses* is a wonderful rendering of the multi-dimensional aspect of modern reality. We read *Ulysses* because the novel can be hilarious, high-spirited, and playful in its language and situations. We read *Ulysses* because of the originality of the rendering of Joyce's characters' unconscious and semi-conscious lives, especially in the fifteenth episode "Circe," written in the form of a play that has been successfully produced as "Ulysses in Nighttown." We also read *Ulysses* because of our pleasure in recognizing and understanding not only literary parallels, parodies, and pastiches but also verbal resonances from the novel's previous episodes. Finally, we read *Ulysses* because in its experiments with literary form, language, styles, and subject matter, it is, along with Picasso's and Matisse's paintings, Kafka's stories, and Eliot's poetry, one of the crystallizing texts of Modernism.

Reading Joyce raises messy questions about the relationship between an author's life and work. For Stephen Dedalus, the major character in *A Portrait of the Artist as a Young Man* and one of the three major figures in *Ulysses*, is based definitively, yet ambiguously, on Joyce's life. We must ask whether we can read *Portrait* or *Ulysses* as if it were possible for Joyce to re-create his life in fiction and to stand objectively detached from the emotional bonds that tie him to the represented experience of his own life. Or, is the explicit and subjective relationship between *Ulysses* and Joyce's life – a life with which we are familiar in great detail because of Richard Ellmann's remarkable biography *James Joyce* – inevitably part of our reading experience? Do we not respond to the teller of *Portrait* and *Ulysses* as a character within the imagined world of the novels, whose full significance depends on a dynamic and varying relationship with the creator? To read Joyce, we need to define the formal relationship between author and novel and to propose an aesthetic which includes the principle that a book's significance may depend in part on knowing something of what happened to the author between the time of the action and the time the book was written.

Writing to his brother Stanislaus, Joyce remarked:

> Don't you think there is a certain resemblance between the mystery of the Mass and what I am trying to do? I mean that I am trying . . . to give people some kind of intellectual pleasure or spiritual enjoyment by converting the bread of everyday life into something that has a permanent artistic life of its own . . . for their mental, moral, and spiritual uplift.[1]

Joyce believed in the significance of seemingly trivial details, and wanted to show that significance to the reader. Thus he establishes parallels between different historical eras, such as turn-of-the-century Dublin and Homeric Greece, and between such radically different characters as Bloom and Stephen.

As we read *Ulysses* and feel the presence of Joyce trying to transform his fictionalized reminiscence into a significant form, and trying to define a voice and values that transcend the perspectives of Bloom, Stephen, and Molly, we understand that, like the reader, Joyce had to struggle between, on the one hand, the pleasures of immersion in the local details of his tale and of his language and, on the other, the demands of interpreting those details. In other words, the reader's odyssey recapitulates in important ways the author's odyssey. Do we not experience an active fictionalized presence not merely trying to transform fact into fiction, but trying to transform the bread and wine of ordinary daily experience into an imagined world with its own teleological significance?

To the extent that we see Stephen as a representation of the younger Joyce, we as readers proceed from the fictional toward the real. Thus Stephen is a version of the immature, self-immersed Joyce who must mature before *Ulysses* can be written, and Bloom represents that part of Joyce which in 1904 had yet to be discovered and developed before *Ulysses* could be written. That the book progresses from Stephen to Bloom and then to Molly – from Stephen's inexperience to Bloom's worldly and practical experience and Molly's sexual experience – illustrates the maturity that must occur before Stephen can become someone who might hope to write *Ulysses*. Even without the knowledge that reading Ellmann's *James Joyce* gives us of the historical Joyce, we understand that the three major figures signify the fictionalized Joyce who is now speaking to us and that, in this crucial sense, to recall a phrase that the narrator uses to point up the amazing parallelism between the minds of Stephen and Bloom, "One life is all" (U.202, 280; IX, 653, 907–8).[2]

In applying Joyce's theory of genres – which I quoted in the last chapter – to his own works, we should think of literary works not as purely lyrical, epical, or dramatic, but as mixed modes that contain aspects of more than one genre. *A Portrait of the Artist as a Young Man* begins in the lyrical mode, but, to the degree to which it is ironic, approaches the epical mode. If we understand the relationship in *Ulysses* among the three genres as a dynamic process – as a dialogue among them – we can better understand the novel's form and meaning.

Thus in *Ulysses* Joyce progresses from the lyrical to the epical and finally to the dramatic. The first three episodes oscillate between the lyrical perspective of Stephen and the epical perspective of Joyce's omniscient but not entirely distanced narrator, a narrator who is never far from Stephen's consciousness and who does not enter into the consciousness of any other characters. By using the lyrical mode, Joyce establishes the continuity with *Portrait* of both

Stephen and the narrative presence, and calls attention to the process of fictionally re-examining and re-creating his own life. By allowing the lyrical mode to dominate over the epical mode with which *Portrait* had concluded, he shows that Stephen has taken a step backward in his artistic development, for the mature artist needs the objectivity Stephen lacks.

In *Ulysses* Joyce progressively distances himself from Stephen and establishes him as a potential character in an epic – the character of the young artist trying to find himself amidst personal and historical confusion so that he might develop into the writer of a novel like *Ulysses*. Presenting Bloom, his intelligent, sensitive, uneducated, empirical, sensual, middle-aged Irish Jew, is the means by which Joyce places his characters – not only Bloom, but Stephen, too – at a distance from himself. Joyce conceived Bloom as a character that would enable him to achieve the epical mode or, in the words from the passage in *Portrait* that we have been discussing, to "prolong and brood upon himself as the center of an epical event."

Perhaps the most notable aspect of the dramatic mode is the protean speaker whose virtuosity enables him to assume various and conflicting voices. For the unique styles that Joyce writes for each episode can be equated with the voices of characters in drama. This ventriloquy calls attention to the presence of an objective artist impersonalizing himself and looking from a detached, ironical perspective at the personae of the plot and at the various tellers. Does not the recurrence of Stephen Dedalus, the major figure of *Portrait*, make particularly striking the contrast between the diverse voices of *Ulysses* and the third-person omniscient narrator of *Portrait*, who renders Stephen's perspective almost exclusively?

Joyce's desire to objectify part of himself in Bloom, a character who seems to be the diametric opposite of Stephen, the artist based on Joyce's younger self, was probably influenced by Oscar Wilde's theory of masks. Wilde believed that we must assume a mask in order to liberate ourselves from our customary, conventional daytime selves. Yet for the very reason that Bloom is still enough of the mature Joyce who is living in Europe and writing *Ulysses*, Joyce had to struggle to achieve the objectivity and distance that are the prerequisites for his dramatic mode, the mode in which, as Joyce puts it, the "personality" of the artist "impersonalizes" itself.

Beginning with the fifteenth episode, "Circe," and climaxing with the eighteenth and final one, "Penelope," the artistic personality becomes – to use Joyce's terms from the passage I quoted above – "impersonalized" and "reprojected from [Joyce's] human imagination." (Although the text does not have chapter titles but only episode numbers, I am following the convention of using the episode titles, suggested by Joyce's schema, to stress the Homeric parallel.) Indeed, it is the depiction of Molly, based on the physicality and ingenuousness of Joyce's beloved Nora Barnacle, that allows him to achieve the necessary objectivity and impersonality to use comfortably the dramatic mode. Molly Bloom displaces the narrative presence, or, to say the same thing differently, the ventriloquy of the voice in "Penelope" is so complete that we at times almost forget that the narrative presence contains all the varied voices – including some, such as the snarling ally of the Citizen in the "Cyclops" episode and the speaker of sentimental pulp in "Nausicaa" – that he assumes only to discredit.

The reader understands that the possibility of discovering an appropriate fictional form for the modern epic novel is itself one subject of *Ulysses*, a subject that self-consciously hovers over the entire novel. Since, for Joyce, inclusiveness is itself an essential prerequisite and a value for the modern epic, he wished to include within *Ulysses* not only his epic mode, but also the lyrical and dramatic. (It is worth noting that Joyce's own definitions of form focus on narrative distance; that they insist on the relation of work to author; and that they assume the imitation of an a priori world.) Central to Joyce's inquiry into the putative form for the modern epic was what voice to assume, what style to employ, and what kind of characters could possibly imply the universality he required.

Since, at the end of *Portrait*, Stephen, as Ellmann nicely puts it in his biography, "could no longer communicate with anyone in Ireland but himself," Joyce could not rely on Stephen's consciousness.[3] In *Ulysses*, Joyce decided to make the creation of the mature artist the subject. But how does he do this? He dramatizes the way the warmth and generosity of an obscure middle-class Jew – a man as marginal as Stephen, the egotistical but self-doubting young artist who has not fulfilled his potential – open doors and windows of experience to the latter. Joyce demonstrates that on one crucial day (June 16, 1904), Stephen began the journey from immature artist to the mature epic artist who was now writing *Ulysses*. Joyce shows that Shakespeare, the artist that Joyce regarded as his major precursor in the English language, also used his own life as his subject.

By distributing his schemata for the novel, and by helping both Frank Budgen write his early biography and Stuart Gilbert write his critical study, Joyce deliberately and willfully shaped the interpretation of *Ulysses*. It is as if God had given both the Holy Word and the subsequent exegeses. Nevertheless, if we approach *Ulysses* as a novel which has important continuities with other novels and with Joyce's prior work, we discover that its meaning and significance depend – as is the case for all literary works – on the relationship among the three basic ingredients of literary experience: author, work, and audience.

I urge you to read Joyce's challenging and difficult, yet funny and compassionate novel that has given me and so many others a lifetime of pleasure.

Because of its difficulty, *Ulysses* is best read in a community, whether it be a class or a reading group. It is also best read over the course of a semester as the one book in a course, so that students can wrestle with it, savor it, learn how to read it, reread it, and have it become part of their lives for several months. Read this way, Joyce's masterwork will accompany them as long as they are sentient. Using Molly Bloom's response – "O Rocks . . . Tell us in plain words" – to Leopold Bloom's explanation of metempsychosis (the transmigration of souls), I shall stress that *Ulysses* is a readable novel rather than an elaborate puzzle or a Rosetta Stone or a hieroglyph (U.64; IV, 343).

II Re-enter Stephen: The Opening Episodes of *Ulysses*

As soon as we enter into the imagined world of *Ulysses*, we realize that Stephen is a man in trouble. He is living with Malachi "Buck" Mulligan, a man he dislikes and who patronizes him, in a Martello tower, which was intended to be a British fortress against a French invasion during the Napoleonic era. Although it is early morning in late spring, a time of hope and promise, the artistic expectations aroused by the ending of *Portrait* remain unfulfilled. By providing a traditional omniscient narrator whose voice is separate and distinct from Stephen's, Joyce uses the opening of *Ulysses* to propose a critique of the lyricism and subjectivity of *Portrait*: "Stately, plump Buck Mulligan came from the stairhead, bearing a bowl of lather on which a mirror and a razor lay crossed" (U.2–3; I, 1–2).

Stephen cannot escape the Catholic epistemology in which he has been educated. Like his creator, Stephen disbelieves as only a former believer can. He is deeply offended by Mulligan's sacrilegious behavior; Mulligan mocks the Eucharist while his gown is open and he is exposing himself. Thus, on the opening page, when Mulligan chants the prayer from the early part of the Mass before the priest or celebrant ascends to the altar, Stephen feels himself placed in the position of the acolyte or altar boy or, in terms of the Catholic liturgy, servant or minister, to the celebrant. He is tortured by the accusation he attributes to his mother: "Ghoul! Chewer of corpses!" (U.10; I, 278).

The riddle that Stephen asks of his students in "Nestor" shows how far he has to go to communicate with his audience:

The Cock crew,
The sky was blue:
The bells in heaven

Were striking eleven.
'Tis time for this poor soul
To go to heaven. (U.26; II, 102–7)

The narcissistic riddle shows us that Stephen is still locked into the "lyrical" mode of *Portrait* and that his imagination cannot reach beyond himself. Given the impenetrable verse query provided by the morbid and self-indulgent Stephen, nobody could have figured out the answer: "The fox burying his grandmother under a holly bush" has no relation to the riddle (U.27; II, 115). But the bathetic disjunction between riddle and solution does engage the reader in a quest to discover what is going on in Stephen's abstruse mind. Stephen's riddle calls attention to the difficulty of reading incomplete and partial texts that do not provide sufficient information for understanding them. His answer is a thinly veiled reference to himself. The grandmother is not only his own mother, but his Irish heritage, indeed, the Old Woman of Ireland for whom, to Stephen, the milklady in "Telemachus" is a symbol. Holly, the traditional evergreen of the Christmas season, represents renewal, but renewal – with its implications of restoration to a prior state – has an ironic aspect since Stephen is trying to put his past behind him. Perhaps he realizes that the artist must be not only an idealistic romantic but also a wily and shrewd man – not unlike, the rereader understands, the foxy Odysseus and his twentieth-century counterpart, Bloom.

The opening of "Proteus," the third episode, calls attention to the artist's creative mission. Just as Menelaus had to wrestle with the continually changing Proteus, Stephen must wrestle with the protean nature of his experience. Under the tutelage of Aristotle, who went as far as possible in exploring the visible world, he is turning away from the Platonism of the Church Fathers and the Celtic Twilight and toward the world of experience which must be the subject of his art: "Ineluctable modality of the visible: at least that if no more, thought through my eyes. Signatures of all things I am here to read" (U.37; III, 1–2).

In *Portrait* Joyce oscillates between objectifying Stephen and using him as a thinly disguised autobiographical figure in a fictionalized memoir – a memoir that contains a quirky combination of Joyce's moral and spiritual autobiography, confession, and artistic credo – even as it provides an occasion for his stylistic experimentation. From the outset of *Ulysses*, Stephen is clearly the result of Joyce's conscious effort to dramatize with some detachment and objectivity a character within the imagined world of the novel.

Put another way, in the opening episodes of *Ulysses*, Stephen has become, in terms of Joyce's theory of genres – articulated in *Portrait* – less of a lyrical figure who can see only in terms of his own needs and more of an epical figure who can achieve some distance in terms of seeing himself as other. Like Telemachus setting out on his journey in search of his father and ultimately his mature identity, Stephen must be a distinct, objectified character, rather than a lyrical figure whose thoughts and emotions reflect Joyce's. Thus, although Stephen's stature within the imagined world is sharply reduced, Joyce's narrator – as opposed to Stephen – has made vast progress toward achieving the artistic goals, defined in *Portrait*, of impersonality, detachment, and stasis.

The richness of these first three episodes of *Ulysses* depends in part on our responding to echoes of prior language and incidents from *Portrait*. In a process not unlike pentimento, Stephen's past, as we know it from *Portrait*, insists on intruding its shadows upon our perception of Stephen in *Ulysses*.

In *Portrait*, the narrator had viewed with gentle irony both Stephen's concluding dialogue with Cranly and his subsequent diary entries. Here it is Stephen who regards himself with bitter, self-conscious irony. In place of the ebullient brilliance and confidence in his role as an artist, which we saw in his dialogue with Cranly that precedes the diary entries in *Portrait*, Stephen reveals, in his opening dialogue with Mulligan, self-hatred, loneliness, and cynicism: "You behold in me, Stephen said with grim displeasure, a horrible example of free thought" (U.20; I, 625–6). Not completely undeserving of Mulligan's diagnosis, "General paralysis of the insane," Stephen is paralytically self-conscious; looking in the mirror he thinks, "As he and others see me. Who chose this face for me? This dogsbody to rid of vermin" (U.6; I, 128–9, 136–7).

When we recall the euphoric expectations of the penultimate diary entry in *Portrait*, we realize that Stephen's artistic career has become stalled: "Welcome, O life! I go to encounter for the millionth time the reality of experience and to forge in the smithy of my soul the uncreated conscience of my race" (p. 253).[4] It is as if the liberation of the concluding pages of *Portrait*, in which he defined himself as a priest of the imagination who would discover the conscience of his race, had not occurred. Because the reality of experience in the form of passionate feelings and empirical knowledge of life is what he lacks, Stephen is not yet ready to be the writer of the epic that Ireland requires. Before he can write an epic of modern Ireland, he must turn his back on various forms of aestheticism that preached "art for art's sake" and glorified a separation between life and art. In his 1922 *Ulysses* Joyce is rejecting the aestheticism and solipsism of Stephen's credo in the 1916 *Portrait*, where he wrote: "I will try to express myself in some mode of life or art as freely as I can and as wholly as I can, using for my defense the only arms I allow myself to use – silence, exile, and cunning" (p. 247).

Unlike his mythical namesake Daedalus, who adapted the arts to the reality of experience, Stephen is lost in the world of his own dreams. Stephen, like Daedalus and his son Icarus, is imprisoned in a labyrinth of his own making, but while Minos imprisoned Daedalus, Stephen imprisons himself. He is an Icarus figure who has flown too near the sun rather than, like his namesake Daedalus, a man who has flown successfully. With its emphasis on drowning images, the first episode, "Telemachus," underlines Stephen's ironic position here as an Icarus figure rather than as the Daedalus figure that he had defined as his model in *Portrait*.

For some time Stephen seems to have acceded to Mulligan's patronizing dominance. He had returned from his exile in Paris for his mother's death, but it is not clear why he remains in Dublin. Morbidly savoring his own misery, he has been wearing black since his mother's death 10 months ago and is still locked in bitterness, self-pity, and melancholy. Like Hamlet, with whom he identifies, Stephen realizes that he is paralyzed but he does not know what to do about it. Like Claudius, Mulligan is a false father who would usurp his affections, were Stephen, like Hamlet, not intent on rejecting him. Stephen's awkward relationship with Mulligan, in which Stephen is displeased with himself and always on guard, accounts for his need for an alter ego to help him overcome loneliness and a sense of isolation, a need which explains his later responsiveness to the kindly, sympathetic Bloom.

Stephen desperately needs an empathetic other, someone who will provide the responsive consciousness that earlier generations found in a prayerful relation with God. Our response to the morbid, humorless Stephen would be different and less sympathetic had we not read *Portrait*. But because we have responded to the development of his creative imagination, we do not so readily abandon him and, at least in part, see him as a victim of an indifferent father, insensitive and at times predatory friends, and a narrow-minded and repressive culture. And by the second half of the second episode, "Nestor," he does become more sympathetic in the conversation with the bigoted and myopic Deasy, an Orangeman who represents the mediocre and materialistic English culture that is infesting Ireland.

III Leopold Bloom: Joyce's Irish Jew

A few facts about Bloom. He is married to Molly but hasn't slept with her since a month before the birth of their son Rudy, who died 11 years ago, 11 days after his birth. His daughter Milly is about to turn 15, and he mourns for his father, who had committed suicide toward the end of June some years ago. He has a sexual pen pal named Martha Clifford, whom he has never met. He incorrectly suspects Molly of multiple affairs and correctly suspects that on this very day, June 16, 1904, she is going to sleep with Blazes Boylan.

Joyce redefines the traditional concept of hero to emphasize not only pacifism but commitment to family ties, concern for the human needs of others, sense of self, tolerance, and decency. Joyce thought Jews embodied the aforementioned qualities. He sees in those values an alternative to the bellicosity of Irish patriotism and the intolerance of Irish Catholicism. Neither circumcised nor the son of a Jewish mother, Bloom is not technically a Jew. But Joyce understands that he has a Jewish identity because, as the son of a Jewish father who emigrated to Ireland, he is regarded as a Jew and outsider by his fellow Dubliners. We realize that he has no choice as to whether he is a Jew or not because he is always *other* to the Dubliners with whom he interacts. Bloom is not only what Stephen requires but what Dublin requires.

That Bloom may be the solution to Stephen's problem is suggested by the opening of "Calypso" with its emphasis upon the nominalistic world of experience: "Mr Leopold Bloom ate with relish the inner organs of beasts and fowls. He liked thick giblet soup, nutty gizzards, a stuffed roast heart, liverslices fried with crustcrumbs, fried hencods' roes. Most of all he liked grilled mutton kidneys which gave to his palette a fine tang of faintly scented urine" (U.55; IV, 1–5). That we are in a radically different world from Stephen's is indicated by the syntax, with its straightforward, vibrant progression from subject to predicate to object. While Stephen interprets or reads the world in terms of his abstractions, Bloom responds in terms of what he has learned from his experience. Bloom is not interested in theories and abstractions for their own sake.

Bloom's imagination and emotional resilience enable him to face the disappointments and frustrations of his life. Yet, as we become aware of his sexual life and Molly's adultery, we understand how partial a loaf he is accepting. Nevertheless, in contrast to Stephen's obsessive preoccupation with the Old Woman of Ireland – figured in his imagination by the milkwoman whom he imagines with "Old shrunken paps" and "wrinkled finger," the midwives on the strand, and the old women of his parable in "Aeolus" – Bloom, after similarly perceiving an old woman as the personification of his people, rejects the metaphor in favor of enriching personal memories and fantasies (U.13–4; I, 398, 401–2). No sooner does reality intrude on his fantasy of reviving the holy land ("No, not like that. A barren land, bare waste. Vulcanic lake, the dead sea: no fish, weedless, sunk deep in the earth. No wind would lift those waves . . . Dead: an old woman's: the grey sunken cunt of the world") than he turns to thoughts of the warmth of sharing his bed with Molly: "Be near her ample bedwarmed flesh. Yes, yes" (U.61; IV, 218–20, 227–8, 238–9).

What Bloom, this modern Odysseus, must do is cast off his thralldom to Molly as Calypso and, by displacing her suitors, restore himself to the position of husband of Penelope. For Bloom, however, Calypso is not so much an external person as a state of mind. The thralldom he must and, indeed, does for the most part overcome is an obsessive preoccupation with three concerns: his personal and racial past, his mortality, and his wife's and 15-year-old daughter's sexuality.

"Lotus-Eaters" is the first of the three public episodes which take place between breakfast and lunch. As we make our way through "Lotus-Eaters," "Hades," and "Aeolus," we realize that most Dubliners seem to have very little work to do. Ironically, Bloom's sexual reveries throughout the day are the lotus leaves which retard his journey. That Joyce calls the technique of "Lotus-Eaters" "narcissism" indicates, among other things, that a certain amount of self-love is necessary to survive in the modern city. One has to be on guard against petty swindlers like M'Coy and potential adulterers like Blazes, and alert to the small pleasures of a public bath or a covert dalliance by correspondence. Befitting an episode whose technique is narcissism, Bloom thinks rather more of his own interests than he does in "Calypso" and "Hades," the preceding and subsequent episodes. Bloom's pride and rationality enable him to resist the narcotics of sloth, gambling, male camaraderie, and Catholicism.

While Stephen's sexual reveries are adolescent, incomplete, narcissistic, and abstract ("Touch me. Soft eyes. Soft soft soft hand. I am lonely here. O, touch me soon, now"), Bloom's memories of passion – drawing upon his first intercourse with Molly on the Howth – are personal and vibrant: "Lips kissed, kissing, kissed. Full gluey woman's lips" (U.49, 67; III, 434–5, IV, 450). After Stephen's effort to escape the demands and responsibilities of his life by living in literary and personal abstractions, Bloom says "Yes" to life. Thinking of the day Rudy might have been conceived he thinks "How life begins" (U.89; VI, 81). Then reluctantly accepting Milly's adolescence and the potential of her having sexual experience with a young student named Bannon, he thinks: "Yes, yes: a woman too. Life, life" (U.89; VI, 89–90). (Are we not to contrast Bloom's worldly acceptance of sexuality and the phases of human life with Stephen's life-denying fixations, which have been shaped by his pride, willed isolation, and rigid Catholic upbringing?) While Bloom accepts his body, takes pleasure in bathing, and is fascinated by the possibility of a woman washing his navel, Stephen is repelled by the idea of someone else giving him a bath: "Bath a most private thing. I wouldn't let my brother, not even my own brother, a most lascivious thing. Green eyes, I see you" (U.43; III, 236–8).

In "Hades," the sixth episode, Bloom uses the occasion of Paddy Dignam's funeral to come to terms with his own mortality. A crucial issue for a post-Christian world – and a focal point of "Hades" – is how one comes to terms with death. In the "Hades" episode we see that for Joyce the stream of consciousness is not merely a technique but a value, a value that affirms the interior space of the mind in contrast to the external world of the Homeric source. We recall that Odysseus descends into the underworld in search of Elpenor's ghost after the latter has fallen off a roof in a drunken stupor. That Bloom's descent into the underworld delves into his memories shows how the modern hero functions in interior psychological space. Haunted by memories of the dead, guilt, morbid associations, and feelings of social alienation from his companions, Bloom's hell is his own consciousness, and the means of extricating himself must also be found there.

The emblem of mortality in "Hades" is the "obese grey rat" that Bloom sees in the graveyard at the end of the episode: "An obese grey rat toddled along the side of the crypt, moving the pebbles. An old stager: greatgrandfather: he knows the ropes. The grey alive crushed itself in under the plinth, wriggled itself in under it. Good hidingplace for treasure" (U.114; VI, 973–5).

Death is the antagonist of "Hades." Not only does the episode mention various kinds of death – suicide, drowning, sudden death in one's sleep, infant death, even the death of a bird – but the texture of the language, as in "The Dead," is imbued with death: "Dead side of the street this" (U.95; VI, 316); "Give us a touch, Poldy. God, I'm dying for it" (U.89; VI, 80–1).

In "Aeolus," an episode in which Stephen's role as developing artist resumes, Joyce uses the perspective of modern journalism to present a moral anatomy of Dublin; he builds on the satire of Dublin life in "Lotus-Eaters" and "Hades." In these three episodes in which Dublin becomes a character in the novel with its own collective character and personality, the organs – genitals ("Lotus-Eaters"), heart ("Hades"), lungs ("Aeolus") – are those necessary for life to continue from moment to moment and from generation to generation. To understand this episode, it may be helpful to think of Stephen as the protagonist and Ireland as the antagonist.

Dublin, as a character in the novel, is suffering from moral paralysis. Its citizens speak of Ireland in empty and hyperbolic rhetoric, including an oft-invoked supposed parallel between the Irish and the Jews. The episode ends with Stephen using his wittily cynical "Parable of the Plums" to debunk bathetically the hyperbolic Irish rhetoric that glibly compares the Irish with the Jews and the Egyptians with the English. Joyce wants us readers to understand that because Stephen's art is progressing here toward the mythic method that is essential to the art of *Ulysses*, and because he now takes public themes as his subject, he is perceptibly developing into the narrative presence who is telling *Ulysses*.

Moreover, Stephen's parable educates us to read the novel metaphorically. In this bitter parable, the midwives – his ironic version of the Old Woman of

Ireland – spit plum pits on the barren ground, while fascinated with the statue of Lord Nelson: "They put the bag of plums between them and eat the plums out of it, one after another, wiping off with their handkerchief the plumjuice that dribbled out of their mouths and spitting the plumstones slowly out between the railings" (U.148; VII, 1024–7). What Ireland needs is fertility and renewal; what these women do is spit seeds upon concrete where they cannot grow. Ireland's seers, the heirs to the Pisgah sight of Paradise, are two self-indulgent old women. That the phallic statue of the adulterous Nelson, England's hero, dominates Dublin emphasizes Ireland's illicit relationship with England. In a sensationalized and corrupt diction deliberately reminiscent of the excesses of yellow journalism, the final headline in this newspaper episode stresses the lewd implications of the scene: "DIMINISHED DIGITS PROVE TOO TITILLATING FOR FRISKEY FRUMPS. ANNE WIMBLES, FLO WANGLES – YET CAN YOU BLAME THEM?" (U.150; VII, 1069–71).

In deference to his Jewish hero, Joyce took as one model the Passover Haggadah; the word "Haggadah" means "telling," and the reading of the Haggadah celebrates the continuity of the Jewish experience and expresses optimism for the future. The technique of the Haggadah is to focus on the essence of the Jewish experience – the Passover narrative with its stress on the flight from Egypt – while using allusions to place the Passover narrative at the center of concentric circles which evoke the entire Jewish experience, including the Diaspora for which the 40 years in the wilderness can be taken as a prefiguration. Indeed the Haggadah traditionally has appropriated to its telling new trials – the Holocaust, pogroms, the establishment of the State of Israel, persecution of the Jews in Russia or any other place. Joyce draws upon this elastic and protean tradition to imply that *Ulysses* is to be regarded as the Haggadah of the Irish experience.

In the eighth episode "Lestrygonians," Bloom recalls his first intercourse on the Howth with Molly, the very scene she recalls in her final reverie as she turns her passionate attention to Bloom:

Ravished over her I lay, full lips full open, kissed her mouth. Yum. Softly she gave me in my mouth the seedcake warm and chewed. Mawkish pulp her mouth had mumbled sweetsour of her spittle Joy: I ate it: joy. Young like, her lips that gave me pouting. Soft warm sticky gumjelly lips. Flowers her eyes were, take me, willing eyes. Pebbles fell. She lay still. A goat. NO-one. High on Ben Howth rhododendrons a nannygoat walking surefooted, dropping currants. Screened under ferns she laughed warmfolded. Wildly I lay on her, kissed her: eyes, her lips, her stretched neck beating, woman's breast full in her blouse of nun's veiling, fat nipples upright. Hot I tongued her. She kissed me. I was kissed. All yielding she tossed my hair. Kissed, she kissed me. (U.176; VIII, 906–16)

Recalling a moment of shared passionate intimacy and tender love, the above recollection gives new meaning to a series of thoughts that Bloom has had. For one thing, it is a kind of ironic Arcadia that momentarily pacifies his anxieties about social violence and allays his fixation on Molly's adultery. Moreover, he has previously associated satisfying his hunger with sexual fulfillment in "Calypso": "To smell the gentle smoke of tea, fume of the pan, sizzling butter. Be near her ample bedwarmed flesh. Yes, yes" (U.61; IV, 237–9). Since warmth is something his intimate life still retains, does not the memory of sharing a bed with Molly help him to overcome gloom in "Hades"? "Feel live warm beings near you. Let them sleep in their maggoty beds . . . Warm beds: warm fullblooded life" (U.115; VI, 1003–5).

In her final reverie, Molly remembers Bloom's calling her "my mountain flower" (U.783; XVIII, 1606). Yet Bloom's memory of the goat's defecating anticipates the analism of his hallucinations and his practice of licking Molly's behind. And, finally, Bloom has trouble sustaining his reverie of better days and poignantly returns to the copulating flies, his metaphor for the copulation of Molly and Blazes:

> Me. And Me now.
> Stuck, the flies buzzed. (U.176; VIII, 917–18)

Bloom's imagination and emotional resilience enable him to face the disappointments and frustrations of his life, including Molly's adultery with Blazes Boylan this very day. Joyce contrasts his characteristic Jewish turn toward tomorrow and acceptance of today – even while being fully conscious of the frustrations and disappointments of the past – with the Irish preoccupation with a romanticized version of the past and the Catholic obsession with dwelling on past sins and measuring every action according to a strict barometer of sins and grace.

IV Episode Nine: The Concept of Artistic Paternity in "Scylla and Charybdis"

To suggest his own biographical relationship to *Ulysses*, Joyce has Stephen propose his expressive theory of the relationship between Shakespeare's art and life. What makes Shakespeare a man of genius is that he encompassed in his vision the "all in all in all of us" (U.213; IX, 1049–50). Joyce re-creates Shakespeare according to his own experience of him, and thus becomes the father of his own artistic father and the artist whose imagination is so inclusive and vast that it contains the "all in all" of Shakespeare plus the very substantial addition – or, in current terminology, the supplement – of his own imagination. Like Joyce, Shakespeare used the details of everyday life for his subject: "All events brought grist to his mill" (U.204; IX, 748). The major creative artist discovers in his actual experience the potential within his imagination: "He found in the world without as actual what was in his world within as possible" (U.213; IX, 1041–2). To activate that potential the artist must have as wide a range of experience as possible; to get beyond the limitations of his own ego in order to achieve the impersonality and objectivity that is necessary for dramatic art, his imagination must have intercourse – and the sexual metaphor is, I think, essential to understanding Joyce's aesthetic – with the world.

For Joyce, homosexuality represents sterile sexuality that must be avoided. He fervently believed that on June 16, 1904, the day he privileged in his imagination as the occasion of his first having walked with Nora, his artistic maturity began. It was, he believed, from that crucial day that he started to overcome paralysis and narcissism and began to move once and for all beyond the purely lyrical in his art, a movement demonstrated by the transformation of the extremely subjective and self-indulgent *Stephen Hero* into the more objective *A Portrait of the Artist*. And it was from this point that he eventually began the artistic journey that climaxed in the epical and dramatic form of *Ulysses*. That he emphasized the crystallizing importance of Nora's willingness to walk with him on June 16, 1904, demonstrates the significance of the seemingly trivial in Joyce's aesthetic and provides a clue to understanding how the climactic meeting between Stephen and Bloom could have vast importance to Stephen's life, and perhaps also to Bloom's.

In the first three episodes, we recall, Joyce calls attention to Stephen as a Hamlet figure. Haunted by the ghost of his mother, estranged from his father, dressed in black, and paralyzed by artistic inaction, Stephen himself identifies with Hamlet all day. It is in *Hamlet*, Joyce believed, that Shakespeare simultaneously writes about universal values even as he writes about himself; thus when Shakespeare "wrote Hamlet he was not the father of his own son merely but, being no more the son, he was and felt himself the father of all his race, the father of his own grandfather, the father of his unborn grandson" (U.208; IX, 867–9).

The "Scylla and Charybdis" episode takes place in the library, an appropriate place to discuss how books should be read and written. From his 1922 vantage point, Joyce has Stephen predict the relationship between his 1904 self and his retrospective fictionalized self: "In the intense instant of imagination, when the mind, Shelley says, is a fading coal, that which I was is that which I am and that which in possibility I may come to be. So in the future, the sister of the past, I may see myself as I sit here now but by reflection from that which then I shall be" (U.194; IX, 381–5). By defining the relationship between the creative imagination of Shakespeare and the biographical Shakespeare whose actual experience is the crucial source for the activity of his creative imagination, the above passage educates the reader to understand that Joyce viewed Stephen as an immature version of the author who wrote *Ulysses*. But with the necessary experience – and for Joyce that included the kind of heterosexual experience that Bloom and Molly, as well as Shakespeare and Ann Hathaway, shared – Stephen has the potential to become a mature artist.

V   The Adventure of Reading: The Odyssey of Styles in Episodes Ten through Fourteen

As Joyce's schema indicates, each of the episodes between ten and fourteen has its own characteristic style. "Wandering Rocks" dramatizes the spiritual and cultural sterility and the moral cannibalism that *Ulysses* must address. By presenting and implicitly discarding the church, personified by Father Conmee, and the secular authority, personified by the viceroy, the earl of Dudley, Joyce is establishing the need for Bloom, the contemporary Elijah figure whose humanistic values offer hope; the need for Stephen, the putative artist whose creative imagination and prophetic vision will redeem Ireland and, in particular, Dublin, its morally paralyzed urban waste land; and the need for Molly, who will redeem Ireland through her sexuality, passion, and the enjoyment of the physical. In its nineteen vignettes, *Ulysses* shows the specific effects of Ireland's position as a servant to England and Roman Catholicism.

The city of Dublin is the major character of "Wandering Rocks," an episode with only the most indirect parallels to the *Odyssey*. The fragmented episode emphasizes the purposeless movement of the city's population at 3 o'clock, a time when the day's work ought to be reaching a climax.

At the very center of the epic, the major characters are relegated to minor roles as if to stress that no one in the modern world can be continually foregrounded as if he or she were an epic hero. But even here Bloom's focus on Molly overcomes Joyce's structural condescension to engage the reader.

The eleventh episode, "Sirens," tests and, on the whole, discards the possibility that language can use the techniques of music. According to Joyce's schema, the organ is the ear and the symbol is music; that he called the technique "Fuga per Canonem" has generated some abstruse commentary analyzing the episode's fugal structure. Joyce, who in 1904 was still thinking of a singing career, explores whether the universal language of music can tell us something about the paradigmatic family relationships – father and son, husband and wife – that, he believed, were common to all cultures and civilization.

Bloom's anxieties, fantasies, and evasions, rather than external figures, are the most important sirens that keep him from returning to Molly and his proper sexual role in his home. Four internal sirens take the form of his imaginative transformations of external sexual stimuli: the letter from Martha Clifford, the playful, anonymous sexuality of the bar girls Misses Douce and Kennedy, the pornographic *Sweets of Sin*, and the approach of Blazes's and Molly's rendezvous. Bloom's imaginative transformation is a version of misreading that Joyce is warning us readers to avoid, even while knowing such misreading in terms of our own hopes and fears is inevitable.

The second half of the episode confirms Joyce's interest in and respect for Bloom's humanity. For Bloom thinks – because he has not had intercourse with Molly since Rudy died – of Blazes and Molly in association with the son he lacks:

> He bore no hate.
> Hate. Love. Those are names. Rudy. Soon I am old. (U.285; XI, 1068–9)

The twelfth episode, "Cyclops," is the climax of the public theme of the novel. It is sandwiched between "Sirens" and "Nausicaa," two episodes in which Bloom is in danger of being diverted by sexual reveries and self-pity not only from his private mission to return home and to re-establish his conjugal relationship with Molly, but also from demonstrating his humanistic community values. It takes place at 5 p.m. in Barney Kiernan's pub, which is presided over by an anonymous boor called the Citizen and "that bloody mangy mongrel" dog, Garryown (U.295; XII, 119–20). The pub is inhabited by a group of bigoted, xenophobic, self-styled patriots whose violent, aggressive behavior contrasts with the humanism and androgyny of Leopold Paula Bloom. Its art is "politics" and its technique is "gigantism." After this episode, the book returns to its emphasis on the interrelationships among the three major characters and between them and the narrative presence.

In this episode the Irish are not only intolerant of any nation other than their own, but are lost in a welter of ineffective rhetoric. Joyce might have expected the reader to recall Homer's description of the Cyclops in section IX of the *Odyssey* as "an overweening / and lawless people, who . . . / Do not sow plants with their hands and do not plow . . . / They have neither assemblies for holding councils nor laws . . . [E]ach one dispenses the laws / For his children and his wives and is not concerned for the others."[5] The Citizen is the most obvious Cyclops figure, a Polyphemus who would physically attack Bloom.

When in his characteristically bitter, cynical tone the Citizen says of Bloom, "A new apostle to the gentiles" and "That's the new Messiah for Ireland," he is unwittingly announcing Bloom's importance (U.333, 337; XII, 1489, 1642). As we shall see, Molly's reacceptance of Bloom in the final paragraph, as her menstruation begins, makes possible the birth of a male child who might be the Messiah in the form of a figure – either hero or artist – who would effectively espouse the humanistic Bloomian values on which Ireland's redemption depends.

Bloom's articulate, eloquent, and courageous response gives an affirmative answer to John Wyse's question, "why can't a jew love his country like the next fellow?" (U.337; XII, 1628–9). Indeed, it is in this episode that Bloom publicly affirms his identity as a Jew, something he deliberately refrained from acknowledging when he encountered a fellow Jew, the pork butcher: "And I belong to a race too . . . that is hated and persecuted. Also now. This very moment. This very instant" (U.332; XII, 1467–8).

Bloom is acknowledging his Jewish identity in such a way that it becomes a return to his racial heritage. That he asserts himself and his values in a hostile environment is part of his growth. His answer also affirms the potential of language – in the face of the attacks on meaning and coherence by the two principle narrators – to communicate values and feelings. His self-respect, concern for others, courage, and tolerance undermine the twin mockery of the snarling, bitter Thersites figure and the hyperbolic blarney of the Irish folk legend. Bloom presents a humanistic alternative to the sterility and paralysis of Dublin. Despite the mockery of the begrudging, petty denizens of the Citizen's pub and the romantic speaker's grandiloquent, bathetic style, Bloom emerges as the vessel of value. His language and values are strikingly different from those of the two narrators and the other characters. In his dialogue with the Citizen and his cohorts, Bloom's syntax and diction affirm the value of a language of direct statement, a language that reflects the speaker's attitude and values – in this case, Bloom's humanity, integrity, and sincerity – with clarity and precision.

Let us turn to the thirteenth episode, entitled "Nausicaa," where Bloom encounters Gerty MacDowell, a 22-year-old woman, on the strand and they mutually masturbate while sexually fantasizing. The exaggerated third-person feminine style of "Nausicaa" – anticipating Molly's breathless, digressive, self-immersed first-person narrative of "Penelope" – is the counterpart of the reductive masculine styles in "Cyclops." The third-person style is appropriate for Gerty's mind; unlike Molly, whose sexual pride enables her to transcend cultural stereotypes and retain an independent identity, Gerty's mind is so steeped in cultural stereotypes that it has lost its capacity for independence. Twenty-two, like Stephen, the virginal but very sexual Gerty is desperate for sexual experiences and, lacking them, substitutes her own poignant fantasies.

Yet Gerty is a far more sympathetic figure than most critics allow. For she refuses to be confined by the clichés of her style, and subconsciously, by asserting her right to her fantasies, comes to terms with, even if she does not quite overcome, the restraints of her Catholicism. Notwithstanding the severe limitations of her perspective, she gradually becomes more complex as she strays from her virginal, romantic ideals in the first paragraphs and begins to express her real emotions and, in her first act of defiant exhibitionism, her sexual needs.

Roman Catholicism is one of the novel's major antagonists, in part because it makes sex and the physical body a problem. In contrast to Gerty and Stephen, the 15-year-old Milly and her father accept sexuality and the body. In Joyce's epic, the bodily functions and the physical life are celebrated.

In the second half of "Nausicaa," the narrator gradually restores Bloom to his stature as a character. For one thing, Bloom's perspective makes his masturbation seem natural, human, and harmless; he rationalizes that he "[m]ight have made a worse fool of [him]self however" (U.372; XIII, 942–3). For another, he now seems to be able to resume his focus on the problems of others – especially Mrs Purefoy – and on Molly.

When in the next episode, "Oxen of the Sun," Bloom is visiting Mrs Purefoy, who is having a baby in the hospital, he sees Stephen carousing with his housemate Mulligan and some other fellows. At the conclusion Bloom follows Stephen into the bawdy district of Dublin because he is worried that Stephen's companions will lead him astray.

That Joyce conceived the episode in part as one in which Bloom metaphorically fertilizes Stephen as an artist is clear from a letter written to Frank Budgen: "Am working hard at *Oxen of the Sun*, the idea being the crime committed against fecundity by sterilizing the act of coition . . . Bloom is the spermatozoon, the hospital, the womb, the nurse the ovum, Stephen the embryo."[6]

The very self-consciousness of the episode calls attention to the relationship between the 1922 teller and the 1904 putative artist. We realize that the 1904 Stephen might have been able to write the pastiche of styles, but it is the fictionalized Joyce of later years who could appreciate Bloom's stature.

In "Oxen of the Sun," Bloom's humanity triumphs over the self-conscious artistry of the narrator's ventriloquism and resists the attempts of the diverse styles to deprive him of stature. Bloom's concern for Mrs Purefoy and Stephen strikingly contrasts with the episode's obsessive interest in stylistic matters.

VI   Circe as the Climax of Joyce's Humanistic Vision

The fifteenth episode, "Circe," explores the subconscious lives of Bloom and Stephen. By refusing to separate clearly the surface events from the hallucinations and fantasies, Joyce demonstrates for us that external events and unconscious life cannot be meaningfully distinguished. "Circe" fulfills the aesthetic theory of "Scylla and Charybdis" in an unexpected form. Rather than dramatizing the conscious lives of Stephen and Bloom, the two halves of his putative artist figure, Joyce presents in dramatic terms their unconscious lives. Are we not supposed to see that these characters are as much an expression of their artistic creator as Shakespeare's characters are of him? Is not the dramatic form of the episode a deliberate effort to achieve the "dramatic form" described in *Portrait,* where the artist depersonalizes himself and regards his characters from a distance? We should think of "Circe" as the fulfillment of the author's odyssey of style – as the kind of turning point that Shakespeare achieved in *Hamlet* – when the artist moves from kinesis to stasis, moves conclusively from a lyrical to a dramatic mode.

That Bloom and Stephen share a vision of Shakespeare shows the reader that these seemingly very different figures – the inexperienced ("beardless") artist and the cuckolded man of experience – have the potential to merge in the figure of the artist. The image of Shakespeare that they see mirrors their artistic frustration – Bloom has literary aspirations as a popular author – and sexual paralysis. Shakespeare's oracular words speak to Stephen's guilt for not praying at his mother's bedside, but Bloom also hears a resonance of the guilt he feels for not preventing in some way his father's suicide: "How my Oldfellow chokit his Thursdaymornun" (U.567; XV, 3828).

At the conclusion of "Circe," Stephen acknowledges Bloom as his spiritual father and Bloom responds to Stephen as his spiritual son. Bloom assumes the role of a protective father when he pays the whores for the chandelier that Stephen has broken, and he comes to Stephen's aid after he has passed out. That Bloom calls Stephen by his first name shows Bloom's desire for intimacy as well as his specific concern for the young man lying prostrate before him: "Mr Dedalus! . . . the name if you call. Somnambulis . . . Stephen! . . . Stephen!" (U.608; X, 4925–8).

At the end of "Circe," Joyce affirms the central place of the father–son relationship. Bloom's vision of his deceased son Rudy is the grace and benediction to Bloom's humanity. As he stands diligently over Stephen – "Silent, thoughtful, alert" – Bloom has a vision of his son Rudy, who died at the age of 11 days. Put in other terms, after Bloom has exorcised his guilt and anxieties, his imagination transforms his actual role as Stephen's guide into the imaginative one as father of his deceased son, Rudy.

Bloom thinks of an 11-year-old Rudy, wearing his yarmulke, following in the Jewish tradition of his own forefathers and re-establishing the tradition he feels guilty for having abandoned. In "Lotus-Eaters," and again in the first part of "Circe," Bloom had imagined his father rebuking him for leaving "the house of his father" and "the god of his father," although it is his father who had changed his name from Virag and abandoned his religion. That Bloom imagines the yarmulke as a "bronze Helmet" may indicate that he has forgotten the word "yarmulke." But it may also indicate that he realizes that the Jews need a helmet to protect them against the kind of anti-Semitism which, as we saw in "Hades," Bloom presumably experiences daily, if not so dramatically as in the climax of "Cyclops."

VII   The Significance of "Eumaeus" and "Ithaca"

"Eumaeus," the sixteenth episode, establishes the father–son relationship between Stephen and Bloom by developing Bloom's paternal attitude toward Stephen and by developing similarities between them: "Though they didn't see eye to eye in everything a certain analogy there somehow was as if both their minds were traveling, so to speak, in the one train of thought" (U.656; XVI, 1579–81). Bloom sees a parallel between his political views at age 22 and Stephen's current ones. Bloom also has poetic aspirations and, like Stephen, loves music.

Bloom and Stephen achieve a significant if far from complete human relationship. They develop an intimacy that neither achieves in his other June 16, 1904, personal interactions. What is most attractive about Bloom to Joyce, himself extremely shy, is that, without being overly concerned with embarrassment or rebuff, he takes chances in personal relationships.

Seeing that Stephen, who has had a hard night, is having trouble walking, Bloom invites him to "Lean on me" and invites Stephen home (U.660; XVI, 1720). Stephen's response emphasizes his need to believe that this is a significant experience: "[H]e thought he felt a strange kind of flesh of a different man approach him, sinewless and wobbly and all that" (U.660; XVI, 1723–4). Perceiving Bloom as something other than an ordinary man – as Fergus, as a black panther, a vampire, a man of strange flesh – is an indication that

Stephen is conferring metaphorical significance on the odyssey of an ordinary man and that he is in the process of becoming the Joyce who will write *Ulysses*.

The conclusion of the episode stresses their companionship; as a driver watches them, they continue "their *tête à tête* ... about sirens, enemies of man's reason, mingled with a number of other topics of the same category, usurpers, historical cases of the kind" (U.665; XVI, 1889–91). We realize that the subjects of their conversation are the subjects of *Ulysses*, the book that results from their metaphorical union.

While the story urges the reader to see the union of Stephen and Bloom as important at the human level, the metaphorical implications point toward their respective roles as artist and hero. Stephen and Bloom find in each other the intimacy that has eluded them all day in their relationships with others. For in this scene, it is the carriage driver who is the outsider rather than Stephen, who earlier had been thinking of following the example of Fergus and turning his back on the real world, or Bloom, who had been the outsider in the carriage at Dignam's funeral.

In "Ithaca," Joyce chooses to present his characters by means of a purportedly scientifically objective catechism. The catechistic style often oversimplifies, as when it reductively categorizes Bloom as representing "The scientific" temperament and Stephen as representing "The artistic" one (U.683; XVII, 560). And the cataloguing tendency of the scientific style recalls that of the romance speaker in "Cyclops"; thus, while Bloom is at first identified with the "universality" as well as the "democratic equality and constancy" of water, the sheer plethora of information about water undermines the comparison and reduces it to bathos (U.671; XVII, 185). The questions and answers are often, but not always, outside the minds of the characters. Yet, as in the "Eumaeus" episode, the humanity of the characters triumphs over the style as we watch Stephen and Bloom find metaphorical significance in each other and discover the friend each needs.

Indeed, as the episode progresses, the narrator becomes increasingly interested in the characters' feelings. When Bloom focuses on Stephen in the oral chronicle of his day that he gives to Molly, his human needs to overcome loneliness and to communicate – the needs that created the mutual relationship with Stephen and which are informing the intimate bedroom scene – are confirmed for the reader as the essence of the novel's values.

Shortly after sharing the vision of "the heaventree of stars," Bloom and Stephen observe simultaneously a "celestial sign": "A star precipitated with great apparent velocity across the firmament from Vega in the Lyre above the zenith beyond the stargroup of the Trees of Berenice towards the zodiacal sign of Leo" (U.703; XVII, 1210–3). The "celestial sign" – a shooting star moving from "Vega in the Lyre" to "the zodiacal sign of Leo" – implies the movement of Stephen, the writer signified by the musical "lyre," toward Leo Bloom. This cosmological sign also predicts the union of Bloom and Stephen in the persona of the maturing artist who will be able to write *Ulysses*.

After Stephen departs, Bloom remains to view the rising sun: "The disparition of three final stars, the diffusion of daybreak, the apparition of a new solar disk" (U.705; XVII, 1257–8). On the metaphorical level, are not the three fixed stars that Bloom sees disappearing the characters of Bloom, Stephen, and Molly and is not the "new solar disk" still another hint of the fully realized artist who will write *Ulysses*?

On one hand, Bloom is the necessary principle that Stephen requires and must assimilate before he can become a mature artist – before Joyce can become the new messiah of Ireland by combining in his transpersonal presence the values of Bloom, Stephen, and Molly. On the other hand, he is a middle-aged man who is fundamentally different in attitudes and values from Stephen, and the brief personal intimacy achieved for a few hours leans on very thin reeds. Thus, given that their communion is based on drinking cocoa and urinating together, should we wonder whether their relationship and its significance may prove ephemeral?

VIII Penelope

Let us turn briefly to the final episode in which Joyce presents Molly's wonderful soliloquy. Molly is the goal of Bloom's odyssean quest to return home and an important paradigm of the mature sexuality that Stephen needs to complete himself. Molly is a bawdy, sexually alive, uneducated woman intent on her own pleasure and appreciative of her husband's qualities. But she is also important to the metaphorical and formal patterns of the novel and helps expand the novel to include an unselfconscious perspective that is an alternative to Stephen's and at times Bloom's Hamletizing. Molly is amoral and libidinous; her monologue is a lyrical explosion that comments on the prior intellectuality of the novel.

The episode begins with her acceding to Bloom's request to get him breakfast the next day. That she accedes to his assertive request indicates that the characteristic pattern of uxorious submission will be reversed on June 17, 1904. Joyce felt that only under the profound influence of Nora Barnacle could he have made the Word flesh. Molly's nominalistic, idiosyncratic narrative confirms the values of the novel – namely that life with all its frustrations, incomprehensibility, quirks, and contradictions must take precedence over the categorizing sensibilities of both Bloom and Stephen. The constant motion and energy of her prose enact the triumph of the "stream of life." Her stream of consciousness becomes the ultimate metaphor for the energy that makes intellectual, spiritual, and artistic growth possible. To use the metaphor that Stephen uses for Shakespeare, her imagination turns everything into grist for her mill.

Within her mind Molly, like her Homeric archetype Penelope, unweaves at night what she has woven by day. What Molly has woven by day is an affair with Blazes, but her reverie in bed, as she sleeps next to Bloom, reaffirms her commitment to Bloom. She slays the suitors when Bloom becomes her primary focus at the end of her monologue. She recalls the great moment of love-making on the Howth that has fed his reveries all day.

The ascendancy of Bloom at the climax of Molly's reverie emphasizes his triumph:

> O and the sea the sea crimson sometimes like fire and the glorious sunsets and the figtrees in the Alameda gardens yes and all the queer little streets and the pink and blue and yellow houses and the rosegardens and the Jessamine and geraniums and cactuses and Gibraltar as a girl where I was a Flower of the mountain yes when I put the rose in my hair like the Andalusian girls used or shall I wear a red yes and how he kissed me under the Moorish wall and I thought well as well him as another and then I asked him with my eyes to ask again yes and then he asked me would I yes to say yes my mountain flower and first I put my arms around him yes and drew him down to me so he could feel my breasts all perfume yes and his heart was going like mad and yes I said yes I will Yes. (U.783; XVIII, 1598–1609)

Within her mind Molly slays the suitors; she recalls when Bloom was, as Blazes is now, a lusty young man who wore a straw hat. Even though Blazes is a vigorous lover, she prefers Bloom: "I dont know Poldy has more spunk in him" (U.742; XVIII, 167–8).

By transforming the sea into a positive sexual image (as opposed to Stephen's hydrophobia and obsessive association of the green sea with his mother's death), and appropriating flowers to her sexual reveries (as opposed to the sterile figure of the pseudonymous Henry Flower), her crescendo is a means of exposing for the reader what has been nay-saying and life-denying in Stephen and Bloom. Does not the breathless movement of her language – emphasized by the increasing frequency of the resounding affirmative "Yes," which is associated with her first intercourse with Bloom on the Howth – itself mime their mutual orgasm? Isn't Joyce's point that Molly's orgasm and epiphany are one? Recreating her memory of the wonderful intercourse with Bloom on the Howth, the very moment that haunts and pleasures Bloom's memory, the ending is a performance, a celebratory enactment, a passionate explosion, of her sexuality. As she says "Yes" to Bloom, she joins Stephen, the various voices created by Joyce, the real Joyce who creates those voices to represent his fictional self, and the reader in saying "Yes" to Bloom's humanistic values and the potential effectiveness of those values. Within the lives of Molly and Bloom, "Yes" suggests the power of the imagination to evoke the presence of the potential fulfillment of the future.

That Molly menstruates indicates that she has not been impregnated by Blazes and that, if Bloom and she resume full sexual relations, the possibility exists of her having the son Bloom desperately desires. Molly's menstruating, her agreeing to make breakfast the next day, and, perhaps most significantly, her returning at the end of her monologue and the entire novel to Bloom and their great sexual moment on the Howth on which Bloom focuses in "Lestrygonians" strongly implies the possibility that on June 17 a new cycle may begin.

In terms of the metaphorical structure, Molly has several purposes. She is the goal of Bloom's odyssean quest to return home and Stephen's quest for mature sexuality to complete himself. She is what Joyce's retrospective presence requires to complete both the Irish epic and his nominalistic, fictionalized account of the crucial day in his life. In this sense, she plays the role of the traditional muse who must inspire the artist's creative process.

The final episode is a tribute to the role that Joyce believed Nora played in the creation of the artist. He wrote to her:

O take me into your soul . . . and then I will become indeed the poet of my race. I feel this, Nora, as I write it. My body will soon penetrate yours, O that my soul could too! O that I could nestle in your womb like a child born of your flesh, be fed by your blood, sleep in the warm and secret gloom of your body.[7]

Reading this passage in which Joyce imagines that Nora gave birth to him, do we not recall Bloom's fetal position at the end of "Ithaca" and realize that Bloom requires Molly to recreate him?

Molly is essential for Joyce's idea that the possibility of mature art, art that depicts a complex knowledge of the world, depends upon the artist's experiencing a passionate sexual relationship. Such a relationship, although frustrating and difficult, becomes, as the lives of Shakespeare and Bloom illustrate, a passport to experience.

IX Conclusion

Ulysses should be read as a social, political, and historical novel. Joyce examines Ireland's dominance by England, Dublin as a city in which there is a dearth of meaningful work, and women whose definition derives from stereotypes created by men's minds. *Ulysses* is Joyce's inquiry into the question of what values are viable in the twentieth-century urban world where, according to Joyce's view, God does not exist and traditional notions of heroism are obsolete. Among other things, *Ulysses* is an effort to redefine the concept of the hero. Joyce uses the marginal Jew Bloom to redefine heroism in secular, humanistic terms. As he examines recent Irish history and culture, Joyce proposes Bloom as an alternative to the contemporary xenophobia and fantasies of the Celtic Renaissance as well as a successor to Parnell.

Joyce's imagined world reflects the reality of British political domination of Ireland. It is worth recalling that prior to 1922 Ireland was not an independent country and stood in the approximate relation to England that Northern Ireland still stands.[8] The world of *Ulysses* also reflects the complexities of evolving urban culture, including how information is transmitted. Among other things *Ulysses* is about marketing the modern city, and the major character, Bloom, is an advertising salesman. Within *Ulysses* characters read and write the city in terms of advertising slogans and jingles, newspaper headlines and articles, and personal notes and letters.

Ulysses teaches us how to read itself. We should think of our experience of reading it as the reader's odyssey. We should be aware of what the novel does to us as we read it and how the ventriloquy of its various styles establishes an unusually complex relationship between text and reader. Unlike some critics, who believe that Joyce's interest in style deflects the reader from his characters, I believe that the focus in every episode returns to the subjects of Stephen, Bloom, Molly, and the Dublin world they inhabit. To be sure, in the episodes from "Sirens" through "Oxen of the Sun," we are aware of a tension in Joyce's imagination between interest in style and interest in character, but in the climax of every episode his focus returns to his major figures and their significance. As odyssean readers turning the pages of the novel and progressing through one crystallizing day in the lives of the major figures, we must overcome the difficulties of style and the opacity of content – just as the modern Ulysses, Bloom, must resist temptations to deflect him from his journey home.

As odyssean readers, we must wend our way through a variety of experiences, but these experiences can best be understood in terms of the novel's two major and contradictory formal principles: on the one hand, its insistence on integration and, on the other, its refusal to allow every word to signify in terms of coherent thematic or structural patterns. Resisting our efforts to understand *Ulysses* in terms of organic unity are a plethora of catalogues, barely relevant details, marginalia, false clues, linguistic games, and playful attempts to undermine the reader's quest for unity. Does not Joyce's insistence on exploring the eccentricities of style for its own sake – its local wit, word games, catalogues, neologisms, and odd typography – urge the reader to pause and enjoy, without imposing interpretive patterns or judgments upon, the peculiarities and oddities of either language or human behavior?

Yet, finally, *Ulysses* insists that its readers interpret every detail in terms of larger patterns, and thus urges the book's own argument that even the most particular details of the individual lives of Bloom and Stephen are important because Bloom and Stephen iterate major historical and mythical figures in Western civilization. *Ulysses* urges the reader to see that if only Bloom's deeds and Stephen's words touch one person, they have an effect, because that one person's behavior and words in turn affect another and so on in an endless sequence. Indeed, that is one reason why the Greek and Jewish cultures have survived and why we continue to read Joyce's *Ulysses* with excitement and pleasure.

Finally, June 16, 1904, is a crystallizing day for all three characters – as it was within Joyce's imagination as the supposed day when he met Alfred Hunter and Nora Barnacle – rather than a gratuitous one. Given Stephen's political parable in "Aeolus," his theory of literature in "Scylla and Charybdis" which echoes Joyce's own, and his expanding his horizons by meeting the Irish Jew Bloom, so different from himself, hasn't Stephen made progress toward becoming the artist who will write the national epic of Ireland?

Chapter 9

Woolf's *Mrs Dalloway*: Sexual Repression, Madness, and Social Form

I Introduction: Reading Virginia Woolf

Reading Virginia Woolf's fiction means participating in the process of sorting out values, for she does not measure her characters by a set of moral principles as, say, Jane Austen does in *Emma*. On every page we experience Woolf's own quest for meaning, her puzzlement over life's riddles, her sense of wonder intermingled with her anxiety and doubt. In the voices of her narrators, we feel the presence of Woolf desperately trying to create meaning from the material within her narrative. This effort mirrors the major subject of her novels: the quest of her characters to create meaning within a world in which time and mortality are the first principles and where order – divine or otherwise – is absent. Woolf is the subject of her fiction, and the form is the correlative to her search for personality, character, and meaning. But because her search is the act of desperation of a person living on the edge, we realize that she is willing to settle for something quite ephemeral for both herself and her characters: moments of apparent unity, temporary states of feeling which inevitably must pass; aesthetic insights that are undermined by the imperfection of art; resting places that are marked by the absence of turmoil rather than by the presence of anything vital except her language.

In other words, Woolf's quest is for islands to which the soul's turmoil might temporarily escape before continuing on its excruciatingly painful mortal journey. Yet she knew that moments of visions, those intense and splendid oases when one could not separate the dancer from the dance, were always more real in their anticipation than their effects. Like Joyce, she felt the gap between word and world; but, even more than for Joyce until *Finnegans Wake*, for her the word was often more real than the world. Writing for Woolf was not merely – as for the other writers in this study – an effort to define her past, but also a refuge and antidote for madness. Writing fiction enabled her to feel that her life had purpose and value: "Now I'm writing fiction again I feel my force glow straight from me at its fullest" (*Diaries*, II, June 19, 1923).[1]

Reading Woolf depends on discarding notions of the biographical fallacy or notions of pure textuality, while responding to the poignant, intense, impulsive, caring presence whose voice speaks and performs the imagined world of the novel. Woolf's aesthetic program enacts the value of feelings and emotions. While she sought in her work an escape from personality, what she actually does is redefine the concept of personality in terms which include moments of feeling. In an important 1920 diary entry she wrote:

> I figure that the approach will be entirely different this time: no scaffolding, scarcely a brick to be seen; all crepuscular, but the heart, the passion, humour, everything as bright as fire in the mist . . . I suppose the danger is the damned egotistical self: which ruins Joyce and [Dorothy] Richardson to my mind: is one pliant & rich enough to provide a wall for the book from oneself without its becoming, as in Joyce and Richardson, narrow & restricting? (*Diaries*, II, January 26, 1920)

For Woolf, realism meant, among other things, sincerity and depth of feeling: "Am I writing *The Hours* [an earlier title for *Mrs Dalloway*] from deep emotion? Of course the mad part tries me so much, makes my mind squint so badly that I can hardly face spending the next weeks at it" (*Diaries*, II, June 19, 1923). Yet she had a fear that she might misuse language:

> One must write from deep feeling, said Dostoevsky. And do I? Or do I fabricate with words, loving them as I do? No I think not . . . I daresay its true, however, that I haven't that "reality" gift. I insubstantise, wilfully to some extent, distrusting reality – its cheapness. But to get further. Have I the power of conveying the true reality? Or do I write essays about myself? (*Diaries*, II, June 19, 1923)

Yet, at times, what is most real to Woolf is the language she uses to create an alternative to the painful reality of the world in which she lives. Put another way, she wanted to intrude into the space between the tick and the tock of passing time and create significant time, to, as she puts it, in the passage I quoted in chapter 1, rescue life from "waste, deadness, superfluity" by "saturat[ing] every atom" with the significance of artistic understanding

(*Diaries*, III, November 28, 1928). (Not only Lily Briscoe, but in their own ways, Mrs Dalloway and Mrs Ramsay are trying to do the same.)

The search for verbal correlatives to non-verbal experience is a characteristic theme of British and Irish Modernism; the search is a function of traditional British empiricism that believes in the power of the mind to control the world as well as a challenge to that empiricism. In Woolf's quest to discover the language for and to give artistic shape to the interior light of the mind, we see a kinship with Lawrence's efforts to dramatize unconscious experience and Joyce's efforts to penetrate beneath levels of conscious behavior. Woolf's web of multiple connections moves toward but never quite reaches unity for the reader, because the reader is always aware that Woolf is obsessively insisting on unity in a world which she knows at the deepest level lacks it. Thus the reader is aware that despite Woolf's desire to imitate unity, she is forced to create it. Because her rhetoric convinces her readers – male and female – that our world is her world, we too are the subjects of Woolf's fiction. The verbal connections become less a signifier of deeper spiritual unity than a substitute for it and, finally, a reminder of what can never be there in a Godless world.

On one hand, Woolf presents a humanism based on multiple subjectivity. On the other, fearing that only the immediacy of her writing could have any meaning for her, she calls in question that humanism. Woolf understood and feared this paradox in her work:

> I think writing must be formal. The art must be respected . . . If one lets the mind run loose, it becomes egotistic: personal, which I detest; like Robert Graves. At the same time the irregular fire must be there; & perhaps to loose it, one must begin by being chaotic, but not appear in public like that. (*Diaries*, II, November 18, 1924)

Like Joyce and Eliot, Woolf wanted to write about her experience in the hope that it represented the experience of others. Woolf – to paraphrase what Joyce in *Ulysses* has Stephen Dedalus say of Shakespeare – "wanted to find in the world without as actual what was in [her] world within as possible."

The novel is, of course, a realistic genre whose central generic and canonical debate has revolved around what constitutes realism – what is real, real truth, and how does one render it if one can locate it? Is "reality" in the details – the specificity – of the lives and conditions of the imagined world? Or is reality based on correlation to an a priori world? Are characters whose thoughts and feelings respond to the social and historical conditions in which they find themselves more real than characters whose minds are not historically defined? Is it the texture – the recognizable nouns, verbs, and adjectives – of the language used by an omniscient narrator that makes a novel real? Or is it the kinship between how we plot our own narrative actions: dreaming, scheming, planning? Or is the true realism – as Sterne implies in *Tristram Shandy* – the digressions from a narrative line, from consistent behavior, and from literal language?

The point of departure for Woolf's reality is Jane Austen's world of English country houses, rigid social customs, and understated feelings and attitudes. In fiction about women, Woolf contends in *A Room's of One's Own*, men prior to nineteenth-century fiction always show women "in their relation to men," and

how small a part of woman's life is that, and how little can a man know even of that when he observes it through the black or rosy spectacles which sex puts upon his nose? Hence, perhaps, the peculiar nature of woman in fiction; the astonishing extremes of her beauty and horror, her alternations between heavenly goodness and hellish depravity. (*Room*, 86)

By contrast, when a middle-class woman like Austen or Emily Brontë or George Eliot wrote, they wrote novels because they were trained "in the observation of character, in the analysis of emotion. Her sensibility had been educated for centuries by the influences of the common sitting-room. People's feelings were impressed on her; personal relations were always before her eyes" (*Room*, 70).

Woolf's "reality" focuses on the individual moments of heightened perceptions, although she does not neglect the physical details of daily life or the historical or economic contexts. For her, "reality" does include a keen awareness of World War I and the permanent change it wrought in England's social fabric.

Like Lily in *To the Lighthouse*, Woolf wishes to isolate events from their temporal dimension and give them pictorial shape. To be sure, the spatial arrangement of her novels owes much to Impressionism's desire to displace the conventional idiom of perception with a fresh human representation of what the eye and mind actually experience, and to Cubism's insistence on seeing a figure or object on its spatial plane and from multiple perspectives. In *Mrs Dalloway*, to emphasize that there is not one reality, she depicts London from the perspective of every character in terms of his or her individual interior space.

Like a Cubist painter using images to define space, Woolf uses words to give definition to not only exterior space but the interior space of her characters' minds. To use terms she uses in a letter to the painter Jacques Raverat, she is one of the writers "who are trying to catch and consolidate and consummate

191

(whatever the word is for making literature) those splashes of yours" (*Letters*, II, October 3, 1924). In her fiction each life is a group of spaces defined by lines (of experience, of family, of social circumstances) but only partially filled with substance. According to Quentin Bell, Woolf "is claiming for herself the ability, or at least the intention, to see events out of time, to apprehend processes of thought and feeling as though they were pictorial shapes."[2]

Woolf is trying to give shape to moments of experience without ordering them any more than is necessary. As do the characters within her novels, she uses memory to draw lines that make sense of experience, but the artist goes one step further and embodies experience in artistic form. The reader is educated by the novels to understand the kinship between memory and artistic sensibility. Like the perceiver of Cubist paintings, the reader must give the space definition in terms that she or he can understand. But Woolf understands that this search for the moment out of time is a quest, not a reachable goal, and that such pictorial shapes (including those achieved by her characters – Lily, for example – or by Woolf herself) inevitably belie the processes that they describe.

As she wrote in a May 6, 1935, diary entry, "[T]he more complex a vision . . . the less it is able to sum up & make linear" (*Diaries*, IV). Mrs Dalloway, for example, needs more from Richard and her daughter than they provide, and is left with rather large gaps to fill with parties, diurnal activity, and, most importantly, memories. For Woolf knew that human memory – in its functions of imposing order and discovering significance – has a kinship with the more developed sensibility of the artist. The artist transforms memory into the formal design of a painting, a novel, a musical composition.

The unity of *Mrs Dalloway* and *To the Lighthouse* – indeed, all Woolf's novels except *Orlando* – depends on a web of connections woven by the narrator outside the mind of the characters. For Woolf, the novel is like a canvas, a material surface on which to place words, to re-create a new reality by verbal strokes of the brush and patches of color. She is concerned with the formal and chromatic effect of the relationship among words and sentences apart from any anterior reality it imitates. Like Lily, she wants to discover a moment out of time, and to weave a texture that might unify the diverse temporal moments into something more. Because unity exists in the mind of the omniscient narrator as it exists in the eye of the painter, Lily's quest to complete her painting parallels the speaker's effort to discover unity in the texture of events she narrates.

Completing the painting not only takes us back to Mrs Ramsay's social choreography, but enacts for the reader the completion of the novel because it accomplishes the aesthetic goal defined from the first page; it enacts how, for those who belong to what we might call Woolf's Sensitive and Aesthetic Elect, "any turn in the wheel of sensation has the power to crystallise and transfix the moment upon which its gloom or radiance rests" (*Lighthouse*, 9). Lily's thought, "he must have reached [the lighthouse]," echoes Mr Ramsay's silent reflection on his finally fulfilling his small quest: "I have reached it" (*Lighthouse*, 308).

The intricate texture of images and echoes enables Woolf's narrator to both overcome and evade the polarities and paradoxes implied by the story. Yet are we not aware that the resolution – depending on spatially arranged verbal relationships that transcend the quests of the characters and the traditional ironic view of the omniscient narrator – is akin to modern painting's resolution of multiple perspectives on a flat plane? The transpersonal moments of epiphanic unity are in a tension with the traditional narrative perspective – in Woolf's case a narrative perspective that often has a paratactic, centrifugal rather than a syntactic, centripetal quality.

On the one hand, in Woolf, the reader experiences a disembodied voice rendering the consciousness of the novel's characters and mediating among their diverse perspectives; on the other, the most physically present aspect of a Woolf novel is often the narrative voice. Of course, the disembodied voice is most and least a presence in the "Time Passes" section of *To the Lighthouse*. As Woolf writes in her diary:

> I cannot make ["Time Passes"] out – here is the most difficult abstract piece of writing – I have to give an empty house, no people's characters, the passage of time, all eyeless and featureless with nothing to cling to . . . Is it nonsense, is it brilliance? Why am I so flown with words, & apparently free to do exactly what I like? . . . this is not made up; it is the literal fact. (*Diaries*, III, April 18, 1926)

The voice is simultaneously more personal and more distant than the traditional omniscient narrator. It is more personal because we feel Woolf's compelling urgency; it is more distant because at times it takes a hawklike or godlike perspective which actively focuses on the pattern at the expense of characters. In doing so, does not Woolf escape the imprisoning conditions of human life and partially fulfill her quest to define herself as artist on a different level of reality? Her escape and quest have continuities with the iconoclastic aestheticism of the 1890s that was a source of Modernism.

In Woolf's novels the narrator's withholding and deferral of significance are as much a part of the narrator's telling as the rendering of significance. One might even say that the narrator mediates rather than renders the multiple points of view, and that in the act of mediation the narrator eschews the traditional ironic perspective that is such a distinctive feature of omniscient narration in the English novel. The quest for meaning is antithetical to conclusive meaning, and, indeed, conclusive meaning is at least partially aligned with Mr Ramsay's autocratic positivism. To the extent that Lily's line carries closure, it, like any vision, has a trace of the certainty that Woolf both sought and wished to avoid. The moment of vision is, then, an intimation of both immortality and mortality, for its suspension of time coexists with its awareness of passing time and, as the vision is assigned to past time, the moment takes us another step toward what the voice of *To the Lighthouse* calls that "fabled land where our brightest hopes are extinguished, our frail barks founder in darkness" (p. 11). If the ecstatic vision, the epiphanic moment, moves to stability and stasis, it must carry the trace of mortality.

Woolf's voice reflects her sense of herself writing not only as a woman in a man's world (including a literary culture dominated by men), but also writing as a Modernist whose beliefs are tentative formulations. She never puts behind her the Victorian world of her parents, a world which values certainty. Even as she seeks a center, even as she strains for a deeper reality and psychology of character than that found in prior fiction, she creates a texture of language that at once seeks and eschews a dialogue with reality. Fusing the narrator and her characters' impressions of events with the actual events, Woolf's novels are a correlative to the flat surfaces of Cubism that resolve foreground and background.

II   Understanding Clarissa

Mrs Dalloway is a lyrical novel rather than a narrative one: while empathetic with the life of Clarissa, the voice transcends her individual perspective and places her in an historical and cultural context of which she is a part. The novel is poised between life and death, war and peace, lyric and narrative, narrator's reflection and character analysis; that poise, that balance, is responsible for the novel's magnificent aesthetic unity. *Mrs Dalloway* is autobiographical because it explores the similarities and differences between what we call madness and what we call sanity. For Woolf, no theme could be more urgent. The novel enables her to examine attitudes and states of mind that are crucial to her experience.

Woolf chooses a day in Clarissa's life in which her past returns with a difference (Peter's and to a lesser extent Sally's return to her life). Woolf juxtaposes past and present through memory and weaves a tautly designed pattern of now and then. As we reread *Mrs Dalloway*, does it not pulsate outward in concentric circles from crucial memories rather than proceed in a linear movement through time? Within those circles are missed opportunities, disappointments, and parallels to other lives. The novel ironically fulfills the title character's wish that she might have her life to live over again, while it urges us to see that she would have made the same decisions if she had such an opportunity.

Mrs Dalloway is Woolf's response to Joyce's *Ulysses*, a work she grudgingly admired, despite what she felt was its tediousness and coarseness. Is not Miss Kilman's mackintosh coat an effort to evoke the enigmatic and marginal Man in the Macintosh in *Ulysses*? Depicting one day in the life of a middle-class woman, Woolf gives the title character no mythic identity. Like *Ulysses*, *Mrs Dalloway* takes place in a large, impersonal city in the month of June; and Woolf chooses a crystallizing day because Peter and Sally return to Clarissa's life and her double, Septimus Smith, commits suicide. Clarissa is no more aware of the parallels to Septimus Smith than Bloom is aware of his mythic identity as the modern Odysseus or the putative Moses.

But while the reader is urged to see Bloom as a humanistic hero whose values and strong sense of self might point the way to redeem Ireland – that is, to see Bloom as a representative figure whose signifying function is established by the novel – Mrs Dalloway never emerges from her own analytic half-light and the narrator's ironic bathos, which reduce her to a ghost or shadow; she "had the oddest sense of being herself invisible; unseen; unknown" (p. 14). She regards her physical appearance with self-contempt: "[S]he had a narrow pea-stick figure; a ridiculous little face, beaked like a bird's" (p. 14).

Despite the apparently monologic or univocal voice, the complexity of Woolf's perceptions gives the novel's omniscient narrator a richly polyphonic or dialogic voice which renders the full complexity of Clarissa, Peter, and even Septimus. Opening *Mrs Dalloway* takes us into an imagined world in which sensibility and feeling count for everything and where traditional manners and morality and their effects count for little. This latter world is presented as a vestige of Victorianism; it is epitomized by Hugh Whitbread, who, as Peter said, "had no heart, no brain, nothing but the manners and breeding of an English gentleman" (p. 8). In this melancholy world, love is not a passionate impulse, but a kind of habit. People in late middle age are conscious of approaching death. The central event is a suicide. There is little promise implied by the young people such as Elizabeth or Miss Kilman. The dawn of a clear June morning is the setting for the novel that is an elegy for Clarissa, for Septimus Smith, and for the ineffectual society to which Clarissa belongs.

Virginia Woolf has captured the agony of Clarissa's loneliness, the results of her sexual repression and frigidity, and her capitulation to social convention. Clarissa's life is a function of a few crucial decisions made years ago. In a sense, her life is over because she has missed her chance for love with both Peter and Sally and settled for something less. Clarissa feared intimacy with Peter because "everything had to be shared; everything gone into" (p. 10); she chooses the separateness that culminates in the room in the attic. Peter recalls that "there was always something cold in Clarissa" (p. 73). Alternatively, had she responded to her impulse to love a woman, she might have been fulfilled. Repressed to the point of frigidity, she is both attracted to and frightened by the spontaneity of Peter and Sally. For her, giving parties provides the possibility of unity that her personal life lacks. She requires the admiration of others to complete her: "How much she wanted it – that people should look pleased as she came in" (p. 13). The passivity of Clarissa, locked into her stereotypical social roles of aging hostess, supportive political wife, and household manager, contrasts with Peter, who remains alive and open to possibilities. Even as Peter confronts aging, disappointment, and loneliness, he lives and speaks according to his feelings.

The novel's efficacy depends on its taut ironic tone and deft stylistic control. Notice how Woolf uses the image of Richard as a spider to urge the reader to see Clarissa as victim:

> And as a single spider's thread after wavering here and there attaches itself to the point of a leaf, so Richard's mind, recovering from its lethargy, set now on his wife, Clarissa, whom Peter Walsh had loved so passionately; and Richard had had a sudden vision of her there at luncheon. (pp. 172–3)

Woolf strikingly contrasts Richard and Peter, whom Mrs Dalloway had loved passionately and who is, like Sally, her missed opportunity. The narrator presents Peter in lucid, straightforward syntax without metaphor. Woolf undermines Richard's stature by having him use words like "vision" and "miracle" bathetically:

> He stopped at the crossing; and repeated – being simple by nature, and undebauched, because he had tramped, and shot; being pertinacious and dogged, having championed the downtrodden and followed his instincts in the House of Commons; being preserved in his simplicity yet at the same time grown rather speechless, rather stiff – he repeated that it was a miracle that he should have married Clarissa; a miracle – his life had been a miracle, he thought; hesitating to cross. (p. 175)

Does not the syntax mock Richard's egotism and conceit by deliberately imitating the pompousness and indecision of a man who is entrusted to be one of the nation's leaders? Does not the diction – "preserved in his simplic-ity," "grown rather speechless," "stiff," "hesitating to cross" – depict a man approaching senility and death?

Like Forster's Fielding, Peter values personal relationships and feels they add to the "infinite richness, this life" (p. 248). Thus he is drawn to Clarissa's party in part because he shares her social values, but much more because he still is attracted to her like a moth to a flame. Yet he feels "something arrogant; unimaginative, prudish" within her, and recalls a moment when her harsh attitude toward a woman who had a baby before marriage had made Peter feel "the death of her soul" (p. 89). That day lives as part of the searing present for Peter because it was the day he and Clarissa had first seen Richard. Peter is a twentieth-century man who believes not in ultimate values, but in the value of experience for its own sake. But he also doubts himself because of his failure to win Clarissa. As much as Clarissa and Septimus, he is beset by self-doubt: "[H]e could not come up to the scratch, being always apt to see round things . . . and to tire very easily of mute devotion and to want variety in love" (p. 241). Yet for all his failings, he has the capacity to love and to renew himself. In Peter's presence, Clarissa feels that she has made little of her life, even while Peter is feeling that he has much life left.

Peter's present life is composed of love affairs, work, and quarrels – what Clarissa's life lacks. When he weeps and she consoles him, she realizes that, "If I had married him, this gaiety would have been mine all day!" but she retreats from the impulse to say, "Take me with you," retreats to the psychological enclosure she has built for herself (p. 70). Peter feels young in his passion for Daisy, just as Clarissa feels old for the lack of passionate love. Is not Woolf implying we are what we love? Peter, like Clarissa, savors his experience, but his, of course, is more recent; Peter thinks, "the compensation of growing old . . . was simply this; that the passions remain as strong as ever, but one has gained – at last! – the power which adds the supreme flavour to existence, – the power of taking hold of experience, of turning it round, slowly, in the light" (p. 119). Yet Peter thinks that the pleasure and meaning of life are much less personal than when he was young; but surely the experience of Septimus and Clarissa contradicts this. Peter's love for Daisy is easy for him; he will not suffer at her hands as Clarissa has made him suffer.

The "solitary traveller" who "by conviction" is "an atheist perhaps" and who thinks "Nothing exists outside us except a state of mind" is not only Peter but Woolf herself (p. 85). In his life Peter has rejected the possibility of surrender ("let me blow to nothingness with the rest"), while Septimus succumbs to this death wish which also has its appeal for Clarissa (p. 87). Peter cannot forget Clarissa, who, for all her faults, still captivates him. Playing with his knife on the day of his visit to Clarissa, Peter Walsh demonstrates considerable anger and hostility. Moreover, although he is engaged to Daisy, he essentially gives Clarissa another try, as if before marrying he will test the waters of his fixation one more time.

As an imaginative man, half-creating what he sees (recalling Austen's *Emma*), Peter is a kind of artist figure; indeed, as he fantasizes about a girl he follows, he reflects that "the better part of life" is "made up" (p. 81), and uses his imagination as a refuge from "this fever of living" (p. 86). His self-image as "an adventurer, reckless, . . . a romantic buccaneer" sustains him (p. 80). Like Septimus and Clarissa, Peter imposes meaning on the sky and branches. Yet his youthful "revelations" about the death of Clarissa's soul and his prediction that she will marry Richard become self-fulfilling prophecies that help create the reality that he now sees. Indeed, we feel that he may have lost Clarissa because, immersed in his myopic perceptions, he was unable to respond to her needs and the competition offered by Richard.

Like Stevens and Yeats, Woolf believes that there is continuity between artistic activity and imaginative activity that sustains all of us. But Mrs Dalloway's belief that she is a refuge and a radiance is an ironic version of this belief. By an act of will she feels she can draw "the parts [of herself] together" and become "a radiancy no doubt in some dull lives, a refuge for the lonely to come to, perhaps" (p. 55). But except for Peter, who has a nostalgic feeling for his first love, does this radiance really matter? Isn't this forced radiance a substitute for passion and creativity? In her characterization of Clarissa, Woolf is examining a life which lacks the certainty of religion or authority, but, which unlike her own, does not have the compensation of art. It is as if she is doing research into the lives of those who do not have, like herself or Lily Briscoe, the artistic activity of creating worlds to sustain them.

The novel's prevailing tone is ironic bathos, a sense that life is far less than religious and literary texts have preached. By incongruous juxtaposition or inflated rhetoric, Woolf undermines the notion that human life yields sublime experience. According to Quentin Bell, "she maintained an attitude sometimes of mild, sometimes of aggressive agnosticism."[3] How, Woolf asks, do we create meaning in "this late age of the world's experience" – a time when airplanes deface the sky with advertisements, and when we poignantly seek to discover an equivalent for the sacraments and rituals of religion by such futile gestures as entertaining the suspicion that a politically prominent figure occupies a chauffeured motor car (p. 13)? Note the narrator's description of the clouds on which humankind has grotesquely written an advertisement for toffee: "the clouds . . . moved freely, as if destined to cross from West to East on a mission of the greatest importance which would never be revealed" (p. 30). Isn't Septimus a parody of romantic visionaries who read the signature of human things upon nature, who anthropomorphize nature, and who see the expression of divine order in nature's disorder? Instead of Christ or instead of Joyce's great humanistic hero, Bloom, Woolf's London has for its "prophet" a pathetic, self-appointed scapegoat who commits suicide.

To the extent that the major British and Irish novels of 1890–1930 reflect disbelief in Christianity's promise of salvation, the anticipation of death – final, conclusive, insignificant death – becomes the determining factor of how humans live. As in Joyce's "The Dead" and Forster's *Howards End*, the major character in *Mrs Dalloway* (as in *To the Lighthouse*) is death. And death – in art and in life – has a seductive attractiveness for Woolf as the mother of beauty. Within Woolf's fiction, death makes it possible to wrench meaning by imposing form (or discourse) on the flux of life (or story).

The process of reading *Mrs Dalloway* shows us that death lurks in every crevice of the imagined world, just as emptiness and loneliness define every life. The novel's world is blighted and darkened by death. The novel is pervaded by constant reminders of the ravages of war, beginning with the early reference to Mrs Foxcroft "eating her heart out because that nice boy was killed" (p. 5). Septimus is, of course, a war victim. Mrs Dalloway has had a bout of influenza which has affected her heart. She has been consigned to an attic room for recuperation. Even though she values this separation as independence, this room leaves her separate from her family and desperately dependent on social ritual and memory to create meaning. Death is never absent from the text for more than a few pages, nor is it absent from the thoughts of Mrs Dalloway or Septimus Smith. Death is in the lines from *Cymbeline* that echo in her mind:

Fear no more the heat o' the sun
Nor the furious winter's rages. (p. 13)

Death is present in Clarissa's opening premonition, a premonition fulfilled by Septimus Smith's suicide: "[S]tanding there at the open window, [knowing] that something awful was about to happen" (p. 3). The candle in her attic room, like the candle in Gretta's and Gabriel's room in "The Dead," suggests death. (Does not Woolf expect us to think of Charlotte Brontë's *Jane Eyre*, in which Rochester confined his wife in the attic?)

Isn't Woolf playing on Clarissa's initials and implying that Clarissa's life is moving toward death – just as surely as Septimus's – and just as surely as in the recitation of the alphabet, C inevitably passes to D? When Clarissa learns that Richard will not return for lunch she feels "shrivelled, aged, breastless" (p. 45). Her enemy is mortality, of which she is acutely conscious: "[S]he feared time itself, and read on Lady Bruton's face, as if it had been a dial cut in impassive stone, the dwindling of life; how year by year her share was sliced" (p. 44).

Mrs Dalloway is the woman Woolf feared that she might become. Aging, lonely, living in the memories of the past, bothered by petty grievances, and regretful of the choices she has made ("Oh if she could have had her life over again!"), she sews as if she were sewing her own shroud (p. 14). Life is reduced to surfaces because she has made the wrong choices.

Woolf uses verbal puns to imbue the reader's consciousness with a sense of imminent death. Recalling the paralytic self-consciousness of Eliot's Prufrock, Clarissa "stiffened a little; so she would stand at the top of her stairs" (p. 25). The recurring old women are reminiscent of the libidinous, often aging figures that Aschenbach confronts in *Death in Venice*. The gray nurse knitting next to Peter, while he dreams, recalls the classical Parcae spinning human fates; Carrie Dempster (whose initials are the same as Clarissa's) suggests Clarissa's mortality. The influenza that may have affected her heart recalls the illness of Hans Castorp in *The Magic Mountain* (1927). The sterility and moral confusion that beset London in 1923 – the bankruptcy of public figures and the absence of private values – anticipate Mann's vision of Europe in 1927. We should think of *Mrs Dalloway*, along with *Women in Love*, as England's Weimar novels, novels of a world that has lost its moorings and in which its inhabitants desperately seek for values or at least sustaining illusions.

III   Historicism and Inclusiveness in *Mrs Dalloway*

The scope of *Mrs Dalloway* belies the view that it is a novel of manners. Its mention of Einstein and Mendel, its focus on the airplane and the limousine in the early pages, the prominence of the war and its effects, as well as the preparation for future battles implied by the young boys in uniform, make it an historical document about England in a period of cultural transformation. The inclusiveness of the novel also depends on historical background (the Roman presence in England), religious contexts (Christianity's origins and promises), and references to English literary culture – Shakespeare and the Romantics – which Woolf wants to use both as points of reference and to modify.

Although Peter conceives of himself as an heir to adventurers of the past, he is not motivated by ideals of service to church or state, for he believes, "Nothing exists outside us except a state of mind" (p. 85). Woolf implies that the social and historical context – with its inconclusiveness, its discontinuities, its erasure of past values and traditions, and especially its violence – *demands* that her subject be the economics of sensibility: the give and take between memories and the present, between the self and other in personal relationships. Woolf's radical inward turn is deliberately post-historical because she feels history has ceased to provide sense-making patterns.

Mrs Dalloway includes every social class. Woolf is very much aware of the schism between the haves and the have-nots. She shows the irony of London's poor people discovering value in the pageantry of the monarchy by thinking "of the heavenly life divinely bestowed upon Kings" (p. 27). Moreover, Clarissa's relation with her servants shows how stratified England still is; servants still have to leave a play in the middle lest they be late. However, after his five years in India, Peter is struck by the change in London. Not only have the positions of the lower classes and the young changed, but social mores have become less rigid; Peter sees a "shift in the whole pyramidal accumulation which in his youth had seemed immovable" (p. 246).

Woolf undermines the assumption that church and state are positive forces in the twentieth-century world. Military training may deprive a man of his uniqueness and turn him "into a stiff yet staring corpse by discipline" (p. 77). Miss Kilman finds in religious fervor and piety an outlet for class resentment: "She in touch with invisible presences! Heavy, ugly, commonplace, without kindness or grace, she know the meaning of life! Miss Kilman stood there . . . (with the power and taciturnity of some prehistoric monster armoured for primeval warfare)" (p. 190). Does not the rhetoric of insult with which the narrative voice dilutes Miss Kilman reveal something about the failure of Woolf's historical consciousness, particularly her lack of range in her class sympathy?

Even more than the other novelists in this study, Woolf challenges nineteenth-century conceptions about a coherent self. She depicts the ironic tension between, on the one hand, elaborate and often vestigial social rules in which people no longer quite believe, and on the other, the incoherence of personalities struggling for definition and meaning in life. To recall my quotation from Wallace Stevens's "An Ordinary Evening in New Haven" in chapter 1, for Woolf, character becomes "the cry of [the] occasion" rather than a stable core of attitudes and values. Continuously, the self reassembles itself in different shapes – shapes that draw upon the range of possibilities stored in the psyche and shaped by prior experience. And the striking parallels between characters show that behavior varies less from person to person than the reader might expect.

In Woolf, the self one presents depends on one's most recent experiences. The self is something one creates and re-creates; each experience brings temporary coherence to one's personality: "That was her self when some effort, some call on her to be her self, drew the parts together, she alone knew how different, how incompatible and composed so for the world only into one centre, one diamond, one . . . meeting-point" (p. 55). But Woolf implies that temporary coherence is like the syntax of our daily discourse, where the next sentence takes precedence over the blurring memory of the last. Clarissa's radical oscillation between depression and exaltation, between past and present, between regret and satisfaction, between longing for an alternative life and glorying in this one, and between nihilism and affirmation of life, does not give her a stable core. Her momentary triumphs must be seen in the context of her living a narrow, constrained existence in which social rituals have replaced values and in which the lack of self-confidence creates erratic lurches of feeling rather than a fully coherent self. Clarissa requires others to complete her, to give her meaning.

Woolf's narrative form presents the temptations of narcissism and solipsism as the central crises of the characters' lives. Woolf understands that Clarissa's curse is the artist's curse – to be detached from life, observing and recording it, but not fully living within it. Clarissa regrets that she has not made more of her life – that she has written a fragmented, disrupted narrative, and that she has scant hopes of writing a different life-narrative. Thus the present is displaced by the past. Clarissa's fear of becoming "invisible; unseen; unknown" reflects Woolf's fear of immersing herself in her art to the point where she becomes remote from life, as well as her concomitant fear that if one ceases to create, life is only emptiness and loneliness. "That is all," the self-contained and reflexive phrase that at times seems to epitomize Clarissa's life, reflects these fears. In Woolf's novels, self-love is the antithesis of the affirmative value of making other people's lives more pleasurable and more meaningful by means of affection, understanding, and tolerance. The novel examines possible alternatives to emptiness, isolation, and disengagement, but offers only the poignant feeling of temporary community achieved by the ersatz social ritual of the concluding party.

To establish the continuity between life and art, Woolf stresses that reading is a mode of perceiving. No one can quite make out the apocalyptic message of the airplane. In every experience Septimus Smith reads confirmation of his own views, namely that "The secret signal which one generation passes, under disguise, to the next is loathing, hatred, despair" (p. 134). That Septimus discovers confirmation of his views is another way Woolf implies that reading texts, like reading experience, is inevitably a subjective experience. But is he any more subjective a reader than Clarissa or Hugh Whitbread? Each character has trouble connecting with her or his own experience and understanding that of others. Each character perceives reflexively. To avoid nihilism, to discover meaning in one's life, one has to become actively aware of others and of the social and historical context of experience in which one is living.

By showing the kinship between disparate people, the narrative presence transcends the parochialism of self-isolation and reaches beyond her own consciousness. For example, when the narrator renders Septimus's feelings in terms of Clarissa's quotation from Cymbeline, "Fear no more, says the heart in the body; fear no more" (p. 211), the reader shares an ironic awareness of which the characters are oblivious. For we realize that Shakespeare's line – simultaneously urging passionate participation in life and submission to the sensual appeal of death – speaks not only to Clarissa but also to Woolf. The urgency of the novel depends upon our realization that in *Mrs Dalloway* Woolf is exploring Septimus's insight that "it might be possible that the world itself is without meaning," a view confirmed by Richard's momentary perception of "the worthlessness of this life" (pp. 133, 172).

At the center of *Mrs Dalloway* is the relationship that never comes off between Peter and Clarissa. She is unable and unwilling to share completely her thoughts and feelings, to become the mutually empathetic other to another person which in the novels of the 1890–1930 period is the one compensation for a world without God. Yet she maintains her independence at a great cost. Isolated from social relations, waiting passively for events, including her husband's return, while keeping herself busy with trivial details, Clarissa's character fulfills Woolf's early paratactic description: "She sliced like a knife through everything; at the same time was outside, looking on" (p. 11). At a crucial time that knife had cut the bond to Peter. Since then, Clarissa's life has narrowed to the kind of social entrapment in which we see her, but it is not the narrative she would have chosen for her life, had she the energy to give her life direction: "Oh if she could have had her life over again! she thought, stepping on to the pavement, could have looked even differently!" (p. 14). In Clarissa's reminiscence, her sterile present contrasts with the past of more hopeful days. Her sensibility seems too fastidious, too delicate for the life around her.

The narrator describes Clarissa's hatred for her daughter's friend – the ugly and religious Miss Kilman – as "a brutal monster," a kind of malevolent beast that inhabits her imagination and seems to undermine her very essence. We think of the threatening finny sea monster lurking at the edge of Woolf's psyche, wanting to devour her rationality and sanity. Clarissa's hatred of Miss Kilman "gave her physical pain, and made all pleasure in beauty, in friendship, in being well, in being loved and making her home delightful rock, quiver, and bend" (p. 17). Her hatred exposes her to the possibility – and for the reader it is a very real possibility enacted by the form of the novel – that "the whole panoply of content [of her life] were nothing but self-love" (p. 17). Yet the hatred is a passionate feeling toward another, and the self-love on which the hatred is based triggers her creative energies, as when she delights in her life and feels "one must pay back from this secret deposit of exquisite moments" (p. 43).

Because Clarissa lacks a central core, she is vulnerable to despair over the smallest occurrences. She realizes that she lacks something essential: "It was not beauty; it was not mind. It was something central which permeated; something warm which broke up surfaces and rippled the cold contact of man and woman, or of women together" (p. 46). She is sexually unresponsive to men – even Peter feels something is amiss – but capable of the pleasure (which she barely acknowledges) of being aroused by women. The constraints of respectability prevent her from following her sexual bent. Sally Seton represents the libidinous, forbidden, unacknowledged self. In the presence of a woman, Clarissa has on occasion felt "some astonishing significance, some pressure of rapture . . . an illumination" (p. 47).

As in Eliot, Conrad, Lawrence, and Joyce, allusions suggest the fullness of the present in comparison to the emptiness of the past, as well as the inevitable passing of the present into the dead past. Woolf was influenced by Joyce's mythic and allusive method, but while he used the past to indict the present and vice versa – after all, Bloom's humanity, pacifism, and eloquence are privileged over the bellicosity, occasional disregard for the lives of others and lack of interiority of Odysseus – Woolf regards Clarissa Dalloway from an ironic perspective defined by a tradition of manners. For example, she implies a comic perspective when she shows Clarissa thinking of her party in terms that would be more appropriate to martyrdom or crises of the soul: "Why seek pinnacles and stand drenched in fire? Might it consume her anyhow! Burn her to cinders! Better anything, better brandish one's torch and hurl it to earth than taper and dwindle away like some Ellie Henderson!" (p. 255).

The party is described as if it were a religious ceremony or an epic battle: Ellie is "weaponless" because she lacks financial means (p. 256). The celebratory occasion deprives Clarissa of her humanity, for she hyperbolically "felt herself a stake driven in at the top of her stairs" (p. 259). Woolf understands that Clarissa not only lacks proportion but importance, for Clarissa expends emotional energies on a minor social occasion which would more appropriately be reserved for more important matters: "Anything, any explosion, any horror was better than people wandering aimlessly, standing in a bunch at a corner like Ellie Henderson, not even caring to hold themselves upright" (p. 255). The prime minister's presence at this social ritual undermines his stature: "[H]oarding secrets he would die to defend, though it was only some little piece of tittle-tattle dropped by a court footman," he is reduced to the same trivial level as Hugh Whitbread (p. 262). If Septimus has fought in the war, Clarissa Dalloway has "acquitted herself honourably in the field of [social] battle" where her parasol is "a sacred weapon" (pp. 43–4). Despite the mock heroic mode, Woolf takes Clarissa very seriously as a sad, poignant figure: on the one hand, she is a social anachronism in a world which no longer will sustain the hierarchies on which her way of life depends; on the other, for Woolf she is a product of a social system which is reluctant to give a place to women.

The imagined world of *Mrs Dalloway* is steeped in death and offers little promise of meaningful life. Woolf understands that the enemy of significance in art and in life is the relentless movement of time, which – by presenting new experience so that one must constantly prepare for what will happen next – refuses to allow the mind to think at length about significance. Art must struggle to locate significant time between the tick-tock of passing time. Yet the repetition of phrases (particularly the ones about death from *Othello* and *Cymbeline*) and episodes creates the possibility of significance. Repetition undermines the sense of continuous movement and progress by emphasizing that human life repeats itself rather than progresses. When we speak of stasis and spatiality in fiction, we are partly expressing our desire to arrest time and the opportunity to "frame" or "confine" action and words within our mental space. As we read *Mrs Dalloway*, our experience has a spatial and temporal dimension.

IV   Doubling: Clarissa and Septimus

Like a Cubist painter, Woolf wants to show different facets of the whole; thus by pulling together past and putative future into a single moment of the present – by rearranging spatial and temporal planes – Woolf discovers order and significance. Her collage method has more in common with modern painting than with the Victorian novel, a form whose emphasis on story and nominalistic representation resembles nineteenth-century narrative painting. Indeed, Woolf's movement from character to character without authorial comment makes the reader assume an active role in discovering the inherent parallelism among characters. It may be that the novel's major revelation is that disparate characters share common bonds: every character has striking resemblances to others, and the major figures – Clarissa Dalloway, Sally Seton, Peter Walsh, Septimus Smith, Elizabeth – are aspects of the voice who for a time shares their perspective.

The parallels within the text, by which each character comes to double the other, emphasize that figures like Septimus, Carrie Dempster, and "a seedy nondescript man" are different in degree but not kind from what we think of as a socially prominent, conventional, upper middle-class matron. Another of Clarissa's doubles is the old lady who survives alone, but is inevitably approaching death in the room opposite Clarissa's house; we realize that the rather infirm and prematurely aging Clarissa in her attic room is moving inevitably in the same direction. Yet, paradoxically, as characters come to more and more resemble one another, we also become more conscious of their subtle differences.

At times, Woolf creates seeming parallels only to draw important distinctions between them. Miss Kilman's probable sexual interest in Elizabeth recalls Clarissa's for Sally. Woolf's narrator shares Clarissa's repugnance to Miss Kilman and renders her fantasy of strangling her: "The agony was so terrific. If she could grasp [Miss Kilman], if she could clasp her, if she could make her hers absolutely and forever and then die; that was all she wanted" (pp. 199–200). Characteristically, Woolf establishes the possibility of parallels, only to step aside and question them. In fact, as her parentheses and qualifications indicate, if we could think of Woolf's temperament in terms of the syntax of a sentence, it would be in a mode that is appositional and interrogative. The narrator insists compulsively on the parallel between Septimus and Clarissa. Like Clarissa, Septimus is pale and beak-nosed (pp. 14, 20). Both are prey to their own imaginations. Clarissa must contend with the "brutal monster" of hatred; for Septimus there is horror which periodically comes "almost to the surface" and threatens to "burst into flames" (p. 21). Both intuitively sense that the world may be without meaning – may be, as Joseph Conrad puts it, "a remorseless process."[4]

Clarissa identifies with Septimus in his suicide: "She felt somehow very like him – the young man who had killed himself. She felt glad that he had done it; thrown it away" (p. 283). She longs for death as a consummation:

> A thing there was that mattered; a thing, wreathed about with chatter, defaced, obscured in her own life, let drop every day in corruption, lies, chatter. This he had preserved. Death was defiance. Death was an attempt to communicate; people feeling the impossibility of reaching the centre which, mystically, evaded them; closeness drew apart; rapture faded, one was alone. There was embrace in death. (pp. 280–1)

She seeks in death what she lacks in life. Put another way, isn't death to Clarissa what painting is to Lily in *To the Lighthouse* and what writing novels was to Woolf?

The parallel between the socially prominent Mrs Dalloway and the insane outsider, Septimus Smith, is both a crucial aesthetic device and a deeply felt insight. It enacts Woolf's perception that a thin line divides sanity and madness, civilization and barbarism, love and hate, isolation and participation in the community, communication and incoherence, form and chaos. Reading *Mrs Dalloway*, we feel that Woolf understands that placement on one side or the other of that line often depends upon circumstances and who is doing the perceiving. In Septimus, Woolf depicts the loneliness, the pathos, the spasmodic energy and apathy of madness as only one who lives with its fear and knowledge can. She wrote in her diary: "Wave crashes. I wish I were dead! I've only a few years to live, I hope. I can't face this horror any more" (*Diaries*, III, September 15, 1926). Is not this passage recalled by Clarissa's perception of her movement into the drawing room in terms of the suspense of diving into the sea, a perception which after at first appearing to be threatening proves benign?

> She . . . felt often as she stood hesitating one moment on the threshold of her drawing-room, an exquisite suspense, such as might stay a diver before plunging while the sea darkens and brightens beneath him, and the waves which threaten to break, but only gently split their surface, roll and conceal and encrust as they just turn over the weeds with pearl. (p. 44)

Both Septimus and Mrs Dalloway, we realize, suffer from a kind of narcissism, and suffer from their lack of interest in things outside themselves.

Septimus Smith has a homosexual fixation on Evans, a man who is "undemonstrative in the company of women" (p. 130). Like Clarissa, who cannot come to terms with her attraction to Sally, Septimus has trouble feeling; he became engaged to Lucrezia because "the panic was on him – that he could not feel" (p. 131). Richard Dalloway's consigning Clarissa to the attic room is not so different from the solution of Bradshaw – which Lucrezia resists – of sending Septimus to a home for the mentally disturbed. In *Mrs Dalloway*, isn't Woolf implying that the social taboo against homosexuality helps create fragmented, unfulfilled lives? Within their stifled claustrophobic worlds, Clarissa and Septimus cannot open the doors and windows of their respective sexual preferences.

In an era which Woolf sees as lacking accepted moral certainties and common political and religious beliefs, she stresses the continuity between the artist's creative process and the necessary process by which each character – mad or sane – creates herself. The theme of imagination is present in the way each person creates her own story and the way characters seek public ceremonies to complete their lives.

The surprising parallels between characters suggest a continuity between the order of art and the kind of ordering that is necessary for a coherent life in the modern world. We see characters as artists trying to discover the plot lines of the tale that they want to tell themselves about themselves, even as they discard from their own individual stories those ingredients that they do not like. Thus, while the novel contradicts her view of herself, Mrs Dalloway perceives herself as creating "a meeting-point [of different selves], a radiancy no doubt in some dull lives, a refuge for the lonely to come to, perhaps" (p. 55). Such stories of reading selves become a metaphor both for the kinds of texts each of us can create and for the knowledge that such stories are functions of our own needs and thus partly apocryphal. Like an artist, Septimus hears the words no one speaks and seeks to convey his visions to others. In the tale he tells himself, Septimus sees himself as a version of Christ as scapegoat and eternal sufferer. Put another way, he hears not the traditional nightingales of Greek myth, but rather sparrows which carry for him God's message that there is no death – a message ironically belied by Woolf's novel.

Septimus identifies with Christ's "eternal suffering," which he equates with "eternal loneliness." But his terrifying sense of isolation is only a radical version of the loneliness felt by Clarissa, his wife, Peter, and even Richard. Peter's vision of death, in which the "fever of living" will cease and he will "blow to nothingness with the rest," establishes a parallel to Septimus; so does his imaginatively endowing the "sky and branches" with images of womanhood (p. 87). "This susceptibility to impressions [that] had been [Peter's] undoing" (p. 107) is even more true for Clarissa and Septimus. Septimus's oscillation between the imaginary world of his madness and the real world is different in degree but not kind from Mrs Dalloway's oscillation between internal depression and her social encounters with other people.

When Lucrezia is making a hat, she and Septimus share moments of intimacy that are as genuine as any between Peter and Clarissa or Richard and Clarissa. Isn't Septimus's message of "universal" love as close as any to the meaning of the novel? And in his moments of intimacy with Lucrezia, Septimus feels that "life is good. The sun was hot," affirming life in the very terms that Clarissa evokes. When she feels "drenched in fire" at the party, we recall the passage in which Septimus experiences ecstasy in his relationship with Lucrezia: "Miracles, revelations, agonies, loneliness, falling through the sea, down, down into the flames, all were burnt out" (p. 216). Even the supposedly stable Richard Dalloway used the word "miracle" to describe his relationship to Clarissa. The reader notices the extremity and desperation of not only Clarissa's but Woolf's quest for meaning in terms of personal relationships – relationships that by their failure undermine that quest. But the reader also notices the apposition of flames with what for Woolf is the amorphous, threatening sea.

Septimus overcomes skepticism with his belief that he has discovered the solution in a divine message. And Clarissa, for all her skepticism, also believed that the "unseen might survive, be recovered somehow attached to this person or that, or even haunting certain places after death" (p. 232) – which is not too different from what Septimus believes about Evans. Clarissa's belief that she and Peter survive even death anticipates that of Septimus Smith, but it is a belief that is not really supported by the values of Woolf's novel:

> Somehow in the streets of London, on the ebb and flow of things, here, there, she survived, Peter survived, lived in each other, she being part, she was positive, of the trees at home; of the house there, ugly, rambling all to bits and pieces as it was; part of people she had never met; being laid out like a mist between the people she knew best, who lifted her on their branches as she had seen the trees lift the mist. (p. 12)

Does she not imagine Peter seeing her as dead in much the same way as Septimus imagines Evans seeing him dead? Dr Holmes assures Septimus that "there was nothing whatever the matter with him" (p. 139). Rather than offer compassion, Sir William Bradshaw, "the ghostly helper, the priest of science," proves to his patients that he "was master of his own actions, which the patient was not" (p. 153). From Leonard Woolf's *Beginning Again: An Autobiography of the Years 1911 to 1918*, we know about Virginia's hostile attitudes toward psychiatrists. In Woolf's time there was nothing but sedatives for depression, and British psychiatry had not welcomed psychoanalysis.[5]

Bradshaw is a surrogate for, and a radical allegorization of, the values of Richard Dalloway and Hugh Whitbread, a point emphasized by his presence at the Dalloway party. But the doctor who counsels others on their private lives is unable to organize his own life. In an interesting sexual image that recalls the wealth of silver that divides the Goulds in *Nostromo* – Conrad's epic novel of imperialism – Lady Bradshaw thinks "sometimes of the patient, sometimes, excusably, of the wall of gold, mounting minute by minute while she waited; the wall of gold that was mounting between them and all shifts and anxieties (she had borne them bravely)" (p. 143). Indeed, Lady Bradshaw, like Lucrezia and Clarissa, has become subsumed into her husband's life, and lost much of her independence. Sir William preaches a credo of proportion, but Woolf emphasizes that Proportion is often accompanied by her sister, Conversion, who "offers help, but desires power; smites out of her way roughly the dissentient or dissatisfied; bestows her blessing on those who, looking upward, catch submissively from her eyes the light of their own" (p. 151). And we realize that in its demanding willfulness the spirit of Conversion threatens tolerance, love, and pluralism – and is epitomized by Miss Kilman's religious zealotry.

V The Significance of the Ending

The ending establishes the validity of Sally's despairing, if not nihilistic image of a human being as an isolated prisoner scratching his or her life on the walls of cells which he or she alone inhabits. The ending is pessimistic and undermines the ecstasy of Peter because we see that people fail to respond to one another. We know from that morning's meeting as well as Clarissa's and Peter's reminiscences that any dialogue between them will end in frustration for both. Peter and Sally do not understand one another or the Dalloways. Sally Seton, the person with whom Clarissa had once connected, is "despairing of human relationships" (p. 293). Sally's question "what can one know even of the people one lives with every day?" emphasizes the difficulty of our understanding one another (p. 293). We see how people try to possess one another in order to confirm their own reality. Richard thinks of Elizabeth as his daughter as Clarissa had thought of Elizabeth as "my Elizabeth." And isn't that why Peter, desperate for confirmation of his decision to marry Daisy, feels "terror" and "ecstasy" at Clarissa's presence (p. 296)? The ecstasy Peter feels for a woman whom he knows is frigid, whom he knows had spoiled his life, is poignantly ironic. We know that nothing will happen between them. Has he, as he believes, really grown in understanding or depth of feeling? Given his fixation with Clarissa, can he make a commitment to Daisy or to anyone? Within the context of the whole novel, can Clarissa's arrival be more than momentarily significant for Peter? Will their ensuing moments not yield the same disappointment as their morning interview?

Thus the final passage must be taken as ironic and reflexive because it will soon be followed by inevitable disappointment. Even though this is the kind of triumph she would welcome, we see the limitations of Clarissa's radiancy. And she herself has reflected that these momentary triumphs were no longer enough, "though she loved it and felt it tingle and sting, still these semblances, these triumphs (dear old Peter, for example, thinking her so brilliant), had a hollowness; at arm's length they were, not in the heart; and it might be that she was growing old but they satisfied her no longer as they used" (p. 265). At the very height of her triumph, she realizes its hollowness and feels the delicious reality of her hatred for Miss Kilman: "Elizabeth's seducer; the woman who had crept in to steal and defile" (p. 266). Pathetically, this is the most sustained emotion in her life: "Kilman was her enemy. That was satisfying; that was real . . . She hated her: she loved her" (pp. 265–9). Doesn't she "love Miss Kilman" because Miss Kilman is the cause of making her feel hatred and anger?

Focusing on the night the memories of Clarissa's past come alive, Woolf's ending is a kind of Walpurgisnacht. The independent clause that echoes through her mind is an anticipation of death ("Fear no more the heat of the sun" [p. 283]) and – because of her use of the phrase in the text's opening pages – emphasizes her lack of progress. Yet the phrase from *Cymbeline* now appears without the ominous accompanying phrase "nor the furious winter's rages" (p. 13). Her identification with Septimus ("She felt somehow very like him – the young man who had killed himself. She felt glad that he had done it; thrown it away" [p. 283]) shows how she is tempted by death and how thin is the line that divides insider from outsider. His death makes her feel the "beauty" and "fun" of life, but is it a morbid beauty that realizes that the possibility of death is in every day and that we are always approaching death.

Peter's image of the soul emerging from obscurity to take part in the surface of life effectively comments on the triviality of the party and the kinds of superficial needs it answers:

> For this is the truth about our soul, he thought, our self, who fish-like inhabits deep seas and plies among obscurities threading her way between the boles of giant weeds, over sunflickered spaces and on and on into gloom, cold, deep, inscrutable; suddenly she shoots to the surface and sports on the wind-wrinkled waves; that is, has a positive need to brush, scrape, kindle herself, gossiping. (p. 244)

The image recalls the insidiously half-submerged Becky Sharp in Thackeray's *Vanity Fair*, hiding her primitive instincts beneath the surface. We see the selfishness of Clarissa's sensibility, for she does not pity Septimus but emotionally feeds off his death to delight narcissistically in her party.

That Clarissa has Peter's admiration is hardly surprising. Away from India, Peter is adrift from his moorings, lonely, and nostalgic. For Peter, Clarissa has "that gift still; to be; to exist; to sum it all up in the moment as she passed" (p. 264). Yet we know that if she has her husband's affection, she does not have his passion and, even while idealizing her and maybe because of that, he has consigned her to the attic. She is, we might say, the mirage, the dream-figure for the solitary traveler – who is not only Peter, but Richard and even Sally, and potentially the reader.

For the reader, much of the real meaning of the party is in the unexpected guests, Sally Seton and Peter Walsh, Clarissa's two possibilities for passionate love, whom Woolf uses to show the reader what Clarissa has passed up. Both Peter and Sally feel that Clarissa lacks something and has sacrificed something in marrying Richard. Even Peter's belief that we understand more as we grow older is hollow in light of what we know of his continuing infatuation with Clarissa, even while trying to convince himself he loves Daisy.

Much has been made of Clarissa's final epiphany: "No pleasure could equal, she thought, . . . this having done with the triumphs of youth, lost herself in the process of living, to find it, with a shock of delight, as the sun rose, as the day sank" (p. 282). But most of the day she has been melancholy, and we should not take this spasm of happiness for the whole. The reader's epiphany is that Mrs Dalloway has had an ersatz epiphany. For what did she make happen, what did she accomplish? She has simply gathered people together for what is primarily banal social conversation.

The party is a social ritual that does not create meaningful feelings of community or opportunities for understanding. She credits Richard for making the social triumph possible ("It was due to Richard" [p. 282]), but her pleasure in this triumph is belied by the sterile and apparently sexless life she settles for. We should not be misled by her momentary happiness from contemplating the quality of life that she has been leading and will continue to lead. At the end we realize that Clarissa has fulfilled Peter's prediction that she will be the perfect hostess:

> Her severity, her prudery, her woodenness were all warmed through now, and she had about her as she said good-bye to the thick gold-laced man who was doing his best, and good luck to him, to look important, an inexpressible dignity; an exquisite cordiality; as if she wished the whole world well, and must now, being on the very verge and rim of things, take her leave. (pp. 264–5)

But the perfection she achieves contains within it the promise of approaching death. Are Septimus's views that charity, faith, and kindness are in short supply really disproved by the ending? If his paranoid fantasy that human nature has condemned him to death is far from the mark, so is Clarissa's view that her party can provide meaning and significance to others.

Chapter 10

Woolf's *To the Lighthouse*: Choreographing Life and Creating Art as Time Passes

I Introduction

To the Lighthouse is a companion novel, if not a sequel, to *Mrs Dalloway*. It is another of Woolf's researches into the form of fiction. But it is also a research into her past, for Mr Ramsay is based on her father, Leslie Stephen, and Mrs Ramsay depends on her mother. As Roger Poole writes:

> Virginia idolised her mother. Julia represented for her everything that was beautiful, life-giving, spontaneous, intuitive, loving and natural. She watched her father impose upon her mother again and again, smiting mercilessly down at her again and again ... [O]n occasion Virginia hated her father in the same way as little James does in the novel which describes their family life together, *To the Lighthouse*.
>
> But also, of course, she loved him and admired him profoundly. This ambiguous swing between admiration for his immensely human and intellectual abilities, and contempt for his unmanly and despotic impositions upon his womenfolk, marked Virginia's view of her father to her dying day.[1]

Thus *To the Lighthouse* is a most personal novel in which Woolf is struggling to come to terms with her past. One feels her trying to do justice to her tyrannical, self-absorbed, but loving – albeit often in an oblique way – and impressive father.

To the Lighthouse enables Virginia Woolf to come to terms with the burden of her past, particularly her dominant father and her elusive but sensitive mother. In probing the needs and desires of the Ramsays and their guests,

Woolf reminds us how the quirks and idiosyncrasies of those who can channel their energies into socially acceptable directions (the masterful but insensitive Mr Ramsay, in particular) are not so different from the fantasies and delusions of those whom society chooses to regard as mad pariahs, such as Septimus Smith. But most of all, *To the Lighthouse* enabled her to inquire into the relationship between art and life, and between memory and experience, and to show how artistic creation is related to the ordering and distorting qualities of memory. Do not memory and artistic creativity both depend upon the mind's ability to create meaning from the past and to inform the present with insights that such meaning can provide?

In Woolf's memory, it is her mother who provided the fecundity and energy, who attended to the children's needs, who made life bearable in a house in which an oppressive, larger-than-life, famous father dominated. In a dualism that recalls the dichotomy Lawrence draws between male and female qualities, Mrs Ramsay represents the subjective – feelings, personal relationships, the possibility of discovering meaning and even unity, if only temporarily. For the children, her husband, the young couple, Charles Tinsley, William Bankes, and Lily, Mrs Ramsay is a kind of minor deity. Thus she has the capacity to create rapture in Mr Bankes: "[T]he sight of her reading a fairy tale to her boy had upon him precisely the same effect as the solution of a scientific problem so that he rested in contemplation of it, and felt . . . that barbarity was tamed, the reign of chaos subdued" (p. 74).[2] By contrast, Mr Ramsay represents objective facts, recognition of life's difficulties, achievements, ambition, and enterprise.

The Ramsays dramatize Woolf's view of the fundamental differences between the male and female minds. As Poole writes, the male is depicted as "egocentric, rough, bruising, insensitive, hammering, dominant, 'fact' obsessed, cynical, reductive, ironical, contemptuous," while the female "esteem[s] insight, vision, beauty, harmony, colour."[3] In her diary on November 28, 1928, Woolf writes: "Father's birthday. He would have been, 1832, 96, yes, today; and could have been 96, like other people one has known; but mercifully was not. His life would have entirely ended mine. What would have happened? No writing, no books; – inconceivable" (*Diaries*, III).[4] In *To the Lighthouse*, Woolf's version of *Sons and Lovers*, she gives the laurel of victory to Mrs Ramsay, whose perspicacity dominates part I; she has a window into the souls and feelings of others and single-handedly creates a feeling of community. Part III of *To the Lighthouse* is in part a not very successful effort to assuage the guilt and disloyalty to her father's memory which she feels for writing part I.

To understand *To the Lighthouse*, one has to feel Woolf as a presence within the text. In a sense, the novel tests and discards a number of values – including intellectual prominence, knowledge, and power – before settling for a tentative affirmation of private values – family, self-knowledge, art for its own sake – even while never losing sight of their limitations. Or, put another way, it discards the male values associated with Mr Ramsay and affirms the female values associated with Lily and Mrs Ramsay. In particular, one hears the voice of a woman who feels her creative energies stifled and engulfed by a male world, who feels that female qualities have been depreciated at the expense of male ones, who feels that women writers are patronized and disregarded, and women's potential subordinated to male needs. Lily notes that Mrs Ramsay "pitied men always as if they lacked something – women never, as if they had something" (p. 129). Yet while she gives life to the men, Mrs Ramsay neglects herself: "she often felt she was nothing but a sponge sopped full of human emotions" (p. 51). In a sense she dies in sacrificial service to her husband, her family and others. She asks "What have I done with my life?" and "wonders" "how she had ever felt any emotion or affection for her husband" (p. 125).

Despite the perfection Mrs Ramsay feels at the end of part I, the set scene cannot displace our understanding of the cost of her *service* to a demanding and willful husband. That Mr Ramsay loves but patronizes his wife informs Woolf's barely suppressed anger, which we feel intermittently bursting through the book's surface: "He liked to think that she was not clever, not book-learned at all" (p. 182). Yet he desperately requires her: "She [looks] at the same time animated and alive as if all her energies were being fused into force, burning and illuminating . . . and into this delicious fecundity, this fountain and spray of life, the fatal sterility of the male plunged itself, like a beak of brass, barren and bare" (p. 58). It is as if Mrs Ramsay were the creative imagination fertilizing the sterile intellect – indeed the male pen(is). Doesn't Woolf want her novel to "burn" and "illuminate" for readers as Mrs Ramsay does for Mr Ramsay?

Mr Ramsay has an eye for the extraordinary, not the ordinary, while Mrs Ramsay has the reverse perspective. He is concerned with the cosmic perspective, she with the human. She needs to marry other people to validate her own life and seems obsessed with arranging matches. Isn't it the fusion of the qualities of Mr and Mrs Ramsay that makes the artist who writes *To the Lighthouse*? Mr Ramsay is a word maker, while Mrs Ramsay favors silence; yet it is she who takes words most seriously: "All this phrase-making was a game, she thought, for if she had said half what he said, she would have blown her brains out by now" (p. 106). Mrs Ramsay provides an island from this world: "[S]he had the whole of the other sex under her protection" (p. 13). Her beauty attracts people to her, but that beauty is a function of other qualities: "her simplicity," "her singleness of mind," and "her spontaneity" (p. 46). For her husband, Mrs Ramsay is a refuge who temporarily offers stability, tranquility, meaning, and significance. She creates not only the possibility of community and relationship but also moments of insight for others. That Mr Ramsay relies upon his wife to renew him, to recreate him, to fertilize his soul is validated by the perception of others. Thus James feels Mrs Ramsay "rise in a rosy-flowered fruit tree laid with leaves and dancing boughs into which the beak of brass, the arid scimitar of his father, the egotistical man, plunged and smote, demanding sympathy" (p. 60).

To the Lighthouse enacts a dialogue between the quest to approach reality or truth or understanding and the possibility that such goals are illusions or mirages. As we have seen, reading major British and Irish novelists in the 1890–1930 period depends on responding to this dialogue. Lily Briscoe seeks truth from Mrs Ramsay, truth in the form of an intimacy that Mrs Ramsay can only occasionally give her. She desperately hopes that intimacy with Mrs Ramsay will unlock "some secret which Lily Briscoe believed people must have for the world to go on at all" (p. 78). She seeks in Mrs Ramsay a secret sharer, an empathetic other to complete herself and "teach [her] everything" (p. 79). Lily regards her as a source of sustenance; Lily "knew knowledge and wisdom were stored up in Mrs Ramsay's heart," but she does not quite know how to reach it (p. 79).

Thinking of how she might reach Mrs Ramsay, Lily describes the process of learning about people in terms of the metaphor of "a bee, drawn by some sweetness or sharpness in the air intangible to touch or taste, one haunted the dome-shaped hive, ranged the wastes of the air over the countries of the world alone, and then haunted the hives with their murmurs and their stirrings; the hives, which were people" (p. 80). Lily is attracted to her for both sexual and spiritual reasons: "Could loving, as people called it, make her and Mrs Ramsay one? for it was not knowledge but unity that she desired, not inscription on tablets, nothing that could be written in any language known to men, but intimacy itself, which is knowledge, she had thought, leaning her head on Mrs Ramsay's knee" (p. 79). As in *Mrs Dalloway*, a central character is more attracted to women than men, but Lily, like Clarissa, reflects what Poole called Woolf's "sexual anesthesia," which he attributes quite convincingly to molestation by the Duckworths: "She could not feel any normal sexual feeling, and sexual matters were attended in her mind with fantasies of horror and dread."[5]

Woolf realized that personal relationships had to provide the order and meaning that religion, empire, and social hierarchies once provided. The personal is all the more important when religion and politics fail; thus the "man of genius," the political leader for whom Bankes waits, will never come (p. 142). Yet Woolf understood that human relationships always fall short and require lies and evasions to sustain them; put another way, Mrs Ramsay reflects her creator's perception that human relations are not only flawed and disappointing, but self-seeking at their best.

To the Lighthouse is, among other things, a defensive effort to find meaning and value in a world where suffering, death, and poverty are dominant factors. The novel's center of values, Mrs Ramsay, sees life as "terrible, hostile, and quick to pounce on you," "her old antagonist," and this view of the self in conflict with the world it inhabits is Woolf's own (pp. 92, 120). Of course, the resistant reader, even while understanding that gloom and depression are not class specific, notices that the Ramsays live, like Woolf herself, in splendor compared to most people – and that Mrs Ramsay's expressions of concern for the poor have an abstract quality.

In *To the Lighthouse*, as in *Mrs Dalloway* and Joyce's "The Dead," death is the major determinant of form. The novel emphasizes the ephemeral quality of life, and the need for human beings to rescue significance and impose meaning. According to Leonard Woolf, "Death, I think, was always very near the surface of Virginia's mind, the contemplation of death. It was part of the deep imbalance of her mind. She was 'half in love with easeful Death.'"[6] If death is the antagonist, the creative memory – the mind's ability to recapture and give shape to the past – is the hero and protagonist. Even in her Isle of Skye retreat Mrs Ramsay feels death as a continual presence. The maid Marie's father is dying of cancer. The pig's skull hanging in the children's room suggests the presence of death and mortality. But, more to the point, the *rereader* knows that for all her vitality Mrs Ramsay herself will soon be dead along with two of her children, and this casts a deep pall of sadness over the novel. Her death lends a special poignancy to her need to arrange marriages and to live her life through her children, for are not these activities futile efforts to impose order on life and thus to forestall death?

Mr Ramsay himself lives with the feeling that "withered old age" and death will forestall his efforts to plod forward in his intellectual quest (p. 55). When he looks from the mountain top he sees not, like Moses, the promised land but "the long wastes of the ages" (p. 56). Is Ramsay not of the class of persons whom Isaiah Berlin calls foxes – those whose thought is "scattered and diffused" and who "pursue many ends" – rather than those whom he calls hedgehogs – those gifted or inspired persons who "relate everything to a single central vision . . . a single, universal, organizing principle in terms of which all that they are and say has significance"?[7] Thus Ramsay is particularly vulnerable to time and mortality, because he needs time to work toward his goal. Yet he has already done his best work, and undoubtedly knows it. He knows that his reputation will not last very long. Within the text, he becomes an objectification of Woolf's own aspirations and fears as a writer; his concern about how "men will speak of him hereafter" is hers (p. 56). Did not Woolf strive to be a hedgehog and to be unlike her father Leslie Stephen, who was a Victorian fox more than a Victorian hedgehog – or sage?

To the Lighthouse is about the problem of creating meaning from the flux and inchoate form of life, and this problem is explored in terms of two kinds of experiences: (1) creating temporary unity within the present by arranging and organizing experience as much as possible; (2) imposing through memory an order upon the past. Woolf's novels are about the process of discovering and creating order and significance in the present from the bits and snips of the past. Woolf understands that we rely on memory and art to meet the challenge thrown down by the philosophically probing questions of William Bankes: "What does one live for? Why, one asked oneself, does one take all these pains for the human race to go on?" (p. 134).

"The Window," the title of part I, represents the division between the outside world and the world created within the house – and the inevitable division within oneself. At the center of "The Window" is the rapport between the Ramsays, which, like all human relationships, has its limitations. "The Window" preserves the intimacy of the present, shuts people off temporarily from night (representing evil, death, and the unknown) and the sea (representing the amoral, indifferent cosmos), and creates an oasis within: "[H]ere, inside the room, seemed to be order and dry land; there, outside, a reflection in which things wavered and vanished, waterily" (p. 147).

As in "The Dead," a story to which Woolf may very well be alluding, a social gathering gives way to a middle-aged couple's moment of intimacy. But unlike Gabriel and Gretta Conroy, the Ramsays do share a special intimacy which continually renews and recreates them. In *To the Lighthouse*, as in *Mrs Dalloway*, reading is a mode of perceiving, and Woolf suggests the parallel between reading texts and reading lives. She stresses the value of reading as a catalyst for deeper feelings and intense moments that prepare the ground for richer human relationships. The reading of Grimm's fairy tale about the fisherman and his wife is testament to the importance of reading as a mode of perception; it is another way that Mrs Ramsay is a lighthouse teaching her family and others how to see. Yet Woolf realizes that reading texts, like reading lives, is a quest toward permanence, understanding, and meaning – a quest that despite its occasional partial successes will always fall short of its goal. The Ramsays, in a quiet, intimate hiatus – and the last time we see Mrs Ramsay alive – at the end of part I of *To the Lighthouse*, read their own books. Reading Scott, Mr Ramsay "forgot himself completely" and enjoys "the astonishing delight and feeling of vigour that it gave him" (p. 180). And reading Shakespeare's ninety-eighth sonnet, Mrs Ramsay has a parallel experience: "All the odds and ends of the day stuck to this magnet; her mind swept, felt clean. And then there it was, suddenly entire; she held it in her hands, beautiful and reasonable, clear and complete, the essence sucked out of life and held rounded here – the sonnet" (p. 181).

In this short period of intimacy, Mrs Ramsay *wants* her husband's reproof for her pessimism about Paul and Minta's marriage, and he wants her "to tell him that she loved him" (p. 184). Although "she never could say what she felt" (p. 185), her smile and her acknowledging the truth of his prophecy have the effect of creating the moment of intimacy for both of them. The end of "The Window" requires a double perspective. True, it ends with her thought, "Nothing on earth can equal his happiness" (p. 186), and their mutual fulfillment. Yet we have seen from what precedes that her life has its limitations, and that her marriage has not only defined but confined her. The echo of "The Dead" has an ironic resonance in view of her approaching death.

Mrs Ramsay is a choreographer of the lives of others, and she is far more successful at it than Clarissa Dalloway; it is she who silently inspires Paul to propose to Minta. Moments after the party is over, she thinks:

> Yes, that was done then, accomplished; and as with all things done, became solemn. Now one thought of it, cleared of chatter and emotion, it seemed always to have been, only was shown now and so being shown, struck everything into stability. They would, she thought, going on again, however long they lived, come back to this night; this moon; this wind; this house; and to her too. It flattered her . . . to think how, wound about in their hearts, however long they lived she would be woven . . . All that would be revived again in the lives of Paul and Minta; "the Rayleys" – she tried the new name over; and she felt, with her hand on the nursery door, that community of feeling with other people which emotion gives as if the walls of partition had become so thin that practically (the feeling was one of relief and happiness) it was all one stream, and chairs, tables, maps, were hers, were theirs, it did not matter whose, and Paul and Minta would carry it on when she was dead. (pp. 170–1)

In arranging the engagement of Paul and Minta, Mrs Ramsay has created "a community of feeling" in which the partitions that divide people have almost broken down. As surely as the artist, Mrs Ramsay has created meaning that lives past her death and shapes the lives of others who in their turn shape the lives of others. That the most intense experience of daily life can have a value and a form is central to the novel's aesthetic: "Here, she felt, putting the spoon down, was the still space that lies about the heart of things, where one could move or rest; could wait now (they were all helped) listening; could then, like a hawk which lapses suddenly from its high station, flaunt and sink on laughter easily" (pp. 158–9). Thus one's sensibility and one's actions have a kind of immortality. And we think of the impression she had made on Tansley as "the most beautiful person he had ever seen . . . [F]or the first time in his life Charles Tansley felt an extraordinary pride" not in scholarship or personal gain, but simply in accompanying Mrs Ramsay (p. 25). And that scene, too, we know will live in his memory. But in the final part of *To the Lighthouse*, we learn that the Rayleys' marriage is hardly a success, and the immortality of which Mrs Ramsay dreams can hardly be said to occur. She seeks the kind of unity in life that she admires in an arrangement of fruit, an arrangement such as Woolf might have seen depicted in a Cézanne painting. Mrs Ramsay's feeling that reaching to take a pear will spoil the fruit arrangement embodies Woolf's regret that perfection is rarely if ever found in life.

For her part Mrs Ramsay needs to mate Lily with William. Lily is divided in the face of romantic love; on the one hand she understands its beauty and exhilaration; but on the other she fears its "degradation" and "dilution." While Mrs Ramsay renews her husband and responds to Bankes and her children, even to Tansley, does she understand Lily, who, in part at least, really does want to retain her independence as a single woman and live for her painting? Furthermore, Lily, like Clarissa, seems asexual. Lily associates Paul with sexual love, but for her such passion has atavistic overtones:

> It rose like a fire sent up in token of some celebration by savages on a distant beach . . . [S]he felt again her own headlong desire to throw herself off the cliff and be drowned looking for a pearl brooch on a beach. And the roar and the crackle repelled her with fear and disgust, as if while she saw its splendour and power she saw too how it fed on the treasure of the house, greedily, disgustingly, and she loathed it. (p. 261)

We think perhaps of how Aschenbach, another repressed adult past 40, associates his passion for Tadzio with primitive lands. Although Lily "loved William Bankes" and "his friendship had been one of the pleasures of her life," Woolf is insisting that love need not be the prelude to marriage, or even to sexual intimacy (p. 263). The putative marital happiness that Mrs Ramsay had created for the Rayleys is belied by their actual lives. She has not, after all, created something that is lasting. For Woolf, only the creative imagination fulfilled by artistic creation can do that.

That Mrs Ramsay remembers a day 20 years ago as if it were yesterday stresses the importance of memory in giving shape to the very day that the characters are living (and the importance to the rereader of his memory of his first reading of *To the Lighthouse*) (p. 132). Mrs Ramsay regrets that James "will remember all his life" his father's prophecy about the weather on the day at age 6 when he planned to go to the lighthouse. In part III, Lily, by making sense of her past experience at the Ramsay house, is trying to discover significance in her present life and art. As in Proust, memory triggers complex emotions about people. For William Bankes the dunes become an elegiac moment for the friendship he once had with Ramsay: "[T]here, like the body of a young man laid in peat for a century, with the red fresh on his lips, was his friendship, in its acuteness and reality, laid up across the bay among the sandhills" (p. 35); the trace of mortality is always present in memory and in art. *To the Lighthouse* is an attempt to immortalize such moments and to unify them into one grand experience. That is why the book stresses memories of experience frozen in time by the mind and why the act of perception is the subject of memories and the narrative.

The entire novel revolves around a contest between death and life, order and flux, creative imagination and the "scraps and fragments" of ordinary experience (p. 136). No sooner does Mrs Ramsay or Lily experience unity than "there was a sense of things having been blown apart, of space, of irresponsibility" (p. 111). *To the Lighthouse* is a novel which, like *Sons and Lovers*, is about the very processes of creating meaning from inchoate personal experience. The struggle for order and meaning within each of the characters' lives is not only the central action of the novel, but the activity that engaged Woolf herself. Doesn't Woolf's own art mime Lily's struggles to render what she sees rather than merely what convention dictates? Woolf's narrator comments: "It was in that moment's flight between the picture and [Lily's] canvas that the demons set on her who often brought her to the verge of tears and made this passage from conception to work as dreadful as any down a dark passage for a child" (p. 32).

Style and form enact and affirm the principles of order, sensibility, and discrimination by which Mrs Ramsay lives. But the possibility of disorder, insensitivity, and personal failure is always threatening to intrude into the novel's imagined world. In "her strange severity, her extreme courtesy," her refusal to "regret her decision, evade difficulties, or slur over duties," Mrs Ramsay not only represents a queenly presence in the social world, a presence that provides standards for others, but also a concept of order which has its correlative in the tight design of the book's structure and texture (p. 14). Yet the process by which the consciousness of characters even within a day, within an hour, oscillates between feelings of unity and disunity creates a tension between formal coherence and the possibility that life lacks meaning. Lily's or Mrs Ramsay's despair at one moment is given meaning by the ecstasy of a subsequent one, and vice versa. Like Woolf herself, the characters often live at the edge of desperation, even madness.

Because for Woolf epiphanic moments which briefly – or even momentarily – order ephemeral perceptions are in themselves values, the readers must not reduce the text to image patterns or mythic echoes; such an approach deprives the novel of its movement and leaves it cold and static.[8] In Woolf, the moments of intense experience take their meaning from the process of chronological experience dramatized within the narrative. Thus, at the center of the novel is Lily, trying to create meaning out of the flux of life. For her, "suddenly the meaning which, for no reason at all, as perhaps [Mr and Mrs Ramsay] are stepping out of the Tube or ringing a doorbell, descends on people, making them symbolical, making them representative, came upon them, and made them in the dusk standing, looking, the symbols of marriage, husband and wife" (pp. 110–11). But such epiphanic and symbolic moments can only be temporary even if they pretend to a permanence that eludes human perceptions; thus in the next instant Lily sees them simply as Mr and Mrs Ramsay watching their children play catch.

Woolf's fictions enact for the reader the ephemeral quality of life. On the one hand, her novels stress significant moments, moments when life coheres into unity and arrests the inevitable flux of time; on the other, these gaps in time undermine the taut plot we expect of traditional fiction and the organic reading that imposes coherent order. Woolf's aesthetic stresses a dialogue between text and reader; the reader, by providing his or her own emotions, completes the novel and knits the strands of the novel together. Thus she wrote to Roger Fry:

> I meant *nothing* by *The Lighthouse*. One has to have a central line down the middle of the book to hold the design together. I saw that all sorts of feelings would accrue to this, but I refused to think them out, and trusted that people would make it the deposit for their own emotions – which they have done, one thinking it means one thing another another. I can't manage Symbolism except in this vague, generalised way. Whether it's right or wrong I don't know; but directly I'm told what a thing means, it becomes hateful to me. (*Letters*, III, 1764, May 27, 1927)

II The Significance of Lily's Paintings

Lily's paintings are crucial to the meaning of *To the Lighthouse*. In this novel painting and writing are metaphors for one another and for the creative process. Painted 10 years later than the first painting and after World War I, Lily's second painting is Postimpressionist. It defines the relationship between line and form, and is more abstract than the painting in part I, which takes its impulse from Impressionism.

Isn't Woolf suggesting that aesthetic assumptions have changed and calling attention to the juxtapositions and non-mimetic quality of her own writing? Lily completes the painting with the line that is a metonymy for both the obsessive linearity of Mr Ramsay and the lighthouse. The line suggests Ramsay's focus on the vertical pronoun – a focus, as is indicated by Lily's employing the same pronoun at a crucial moment ("I have had my vision"), that she, at the age of 44 and without supporting love relationships, so desperately needs. She begins and ends her painting with a single line, perhaps suggesting Japanese ink drawings: "One line placed on the canvas committed her to innumerable risks, to frequent and irrevocable decisions" (p. 235). As she paints she loses herself in her vision, but does not completely lose touch with life. She wants to balance "two opposite forces; Mr Ramsay and the picture; which was necessary. There was something perhaps wrong with the design? Was it, she wondered, that the line of the wall wanted breaking, was it that the mass of the trees were too heavy?" (p. 287). In a sense the final line discovers for her – and for her creator – the relationship between art and life. For Woolf, the line also stands for the completion of the novel. Indeed, if the impulse for the first painting was what Lily sees, the impulse for the second is a dialogue between her imagination and experience, and between her sense of form and what she wants to include. The concern with mass and line shows the influence of Roger Fry's two London exhibits in 1910 to 1912 of Postimpressionist painters, particularly Cézanne, who "drew" not only with line but with mass, with blocks of color.

An artist who relies on her inner vision, rather than external reality, Lily Briscoe paints what she knows, not what she sees. If her concept of form requires it, she paints a tree or a line although it may exist only in the mind's eye: "I shall put the tree further in the middle; then I shall avoid that awkward space" (p. 128). Yet her artistic epiphany is created by human emotion – a vision that, notwithstanding Mrs Ramsay's pity for William Bankes, he "is not in the least pitiable. He had his work, Lily said to herself. She remembered, all of a sudden as if she had found a treasure, that she had her work" (p. 128). Thus the ground for Lily's epiphanic moment of wholeness depends on her personal, independent critique of Mrs Ramsay's pity for Bankes. By showing that Lily's art requires the impetus of human feeling, Woolf urges the reader to see that non-representational art is neither merely second-hand copying of the insights of others nor cold geometric forms. That Lily's formal, non-realist's aesthetic depends on humanistic values helps us understand how we should read.

For Lily Briscoe the Postimpressionist, "the question [is] one of the relations of the masses, of lights and shadows" – as it is for Cézanne – but for her, art is much more than that (p. 82). Art for Lily – as for Woolf – is "the deposit of each day's living mixed with something more secret than she had ever spoken or shown," and that deposit expresses her deepest feelings (p. 81). One might say that Mrs Ramsay influences or educates Lily's aesthetic values, as Lily educates the reader to respond to those of the narrative presence of the novel:

> Aren't things spoilt then, Mrs Ramsay may have asked (it seemed to have happened so often, this silence by her side) by saying them? Aren't we more expressive thus? The moment at least seemed extraordinarily fertile. She rammed a little hole in the sand and covered it up, by way of burying in it the perfection of the moment. It was like a drop of silver in which one dipped and illumined the darkness of the past. (p. 256)

Storing up the past serves as a metaphor not only for what Lily has done and is doing now, but for what Woolf's narrator is doing as she writes of Lily's triumph. The view that saying too much can spoil things is not only Mrs Ramsay's, but her creator's. Thus Woolf's presence shapes our reading.

Lily's impulse for the second painting is the intertextual memory of the first painting:

> There was something . . . something she remembered in the relations of those lines cutting across, slicing down, and in the mass of the hedge with its green cave of blues and browns, which had stayed in her mind; which had tied a knot in her mind so that at odds and ends of time, involuntarily, as she walked along Brompton Road, as she brushed her hair, she found herself painting that picture, passing her eye over it, and untying the knot in imagination. But there was all the difference in the world between planning airily away from the canvas and actually taking her brush, and making the first mark. (pp. 234–5)

For her, colors – "its green cave of blues and browns" – are at least partially freed from the morphology of representation. From her emphasis on spatial relations, we can certainly assume that Woolf had seen the work of Cézanne, Gauguin, and Matisse. We might think of what Elderfield wrote of Matisse's style in the 1908 to 1912 period: "at times, he did not just adjust form as he adjusted color, but drew everything in advance and then carefully filled in the picture with colors appropriate to the size of the compartments they occupied."[9] The stress in the second painting is on imbuing everyday experience with the magic of meaning and form: "One wanted, she thought, dipping her brush deliberately, to be on a level with ordinary experience, to feel simply that's a chair, that's a table, and yet at the same time, it's a miracle, it's an ecstasy" (pp. 299–300). She seeks an epiphany through her art. Lily's creative imagination not only recalls Mrs Ramsay from the past but transforms her into a symbolic, if ambiguous, figure in the present. As an artist she wants to achieve the kind of unity that Mrs Ramsay achieves in her life. To inform ordinary experience with meaning is a crucial goal of Woolf's art – a goal that can be approached but never reached.

Woolf is embodied in Lily's quest for artistic values and Mrs Ramsay's quest for personal ones. The equation between Lily's painting and Woolf's writing is crucial, but so is the equation between Mrs Ramsay's effects on people and the goals that Woolf wants to achieve. Woolf establishes a relationship between Mrs Ramsay's quest to achieve wholeness and unity in personal relationships and Lily's quest to complete her picture. Mrs Ramsay is expected and expects herself to create the unity that will give her dinner party meaning: "And the whole of the effort of merging and flowing and creating rested on her" (p. 126). And she thinks of her task in terms of the crucial image of sailing a ship:

[I]n pity for [William Bankes], life being now strong enough to bear her on again, she began all this business, as a sailor not without weariness sees the wind fill his sail and yet hardly wants to be off again and thinks how, had the ship sunk, he would have whirled round and round and found rest on the floor of the sea. (p. 127)

The image captures the continuing and finally futile quest to keep one's bearings in the cosmos – represented by the sea – which is indifferent toward both quest and goal.

Does not Lily's final vision emphasize its transitoriness, its consignment to the past?: "I have *had* my vision" (p. 310; emphasis mine). We know from the novel's narrative code – specifically, no sooner do we read of Mrs Ramsay's epiphany than we learn both of her death and of her failure to shape the relationship between Paul and Minta – that visions cannot wrench themselves from temporality. Since Mrs Ramsay's triumphant vision had given "The Window" a similar closure and since Lily had conceived the resolving line at the end of that section, the narrative code warns us not to be seduced by Lily's epiphany or even the narrative voice's visionary experience. Woolf implicitly asks her readers, are not secular visions always ironized by what is missing: the deeply felt passionate relationship with God in which the seeker completes himself or herself, or, in other terms, in which the world and word become one?

That Lily's final thoughts ("It was done; it was finished") echo Christ's words on the cross ("*Consummatum est*") emphasizes Woolf's awareness of this irony. The verticals – Lily's line parodying Mr Ramsay and the ego represented by the vertical pronoun "I," the lighthouse (a man-made substitution for God's creation of light), Mr Carmichael standing – are equated with the quest to discover meaning in a world where God is no longer a factor. As with all the major writers of our period, the concept of God is the absent signifier hovering over the text and the imagined world created by the text. We recall Mrs Ramsay's religious skepticism, as she thinks, as her creator might of death and suffering: "How could any Lord have made this world?" (p. 98). As in *Mrs Dalloway*, the absence of Christian belief is a striking fact in the novel. But unlike Hardy, Lawrence, Joyce, and Yeats, Woolf's unbelief really does not struggle with belief. When Mrs Ramsay hears herself muttering the conventional Victorian shibboleth, "We are in the hands of the Lord," she dismisses it as a lie (p. 97): "With her mind she had always seized the fact that there is no reason, order, justice: but suffering, death, the poor. There was no treachery too base for the world to commit; she knew that" (p. 98).

When she becomes like an artist surveying her creation, Mrs Ramsay creates a kind of unity, a moment of *kairos*, a significance, of the kind that used to be associated with religion: "She looked at the window in which the candle flames burnt brighter now that the panes were black, and looking at that outside the voices came to her very strangely, as if they were voices at a service in a cathedral, for she did not listen to the words" (pp. 165–6). But verticals and linearity also are equated with the masculine need to progress, dominate, and conquer – with Mr Ramsay's need to move "from start to finish" through the letters of the alphabet (p. 55) – in contrast to the novel's intense effort to render somehow the dynamic, evanescent, shifting, interconnecting and intersecting planes and spheres of reality. Thus the equation of the journey to the lighthouse with the completion of the painting is itself an acknowledgment of the paradox that completing a work – fixing an impression in time – belies the flux and hence the infinite possibilities of reality. In Woolf's imagined world, as in Lawrence's, to be complete or finished is equated with death, while the flux of the quest for values is itself a value aligned with being fully alive. It is the movement toward the goal that gives life significance – reaching toward the lighthouse, pressing on in the attempt to solve the problem of the painting, trying to pull together the novel. Put another way, as in the series with which I concluded the prior sentence, the verb takes precedence over its object. Ultimately, the verticals of the lighthouse become ironized by temporality, by the inability of the characters or the narrator to close the gap between the signifier and the signified. Indeed, reaching the lighthouse and completing the painting, like Mrs Ramsay's vision, is another poignant and very emphatic step toward death. Just as the second section, "Time Passes," dramatized how time preys on things human, the narrative shows us that not only Lily's painting but Woolf's writing is not immune to time. Yet, unlike a painting, the collective reading experience of a literary text, if and when published, can be repeated often enough so that it has the chance to survive time.

In section V, part II, "The Lighthouse," Woolf specifically equates the act of memory with the act of Lily's artistic creation: "And as she dipped into the blue paint, she dipped too into the past there. Now Mrs Ramsay got up, she remembered" (p. 256). But memories of Mrs Ramsay *are* the catalyst for Lily's intense experience. The powerful presence of the past in human lives is a Woolf theme. Lily half expects Mrs Ramsay to return from the past to the present:

> For the whole world seemed to have dissolved in this early morning hour into a pool of thought, a deep basin of reality, and one could almost fancy that had Mr Carmichael spoken, for instance, a little tear would have rent the surface of the pool. And then? Something would emerge. A hand would be shoved up, a blade would be flashed. (pp. 266–7)

Lily wants to believe in the immortality of art – "How 'you' and 'I' and 'she' pass and vanish; nothing stays; all changes; but not words, not paint" (p. 267) – but she fears that her paintings will be hung in attics and stored under a sofa. Lily dissolves into tears for Mrs Ramsay, for the immortality that she herself will never achieve, and for her own realization that she, too, will die. Now that she cannot seek consolation from either Mrs Ramsay or Bankes – about whom we have no idea whether he is living or dead – Lily silently asks Mr Carmichael, who by his presence had become objectified into the other she seeks:

> What was it then? What did it mean? Could things thrust their hands up and grip one; could the blade cut; the fist grasp? Was there no safety? No learning by heart of the ways of the world? No guide, no shelter, but all was miracle, and leaping from the pinnacle of a tower into the air? Could it be, even for elderly people, that this was life – startling, unexpected, unknown? (p. 268)

Is not Lily's perception – that the real significance of life is these moments that contain the "startling," the "unexpected," and the "unknown" – central to Woolf's aesthetic? The text enacts this in Lily's tears and her desperate insistence on meaning in a life "so short" and "so inexplicable." In the pathos of Lily's quest, we feel Woolf's own:

> For one moment she felt that if they both got up, here, now on the lawn and demanded an explanation, why was it so short, why was it so inexplicable, said it with violence, as two fully equipped human beings from whom nothing should be hid should speak, then, beauty would roll itself up; the space would fill; those empty flourishes would form into shape; if they shouted loud enough Mrs Ramsay would return. (p. 268)

The beauty of art confers meaning by the filling of empty spaces, by organizing unity among details, and by providing the coherence of epiphanic insight. But, as in many Modernist texts, moments of order and beauty are temporary and not sufficient to provide plenitude.

We feel Woolf's identification with Lily when the latter thinks of literary responses in painterly terms: "[L]ike everything else this strange morning the words became symbols, wrote themselves all over the grey-green walls. If only she could put them together, she felt, write them out in some sentence, then she could have got at the truth of things" (p. 219). Lily's mind works in terms of shapes and color. Her perceptions might be those of Woolf if we substitute writing for painting: "It was a miserable machine, an inefficient machine, she thought, the human apparatus for painting or for feeling; it always broke down at the critical moment; heroically, one must force it on" (p. 287).

Woolf depicts acts of memory as kinds of narratives. The prototype for the way memory both recaptures and permanently loses experience is Mrs Ramsay's recollection of the Mannings: "[N]ow she went among them like a ghost; and it fascinated her, as if, while she had changed, that particular day, now become very still and beautiful, had remained there, all these years" (p. 132). This image describes not only the position of Lily, Mr Ramsay, and his returning children in part III, but also Woolf's position as she returned to the memories of her parents' home and family relationships. In a reversal that privileges reading over living, imagination over results, the experience of memory is specifically equated with reading a book. During the dinner party, the narrator renders Mrs Ramsay's desire to

> return to that dream land, that unreal but fascinating place, the Mannings' drawing-room at Marlow twenty years ago; where one moved about without haste or anxiety, for there was no future to worry about. She knew what happened to them, what to her. It was like reading a good book again, for she knew the end of the story, since it happened twenty years ago, and life, which shot down even from this dining-room table in cascades, heaven knows where, was sealed up there, and lay, like a lake, placidly between its banks. (p. 140)

Yet, finally, Mrs Ramsay censors the escapism of fantasy with the lesson of reason; she acknowledges that the Mannings have had a life beyond her consciousness and she had one beyond theirs, and finds the thought "strange and distasteful" (p. 133).

In the face of insecurity, Lily holds onto what she sees: "The jacmanna was bright violet; the wall staring white. She would not have considered it honest to tamper with the bright violet and the staring white, since she saw them like that, fashionable though it was . . . to see everything pale, elegant, semitransparent" (pp. 31–2). At times it seems as if she were influenced by Matisse's ethos, but did not know how to soar from her physical position on the ground. Yet she is able to draw upon her imagination: "In a flash she saw her picture, and thought, Yes, I shall put the tree further in the middle; then I shall avoid that awkward space . . . She took up the salt cellar and put it down again on a flower in pattern in the table-cloth, so as to remind herself to move the tree" (p. 128). *To the Lighthouse* is about the writing of itself, and a major trope is Lily's creation of a painting.

To the Lighthouse enacts a dialogue between feelings of emptiness and the search for compensating plenitudes – plenitudes provided by memories and, for the artist, the consolation of form. Lily feels, as Mrs Ramsay had, the impotence of language to describe feeling: "For how could one express in words these emotions of the body? express that emptiness there?" (p. 265). But, at a crucial moment – almost like the lines that define the shape of her painting – she recalls Mrs Ramsay's presence so vividly that it defines her own present space and significance. For a moment – but only a moment – she believes that memory can renew Mrs Ramsay and that the power of her feelings is enough to recreate the past. Yet the effect of the memory enables her to complete her picture.

The sailing image is fulfilled – by *fulfillment* I mean the image is given its significance in terms of the evolving pattern and the retrospective spatial dimension – by Mrs Ramsay's figuratively reaching the lighthouse at the end of "The Window" (and later, in part III, the sailing image is recalled by the successful, yet ironic, voyage of Mr Ramsay with which the novel concludes). As her dinner party coheres, Mrs Ramsay experiences a moment of perfect rapture:

Nothing need be said; nothing could be said. There it was, all round them. It partook, she felt, carefully helping Mr Bankes to a specially tender piece, of eternity; as she had already felt about something different once before that afternoon; there is a coherence in things, a stability; something, she meant, is immune from change, and shines out (she glanced at the window with its ripple of reflected lights) in the face of the flowing, the fleeting, the spectral, like a

229

ruby; so that again tonight she had the feeling she had had once today, already, of peace, of rest. Of such moments, she thought, the thing is made that endures. (p. 158)

The stability that Mrs Ramsay feels is very much what Lily seeks in her painting and Woolf seeks in her fiction – the subduing of diverse impressions to the unity of the whole. It is what Woolf is trying to achieve for her reader, and it is imaged by the lighthouse, pointedly evoked by the verb "shines out." As I have been arguing, Woolf's novels are both a quest to define those epiphanic moments and to achieve them within her text, and an acknowledgement that such moments must be ephemeral.

For these moments are inevitably transitory. As in Joyce we should think of the quest for epiphany as more important than the epiphanic moment. The epiphanic moment is always to occur and has occurred. Here the unity is threatened by versions of male insecurity: Mr Ramsay's "extreme anxiety about himself" (p. 162) and Tansley's self-doubt: "Am I saying the right thing? Am I making a good impression?" (p. 163). As soon as the people leave the room, the party is consigned to the "past" – the word with which section XVIII closes. In light of her own death and that of two of her children a few pages later, Mrs Ramsay's epiphany is particularly ironic and shows the futility of forestalling time. Even the great moment inevitably fades into the past. The very conditions of mortality, Woolf implies, make the quest for these moments of perfection, of coherence, of significance, all the more important. Such moments are as close as life comes to art.

III "Time Passes"

In part II, "Time Passes," the perspective becomes impersonal, detached, hawklike. Death is an insistent presence. At first the "airs" – Woolf's metaphor for indifferent, relentless time – have little effect on the house when it is uninhabited, but, after the family fails to return, the "airs" begin to reclaim the house as their own, and the house and its contents decay. Part II responds to Mrs Ramsay's allegorical question, "What was the value, the meaning of things?," with an allegorical answer (p. 183). To the detached perspective, Mrs Ramsay's death and the deaths of Prue and Andrew are mere parentheses to the larger processes of life it records. The omniscient, distanced, and ironic voice is the antithesis of the personal, subjective presence which was something of a window into the consciousnesses of the characters, especially Mrs Ramsay and Lily. But here the focus is on the house, from which human life is absent, and this is all the more moving and effective because of part I.

At times in "Time Passes," one aspect of the polyphonic narrative voice has a vatic tone. It does not speak of a benevolent order but of nature that is indifferent to human presence and aspiration, even as the human mind desperately needs to understand nature and discover its significance: "[I]t seemed as if the universe were battling and tumbling, in brute confusion and wanton lust aimlessly by itself . . . [T]he stillness and the brightness of the day were as strange as the chaos and tumult of night, with the trees standing there, and the flowers standing there, looking before them, looking up, yet beholding nothing, eyeless, and so terrible" (p. 203). Nature reclaims the house until the residents give word that they will return; then the house is described in terms suggesting rebirth: "some rusty laborious birth seemed to be taking place" (p. 210). With the return of people, the setting is humanized and given its meaning; in the absence of humankind, nature is chaotic. Indeed, another aspect of the voice seeks to verbalize the responses of the non-verbal experience of "the mystic, the visionary," who regrets her failure to compose order from fragments and to discover meaning in the night and is denied an answer to such basic questions as "What am I, What is this?" (p. 198). In "Time Passes" the world is presented as an unreadable hieroglyph that cannot be allegorized except as impenetrable signifiers: "[I]t seems impossible . . . that we should ever compose from their fragments a perfect whole or read in the littered pieces the clear words of truth" (p. 193).

Woolf is mocking the visionary romantic voice which proclaims with confidence that "good triumphs, happiness prevails, order rules" (p. 199), or that nature contains "some absolute good" or has "a knowledge of the sorrows of mankind" (p. 199) – and the reader who reads in search of conclusive interpretations of reality from her work. World War I has made such a quest impossible. The war undermines the position that we live in a benign cosmos, for seekers on the beach would find

something out of harmony with this jocundity and this serenity. There was the silent apparition of an ashen-coloured ship for instance, come, gone; there was a purplish stain upon the bland surface of the sea as if something had boiled and bled, invisibly, beneath . . . It was difficult blandly to overlook them; to abolish their significance in the landscape; to continue, as one walked by the sea, to marvel how beauty outside mirrored beauty within . . . That dream, of sharing, completing, of finding in solitude on the beach an answer, was then but a reflection in a mirror, and the mirror itself was but the surface glassiness which forms in quiescence when the nobler powers sleep beneath? Impatient, despairing yet loth to go (for beauty offers her lures, has her consolations), to pace the beach was impossible; contemplation was unendurable; the mirror was broken. (pp. 201–2)

Thus humans must create their own order in art (Lily's paintings) if they are to fulfill their dream of sharing and completing reality. Woolf is turning the traditional image of a mirror held up to nature inside out and using it as an image of narcissism and solipsism. She is also implying that in the modern world – despoiled by war – a conception of a benevolent cosmos ordered by a "divine goodness" (a phrase she uses ironically) is apocryphal (p. 192). People seek order, perhaps in a walk by the sea, but

[N]o image with semblance of serving and divine promptitude comes readily to hand bringing the night to order and making the world reflect the compass of the soul . . . Almost it would appear that it is useless in such confusion to ask the night those questions as to what, and why, and wherefore, which tempt the sleeper from his bed to seek an answer. (p. 193)

The pacers on the beach disappear at this point as nature reclaims the house; nevertheless, the continuation of life is its own answer both to cosmic questions and to such disruptions of human continuity as those created by the Great War.

IV Conclusion: "The Lighthouse"

In the final part entitled "The Lighthouse," Lily has a strong feeling that this is a crucial day in her life, but she is frustrated with her painting. Mr Ramsay stalks about muttering "Perished. Alone" and Lily thinks of the picture which she had been working on 10 years ago (p. 220). Mr Ramsay turns to Lily as he had formerly turned to Mrs Ramsay; but she is unresponsive to his need not only because she is inexperienced with the supplicating male, but because he is interfering with her work: "She hated playing at painting. A brush, the one dependable thing in a world of strife, ruin, chaos – that one should not play with, knowingly even: she detested it" (p. 224). Ironically, praising his boots is enough to fulfill his need – his pathetic masculine need for admiration – although she does not feel sympathy: "They had reached, she felt, a sunny island where peace dwelt, sanity reigned and the sun forever shone, the blessed island of good boots" (p. 230). Until she praises his boots, she had, as his children will on the boat, resented his demands. Yet masculinity triumphs in all its crassness and insensitivity. While earlier he had been described as "the leader of the doomed expedition," he now leads a successful expedition which comes together as surely as did his wife's party 10 years earlier (p. 57).

The memory of Mrs Ramsay is a catalyst for Lily's personal growth. She recalls how Mrs Ramsay's life had refuted and now refutes Lily's prejudice about "the ineffectiveness of action, the supremacy of thought" (p. 292), and modified her grotesque idea of Charles Tansley: "Half one's notions of other people were, after all, grotesque. They served private purposes of one's own" (p. 293). In Lily's mind, past and present merge; she imagines Mrs Ramsay sitting in her house as she might have 10 years ago, solicitous of the happiness of others but needing to affirm her own life by bringing others together in marriage: Paul and Minta, Lily and Bankes, Prue and a future lover. But Lily understands that time prevented Mrs Ramsay from imposing order on life, as her death and the failure of the Rayleys' marriage make clear.

As in Wordsworth, past memories affect current emotions and attitudes. Shaped by her memory of Mrs Ramsay, Lily is – at least on this day – better able to relate to people and to get outside of herself and the protection of her art. She now takes part in the kind of meaningful silent speech that had been the basis of Mrs Ramsay's ability to achieve empathy. She feels that Mr Carmichael and she "had not needed to speak. They had been thinking the same things and he had answered her without her asking him anything. He stood there as if he were spreading his hands over all the weakness and suffering of mankind; she thought he was surveying, tolerantly and compassionately, their final destiny" (p. 309).

Hasn't Lily achieved a moment of community and sense of unity like those of Mrs Ramsay? It is as if she were adopting Mrs Ramsay's values at last. She has grown in tolerance, sympathy, understanding, and the ability to feel. She understands Mr Ramsay as a human being rather than a symbol and feels the empathy that he required that morning. In the last section this heightened emotional life informs her painting: "She looked at the steps; they were empty; she looked at her canvas; it was blurred. With a sudden intensity, as if she saw it clear for a second, she drew a line there, in the centre. It was done; it was finished. Yes, she thought, laying down her brush in extreme fatigue, I have had my vision" (p. 310). And it is as if the novel coheres; for isn't the complete painting the necessary metaphor for the art of writing the novel? The painting concludes a series of perceptions and fulfills a number of formal patterns: Mr Ramsay's physical quest to take his son to the lighthouse and pay his penance to the memory of his wife; his quest to relate to his children; Lily's aesthetic and emotional maturation; James and Cam's passage from childhood to adulthood; the fulfillment of the symbol of the lighthouse as light, truth, immortality, and as counter to the flux and relativity of life – and, for Woolf, the painful process of writing the novel.

The intermingling of the ordinary with the metaphorical is Woolf's characteristic way of telling. At times, however, she creates comparisons that urge a response that the literal level does not justify. Put another way, the intensity and energy of metaphors and allusions (discourse) do not merely complement the action (story), but also violate the conventions of the novel of manners and morals. Such meaning, unsupported by and even at odds with the action, gives Woolf's novel its polyphonic character despite the wonderfully idiosyncratic monologue of the narrative voice.

Such a technique enables her to give individuality and complexity to a character's perception – to create a dialogic effect – without fully surrendering the sensibility and perspicacity of her narrative voice. For example, to stress James's anxiety, even paranoia, Woolf has James think of his father as a wagon wheel crushing someone's foot:

> Suppose then that as a child sitting helpless in a perambulator, or on some one's knee, he had seen a waggon crush ignorantly and innocently, some one's foot? Suppose he had seen the foot first, in the grass, smooth, and whole; then the wheel; and the same foot, purple, crushed. But the wheel was innocent. So now, when his father came striding down the passage knocking them up early in the morning to go to the Lighthouse down it came over his foot, over Cam's foot, over anybody's foot. (p. 275)

But does Mr Ramsay's conduct justify James's bizarre oedipal fantasy of killing his father?

> [I]t was not him, that old man reading, whom he wanted to kill, but it was the thing that descended on him – without his knowing it perhaps: that fierce sudden black-winged harpy, with its talons and its beak all cold and hard, that struck and struck at you (he could feel the beak on his bare legs, where it had struck when he was a child), and then made off, and there he was again, an old man very sad, reading his book. (pp. 273–4)

Of course, James's response reflects Woolf's ambivalence toward her own father.

Indeed, is not such a metaphor a sublimated version of the violence which finally results in the World War? True, James recalls his father's disturbing prophecy of rain years ago – the prophecy that blasted his expectations of a perfect childhood day. Even if we accept James's deep oedipal love for his mother ("she alone spoke the truth; to her alone could he speak it" [p. 278]), the image of his mother as a flowering tree fertilizing his father's sword – an image that in part III takes the form of the sword smiting through the tree – is inappropriate to the responses of a young boy and not really justified by the adolescent's felt experience as we see it: "[S]omething flourished up in the air, something arid and sharp descended even there, like a blade, a scimitar, smiting through the leaves and flowers even of that happy world and making it shrivel and fall" (p. 276). By urging a metaphorical significance that action and characterization do not justify, Woolf sets up a tension between the language and the action that it comments upon, a tension that becomes central to our experience of reading her novels. (By contrast, metaphors in traditional novels such as *Emma* or *Tom Jones* do not create alternative effects, but reinforce the effects of action that is described.)

By having her narrator use questions and parentheses, Woolf qualifies the authority of her speaker's commentary and even her presentation of narrative vignettes, while suggesting the possibility of alternative commentary and episodes which would provide different perspectives. For Woolf knew that reading lives, even more than reading complex texts, is an insuperable task. Her narrator, like her implied reader or imagined narratee, is always marginal and always something of an outsider. Woolf is empathetic with those who, like all of us, are excluded from the plenitude of understanding, whether it be Bankes, who feels nothing at dinner; Tansley, who enters into conversation with Lily, who withholds obvious deference to his masculine role; Lily, who resents that she is patronized as a woman by Tansley as well as by Mrs Ramsay as a single woman – or the omniscient narrator, who is at one remove from the imagined world she describes, and the reader, who is at a still further remove from Woolf's imagined world, a world that includes the narrator – a surrogate self. The lighthouse is an ordering principle within the sea; the sea suggests to Mrs Ramsay (and Woolf, as we know from her *The Waves* [1931]) what Conrad calls the "remorseless process" of the indifferent cosmos. But the amorphous, immeasurable sea also represents the resolution of death that Woolf both feared and sought:

> The monotonous fall of the waves on the beach . . . remorselessly beat the measure of life, made one think of the destruction of the island and its engulf-ment in the sea, and warned her whose day had slipped past in one quick doing after another that it was all ephemeral as a rainbow – this sound which had been obscured and concealed under the other sounds suddenly thundered hollow in her ears and made her look up with an impulse of terror. (pp. 27–8)

As Poole notes, Rhoda in *The Waves* thinks of the waves in these terms: "Rolling me over the waves will shoulder me under. Everything falls in a tremendous

Chapter 11

Forster's *Passage to India*: The Novel of Manners as Political Novel

I Introduction

After I visited India on a brief tour a few years ago, I began to understand the immensity and infinite variety and cultural complexity of India's history and people. While Hinduism is the dominant religion, the Muslim minority is the world's second largest Muslim population. A few centuries before the English imposed their will upon India, Muslims conquered India and established their own empire. Under the leadership of Mahatma Gandhi and Jawaharlal Nehru, India freed itself from nearly two centuries of British domination after World War II and, after becoming an independent dominion in 1947 (and after dividing itself into a mostly Hindu India and Muslim Pakistan), became on January 26, 1950, a fully independent country. India has become the world's largest democracy.

E. M. Forster's *A Passage to India* (1924) depends upon the ever-shifting relations among Hindus, Muslims, and English Christians. The caste system regulates many aspects of the Hindu behavior. In 1947 India legally – but not quite effectively as yet – abolished the caste system and the category of untouchables. But in 1924, the year of *A Passage to India*, the caste system played an even larger role than it does today.

II Forster's Contribution to the English Novel

Although his novels superficially resemble Victorian novels, it is not too much to say that E. M. Forster permanently changed the English novel. Perhaps his not having written longer fiction for the last four decades of his life has inhibited our recognition of the seminal role he played in the transformation of the Victorian novel into what we know as the modern novel. For example, Lionel Stevenson barely mentions E. M. Forster's contribution,[1] and Walter Allen asserts that Forster cannot "be regarded as a pioneer" and places him "in the older English tradition which, beginning with Fielding, ends, we normally assume, with Meredith."[2] In this chapter, I shall make rather more substantial claims for Forster's originality as an artist than are usually made. This originality is based on four major achievements:

1 In the guise of writing objective novels, he wrote personal, subjective ones. He used the conventional omniscient narrator in novels which have a large expressive component. For Forster's novels, like those of the other great modern British and Irish novelists – Joyce, Lawrence, Woolf, and Conrad – are the history of his soul, are metaphors of the self. His novels not only dramatize his characters' search for values, but structurally are quests for values, quests that reflect his own doubt and uncertainty.

2 Forster conceived of the structure of a novel as a continuous process by which values are presented, tested, preserved, or discarded, rather than as the conclusion of a series that clarifies and reorders everything that precedes. Thus his final scene is merely one in a series of events; it just happens to be the last that the reader will experience. Consequently, the issues raised in the novel remain unresolved and the future directions of the surviving characters are often open to speculation.

3 In his novels, Forster challenges not only the artistic and thematic conventions of the novel of manners, but the traditions of manners and morals on which British life and fiction depended. His novels test accepted Victorian shibboleths about proper and decorous behavior, about the importance of reason as necessary to controlling unruly passions and instincts, and about the relationships among social classes. His characters do not discover a place within the community but remain outside the community. When they acknowledge their sexuality in the face of conventions, they are not, as in prior novels, punished for it. The plots establish the validity of instinct, passion, and inner life.

4 Forster expanded the novel's range beyond the drawing rooms that provide the setting for so much of the English novel. In his effort to reach for poetry and passion, he expanded the novel geographically (India, Italy), sociologically (Leonard Bast; the schisms that divide classes, races, and religions), and cosmologically (the mysterious Marabar caves and the Hindu perspective in *A Passage to India*).

III   Forster's Originality

The debt of the Victorian novel to the eighteenth-century novel includes a debt to Neoclassic – what we think of as Aristotelian – assumptions about the plot's central role in a novel's form. But Forster is not an Aristotelian. He thinks of plot as a series of circumstances – often arbitrarily selected and arranged – which enables the author to explore the characters' personal lives and values. In a Forster novel plot is important, but no more than voice or setting, and less than the moral and emotional life of the characters. His plots, in fact, mime the quest of his principal characters to escape social entrapment by expressing feelings and passions and by creating personal ties. It is characteristic of Forster that the ending is another in a series of episodes in which human limitations are exposed rather than an apocalyptic episode which resolves prior social and moral problems. In *Aspects of the Novel*, he wrote rather critically: "Nearly all novels are feeble at the end. This is because the plot requires to be wound up" (p. 66).[3] But Forster ended his novels without resolving them in order to imply that life was a continuous process that could not be arbitrarily summarized by a climactic incident (other than death) at the end of a narrative.

Like the other major British and Irish Modernists – Conrad, Lawrence, Joyce, and Woolf – Forster understood human character as a continually changing flux of experience rather than fixed and static as in the traditional novel of manners, and sought to dramatize states of mind at crucial moments. The essence of a Forster novel is contained in crystallizing moments that give that flux meaning. He believed that within the flux of each person's experience were crucial symbolic moments, watersheds of experience, when, as he put it in *Aspects of the Novel*, "life in time" gives way to "life by values" and the significance of a character's life reveals itself. But these moments, akin to Joyce's epiphanies, are often not complete in themselves or clearly understood by the character experiencing them, even though the narrator and reader understand them. In part, Forster's novels are a concatenation of these significant moments in the lives of his major characters.

For Forster, fiction provided the only possible principle of order in the face of major historical forces that seemed to have deprived humans of their significance – the Industrial Revolution, imperialism, urbanization, and the intensifying organization and systemization of English life. He is interested in these historical phenomena insofar as they affect the quality of feelings, imagination, and personal relationships. Flux is both an inevitable part of life with which we must come to terms and an enemy which we must combat. It makes anachronistic the social solutions of the past. And Forster thought that the kind of novel that a conservative, hierarchical society produced is also anachronistic. In the face of the instability of personal relations, of class structure, and of accepted standards of social behavior, the novel of manners, which depends upon the author's reliance upon her or his audience to recognize violations of decorum and propriety, begins to break down. In Lawrence, Joyce, and Woolf, as well as in Forster, characters are judged more on whether they are true to their best impulses than on how they function in the community.

Forster's novels enact his quest for the inner life as well as his attempt to rescue himself from the curse of Modernism. Forster wrote in "The Challenge of Our Time":

> I belong to the fag-end of Victorian liberalism, and can look back to an age whose challenges were moderate in their tone, and the cloud on whose horizons was no bigger than a man's hand. In many ways, it was an admirable age. It practised benevolence and philanthropy, was humane and intellectually curious, upheld free speech, had little colour-prejudice, believed that individuals are and should be different, and entertained a sincere faith in the progress of society. (*Two Cheers for Democracy*, p. 54)

In a sense, his novels are elegiac and nostalgic. Like Eliot, Joyce, Conrad, and Lawrence, he juxtaposes the present to the past, in part to define the present, in part out of nostalgia for the past.

Forster's novels, like Hardy's and Lawrence's, seek to create an English pastoral, a mythology with tales of English heroes, which would invigorate the culture and the language. Like Lawrence, Conrad, and Hardy, Forster stands with the Coleridgeans against the Utilitarians. Thus, rural life – the myth of the English countryside – is a source of values. In *Howards End* he writes: "In these English farms, if anywhere, one might see life steadily and see it whole, group in one vision its transitoriness and its eternal youth, connect – connect without bitterness until all men are brothers" (p. 266). Like Arnold, Forster's goal was "to see life steadily and see it whole." Forster is, above all, a humanist who does not believe that a god directs human destiny. As in Arnold's case, art was a surrogate for religion. Wilfred Stone writes: "[Forster's] art, and his belief in art, are his religion . . . The religion *is* a coming together, of the seen and the unseen, public affairs and private decencies. Another name for this religion is humanism."[4] With its carefully constructed patterns and symbolic scenes, the artificial order of the novel was for Forster an alternative to belief in traditional religions.

Beginning with Hardy and Conrad, the major British and Irish writers frequently examine the events of the narrative in the context of vast historical perspectives. Lawrence, Conrad, Joyce (and, of course, Yeats and Eliot) also dramatize the present through the lens of the past. Frazer's *The Golden Bough* (1890) extended the range of the past beyond biblical time and even beyond historical time; later, Jung's emphasis on archetypes stressed that all cultures share common anthropological experience and psychological traits. And Forster wished to show that, despite differences in breeding, customs, and values, a common heritage united humankind. Crucial aspects of Forster's values rest in what he calls "the inner life" and the "unseen," both of which resist language.

By the "inner life," he means passions and feelings, those aspects of life in which humans may experience poetry and romance. For Forster, the "unseen" means not the traditional Christian God but a world beyond things, a world that can be reached by passions, imagination, intelligence, and affection. Like Conrad, Lawrence, and Joyce, Forster sees the need to revivify family ties and personal relationships that form the basis of both ancient cultures and British civilization. Forster wants the novel to move beyond local, nominalistic insight and toward universal truths. As he puts it in *Aspects of the Novel*, he wants his fiction to "[reach] back . . . to join up with all the other people far back" (pp. 92–3).

Whereas Victorian novelists usually wrote of how humans lived in the community and examined the values for which humans lived, their successors, including Forster, wrote about themselves. Influenced by Impressionism and Postimpressionism, which stressed the uniqueness of each human's perception, as well as by the dissolution of moral and political certainties in the 1890–1910 period, Forster wrote fiction that expressed his private feelings, the idiosyncrasies of his personality, and the anxieties and frustrations of his psyche. As Stone writes: "His novels are not only chapters in a new gospel, they are dramatic installments in the story of his own struggle for selfhood – and for a myth to support it. They tell of a man coming out in the world, painfully emerging from an encysted state of loneliness, fear, and insecurity."[5] Like Conrad, Lawrence, Joyce, and Woolf, Forster wished to create the order in art that the world lacked; like them, he wished to create himself in his art and to export that created self back into his life; like them, he wrote fiction as a way of defining himself. The dissolution of distance between author and protagonist in autobiographical fiction recurs in this period ("The Secret Sharer," *Jude the Obscure*, *Sons and Lovers*, and *A Portrait of the Artist as a Young Man*). For, in the face of rapid social changes and the resultant confusion of values, authors are trying to create themselves and rescue versions of their youthful selves.

Even if Forster at first seems a far less prominent presence than Conrad, Lawrence, Joyce, and Woolf, he reveals his psyche and values on every page.

Rather than establishing a fixed standard of values by which he measures his characters, his technically omniscient voice undergoes a quest for values as well as a quest for self-understanding. An often lonely man dealing with his homosexuality and resulting anxieties in a hypocritical culture, Forster creates characters who often do not understand their sexuality or motives in relationships – and at times it is not clear whether Forster's narrator understands them either. In *The Longest Journey* (1907), Forster is unable to separate himself from the homosexual character Rickie whose implicit connection to Stewart Ansell represents not only the road not taken, but the better path. In *Where Angels Fear to Tread* (1905), Philip, the self-conscious, disengaged man who has difficulty feeling, is not only a precursor of Fielding but a latent homosexual.

Forster may well have stopped writing novels after *A Passage to India* in part because of his resistance to repressing homosexual intimacy. In *Maurice*, the homosexual novel that Forster finished in 1913 and was not published until after his death in 1971, Maurice and his lover are forced to become "outlaws" (p. 254), although Forster had written in a 1960 "Terminal Note" to *Maurice*: "A happy ending was imperative. I shouldn't have bothered to write otherwise. I was determined that in fiction anyway two men should fall in love and remain in it for the ever and ever that fiction allows, and in this sense Maurice and Alex still roam the greenwood" (p. 250). Finally, are we not left with the impression that future Maurices will experience his confusion and loneliness and will seek advice from intolerant and incredulous doctors and well-meaning but often ineffectual hypnotists? Isn't the "disgusting and dishonourable old age" of the person who propositions Maurice on the train a real possibility for a man who was, in a parallel scene, once tempted to make similar advances to a man? Forster shows that because – in his day – homosexual males are denied love and must repress their needs, they desperately seek love in any way they can.

Forster's own spiritual quest determines the form of his novels. His aesthetic values cannot be separated from his moral ones. With their elegant phrasing, tact, balance, and sensibility, his novels enact his values. The novels are the objective correlative for the keen sensibility, the personal relationships, and the delicate discriminations of feeling that he sought. Forster believed in the therapeutic value of the aesthetic. By sustained and successful creative activity, the artist may discover temporary unity and coherence in his or her own life; moreover, the completed work of art provides for a brief time a measure of unity and coherence for readers.

Forster sought to move beyond the subjective and to create an impersonal art out of his own experiences and feelings. But he never quite succeeded in getting outside of himself, and it may be that his novels are more exciting because of this. Although he grew as a novelist and gradually enlarged his scope, he never suppressed his own doubts and anxieties simply to create an objective vision for himself and his reader.

In *Aspects*, he expressed his admiration for Hardy: "The work of Hardy is my home" (p. 66). This has been taken to mean Forster is an heir to the Victorian novel, but Forster, like Lawrence, realized that Hardy was one of the great innovators in the English novel. Hardy taught Forster, particularly in *Jude the Obscure*, that the author did not have to separate the omniscient narrator from the protagonist's perspective. Like Hardy, Forster uses an omniscient voice that often becomes an empathetic spokesman for major characters. Like Hardy, he creates an alternative to the benevolent cosmos that dominated English fiction prior to Hardy. Like Hardy, he gave up writing novels in the middle of his career.

Forster was influenced not only by Hardy's skeptical world view and his sense of story, but by his stress on various kinds of sexual exploitation. Forster transfers Hardy's sexual themes primarily to the upper middle class. *Howards End* (1910) is a kind of retelling of *Tess of the d'Urbervilles*, with both Jackie and Helen playing variations of Tess's role with Wilcox. Wilcox's son, Paul, is a version of Alec, and Leonard Bast is a parody of Angel. Forster is criticizing the hypocrisy and insanity of the sexual morality which allows Henry Wilcox, twice a seducer, to condemn Helen Schlegel's sexual peccadillo.

Howards End turns the novel of manners upside down and dramatizes that in the modern world there is a separation between, on the one hand, culture, tradition, and courtesy and, on the other hand, wealth. Indeed, *Howards End*, like *The Rainbow*, is conceived in terms of a dualism between the forces of light and those of darkness: the Schlegels and Wilcoxes, manners and money, love and truth, things as they are and things as they ought to be, personal life and the world of commerce and industry, imagination and reason, the surface life and the inner life. In this book Forster goes beyond the novel of manners to examine the relation of public life to private virtue. England becomes a character and its health is a major focus. Forster shows the impossibility of the Schlegels' desire "that public life should mirror whatever is good in the life within" (*Howards End*, 25). The Schlegel sisters are unable to stop the advance of materialism, mediocrity, and the empirical intellect that responds only to facts. In the character of Leonard Bast, Forster uncharacteristically reaches down into the lower middle class to show how the energy and pretension of the new urban class are synonymous with that of London; we cannot but think of Eliot's speaker's remarking in *The Waste Land*: "I had not thought death had undone so many." The Schlegels want to create Leonard as one of their sort, but they pathetically fail. Because Bast is the kind of raw, feral male figure that both repels and fascinates the homosexual Forster, his depiction of Bast shows Forster's awkwardness and even arrogance.

Like *Nostromo*, *Women in Love*, and *The Magic Mountain*, the plot of *Howards End* is a vision of the world in disintegration. As it moves from house to house, *Howards End*, like *Women in Love*, gradually discards or discredits major aspects of English civilization.

Forster's view of humankind is somewhere between Hardy's pessimism and Lawrence's optimism; Forster doubts humankind's capacities, but believes that they will muddle through, and that the artist provides a model for the potential of the individual imagination to create meaning and for the individual heart to respond, on occasion, in a humane way. He shares with the other great Modernists the belief that language can create meaning, can exorcise chaos when all else fails. He is often a polite version of Lawrence, of whom he wrote admiringly in *Aspects*. According to Forster, Lawrence is "the only living novelist in whom the song predominates, who has the rapt bardic quality" (*Aspects*, 99).

Like Lawrence, Forster saw himself in the tradition of the English Romantics, who sought to combine the visionary and realistic mode, the prophetic and the personal. Both frequently sound an elegiac and nostalgic note. Both regretted that humans were no longer in harmony with nature and that the Industrial Revolution had deprived humans of their individuality. Forster anticipates Lawrence in dramatizing what industrialism and commercialism has taken from the modern world. Doesn't Forster's Wilcox in *Howards End* suggest Lawrence's Gerald Crick in *Women in Love*? The former thinks that the force of his will can reshape the world to his own image; he is "broken" when circumstances, in the form of a manslaughter charge against his son, get beyond his control.

IV   The Modernity of *Passage to India*: Leaving Jane Austen's World Behind

Discussing how Forster's novels differ from their predecessors not only enables us to appreciate his uniqueness as an artist, but places the relationship between his values and techniques in a new perspective. Even in *A Passage to India* and *Howards End*, his voice rarely has the certainty of the authoritative, omniscient voice of Victorian fiction. Thus the reader of a Forster novel must be especially attentive to irony and the psychological nuances of character. Part of Forster's modernity is his expectation that the reader will discover relationships and significance. His reticence, the sparseness of his analysis in comparison to such contemporaries as Bennett or Galsworthy, is part of his technique.

We best understand the originality of *A Passage to India*, a seemingly traditional novel, if we compare it briefly with an Austen novel, for *A Passage to India* is a modern version of the novel of manners. We recall that in *Aspects of the Novel*, Forster respects Austen as a writer who "pass[es] the creative finger down every sentence and into every word" (p. 50).

Let us think about *Emma* and *Pride and Prejudice* for a moment. Like many of her contemporaries, Austen believed that characters in novels, like people in real life, could approach ideals of self-understanding and self-control. But Forster's fiction testifies that contemporary men and women live in a world which has lost its grace, dignity, and humanity. That loss is accentuated in the apparent disarray of India, where the Muslim and Hindu cultures restlessly strive to find an equilibrium while under British control.

Forster understood that, whatever the original articulated ideals for the British presence in India – such as improving the economic lot of the backward colonized nation by introducing commerce, even as Britain administered justice and introduced a better education system – the purposes of the British empire had become (as is always the case with imperialism) the preservation of power. As Fareed Zakaria notes, "[M]any of the Britons – almost all Scots, Irish, or Welsh – who ran India approached their tasks with Enlightenment ideas about science, free trade and constitutional government."[6] *A Passage to India* is based in part on Forster's desire to show that it is no longer possible – and certainly not possible in writing about a land suffering from British conquest – to write an Austen-like novel without sacrificing artistic integrity.

I should stress that Forster's focus is on the English, not the Scots, Irish, or Welsh. What, he asks, do English ideas of personal relationships have to do with Godbole the Hindu Brahmin or the non-verbal, handsome untouchable who turns the fan at Aziz's trial? For where there is empire, the tradition of manners becomes so skewed – we recall the bathetic bridge party at the English club in chapter 5 – as to become unrecognizable.

Articulating his view that India is no place for British niceties, Ronny Heaslop ironically reveals what happens to those – usually not Britain's best and brightest but those who for one reason or another are unlikely to excel in Britain – sent out to govern India or other colonies: "We're not out here for the purpose of behaving pleasantly!" (p. 43). While Heaslop and his colleagues are referring to a country that they regard as chaotic and underdeveloped, Forster implies in his novel that the politics of imperialism and the concomitant imaginative failure of the English to understand India's people and culture are the source of much of the difficulty in India. But he does not minimize the cultural differences between Hindu and Muslim, or totally exculpate either of those cultures from responsibility.

Forster not only shows how the tradition of manners fails when it leaves the insularity of an English village, but hints at its obsolescence. We should recall that the hierarchical relationships and a stifling class system have been a concern of his in his prior novels, *Where Angels Fear to Tread, The Longest Journey, A Room with a View* (1908), and *Howards End.* Adela's poignant comment about a tradition of personal relationships may underline Forster's nostalgia for a time when they flourished: "What is the use of personal relationships when everyone brings less and less to them?" (*Passage,* 188). But her comment reminds us that Forster as homosexual outsider did not feel included in personal relationships and felt the need to wear a social mask. It also reminds the resistant reader aware of English class structure in the nineteenth and early twentieth centuries that many others were also excluded.

While hardly rivaling Gandhi, Forster played an important role in raising British consciousness about the effects of colonialism and helped pave the way for British withdrawal. His writing – his novel-length *passage* of writing – provided eloquent testimony to how English ideals were corrupted by self-created imperialistic myths often based upon racist assumptions. The English and Indians are in an imperialistic relationship based on dominance and subservience. Members of both the conquering and conquered nation are corrupted and diminished when a relatively small number of representatives of the dominant nation willfully exercise power to keep the entire population of the subservient nation in humiliating circumstances. For Forster, India is not only the setting for a novel, or even a metaphor for British imperialism, but an essential and troubling reality that he knows from personal experience.

Because the omniscient narrator expresses Forster's quest for values, he is a different kind of figure from the omniscient narrator in eighteenth-century fiction or Victorian fiction prior to Hardy. While Austen's values within her imagined world are relatively static, Forster's are continually undergoing change. Unlike Austen, he tests and sympathizes with a variety of value systems. While Austen *knows* from the outset the standards by which Emma falls short, and tells us in the first pages, Forster tentatively adopts, *seriatim,* the perspective of Fielding, Mrs Moore, and Godbole as he frustratingly searches not only for ways to alleviate the cultural and human gulf among Muslims, Hindus, and English, but also for a set of values to replace those that are dismayingly unsatisfactory in the face of what he is narrating. Thus we can say that whereas Austen's focus is on the moral development of her characters, Forster's is on making sense not only of the imagined world he has created but of the real or anterior world that informs it.

Forster dramatizes the transformation of his surrogate, the narrator. As the narrator learns that evil is as much in the human psyche – regardless of race – as in the caves, he realizes the England of Austen's novels – the customs and manners she evokes – is irrelevant to India. The telling becomes a *passage* if not to enlightenment, at least to understanding. That the narrator changes his values urges the narratee – the implied reader whom he addresses – to reconsider his or her attitudes toward India; thus the narrator's change of values becomes part of the novel's rhetoric of persuasion.

Unlike Austen's Highbury, India is more than a background for events in an imagined world. For Forster, India represents passion, poetry, and sexuality and thus offers the possibility of intimacy. India is often the novel's major character; as with Hardy's coming to terms with Sue or even Jude, Forster's coming to terms with his character India is presented in a complicated and even contradictory way that reflects the author's ambivalence. One might say that the difference between Austen's Highbury and Forster's India is the difference between Constable's eighteenth-century landscapes, depicting a scene such as Salisbury cathedral as it might have looked at an ideal moment, and the landscapes of such Postimpressionists as Cézanne and Van Gogh, who express the emotions of the painter more than they depict the actual or even idealized physical scene.

When we open a novel we enter an imagined world with its own cosmology and grammar of motives. *A Passage to India* has one of the most wonderful openings in the English novel. Its first chapter dramatizes the grim schisms that divide India, separating it into different nations occupying the same space at the same time but divided along racial, ethnic, and religious grounds. Forster has invented the geography, for there is no Chandrapore along the Ganges; nor do the caves he describes exist as the Marabar Caves.

In the first paragraph of part one of the three-part novel, entitled "Mosque," Chandrapore is defined by the narrator, as if he were within the streets, in terms of what the city is not:

Edged rather than washed by the river Ganges, it trails for a couple of miles along the bank, scarcely distinguishable from the rubbish it deposits so freely. There are no bathing-steps on the river front, as the Ganges happens not to be holy here; indeed there is no river front, and bazaars shut out the wide and shifting panorama of the stream. The streets are mean, the temples ineffective... The very wood seems made of mud, of mud moving... [T]he general outline of the town persists, swelling here, shrinking there, like some low but indestructible form of life. (p. 2)

Until the eighteenth century, Chandrapore had some stature, but it seems to be in a long period of continuing decline. Those readers who know the awesome beauty of India's geography and historical sites will respond to the deliberate reductive bathos – what we might call the rhetoric of nullification, dominated by words like "filth," "mud," and "low" – with which Forster describes this place. Within this India there seems to be no distinction between Muslim and Hindu.

But in the second paragraph the narrator, adopting a hawk's perspective and changing his optics to a view from above, introduces the reader to a different world; on the first rise are the houses of the Euro-Asians, and on the second the English rulers, and from their perspective Chandrapore looks entirely different: "It is a city of gardens. It is no city, but a forest sparsely scattered with huts. It is a tropical pleasance washed by a noble river" (p. 3). Trees soar

> to build a city for birds. Especially after the rains do [the trees] screen what passes below, but at all times, even when scorched and leafless, they glorify the city to the English people who inhabit the rise, so that new-comers cannot believe it to be as meagre as it is described, and have to be driven down to acquire disillusionment. (p. 3)

But the civil station on the second rise is itself described by negatives as if to emphasize its kinship with the land below and the people which it suppresses: "It charms not" and the best the narrator can concede is that "It has nothing hideous in it" (p. 3).

Within the first two paragraphs the narrator's perception of geography enacts the unbridgeable schism between the English and Indians, imperialists and colonial subjects. The dialogue between the Ganges river, vegetation, and sky – between the mud of Chandrapore, the ordering gardens, and the indifferent cosmos – mirrors the dialogue between three cultures that is the essence of the novel. Describing the sky, the stars, and the sun, the last two paragraphs of the opening chapter move to an even more distant perspective, one that anticipates the narrator's cosmological perspective which emphasizes the diminutive nature of humans and their relatively short presence on earth not merely as individuals but as a species. And, after stressing the "prostrate earth" with "no mountains," the chapter's last sentence introduces the last crucial element of the novel's geography: "League after league the earth lies flat, heaves a little, is flat again. Only in the south, where a group of fists and fingers are thrust up through the soil, is the endless expanse interrupted. These fists and fingers are the Marabar Hills, containing the extraordinary caves" (p. 4). Poignantly the narrator tries to anthropomorphize geography.

The caves become a metaphor for the timelessness of the geological cosmos and for the non-verbal world that preceded and will outlast humankind. Like

Hardy's Wessex geography, the caves are indifferent to human aspirations. Forster's narrator's description reveals the author's imaginative effort and even personal agony. It is as if the caves resist human description even though we are told that they are "readily described": "Nothing, nothing attaches to them and their reputation – for they have one – does not depend upon human speech" (p. 117). On the one hand, the caves depend upon oral and written language for their reputation and their significance. On the other hand, the very inadequacy of the language illustrates the mind's limitations as it confronts the unknown. Forster understands how we need to domesticate the sublime; thus the narrator recoils to personification as a way of containing and comprehending the caves: "Fist and fingers thrust above the advancing soil – here at last is their skin, finer than any covering acquired by the animals, smoother than windless water, more voluptuous than love. The radiance increases, the flames touch one another, kiss, expire. The cave is dark again, like all caves" (p. 118). By placing human events in a vast geological context, Forster reduces their proportion.

V   The Transformation of Values within *A Passage to India*

At the outset Forster embraces the code of Fielding, the teacher and liberal humanist who befriends Aziz. At first glance Fielding's code would not be out of place in an Austen novel: "The world, he believed, is a globe of men who are trying to reach one another and can best do so by the help of goodwill plus culture and intelligence – a creed ill suited to Chandrapore, but he had come out too late to lose it" (p. 56). Forster admires Fielding's self-control, decency, and fundamental courage (what he called "pluck" in the essay "What I Believe"). Fielding – the "holy man minus the holiness" – embodies the spirit of Bloomsbury's ideal of personal relationships. He is the epitome of liberal England, and the heir to the tradition of manners and morals: "I believe in teaching people to be individuals, and to understand other individuals. It's the only thing I do believe in" (p. 132). But no sooner do we think that the narrator has adopted or even fully endorsed the values of Fielding than he steps back and re-examines them.

Although not recognizing the homosocial and latent homosexual feelings that draw him to Aziz, Fielding himself is at least dimly aware that he lacks Aziz's passionate intensity and intuitive generosity: "[Fielding] wished that he too could be carried away on waves of emotion" (p. 109). Even though Forster later marries Fielding off, Fielding has no real interest in women and, indeed, "took no notice" of the wives of his colleagues (p. 56). Nor does Forster

249

acknowledge in his commentary that the attraction between Fielding and Aziz is mutual.

Even while *A Passage to India* provides a room with a view – to borrow from the title of Forster's 1908 novel set at the outset in Italy – Forster is redefining the equation of travel with learning *and* moral growth. That equation is an essential premise of much eighteenth- and nineteenth-century fiction and travel literature, from *Moll Flanders* and *Tom Jones* to *Jane Eyre* and *Great Expectations*. The equation is a version of the Protestant myth of self-improvement through experience and hard work.

In *Passage to India*, for the more perceptive of the English, travel is equated with education about the corrosive effects of imperialism. If we think of Fielding's self-image as a traveler, we realize the concept of traveling as an experience of learning but not necessarily growth or self-development is central to *A Passage to India*. Fielding's stature is reduced when he returns to England, marries, and becomes part of the hierarchy of English education in India, ironically proving his own contention that "Any man can travel light until he has a wife or children" (p. 112).

Even before Aziz's trial, after he has been wrongfully accused by Adela of molesting her, Forster's narrator begins to separate himself from Fielding and to reveal that Fielding's values provide only a partial perspective to understanding India and that his truths are partial truths. For the narrator shows us that Fielding lacks imagination, passion, and spiritual depth. We see this clearly when Fielding sees the caves from a distance. Failing to apprehend the sublime if terrifying beauty of the caves, he questions his life and values:

> After forty years' experience, he had learned to manage his life and make the best of it on advanced European lines, had developed his personality, explored its limitations, controlled his passions – and he had done it all without becoming either pedantic or worldly. A creditable achievement, but as the moment passed he felt he ought to have been working at something else the whole time – he didn't know at what, never would know, never could know, and that was why he felt sad. (p. 181)

Forster's style parodies the self-control and balance of Fielding's mind. Words like "manage," "developed," "explored," and "controlled" capture the essence of the liberal humanist view that life can be understood and mastered as if it were a space – or colony – to be mapped, explored, and conquered. Fielding avoids the Scylla and Charybdis of worldliness and pedantry. Yet the last sentence of the aforementioned quotation opens to Fielding and the reader the possibility that something more exists; a series of inconclusive and imprecise clauses give way to a recognition – indeed, a revelation – that his way is only one possible way and a limited one at that.

If I were to choose a paradigmatic vignette to show how Forster turns the novel of manners upside down, it would be this moment when he exposes the limitations of his erstwhile surrogate Fielding. Could we imagine Austen's Knightley in a moment of self-doubt, alone in a moral desert bereft of values? Finally, Fielding in India has no tradition of manners on which to rely; nor can he as an agnostic fall back on belief in a benevolent cosmos or the presence of God's Holy Plan. Fielding, we realize, is exposed and contained within a text in which, by tradition, he should be the hero. For has he not risked career and perhaps even his physical well-being in the interests of truth and fairness? Yet this apparently is not enough.

In his prior novels, Forster focused upon the plagues of moral relativism, materialism, and social snobbery, plagues which could be contained and perhaps partially controlled by the kind of values Fielding represents and articulates. But after the trial at which Aziz is exonerated, the narrator stresses that Fielding's liberal humanism is one of several possible sets of values. In the last part of "Caves" and in "Temple," Forster is questioning not only Fielding's values but the values to which he had dedicated his prior novels – the primacy of personal relationships and the necessity of understanding one another; these values are epitomized by the famous epigraph to *Howards End*, "Only connect."

Yet finally in *A Passage to India* humanism triumphs, if in a reduced and more modest version. As Godbole and Mrs Moore are tested and ultimately discarded as prophets, the narrative voice again becomes the spokesman for the values of humanism – moderation, tolerance, tact, integrity, and respect for others. The narrator's own language presents the unity and balance that life in India – life anywhere – lacks.

Despite Mrs Moore's early empathy for Aziz, she ultimately deserts him as she puts aside relations with people and withdraws into her self. After her experience in the caves, she turns her back on human ties:

What had spoken to her in that scoured-out cavity of granite? What dwelt in the first of the caves? Something very old and very small. Before time, it was before space also. Something snub-nosed, incapable of generosity – the undying worm itself . . . Visions are supposed to entail profundity, but – wait till you get one, dear reader! The abyss also may be petty, the serpent of eternity made of maggots. (p. 198)

Godbole's Hindu vision in "Temple" is an effort to overcome the implications of her vision and transcend the time and space that define existence and most human consciousness. While the narrator understands Mrs Moore's impatience with life he cannot endorse it because finally it involves selfish desertion of her friend Aziz: "She had come to that state where the horror of the universe and its smallness are both visible at the same time – the twilight of the double vision in which so many elderly people are involved" (p. 197). For Forster, spiritual self-realization cannot come at the expense of human relations. Indeed, he may be indicting the sanctimony of Christianity: "Her Christian tenderness had gone, or had developed into a hardness, a just irritation against the human race: she had taken no interest at the arrest, asked scarcely any questions" (p. 190).

Her mythic identity as "Esmiss Esmoor" that she takes on for Indians – as if she were a kind of minor Hindu goddess – has nothing to do with her actual behavior. That her disdain for human relations parallels Godbole's cosmic perspective is strongly ironic. Forster's characterization of Mrs Moore is a wonderful and rare depiction of the process of the later stages of aging as subtraction from community and preparation for death. Her self-immersion represents a serious failure of the "connection" – to use Forster's term – that binds one human to another. Whatever the excuse, does Mrs Moore not commit what for Forster is the heresy of deserting her friend?

A fundamental paradox of the text is that Forster's own prose has difficulty aligning itself with unspoken mysteries and spiritual values. Yet the celebratory and performative religious ritual of "Temple" is an effort to move beyond the concatenation of events on which traditional Western narrative is based. Within "Temple," we might (somewhat reductively) say that we can locate a double perspective: (1) the external perspective of a secular but open-minded skeptic, whose view, like Fielding's, is predicated on interest in other cultures and who earnestly desires to understand the unfathomable mysteries of other cultures; (2) the inner vision of someone, who, like Godbole, is experiencing a revelation of the transcendent unity of the cosmos as he participates in the performance ritual of the birth of SHRI KIRISHNA. (It is worth remembering that Krishna, the seventh incarnation of Vishnu, is with Rama one of the two gods who embodies humanity and, in the epic *Mahabharata*, is the god who intercedes on behalf of heroes).

The dialectic between the echo in the cave – representing inexplicable evil and the absence of good – and the Hindu religion – representing a quest to transcend the individual by overcoming the limitations of space and time and unite with a universal soul – is central to Forster's effort to introduce what he calls "prophecy" in his *Aspects of the Novel*. In the ending to *A Passage to India*, he strives for "expansion" and "opening out," by which he means a movement that takes the reader beyond space and temporal limitations of narrative to a performative ecstasy: "Expansion. That is the idea that the novelist must cling to. Not completion. Not rounding off but opening out. When the symphony is over we feel that the notes and tunes composing have been liberated, they have found in the rhythm of the whole their individual freedom" (*Aspects*, 116).

Godbole's stature as a prophetic figure is undermined by his human failures. As a Brahmin, he "had never been known to tell anyone anything" (p. 295). He is no help to Aziz when he is falsely accused; later he allows Aziz to believe Fielding has married Adela when in fact Fielding has married Mrs Moore's daughter. Aziz's misconception leads him into foolish and even humiliating behavior. Although Forster's narrator does at times take a geological and historical perspective that minimizes human presence as a small blip in time, the novel finally rejects Godbole's hawk's-eye view of human behavior or at the most sees it as one discursive formation. According to Godbole:

> When evil occurs, it expresses the whole of the universe. Similarly when good occurs . . . Good and evil are different, as their names imply. But, in my humble opinion, they are both aspects of my Lord. He is present in the one, absent in the other, and the difference between presence and absence is great, as great as my feeble mind can grasp. Yet absence implies presence, presence is not non-existence, and we are therefore entitled to repeat, "Come, come, come, come." (p. 169)

Just as Fielding's rationalism and control have their limits, so do Godbole's ascetic spirituality and ability to thrust himself out of himself. With gentle irony, Forster examines the Hindu concept that supreme divinity can be found in any object by being worshipped at one moment by one particular person. For even Godbole cannot meditate upon the stone: "He loved the wasp equally, he impelled it likewise, he was imitating God. And the stone, where the wasp clung – could he . . . no, he could not, he had been wrong to attempt the stone, logic and conscious effort had seduced" (p. 277).

Godbole's long view seems to be patronizing if not dismissive of the manners and passions of individuals, and human life is what interests Forster. He views Godbole's spiritualism as another of humankind's working arrangements. The Hindu celebration is an outlet for very human and even animal passions and instincts. To perform the rajah's holy journey after he dies, the Hindus simply – and to skeptical Western eyes perhaps bathetically – make an effigy of him, but is that so different from the faith required to believe in the Eucharist? If at first the novel seems to reject Fielding's liberal humanism, it gradually shows that the alternatives are no better. That religion is not a living force binding humans to one another within a community is illustrated by

Godbole's human failures. Like Mrs Moore, he has subtracted himself from a human community in his search for something more. Thus Fielding's humanism may have a qualified triumph, after all, when we realize the effects of being "one with the universe" as exemplified by Mrs Moore's and Godbole's indifference to other people (p. 198).

Mrs Moore's son Ralph is the Western correlative to the "untouchable" Indian who turns the fan in the courtroom. Do not Ralph's simple vocabulary, depth of feeling, and intuitive understanding of Hindu rituals comment upon the verbosity of the Muslims and the complicated motives of the English? Although he "appeared almost an imbecile," Ralph instinctively understands Aziz's hostility; by telling Aziz that his mother loved him, he is the catalyst for Aziz's temporary, if tense, reconciliation with Fielding. And perhaps he anticipates Forster's final verdict – "not yet" – on the possibility of lasting reconciliation. That wisdom becomes the province of the unwitting in Ralph – and in several figures such as Emerson (*Room with a View*), Gino (*Where Angels Fear to Tread*), Stephen Wonham (*The Longest Journey*) – is an aspect of Forster's rebellion against utilitarianism, progress, and moral education.

VI Conclusion

Forster needs to be understood in the context of the other major Modernists. He found Hardy a most congenial novelist because Hardy's third-person narrator is an evolving character and because Hardy transformed apparent realism into mythic episodes by means of illuminating distortion. If in *A Passage to India* we hear Lawrence's bardic voice and prophetic tones, we also realize that Forster, like Conrad, is fascinated by non-Western cultures and faces the problem of how to cope with a purposeless, amoral, indifferent universe.

Forster's originality has to be seen in the context of the other major writers of the period – Conrad, Lawrence, Joyce, and Woolf. In Victorian fiction, characters are defined by their relationship within a community. In modern British and Irish fiction the characters are defined by alienation from that community. In *The Turn of the Novel*, Alan Friedman writes:

> It may not be too soon to suggest that whatever the causes, older assumptions about character, society, and career have already given place to newer ones; that self and world, sequence and consequence, if not in life at least in fiction, have been restructured; that, in short, we have been witnessing a mutation in the form of the novel which corresponds to a mutation in the ends of culture. (p. xiii)[7]

The major Modernists, like their characters, oscillate among contradictory attitudes: longing for a past that cannot be recaptured and detesting the world that has displaced that past, while welcoming social change and trying to come to terms with a more complex present. The major characters' quest for self-understanding is still the essence of the English novel from 1890 to 1930, but the focus now is on the desperation of that quest, not the attainment of that goal. That quest reflects the authors' own uncertainty, frustration, and anxiety.

The stress on private values, on restoring family relationships, and on developing personal relationships that matter is another characteristic of the novel in the 1890–1930 period; it is an alternative to the Victorian novel's faith that community life can provide a social and moral fabric for each individual. The traditional novel's omniscient narrator depends for its effects upon the incongruity between what the narrator says and what the character thinks. But when the narrator's values are not stable and consistent, that irony breaks down and we feel the author as a formal presence within the text. Like his contemporaries Conrad, Lawrence, and Joyce, Forster believed that human truth must inevitably be partial, a matter of perspective.

Writing in 1924, Virginia Woolf insisted in "Mr Bennett and Mrs Brown" that the Georgian writers needed to abandon the "tools" and "conventions" of their Edwardian predecessors because the latter "have laid an enormous stress on the fabric of things": "At the present moment we are suffering, not from decay, but from having no code of manners which writers and readers accept as a prelude to the more exciting intercourse of friendship . . . Grammar is violated, syntax disintegrated."[8] Forster does not violate grammar and syntax. His style has more in common with Austen, Fielding, and James than with the comparatively pedestrian journalistic prose of Bennett, Wells, and Galsworthy or the experiments with diction and syntax of Joyce and Lawrence. He shows how polished, precise use of literate discourse can both render the inner life – feelings, passions, subconscious needs – and, particularly in his last two novels, create the prophetic note that he sought. Forster's conversational prose, his leisurely pace, his self-confidence, his lucid, unpretentious diction and poised syntax, imply the very humanistic values he espoused. While Conrad, Lawrence, Joyce, and Woolf sought new forms and syntax, Forster shows that the English language and its novel genre already had the resources to examine the life of instincts and passions.

Notes

Introduction: Reading the Modern British and Irish Novel 1890–1930

1 John Elderfield, *Henri Matisse: A Retrospective* (New York: Museum of Modern Art, 1992), p. 26.
2 Charles Altieri, *Painterly Abstraction in Modernist American Poetry: The Contemporaneity of Modernism* (Cambridge: Cambridge University Press, 1989), p. 378.
3 David Richards, "The Jackhammer Voice of Mamet's 'Oleanna,'" *New York Times Arts and Leisure* (November 8, 1992), p. 5.
4 Paul Fussell, *The Great War and Modern Memory* (Oxford: Oxford University Press, 1975), p. 8.
5 Kenneth Silver, *Esprit de Corps: The Art of the Parisian Avant-Garde and the First World War, 1914–25* (Princeton, NJ: Princeton University Press, 1989), p. 35.
6 James Clifford, *The Predicament of Culture: Twentieth-Century Ethnography, Literature, and Art* (Cambridge, MA: Harvard University Press, 1988), p. 117.
7 Clifford, *Predicament*, pp. 92–3.
8 Elderfield, *Matisse*, p. 203.
9 T. S. Eliot, *Selected Essays* (New York: Harcourt, Brace and World, 1960), p. 4.
10 Quoted in Phillip Marcus, *Yeats and Artistic Power* (New York: New York University Press, 1992), p. 1.
11 Marcus, *Yeats*, p. 8.
12 Quoted in G. di San Lazzaro, *Klee: His Life and Work* (London: Thames and Hudson, 1957), p. 112.
13 Pepe Karmel, "Symbolism's Voyage into Despair and Back," *New York Times* (August 27, 1995), p. 31.
14 Quoted in di San Lazzaro, *Klee*, p. 105.
15 Quoted in Richard Ellmann and Charles Feidelson Jr (eds.), *The Modern Tradition: Backgrounds of Modern Literature* (New York: Oxford University Press, 1965), p. 145.
16 Quoted in Ellmann and Fiedelson, *Modern Tradition*, p. 725.
17 Ibid., p. 725.

18 See Richard Ellmann, *Oscar Wilde* (New York: Alfred A. Knopf, 1988).

19 Quoted by Jack Flam, *Matisse: The Man and his Art, 1869–1918* (Ithaca, NY, and London: Cornell University Press, 1986), p. 37.

20 Flam, *Man and his Art*, p. 17.

21 Julian Barnes, "The Proudest and Most Arrogant Man in France," *New York Review of Books*, 39:17 (October 22, 1992), 3–5, see p. 3.

22 Quotations refer to *Ulysses: A Critical and Synoptic Edition*, ed. Hans Walter Gabler with Wolfhard Steppe and Claus Melchior (New York and London: Garland, 1984). Episode and line number refer to the Gabler edition. Where there is a change in the Gabler edition from the 1961 Random House edition, I have underlined the episode and line number.

Chapter 1 "I Was the World in Which I Walked": The Transformation of the British and Irish Novel, 1890–1930

1 Quoted in Alfred E. Elsen, *Rodin* (New York: Museum of Modern Art, 1963), p. 93.

2 Elsen, *Rodin*, p. 101.

3 Quoted in Elsen, p. 102.

4 F. H. Bradley, *Appearance and Reality: A Metaphysical Essay*, 2nd edn (London: S. Sonnechein, 1908), p. 346.

5 J. Hillis Miller, *The Form of Victorian Fiction* (Notre Dame: University of Notre Dame Press, 1968), p. 5.

6 Patricia Meyer Spacks, "Introduction," in *The Author in his Work*, eds. Louis L. Martz and Aubrey Williams (New Haven, CT: Yale University Press, 1978), p. xv.

7 Virginia Woolf, "Mr Bennett and Mrs Brown" (1924), in *The Captain's Death Bed and Other Essays* (New York: Harcourt, Brace, 1950), p. 117.

8 Joseph Conrad, *A Personal Record* (1912) (New York: Doubleday, 1926), p. xv.

9 *The Letters of D. H. Lawrence*, ed. Aldous Huxley (New York: Viking Press, 1932), April 22, 1914, p. 19.

10 Spacks, "Introduction," p. xii.

11 Woolf, "Mr Bennett and Mr. Brown," pp. 96–7.

12 Samuel Hynes, *The Edwardian Turn of Mind* (Princeton, NJ: Princeton University Press, 1968), p. 326.

13 Vincent Van Gogh, fall 1995 exhibition comment accompanying "Self-Portrait with Straw Hat" (1887), André Meyer Galleries of Metropolitan Museum of Art, New York.

14 *Great Victorian Paintings* (London: Arts Council, 1968), p. 7.

15 Woolf, "The Russian Point of View," in *The Common Reader: First Series* (New York: Harcourt, Brace and World, 1925), p. 182.

16 Woolf, *The Common Reader*, p. 157.

17 See E. M. Forster, *Aspects of the Novel* (New York: Harcourt, Brace and World, 1954; orig. edn 1927), pp. 130–5.

18 George Dangerfield, *The Strange Death of Liberal England* (New York: Putnam, 1980), p. 366.
19 Noel Annan, "The Intellectual Aristocracy," in J. H. Plumb (ed.), *Studies in Social History: A Tribute to George Trevelyan* (London and New York: Longmans, Green, 1955), pp. 252–3.
20 Wilfred Stone, *The Cave and the Mountain: A Study of E. M. Forster* (Palo Alto, CA: Stanford University Press, 1966), p. 19.
21 Woolf, "Mr Bennett and Mrs Brown," p. 105.
22 Malcolm Bradbury, *Possibilities: Essays on the State of the Novel* (New York: Oxford University Press, 1973), p. 84.
23 Miller, *Victorian Fiction*, p. 63.
24 Quoted in Quentin Bell, *Virginia Woolf: A Biography* (New York: Harcourt, Brace, Jovanovich, 1972), vol. II, p. 73.
25 Virginia Woolf, *To the Lighthouse* (New York: Harcourt, Brace and World, 1927), p. 236.
26 Woolf, *To the Lighthouse*, p. 241.
27 Hilton Kramer, "The Picasso Show," *New York Times* (October 12, 1980).
28 *The Diary of Virginia Woolf*, vol. III: 1925–30, ed. Anne Oliver Bell with Andrew McNeillie (New York: Harcourt, Brace, Jovanovich, 1980), November 28, 1928, pp. 209–10.
29 Wallace Stevens, *Collected Poems* (New York: Alfred A. Knopf, 1954), pp. 473–4
30 *The Letters of D. H. Lawrence*, January 29, 1914, p. 180.

Chapter 2 Hardy's *Jude the Obscure*: The Beginnings of the Modern Psychological Novel

1 Florence Emily Hardy, *The Early Life of Thomas Hardy, 1840–1891* (London and New York: Macmillan, 1928), p. 293.
2 See Scott Elledge (ed.), Norton Critical Edition of *Tess of the d'Urbervilles* (New York: Norton, 1965), p. 19.
3 M. H. Abrams, "English Romanticism: the Spirit of the Age," in Harold Bloom (ed.), *Romanticism and Consciousness* (New York: Norton, 1970), p. 103.
4 *Joseph Conrad's Letters to R. B. Cunninghame Graham*, ed. C. T. Watts (Cambridge: Cambridge University Press, 1969), pp. 56–7.
5 Ian Gregor, "What Kind of Fiction did Hardy Write?," *Essays in Criticism*, 16 (1966), 290–308.
6 Page references are to *Jude the Obscure*, ed. Norman Page, Norton Critical Edition, 2nd edn (New York: Norton, 1999).
7 Elizabeth Langland, "Becoming a Man in *Jude the Obscure*," in Margaret R. Higonnet (ed.), *The Sense of Sex: Feminist Perspectives in Hardy* (Urbana and Chicago: University of Illinois Press, 1992), p. 34.
8 Langland, "Becoming a Man," p. 36.

9   Langland, "Becoming a Man," p. 43.

10 For a somewhat different version of why Hardy stopped writing, a version that stresses his search for camaraderie as a basis for relationships between sexes, see H. M. Daleski, *Thomas Hardy: Parodoxes of Love* (Columbia, MO, and London: University of Missouri Press, 1990), especially p. 204.

Chapter 3   Conrad's *Heart of Darkness*: "We Live, as We Dream – Alone"

1   Page numbers in parentheses refer to Joseph Conrad, *Heart of Darkness*, Kent edition (Garden City, NY: Doubleday, 1926).

2   Letter of March 26, 1897, in *Collected Letters of Joseph Conrad, vol. 1, 1861–1897*, eds. Frederick Karl and Laurence Davies (New York: Cambridge University Press, 1983), p. 347.

3   Ernst Cassirer, *The Logic of the Humanities*, trans. Clarence Smith Howe (New Haven, CT: Yale University Press, 1961), p. 58.

4   See Adam Hochschild, *King Leopold's Ghost: A Story of Greed, Terror, and Heroism in Central Africa* (Boston: Houghton Mifflin, 1998).

5   Chinua Achebe, "An Image of Africa," *Massachusetts Review*, 18 (1977), 782–94.

6   Letter to Edward Noble, November 2, 1895, in *Collected Letters, vol. 1*, p. 253.

7   Cleo McNelly, "Natives, Women, and Claude Lévi-Strauss: A Reading of Tristes Tropiques as Myth," *Massachusetts Review*, 16 (1975), 7–29, p. 25.

8   Edward Said, *Culture and Imperialism* (New York: Alfred A. Knopf, 1993), p. 25.

9   Said, *Culture and Imperialism*, p. 30.

10 F. H. Bradley, *Appearance and Reality: A Metaphysical Essay*, 2nd edn (London: S. Sonnechein, 1908), p. 346.

11 Letter to R. B. Cunninghame Graham, December 20, 1897, in *Collected Letters, vol. 1*, p. 425.

12 Patrick Brantlinger, *Rule of Darkness: British Literature and Imperialism, 1830–1914* (Ithaca, NY: Cornell University Press, 1988), p. 271.

13 Martha Nussbaum, "Perceptive Equilibrium: Literary Theory and Ethical Theory," in Ralph Cohen (ed.), *The Future of Literary Theory* (New York: Routledge, 1988), p. 61.

Chapter 4   Conrad's *Lord Jim*: Reading Texts, Reading Lives

1   J. Hillis Miller, *Fiction and Repetition: Seven English Novels* (Cambridge, MA: Harvard University Press, 1982), pp. 39–40.

2   In *Collected Letters of Joseph Conrad, vol. I, 1861–1897*, eds. Frederick Karl and Laurence Davies (New York: Cambridge University Press, 1983), p. 425.

3   Ibid., p. 253.

4 Page numbers in parentheses refer to the Norton Critical Edition of *Lord Jim*, ed. Thomas Moser (New York: Norton, 1968).
5 I discuss Marlow's shortcomings in greater detail in my book *Conrad: "Almayer's Folly" Through "Under Western Eyes"* (Ithaca, NY: Cornell University Press; London: Macmillan, 1980). See my *Lord Jim* chapter, pp. 76–97.
6 Douglas Hofstadter, *Gödel, Escher, Bach: An Eternal Golden Braid* (New York: Basic Books, 1979).
7 Geoffrey Hartman, "The Culture of Criticism," *PMLA*, 99:3 (May 1984), 371–97, p. 386.

Chapter 5 Lawrence's *Sons and Lovers*: Speaking of Paul Morel: Voice, Unity, and Meaning

1 The first quotation is from a review that appeared in the *Saturday Review* (London), June 21, 1913, and the second from an anonymous review in the *Athenaeum*, June 21, 1913. Both are reprinted in *Sons and Lovers: Text, Background, and Criticism*, ed. Julian Moynahan (New York: Viking Press, 1968). Page numbers in parentheses refer to the Moynahan edition.
2 See Schorer's brilliant essay "Technique as Discovery," *Hudson Review*, 1 (spring 1948), 67–87; partially repr. in E. W. Tedlock, Jr (ed.), *D. H. Lawrence and Sons and Lovers* (New York: New York University Press, 1965), pp. 164–9.

   According to Schorer, the problem derives from Paul and his creator simultaneously loving the mother and hating her for "compelling" his love:

> This is a psychological tension which disrupts the form of the novel and obscures its meaning, because neither the contradiction in style nor confusion in point of view is made to right itself. Lawrence is merely repeating his emotions, and he avoids an austerer technical scrutiny of his material because it would compel him to master them. He would not let the artist be stronger than the man . . .
>
> Lawrence could not separate the investigating analyst, who must be objective, from Lawrence, the subject of the book; and the sickness was not healed, the emotion not mastered, the novel not perfected. All this, and the character of a whole career, would have been altered if Lawrence had allowed his technique to discover the fullest meaning of his subject. (Tedlock, *Lawrence and Sons and Lovers*, pp. 168–9)

3 Louis L. Martz, "Portrait of Miriam: A Study in the Design of *Sons and Lovers*," in Maynard Mack and Ian Gregor (eds.), *Imagined Worlds: Essays on Some English Novels and Novelists in Honour of John Butt* (New York: Methuen, 1968), p. 351.

4   *The Collected Letters of D. H. Lawrence*, ed. Harry T. Moore, 2 vols. (New York: Viking Press, 1962); repr. in Tedlock, *Lawrence and Sons and Lovers*, p. 14.

5   In part two, Lawrence is experimenting with the heightened imagistic language that becomes so characteristic of his technique. When Lawrence's prose becomes incantational and lyrical, and ceases to concern itself with presentation of dramatic scenes or with descriptions, *Sons and Lovers* most approaches the great prophetic novels, *The Rainbow* and *Women in Love*. The cancelled foreword shows how even with regard to his autobiographical novel, he was attracted to mystical and visionary explanations disguised as polemic and dialectical argument.

6   Twice within a few pages, the narrator tries to place Paul's situation within a dialectical framework. First, he argues that Paul's sexual problem is a common one: "He was like so many young men of his own age. Sex had become so complicated in him that he would have denied that he could ever want Clara or Miriam or any woman that he *knew*" (p. 276; emphasis Lawrence's). A few moments later he pursues this point:

> He looked around. A good many of the nicest men he knew were like himself, bound in by their own virginity, which they could not break out of. They were so sensitive to their women that they would go without them forever rather than do them a hurt, an injustice. Being the sons of mothers whose husbands had blundered rather brutally through their feminine sanctities, they were themselves too diffident and shy. They could easier deny themselves than incur any reproach from a woman; for a woman was like their mother, and they were full of the sense of their mother. (p. 279)

7   D. H. Lawrence, *Psychoanalysis and the Unconscious* and *Fantasia of the Unconscious* (New York: Viking Press, 1960), pp. 155–6.

8   While writing his next novel, *The Rainbow*, Lawrence was still very much concerned with convincing himself of the frequency of sexual and passionate relationships between parent and child of the opposite sex; witness Tom Brangwen's love for his stepdaughter Anna and Will's for Ursula.

9   The extent to which atonement to his father is important to Lawrence is indicated by both the substance and tone of the following remarks in *Fantasia of the Unconscious*: "It is despicable for any one parent to accept a child's sympathy against the other parent. And the one who *received* the sympathy is always more contemptible than the one who is hated" (p. 131; emphasis Lawrence's).

10 *Collected Letters* I, pp. 160–1; repr. in Moynahan, *Sons and Lovers: Text, Background, and Criticism*, p. 492.

11 As Harry T. Moore has pointed out, the word should probably be "whimpered" instead of "whispered," because it occurs in Lawrence's final manuscript and "in the first and several other editions published in his lifetime" (Tedlock, *Lawrence and Sons and Lovers*, p. 63).

12 One cannot dismiss Jessie Chamber's perceptive complaint:

Either he was aware of what he was doing and persisted, or he did not know, and in that case no amount of telling would enlighten him. It was one of the things he had to find out for himself. The baffling truth, of course, lay between the two. He was aware, but he was under the spell of the domination that had ruled his life hitherto, and he refused to know. So instead of a release and a deliverance from bondage, the bondage was glorified and made absolute. His mother conquered indeed, but the vanquished one was her son. In *Sons and Lovers* Lawrence handed his mother the laurels of victory. (Jessie Chambers, *D. H. Lawrence: A Personal Record, by "E. T."*, 2nd rev. edn [New York: Barnes and Noble, 1965]; repr. in Moynahan, *Sons and Lovers: Text, Background, and Criticism*, p. 482).

Chapter 6   Lawrence's *The Rainbow*: Family Chronicle, Sexual Fulfillment, and the Quest for Form and Values

1   *The Letters of D. H. Lawrence*, ed. Aldous Huxley (New York: Viking Press, 1932), p. 191.
2   *Phoenix: The Posthumous Papers of D. H. Lawrence*, ed. Edward P. McDonald (New York: Viking Press, 1936), pp. 529, 532, 535. Published as "Morality and the Novel," in *Calendar of Modern Letters* (December 1925). Unless otherwise indicated, selections from *Phoenix* were unpublished in Lawrence's lifetime. See also Lawrence, *Study of Thomas Hardy and Other Essays*, ed. Bruce Steele (Cambridge: Cambridge University Press, 1985).
3   For a splendid discussion of the evolution of *The Rainbow* and *Women in Love*, see Mark Kinkead-Weekes, "The Marble and the Statue: The Exploratory Imagination of D. H. Lawrence," in Maynard Mack and Ian Gregor (eds.), *Imagined Worlds: Essays on Some English Novels and Novelists in Honor of John Butt* (London: Methuen, 1968), pp. 371–418.
4   Emile Delavenay, *D. H. Lawrence, The Man and his Work: The Formative Years 1885–1919*, trans. Katherine M. Delavenay (Carbondale: Southern Illinois University Press, 1972), p. 255.
5   Page references are to D. H. Lawrence, *The Rainbow* (New York: Viking Press, 1962).
6   Quoted in Kinkead-Weekes, "Marble and the Statue," p. 372, from an autumn 1913 letter in *The Collected Letters of D. H. Lawrence*, 2 vols., ed. Harry T. Moore (New York: Viking Press, 1962), I, p. 241.
7   For a fuller discussion of *kairos* and *chronos*, see Frank Kermode, *The Sense of an Ending: Studies in the Theory of Fiction* (New York: Oxford University Press, 1967).
8   See Lawrence, "The Study of Thomas Hardy," in *Phoenix*, pp. 446–8.
9   For discussion of how "Study of Thomas Hardy," written in 1914 but unpublished until after Lawrence's death, is central to Lawrence, see H. M. Daleski's *The*

Forked Flame (Evanston, IL: Northwestern, 1965), pp. 18–41. For discussion of how "Study of Thomas Hardy" specifically informs *The Rainbow*, see Daleski, *Forked Flame*, pp. 74–125.

10 In "Study of Thomas Hardy," Lawrence writes, "[the wild poppy] has . . . achieved its complete poppy-self . . . It has uncovered its red. Its light, itself, has risen and shone out, has run on the winds for a moment. It is splendid" (*Phoenix*, pp. 403–4).

Chapter 7   Joyce's *Dubliners*: Moral Paralysis in Dublin

1 Mary Gordon, "How Ireland Hid its Own Dirty Laundry," *New York Sunday Times*, section II, (3 August, 2003), 1–18, see p. 18.

2 Quoted by Mary Reynolds, *Dante and Joyce* (Princeton, NJ: Princeton University Press, 1981), p. 220.

3 James Joyce, *A Portrait of the Artist as a Young Man*, Viking Critical Edition, ed. Chester G. Anderson (New York: Viking Press, 1968).

4 Bakhtin's concept of heteroglossia is particularly useful to discuss the dialogues among styles in "Araby" (see M. M. Bakhtin, *The Dialogic Imagination*, ed. Michael Holquist, trans. Caryl Emerson and Michael Holquist [Austin: University of Texas Press, 1981], pp. 261–3, 291–2).

5 Gordon, "How Ireland Hid its Own Dirty Laundry," p. 18.

6 Richard Ellmann, *James Joyce*, rev. edn (New York: Oxford University Press, 1984), p. 247.

7 Page references are to *James Joyce's "The Dead,"* ed. Daniel R. Schwarz (New York: Bedford Books of St Martin's, 1996).

8 R. D. Laing, *The Divided Self: An Existential Study in Sanity and Madness* (Baltimore: Penguin, 1965), p. 4.

9 Jacques Lacan, *The Four Fundamental Concepts of Psycho-Analysis*, ed. Jacques-Alain Miller, trans. Alan Sheridan (New York: Norton, 1981), p. 101.

10 Garry Leonard, "Joyce and Lacan: The 'Woman' as a Symptom of 'Masculinity' in 'The Dead,'" *James Joyce Quarterly*, 28.2 (1991), 451–72, pp. 451, 460.

11 T. S. Eliot, "*Ulysses*, Order, and Myth," *Dial*, 75 (November 1923), 480–3; repr. as "Myth and Literary Classicism," in Richard Ellmann and Charles Feidelson, Jr (eds.), *The Modern Tradition: Backgrounds of Modern Literature* (New York: Oxford University Press, 1965), pp. 675–81.

12 Vincent P. Pecora, "'The Dead' and the Generosity of the Word," *PMLA*, 101.2 (1986), 233–45, p. 243.

13 Florence Walzl, "Gabriel and Michael: The Conclusion to 'The Dead,'" *James Joyce Quarterly*, 4 (1966), 17–31; quoted in *Dubliners: Text, Criticism, and Notes*, eds. Robert Scholes and A. Walton Litz. (New York: Viking Press, 1968), p. 433.

14 In *Portrait*, we recall Stephen dreams that he no longer exists: "How strange to think of him passing out of existence in such a way, not by death but by fading out in the sun or being lost or forgotten somewhere in the universe" (p. 89).

And in the "Hades" episode of *Ulysses*, Bloom descends into his own hell which includes the fear that he will no longer exist, but Bloom – far more emphatically than Gabriel – returns because of his resilience and coherence, because his ego negotiates effectively between his id and superego.

Chapter 8 Joyce's *Ulysses*: The Odyssey of Leopold Bloom and Stephen Dedalus on June 16, 1904

1 Quoted in Richard Ellmann, *James Joyce* (New York: Oxford University Press, 1982; orig. edn 1959), p. 163; from Stanislaus Joyce, *My Brother's Keeper: James Joyce's "Early Years,"* ed. Richard Ellmann (New York: Viking Press, 1958), pp. 103–4.
2 Quotations refer to *Ulysses: A Critical and Synoptic Edition*, eds Hans Walter Gabler with Wolfhard Steppe and Claus Melchior (New York: Vintage, 1984). I have included page references to the 1961 Random House edition, prefixed "U." Where there is a change in the Gabler edition from the Random House edition, I have underlined the episode and line number.
3 Ellmann, *James Joyce*, p. 358.
4 Page references are to the Viking Critical Edition of *A Portrait of the Artist as a Young Man*, text corrected Chester G. Anderson and ed. Richard Ellmann (New York: Viking Press, 1964). A capital "P" will indicate future references to *Portrait*.
5 *The Odyssey*, trans. and ed. Albert Cook (New York: Norton, 1967), IX.106–13.
6 *The Letters of James Joyce*, vol. 1, ed. Stuart Gilbert (New York: Viking Press, 1957), pp. 138–9.
7 *Selected Letters of James Joyce*, ed. Richard Ellmann (New York: Viking Press, 1975), p. 169.
8 Among the important more recent work done on Irish contexts is Maria Tymoczko's *The Irish "Ulysses"* (Berkeley: University of California Press, 1994), and Vincent J. Cheng has written well about the post-colonial implications of *Ulysses* in *Joyce, Race, and Empire* (Cambridge: Cambridge University Press, 1995).

Chapter 9 Woolf's *Mrs Dalloway*: Sexual Repression, Madness, and Social Form

1 I quote from *The Diaries of Virginia Woolf*, 4 vols., ed. Anne Oliver Bell (New York: Harcourt, Brace, Jovanovich, 1977–82) and *The Letters of Virginia Woolf*, 6 vols., ed. Nigel Nicholson (New York: Harcourt, Brace, Jovanovich, 1975–80). I also quote from *A Room of One's Own* (New York: Harcourt, Brace and World, 1929). When I quote from the text of Woolf's novels, page numbers in parentheses refer to *Mrs Dalloway* (New York: Harcourt, Brace and World, 1925), and *To the Lighthouse* (New York: Harcourt, Brace and World, 1927).

2   See Quentin Bell, *Virginia Woolf: A Biography*, 2 vols. (New York: Harcourt, Brace, Jovanovich, 1972), II, 107.
3   Quentin Bell, *Virginia Woolf*, II, 135–6.
4   December 20, 1897, letter to Cunninghame Graham, in *Collected Letters of Joseph Conrad, vol. 1, 1861–1897*, eds. Frederick Karl and Laurence Davies (New York: Cambridge University Press, 1983).
5   Leonard Woolf, *Beginning Again: An Autobiography of the Years 1911 to 1918* (New York: Harcourt, Brace and World, 1964).

Chapter 10   Woolf's *To the Lighthouse*: Choreographing Life and Creating Art as Time Passes

1   Roger Poole, *The Unknown Virginia Woolf* (New York: Cambridge University Press, 1978), p. 14.
2   When I quote from the text of Woolf's novels, page numbers in parentheses refer to *Mrs Dalloway* (New York: Harcourt, Brace and World, 1925) and *To the Lighthouse* (New York: Harcourt, Brace and World, 1927). See Quentin Bell, *Virginia Woolf: A Biography*, 2 vols. (New York: Harcourt, Brace, Jovanovich, 1972), II, 107, and II, 135–6.
3   Poole, *Unknown Virginia Woolf*, pp. 260–1.
4   I quote from *The Diaries of Virginia Woolf*, 4 vols., ed. Anne Oliver Bell (New York: Harcourt, Brace, Jovanovich, 1977–82), and *The Letters of Virginia Woolf*, 6 vols., ed. Nigel Nicholson (New York: Harcourt, Brace, Jovanovich, 1975–80).
5   Poole, *Unknown Virginia Woolf*, p. 33.
6   Leonard Woolf, *The Journey Not the Arrival Matters: An Autobiography of the Years 1939–1969* (New York: Harcourt, Brace, Jovanovich, 1970), p. 73; quoted in Poole, *Unknown Virginia Woolf*, p. 23.
7   Sir Isaiah Berlin, *The Hedgehog and the Fox: An Essay on Tolstoy's View of History* (New York: Simon and Schuster, 1955), p. 1.
8   See, for example, Avrom Fleishman's discussion of *To the Lighthouse* in his *Virginia Woolf: A Critical Reading* (Baltimore: Johns Hopkins University Press, 1975).
9   John Elderfield, *Henri Matisse: A Retrospective* (New York: Museum of Modern Art, 1992), p. 60.
10 See Poole, *Unknown Virginia Woolf*, p. 269.
11 See Bell, *Virginia Woolf*, II, 109–10.

Chapter 11   Forster's *Passage to India*: The Novel of Manners as Political Novel

1   Lionel Stevenson, *The English Novel: A Panorama* (Boston: Houghton Mifflin, 1960).
2   Walter Allen, *The English Novel* (New York: E. P. Dutton, 1954), p. 400.

3 Page numbers in parentheses refer to *The Abinger Edition of E. M. Forster*, ed. Oliver Stallybrass (London: Edward Arnold, 1972–).

4 See Wilfred Stone, *The Cave and the Mountain: A Study of E. M. Forster* (Palo Alto, CA: Stanford University Press, 1966), pp. 18–19.

5 Stone, *The Cave and the Mountain*, p. 19.

6 Fareed Zakaria, "The Previous Superpower," review of Simon Schama's *A History of Britain: The Fate of Empire, 1776–2000*, *New York Times Book Review* (July 27, 2003), 11–12, p. 12.

7 Alan Friedman, *The Turn of the Novel* (New York: Oxford University Press, 1966), p. viii.

8 Virginia Woolf, "Mr Bennett and Mrs Brown," *The Captain's Death Bed and Other Essays* (New York: Harcourt, Brace, 1950), pp. 112, 115.

Select Bibliography

I have included all the critical and scholarly studies cited in my notes plus a selection of works that are essential to the study of the early modern British and Irish novel and to understanding the current critical mindscape.

General works

Abrams, M. H., "The Deconstructive Angel," *Critical Inquiry*, 4 (1977), 425–38.

——, *Doing Things with Texts: Essays in Criticism and Critical Theory*, ed. with intro. Michael Fisher (New York: Norton, 1989).

——, "How to Do Things with Texts," *Partisan Review*, 46 (1979), 366–88.

——, *The Mirror and the Lamp: Romantic Theory and the Critical Tradition* (New York: Oxford University Press, 1953).

——, *Natural Supernaturalism: Tradition and Revolution in Romantic Literature* (New York: Norton, 1971).

Allen, Walter, *The English Novel* (New York: E. P. Dutton, 1954).

Altieri, Charles, *Painterly Abstraction in Modernist American Poetry: The Contemporaneity of Modernism* (Cambridge: Cambridge University Press, 1989).

Aristotle, *Poetics*, trans. Preston H. Epps (Chapel Hill, NC: University of North Carolina Press, 1942; repr. 1970).

Auerbach, Erich, *Mimesis: The Representation of Reality in Western Literature*, trans. Willard Trask (Princeton, NJ: Princeton University Press, 1953).

Bakhtin, Mikhail, *The Dialogic Imagination*, ed. Michael Holquist, trans. Caryl Emerson and Michael Holquist (Austin: University of Texas Press, 1981).

——, *Problems of Doestoevsky's Poetics*, ed. and trans. Caryl Emerson (Minneapolis: University of Minnesota Press, 1984).

Barnes, Julian, "The Proudest and Most Arrogant Man in France," *New York Review of Books*, 39:17 (October 22, 1992), 3–5.

Barthes, Roland, "Introduction to the Structural Analysis of Narrative," in *Image–Music–Text*, trans. Stephen Heath (New York: Hill and Wang, 1977), 79–124.

——, *The Pleasure of the Text* (New York: Hill and Wang, 1974).

——, *S/Z* (New York: Hill and Wang, 1974).

Batchelor, John, *The Edwardian Novelists* (New York: St Martin's Press, 1982).

Beach, Joseph Warren, *The Twentieth Century Novel: Studies in Technique* (New York: Appleton-Century, 1932).

Beja, Morris, *Epiphany in the Modern Novel* (Seattle: University of Washington Press, 1971).

Benjamin, Walter, *Illuminations*, trans. Harry Zohn (New York: Schocken, 1969).

Berlin, Sir Isaiah, *The Hedgehog and the Fox: An Essay on Tolstoy's View of History* (New York: Simon and Schuster, 1955).

Bloom, Harold, *The Anxiety of Influence: A Theory of Poetry* (New York: Oxford University Press, 1973).

——, *A Map of Misreading* (New York: Oxford University Press, 1975).

—— (ed.), *Romanticism and Consciousness* (New York: Norton, 1970).

Booth, Wayne, "Between Two Generations: The Heritage of the Chicago School," *Profession*, 82 (1982), 19–26.

——, *Critical Understanding: The Powers and Limits of Pluralism* (Chicago: University of Chicago Press, 1979).

——, *Now Don't Try to Reason With Me: Essays and Ironies for a Credulous Age* (Chicago: University of Chicago Press, 1970).

——, *The Rhetoric of Fiction* (Chicago: University of Chicago Press, 1961; rev. edn. 1983).

——, "The Rhetoric of Fiction and the Poetics of Fiction," *Novel*, 1:2 (winter 1968), 105–13.

——, *The Rhetoric of Irony* (Chicago: University of Chicago Press, 1974).

——, "Ten Literal 'Theses,'" in Sheldon Sacks (ed.), *On Metaphor* (Chicago: University of Chicago Press, 1979).

Bradbury, Malcolm, *Possibilities: Essays on the State of the Novel* (New York: Oxford University Press, 1973).

Bradley, F. H., *Appearance and Reality: A Metaphysical Essay*, 2nd edn (London: S. Sonnechein, 1908).

Brooks, Peter, *Reading for the Plot* (New York: Alfred A. Knopf, 1984).

Burke, Kenneth, *The Philosophy of Literary Form* (New York: Vintage, 1957).

Cain, William E., *The Crisis in Criticism: Theory, Literature, and Reform in English Studies* (Baltimore: Johns Hopkins University Press, 1984).

Calderwood, James L. and Toliver, Harold E., *Perspectives on Fiction* (New York: Oxford University Press, 1968).

Cassirer, Ernst, *The Logic of the Humanities*, trans. Clarence Smith Howe (New Haven, CT: Yale University Press, 1961).

Chatman, Seymour Benjamin, *Story and Discourse: Narrative Structure in Fiction and Film* (Ithaca, NY: Cornell University Press, 1978).

Crane, R. S., "The Concept of Plot and the Plot of *Tom Jones*," in R. S. Crane (ed.), *Critics and Criticism* (Chicago: University of Chicago Press, 1957).

Culler, Jonathan, *On Deconstruction: Theory and Criticism After Structuralism* (Ithaca, NY: Cornell University Press, 1982).

——, *The Pursuit of Signs: Semiotics, Literature, Deconstruction* (Ithaca, NY: Cornell University Press, 1981).

——, *Structuralist Poetics: Structuralism, Linguistics and the Study of Literature* (Ithaca, NY: Cornell University Press, 1975).

De Man, Paul, *Allegories of Reading: Figural Language in Rousseau, Nietzsche and Proust* (New Haven, CT: Yale University Press, 1979).

——, *Blindness and Insight: Essays in the Rhetoric of Contemporary Criticism* (New York: Oxford University Press, 1971).

——, "Semiology and Rhetoric," in Josue Harari (ed.), *Textual Strategies: Perspectives in Post-Structuralist Criticism* (Ithaca, NY: Cornell University Press, 1979).

Derrida, Jacques, "The Supplement of Copula: Philosophy Before Linguistics," in Josue Harari (ed.), *Textual Strategies: Perspectives in Post-Structuralist Criticism* (Ithaca, NY: Cornell University Press, 1979).

——, *Writing and Difference* (Chicago: University of Chicago Press, 1978).

Di San Lazzaro, G., *Klee: His Life and Work* (London: Thames and Hudson, 1957).

Eagleton, Terry, *Literary Theory: An Introduction* (Minneapolis: University of Minnesota Press, 1983).

Eco, Umberto, *The Name of the Rose*, trans. William Weaver (New York: Warner Books, 1983).

Eliot, T. S., *Selected Essays* (New York: Harcourt, Brace and World, 1960).

Elderfield, John, *Henri Matisse: A Retrospective* (New York: Museum of Modern Art, 1992).

Ellmann, Richard, *Eminent Domain* (New York: Oxford University Press, 1967).

——, *Oscar Wilde* (New York: Alfred A. Knopf, 1988).

—— and Charles Feidelson, Jr (eds.), *The Modern Tradition: Backgrounds of Modern Literature* (New York: Oxford University Press, 1965).

Elsen, Albert E., *Rodin* (New York: Museum of Modern Art, 1963).

Fish, Stanley, *Is There a Text in the Class?* (Cambridge, MA: Harvard University Press, 1980).

Flam, Jack, *Matisse: The Man and his Art, 1869–1918* (Ithaca, NY, and London: Cornell University Press, 1986).

Forster, E. M., *Aspects of the Novel* (New York: Harcourt, Brace and World, 1954; orig. edn 1927).

Foucault, Michel, *Language, Counter-Memory, Practice: Selected Essays and Interviews*, trans. Donald F. Bouchard and Sherry Simon (Ithaca, NY: Cornell University Press, 1977).

Frank, Joseph, "Spatial Form: An Answer to Critics," *Critical Inquiry*, 4 (winter 1977) 231–52.

——, "Spatial Form in Modern Literature," *Sewanee Review*, 53 (1945), 221–40, 435–56, 643–53.

——, *The Widening Gyre: Crisis and Mastery in Modern Literature* (New Brunswick, NJ: Rutgers University Press, 1963).

Friedman, Alan, *The Turn of the Novel* (New York: Oxford University Press, 1966).

Frye, Northrop, *Anatomy of Criticism: Four Essays* (Princeton, NJ: Princeton University Press, 1957).

Genette, Gerard, *Narrative Discourse: An Essay in Method*, trans. Jane E. Lewin (Ithaca, NY: Cornell University Press, 1980).

Girard, Rene, *Deceit, Desire, and the Novel: Self and Other in Literary Structure*, trans. Yvonne Freccero (Baltimore: Johns Hopkins University Press, 1965).

Glueck, Grace, "Joan Miro Exhibit, Sculpture and Ceramics," *New York Times* (May 4, 1984), C24.

——, "A Lively Review of the Futurist Experience," *New York Times*, "Arts and Leisure" (May 1, 1983), section 2, 29.

Gould, Stephen Jay, Review of Evelyn Fox Feller, *A Feeling for Organism: The Life and Work of Barbara McClintock*, *New York Review of Books*, 31:5 (March 20, 1984), 3–6.

Graff, Gerald, *Literature Against Itself: Literary Ideas in Modern Society* (Chicago: University of Chicago Press, 1979).

——, *Professing Literature* (Chicago: University of Chicago Press, 1987).

Harari, Josue (ed.), *Textual Strategies: Perspectives in Post-Structuralist Criticism* (Ithaca, NY: Cornell University Press, 1979).

Hardy, Barbara Nathan, "Toward a Poetics of Fiction: An Approach Through Narrative," *Novel*, 2:1 (autumn 1968), 5–14.

Hartman, Geoffrey, *Criticism in the Wilderness* (New Haven, CT: Yale University Press, 1980).

——, "The Culture of Criticism," *PMLA*, 99:3 (May 1984), 371–97.

——, *Saving the Text: Literature, Derrida, Philosophy* (Baltimore: Johns Hopkins University Press, 1981).

Harvey, W. J., *Character and the Novel* (Ithaca, NY: Cornell University Press, 1965).

Hirsch, E. D., *The Aims of Interpretation* (Chicago: University of Chicago Press, 1976).

——, *Validity in Interpretation* (New Haven, CT: Yale University Press, 1967).

Hofstadter, Douglas, *Gödel, Escher, Bach: An Eternal Golden Braid* (New York: Basic Books, 1979).

Holland, Norman M., *The Dynamics of Literary Response* (New York: Oxford University Press, 1968).

Iser, Wolfgang, *The Act of Reading: A Theory of Aesthetic Response* (Baltimore: Johns Hopkins University Press, 1978).

——, *The Implied Reader: Patterns of Communication in Prose Fiction from Bunyan to Beckett* (Baltimore: Johns Hopkins University Press, 1974).

James, Henry, "The Art of Fiction" (1884), in James E. Miller (ed.), *Theory of Fiction: Henry James* (Lincoln, NE: University of Nebraska Press, 1972).

——, *The Art of the Novel: Critical Prefaces*, ed. R. P. Blackmur (New York: Charles Scribner's Sons, 1934).

——, *Notes on Novelists* (New York: Charles Scribner's Sons, 1914).

Kenner, Hugh, *The Pound Era* (Berkeley and Los Angeles: University of California Press, 1971).

Kermode, Frank, *The Art of Telling: Essays on Fiction* (Cambridge, MA: Harvard University Press, 1983).

——, *The Genesis of Secrecy: An Interpretation of Narrative* (Cambridge, MA: Harvard University Press, 1979).

——, *Romantic Image* (London: Routledge and Kegan Paul, 1957).

——, "Secrets and Narrative Sequence," in W. J. T. Mitchell (ed.), *On Narrative* (Chicago: University of Chicago Press, 1981).

——, *The Sense of an Ending: Studies in the Theory of Fiction* (New York: Oxford University Press, 1967).

Kiely, Robert, *Beyond Egotism* (Cambridge, MA: Harvard University Press, 1980).

Langbaum, Robert, "The Epiphanic Mode in Wordsworth and Modern Literature," *New Literary History* 14:2 (winter 1983), 335–8.

——, *The Modern Spirit: Essays on the Continuity of Nineteenth and Twentieth Century Literature* (New York: Oxford University Press, 1970).

Langland, Elizabeth, *Society in the Novel* (Chapel Hill, NC: University of North Carolina Press, 1989).

Leavis, F. R., *The Great Tradition: George Eliot, Henry James, Joseph Conrad* (London: Chatto and Windus, 1948).

Lentricchia, Frank, *After the New Criticism* (Chicago: University of Chicago Press, 1980).

Levenson, Michael, *Modernism and the Fate of Individuality: Character and Novelistic Form from Conrad to Woolf* (Cambridge and New York: Cambridge University Press, 1991).

Levine, George, *The Realistic Imagination: English Fiction from Frankenstein to Lady Chatterley* (Chicago: University of Chicago Press, 1981).

Lodge, David, *Language of Fiction: Essays in Criticism and Verbal Analysis of the English Novel* (New York: Columbia University Press, 1966).

——, *The Modes of Modern Writing: Metaphor, Metonymy, and the Typology of Modern Literature* (Ithaca, NY: Cornell University Press, 1977).

——, *Working with Structuralism: Essays and Reviews on Nineteenth- and Twentieth-Century Literature* (London: Routledge and Kegan Paul, 1981).

London, Bette, *The Appropriated Voice: Narrative Authority in Conrad, Lawrence, and Woolf* (Ann Arbor, MI: University of Michigan Press, 1990).

Lubbock, Percy, *The Craft of Fiction* (New York: Viking Press, 1957; orig. edn 1921).

Lukàcs, Georg, *Studies in the European Novel* (New York: Grossett and Dunlap, 1964).

Mack, Maynard and Ian Gregor (eds.), *Imagined Worlds: Essays in Honour of John Butt* (London: Methuen, 1968).

Marcus, Phillip, *Yeats and Artistic Power* (New York: New York University Press, 1992).

Marcus, Steven, *The Other Victorians: A Study of Sexuality and Pornography in Mid-Nineteenth-Century England* (New York: Basic Books, 1966).

Martz, Louis L. and Aubrey Williams (eds.), *The Author in his Work* (New Haven, CT: Yale University Press, 1978).

McKeon, Richard, *Thought, Action, and Passion* (Chicago: University of Chicago Press, 1981).

Miller, D. A., *Narrative and its Discontents: Problems of Closure in the Traditional Novel* (Princeton, NJ: Princeton University Press, 1981).

Miller, J. Hillis, *The Disappearance of God: Five Nineteenth-Century Writers* (Cambridge, MA: Harvard University Press, 1963).

——, *Fiction and Repetition: Seven English Novels* (Cambridge, MA: Harvard University Press, 1982).

——, *The Form of Victorian Fiction* (Notre Dame: University of Notre Dame Press, 1968).

——, *Poets of Reality: Six Twentieth Century Writers* (Cambridge: Belknap Press of Harvard University Press, 1965).

Mitchell, W. J. T. (ed.), *On Narrative* (Chicago: University of Chicago Press, 1981), repr. of articles from *Critical Inquiry*, 7:1 (autumn 1980) and 7:4 (summer 1981).

Newton, Adam Zachary, *Narrative Ethics* (Cambridge, MA: Harvard University Press, 1995).

Norris, Margot, *Beasts of the Modern Imagination: Darwin, Nietzsche, Kafka, Ernst, and Lawrence* (Baltimore: Johns Hopkins University Press, 1985).

Nussbaum, Martha, "Perceptive Equilibrium: Literary Theory and Ethical Theory," in Ralph Cohen (ed.), *The Future of Literary Theory* (New York: Routledge, 1988).

Nuttal, A. D., *A New Mimesis: Shakespeare and the Representation of Reality* (New York: Methuen, 1983).

Plato, *Symposium*, trans. Walter Hamilton (New York: Penguin, 1951).

Poulet, Georges, "Criticism and the Experience of Interiority," in Richard Macksey and Eugene Donato (eds.), *The Structuralist Controversy: The Languages of Criticism and the Sciences of Man* (Baltimore: Johns Hopkins University Press, 1970).

——, "Phenomenology of Reading," *New Literary History*, 1:1 (October 1969), 53–68.

Pratt, Mary Louise, *Towards a Speech Act Theory of Literary Discourse* (Bloomington: Indiana University Press, 1977).

Price, Martin, *Forms of Life: Character and Moral Imagination in the Novel* (New Haven, CT: Yale University Press, 1983).

Riffaterre, Michael, "Interpretation and Descriptive Poetry: A Reading of Wordsworth's 'Yew-Tree,'" *New Literary History*, 4 (winter 1973), 229–56.

Rosenbaum, S. P. (ed.), *The Bloomsbury Group* (Toronto: University of Toronto Press, 1975).

Russell, John, *The Meaning of Modern Art* (New York: Museum of Modern Art, 1981).

Sacks, Sheldon, *Fiction and the Shape of Belief* (Berkeley and Los Angeles: University of California Press, 1967).

—— (ed.), *On Metaphor* (Chicago: University of Chicago Press, 1979).

Said, Edward, *Beginnings: Intention and Method* (New York: Basic Books, 1975).

Scholes, Robert (ed.), *Approaches to the Novel* (San Francisco: Chandler, 1961; rev. edn 1966).

—— and Robert Kellogg, *The Nature of Narrative* (New York: Oxford University Press, 1966).

Schorer, Mark, "Technique as Discovery," *Hudson Review*, 1 (spring 1948), 67–87, repr. in James L. Calderwood and Harold E. Toliver (eds.), *Perspectives on Fiction* (New York: Oxford University Press, 1968).

——, *The World We Imagine* (New York: Farrar, Straus, Giroux, 1968).

——, Josephine Miles, Gordon McKenzie (eds.), *Criticism: The Foundation of Modern Literary Judgement*, rev. edn (New York: Harcourt, Brace, 1958).

Schwarz, Daniel R., *The Case for a Humanistic Poetics* (Philadelphia: University of Pennsylvania Press, 1991).

——, "Culture, Canonicity and Pluralism: A Humanistic Perspective on Professing English," *Texas Studies in Language and Literature*, 34 (spring 1992), 149–75.

——, "The Ethics of Reading: The Case for Pluralistic and Transactional Reading," *Novel*, 12 (winter–spring 1988), 197–218, repr. in Mark Spilka and Caroline McCracken-Flesher (eds.), *Why the Novel Matters* (Bloomington: Indiana University Press, 1990).

——, *The Humanistic Heritage: Critical Theories of the English Novel From James to Hillis Miller* (London: Macmillan; Philadelphia: University of Pennsylvania Press, 1986).

Searle, John R., *Expression and Meaning: Studies in the Theory of Speech Acts* (Cambridge and New York: Cambridge University Press, 1979).

——, Review of Jonathan Culler, *On Deconstruction, New York Review of Books* (October 27, 1983), 74–9.

——, *Speech Acts: An Essay in the Philosophy of Language* (London: Cambridge University Press, 1969).

——, Ference Kiefer, and Manfred Bierwisch (eds.), *Speech Act Theory and Pragmatics* (Dordrecht and Boston: D. Reidel, 1980).

Silver, Kenneth, *Esprit de Corps: The Art of the Parisian Avant-Garde and the First World War, 1914–25* (Princeton, NJ: Princeton University Press, 1989).

Smith, Barbara Herrnstein, "Narrative Versions, Narrative Theories," in W. J. T. Mitchell (ed.), *On Narrative* (Chicago: University of Chicago Press, 1981).

——, *Poetic Closure: A Study of How Poems End Narrative* (Chicago: University of Chicago Press, 1968).

Stevenson, Lionel, *The English Novel: A Panorama* (Boston: Houghton Mifflin, 1960).

Sturrock, John, *Structuralism and Since: From Lévi-Strauss to Derrida* (Oxford: Oxford University Press, 1979).

Suleiman, Susan and Inge Crosman (eds.), *The Reader in the Text: Essays on Audience and Interpretation* (Princeton, NJ: Princeton University Press, 1980).

Sumner, Rosemary, *A Route to Modernism: Hardy, Lawrence, Woolf* (New York: St Martin's, 2000).

Thickstun, William, *Visionary Closure in the Modern Novel* (London: Macmillan, 1987).

Todorov, Tzvetan, *The Poetics of Prose*, trans. Richard Howard (Ithaca, NY: Cornell University Press, 1977).

——, "Structural Analysis of Narrative," *Novel*, 3:1 (autumn 1969), 70–6.

Tompkins, Jane P. (ed.), *Reader Response Criticism* (Baltimore: Johns Hopkins University Press, 1980).

Torgovnick, Marianna, *Closure in the Novel* (Princeton, NJ: Princeton University Press, 1981).

Trilling, Lionel, *The Liberal Imagination* (New York: Viking Press, 1950).

——, *The Opposing Self: Nine Essays in Criticism* (New York: Viking Press, 1955).

——, ed. and intro., *The Portable Matthew Arnold* (New York: Viking Press, 1949).

Van Ghent, Dorothy, *The English Novel: Form and Function* (New York: Harper and Row, 1953).

Watt, Ian, *The Rise of the Novel* (Berkeley and Los Angeles: University of California Press, 1957).

Weinstein, Philip M., *The Semantics of Desire: Changing Models of Identity from Dickens to Joyce* (Princeton, NJ: Princeton University Press, 1984).

White, Hayden, "The Value of Narrativity in the Representation of Reality," in W. J. T. Mitchell (ed.), *On Narrative* (Chicago: University of Chicago Press, 1981).

Williams, Raymond, *The English Novel from Dickens to Lawrence* (New York: Oxford University Press, 1970).

——, *Politics and Letters* (London: New Left Books, 1979).

Wilson, Edmund, *Axel's Castle: A Study in the Imaginative Literature of 1870–1930* (New York: Charles Scribner's Sons, 1959).

Woolf, Virginia, "Mr Bennett and Mrs Brown" (1924), in *The Captain's Death Bed and Other Essays* (New York: Harcourt, Brace, 1950).

Historical

Annan, Noel, "The Intellectual Aristocracy," in J. H. Plumb (ed.), *Studies in Social History: A Tribute to George Trevelyan* (London and New York: Longmans, Green, 1955).

Clifford, James, *The Predicament of Culture: Twentieth-Century Ethnography, Literature, and Art* (Cambridge, MA: Harvard University Press, 1988).

Cox, C. B. and A. E. Dyson (eds.), *The Twentieth-Century Mind*, 3 vols. (London: Oxford University Press, 1972).

Dangerfield, George, *The Strange Death of Liberal England* (New York: Putnam, 1980).

Ford, Boris (ed.), *The Modern Age*, vol. 7 of the Pelican Guide to English Literature, 3rd edn (Baltimore: Penguin, 1973).

Fussell, Paul, *The Great War and Modern Memory* (New York: Oxford University Press, 1975).

Great Victorian Paintings (London: Arts Council, 1968).

Houghton, Walter E., *The Victorian Frame of Mind* (New Haven, CT: Yale University Press, 1957).

Hynes, Samuel, *The Edwardian Turn of Mind* (Princeton, NJ: Princeton University Press, 1968).

Lester, John A., Jr, *Journey Through Despair 1880–1914* (Princeton, NJ: Princeton University Press, 1968).

Zakaria, Fareed, "The Previous Superpower," review of Simon Schama's *A History of Britain: The Fate of Empire, 1776–2000*, *New York Times Book Review* (July 27, 2003), 11–12.

Feminist criticism and theory

Abel, Elizabeth (ed.), *Writing and Sexual Difference*, special issue of *Critical Inquiry*, 8 (1981). See especially "Editor's Introduction," 173–8; and Elaine Showalter, "Feminist Criticism in the Wilderness," 79–205.

Felman, Shoshana (ed.), *Literature and Psychoanalysis* (Baltimore: Johns Hopkins University Press, 1982).

Fetterley, Judith, *The Resisting Reader: A Feminist Approach to American Fiction* (Bloomington: Indiana University Press, 1978).

Frye, Joanne S., *Living Stories, Telling Lives: Women in the Novel* (Ann Arbor, MI: University of Michigan Press, 1985).

Gallop, Jane, *The Daughter's Seduction: Feminism and Psychoanalysis* (Ithaca, NY: Cornell University Press, 1982).

Gilbert, Sandra M. and Susan Gubar, *The Madwoman in the Attic: The Woman Writer and the Nineteenth-Century Imagination* (New Haven, CT: Yale University Press, 1979).

Heilbrun, Carolyn and Margaret R. Higonnet (eds.), *The Representation of Women in Fiction* (Baltimore: Johns Hopkins University Press, 1983).

Jacobus, Mary, *Reading Woman: Essays in Feminist Criticism* (New York: Columbia University Press, 1986).

—— (ed.), *Women Writing and Writing about Women* (New York: Barnes and Noble, 1979).

Kolodny, Annette, "Dancing Through the Minefield: Some Observations on the Theory, Practice and Politics of a Feminist Literary Criticism," *Feminist Studies*, 6 (1980), 1–25.

Lacan, Jacques, *Feminine Sexuality*, eds. J. Mitchell and J. Rose (London: Macmillan, 1982).

Marks, Elaine and Isabelle de Courtivron (eds.), *New French Feminisms: An Anthology* (Amherst: University of Massachusetts Press, 1980).

McConnell-Ginet, Sally and Nelly Furman (eds.), *Women and Language in Literature and Society* (New York: Praeger, 1980).

Miller, Nancy K., "Emphasis Added: Plots and Plausibilities in Women's Fiction," *PMLA*, 96 (1981), 36–48.

Millett, Kate, *Sexual Politics* (New York: Doubleday, 1970).

Scott, Bonnie Kim, *Refiguring Modernism*, Vol. I: *The Women of 1928* (Bloomington and Indianapolis: University of Indiana Press, 1995).

Showalter, Elaine, *A Literature of their Own: British Women Novelists from Brontë to Lessing* (Princeton, NJ: Princeton University Press, 1977).

Woolf, Virginia, *A Room of One's Own* (New York: Harcourt, Brace and World, 1957; orig. edn 1929).

Marxism, new historicism, and cultural studies

Brantlinger, Patrick, *Crusoe's Footprints: Cultural Studies in Britain and America* (New York: Routledge, 1990).

——, *Rule of Darkness: British Literature and Imperialism, 1830–1914* (Ithaca, NY: Cornell University Press, 1988).

Demetz, Peter, *Marx, Engels, and the Poets*, trans. Jeffrey L. Sammons (Chicago: University of Chicago Press, 1967).

Eagleton, Terry, *Criticism and Ideology* (London: New Left Books, 1976).

——, *Marxism and Literary Criticism* (London: Methuen, 1976).

Jameson, Frederic, *Marxism and Form* (Princeton, NJ: Princeton University Press, 1972).

——, *The Political Unconscious* (Ithaca, NY: Cornell University Press, 1981).

Williams, Raymond, *Marxism and Literature* (Oxford: Oxford University Press, 1977).

Thomas Hardy

Daleski, H. M., *Thomas Hardy: Paradoxes of Love* (Columbia, MO, and London: University of Missouri Press, 1990).

De Laura, David J., "'The Ache of Modernism' in Hardy's Later Novels," *ELH*, 22 (1967), 380–99.

Eliot, T. S., *After Strange Gods* (New York: Harcourt, Brace, 1934).

Friedman, Alan, "Thomas Hardy: 'Weddings Be Funerals,'" in *The Turn of the Novel* (New York: Oxford University Press, 1966).

Gatrell, Simon, *Thomas Hardy and the Proper Study of Mankind* (Charlottesville, VA: University of Virginia Press, 1993).

Gittings, Robert, *Thomas Hardy's Later Years* (Boston: Little, Brown, 1978).

——, *Young Thomas Hardy* (Boston: Little, Brown, 1975).

Gregor, Ian, *The Great Web: The Form of Hardy's Major Fiction* (London: Faber and Faber, 1974).

——, "What Kind of Fiction Did Hardy Write?," *Essays in Criticism*, 16 (1966), 290–308.

Guerard, Albert J. (ed.), *Hardy: A Collection of Critical Essays* (Englewood Cliffs, NJ: Prentice-Hall, 1973).

——, *Thomas Hardy: The Novels and Stories* (Cambridge, MA: Harvard University Press, 1949).

Hardy, Florence Emily, *The Early Life of Thomas Hardy, 1840–1891* (London and New York: Macmillan, 1928).

——, *The Later Years of Thomas Hardy* (New York: Macmillan, 1930).

Higonnet, Margaret R. (ed.), *The Sense of Sex: Feminist Perspectives in Hardy* (Urbana and Chicago: University of Illinois Press, 1992).

Howe, Irving, *Thomas Hardy* (New York: Macmillan, 1967).

Johnson, Bruce, *True Correspondence: A Phenomenology of Thomas Hardy's Novels* (Jacksonville: Florida State University Press, 1983).

Kramer, Dale (ed.), *Critical Approaches to the Fiction of Thomas Hardy* (London: Macmillan, 1979).

—— (ed., with the assistance of Nancy Marck), *Critical Essays on Thomas Hardy: The Novels* (Boston, MA: G. K. Hall, 1990).

Langbaum, Robert, *Thomas Hardy in Our Time* (New York: St Martin's, 1995).

Langland, Elizabeth, "Becoming a Man in *Jude the Obscure*," in Margaret R. Higonnet (ed.), *The Sense of Sex: Feminist Perspectives in Hardy* (Urbana and Chicago: University of Illinois Press, 1992).

Miller, J. Hillis, *Thomas Hardy: Distance and Desire* (Cambridge, MA: Harvard University Press, 1970).

Millgate, Michael, *Thomas Hardy: A Biography* (New York: Random House, 1982).

——, *Thomas Hardy: His Career as a Novelist* (New York: Random House, 1971).

Modern Fiction Studies, Thomas Hardy issue, VI (fall 1960).

Morgan, Rosemarie, *Women and Sexuality in the Novels of Thomas Hardy* (New York and London: Routledge, 1988).

Pinion, F. B., *A Hardy Companion: A Guide to the Works of Thomas Hardy and their Background* (New York: St Martin's, 1968).

Seymour-Smith, Martin, *Hardy* (New York: St Martin's, 1994).

Southern Review, Thomas Hardy centennial issue, VI (summer 1940).

Squires, Michael, *The Pastoral Novel: Studies in George Eliot, Thomas Hardy, and D. H. Lawrence* (Charlottesville, VA: University of Virginia Press, 1974).

Vigar, Penelope, *The Novels of Thomas Hardy: Illusion and Reality* (London: Athlone Press, 1974).

Webster, Harvey Curtis, *On a Darkling Plain: The Art and Thought of Thomas Hardy* (Chicago: University of Chicago Press, 1947).

Woolf, Virginia, "The Novels of Thomas Hardy," in *The Second Common Reader* (New York, 1932; first published in *The Times Literary Supplement*, January 19, 1928).

Joseph Conrad

Achebe, Chinua, "An Image of Africa," *Massachusetts Review*, 18 (1977), 782–94.

Armstrong, Paul B., *The Challenge of Bewilderment: Understanding and Representation in James, Conrad, and Ford* (Ithaca, NY: Cornell University Press, 1987).

Baines, Jocelyn, *Joseph Conrad: A Critical Biography* (New York: McGraw-Hill, 1960).

Bretell, Richard, *The Art of Paul Gauguin* (Washington, DC: National Gallery of Art, 1988).

Conrad, Joseph, *Collected Letters of Joseph Conrad, vol. 1, 1861–1897*, eds. Frederic Karl and Laurence Davies (New York: Cambridge University Press, 1983).

Daleski, H. M., *Joseph Conrad: The Way of Dispossession* (New York: Holmes and Meier, 1976).

Demory, Pamela H., "*Nostromo*, Making History," *Texas Studies in Literature and Language*, 35:3 (fall 1993), 315–46.

Ducharme, Robert, "The Power of Culture in *Lord Jim*," *Conradiana*, 22 (1990), 3–24.

Erdinast-Vulcan, Daphna, *Joseph Conrad and the Modern Temper* (Oxford: Clarendon Press, 1991).

Fleishman, Avrom, *Conrad's Politics: Community and Anarchy in the Fiction of Joseph Conrad* (Baltimore: Johns Hopkins University Press, 1967).

Fogel, Aaron, *Coercion to Speak: Conrad's Poetics of Dialogue* (Cambridge, MA: Harvard University Press, 1985).

Guerard, Albert, *Conrad the Novelist* (Cambridge, MA: Harvard University Press, 1958).

Guetti, James, *The Limits of Metaphor: A Study of Melville, Conrad, and Faulkner* (Ithaca, NY: Cornell University Press, 1967).

Hay, Eloise Knapp, *The Political Novels of Joseph Conrad* (Chicago: University of Chicago Press, 1963).

Hochschild, Adam, *King Leopold's Ghost: A Story of Greed, Terror, and Heroism in Central Africa* (Boston: Houghton Mifflin, 1998).

Jean-Aubry, G. *Joseph Conrad: Life and Letters*, 2 vols. (Garden City, NY: Doubleday, Page, 1927).

Johnson, Barbara, and Marjorie Garber, "Secret Sharing: Reading Conrad Psychoanalytically," *College English*, 49:6 (1987), 628–40.

Johnson, Bruce, *Conrad's Models of Mind* (Minneapolis: University of Minnesota Press, 1971).

Karl, Frederick, *Joseph Conrad: The Three Lives* (New York: Farrar, Straus and Giroux, 1979).

McNelly, Cleo, "Natives, Women, and Claude Lévi-Strauss: A Reading of *Tristes Tropiques* as Myth," *Massachusetts Review*, 16 (1975), 7–29.

Meyer, Bernard, *Joseph Conrad: A Psychoanalytic Biography* (Princeton, NJ: Princeton University Press, 1967).

Moser, Thomas, *Joseph Conrad: Achievement and Decline* (Cambridge, MA: Harvard University Press, 1957).

Murfin, Ross (ed.), *Heart of Darkness: A Case Study in Contemporary Criticism* (New York: St Martin's, 1989).

Nadjer, Zdzislaw, *Conrad's Polish Background* (London: Oxford University Press, 1964).

——, *Joseph Conrad: A Chronicle*, trans. Halina Carroll-Najder (New Brunswick, NJ: Rutgers University Press, 1983).

Rosenfield, Claire, *Paradise of Snakes: An Archetypal Analysis of Conrad's Political Novels* (Chicago: Chicago University Press, 1967).

Said, Edward, *Culture and Imperialism* (New York: Alfred A. Knopf, 1993).

Schwarz, Daniel, *Conrad: "Almayer's Folly" Through "Under Western Eyes"* (Ithaca, NY: Cornell University Press; London: Macmillan, 1980).

——, *Conrad: The Later Fiction* (New York: Humanities Press; London: Macmillan, 1980).

—— (ed.), *Conrad's "The Secret Sharer": A Case Study in Contemporary Criticism* (New York: St Martin's, 1997).

——, *Rereading Conrad* (Columbia, MO: University of Missouri Press, 2001).

Van Ghent, Dorothy, "Introduction," in *Nostromo* by Joseph Conrad (New York: Holt, Rhinehart and Winston, 1961).

Watt, Ian, *Conrad in the Nineteenth Century* (Berkeley and Los Angeles: University of California Press, 1979).

Watts, C. T. (ed.), *Joseph Conrad's Letters to R. B. Cunninghame Graham* (Cambridge: Cambridge University Press, 1969).

Wollaeger, Mark A., *Joseph Conrad and the Fictions of Skepticism* (Stanford, CA: Stanford University Press, 1990).

D. H. Lawrence

Balbert, Peter and Phillip L. Marcus (eds.), *D. H. Lawrence: A Centenary Consideration* (Ithaca, NY: Cornell University Press, 1985).

Bell, Michael, *D. H. Lawrence: Language and Being* (Cambridge: Cambridge University Press, 1991).

Cavitch, David, *D. H. Lawrence and the New World* (New York and London: Oxford University Press, 1969).

Daleski, H. M., *The Forked Flame* (Evanston, IL: Northwestern, 1965).

Delavenay, Emile, *D. H. Lawrence, the Man and his Work: The Formative Years: 1885–1919*, trans. Katharine M. Delavenay (Carbondale: Southern Illinois University Press, 1972).

Gordon, David J., *D. H. Lawrence as a Literary Critic* (New Haven, CT: Yale University Press, 1960).

Hamalian, Leo, *D. H. Lawrence in Italy* (New York: Taplinger, 1982).

Herzinger, Kim, *D. H. Lawrence in his Time: 1908–1915* (Lewisberg, PA: Bucknell University Press, 1982).

Kermode, Frank, *D. H. Lawrence* (New York: Viking Press, 1973).

Kinkead-Weekes, Mark, *D. H. Lawrence: Triumph to Exile, 1912–1922* (Cambridge: Cambridge University Press, 1996).

——, "The Marble and the Statue: The Exploratory Imagination of D. H. Lawrence," in Maynard Mack and Ian Gregor (eds.), *Imagined Worlds: Essays on Some English Novels and Novelists in Honor of John Butt* (London: Methuen, 1968).

Lawrence, D. H., *Apocalypse and the Writings on Revelation* (1932), ed. Mara Kalnins (New York: Cambridge University Press, 1980).

——, *The Collected Letters of D. H. Lawrence*, ed. Harry T. Moore, 2 vols. (New York: Viking Press, 1962).

——, *D. H. Lawrence and Sons and Lovers*, ed. E. W. Tedlock, Jr (New York: New York University Press, 1965).

——, *Fantasia of the Unconscious* (1922; repr. New York: Viking Press, 1960).

——, *The Letters of D. H. Lawrence*, ed. Aldous Huxley (New York: Viking Press, 1932).

——, *The Letters of D. H. Lawrence*, vol. I, ed. James T. Boulton (1979); vol. II, eds. George J. Zytaruk and James T. Boulton (1981); vol. III, eds. James T. Boulton and Andrew Robertson (New York: Cambridge University Press, 1984).

——, *Phoenix: The Posthumous Papers of D. H. Lawrence*, ed. Edward P. McDonald (New York: Viking Press, 1936).

——, *Phoenix II* (New York: Viking Press, 1968).

——, *Psychoanalysis and the Unconscious* (1921; repr. New York: Viking Press, 1960).

——, *Study of Thomas Hardy and Other Essays*, ed. Bruce Steele (Cambridge: Cambridge University Press, 1985).

Martz, Louis, "Portrait of Miriam: A Study in the Design of *Sons and Lovers*," in Maynard Mack and Ian Gregor (eds.), *Imagined Worlds: Essays on Some English Novels and Novelists in Honor of John Butt* (London: Methuen, 1968).

Meyers, Jeffrey, *D. H. Lawrence and the Experience of Italy* (Philadelphia: University of Pennsylvania Press, 1982).

—— (ed.), *D. H. Lawrence and Tradition* (Amherst: University of Massachusetts Press, 1985).

Moore, Harry T. (ed.), *A D. H. Lawrence Miscellany* (Carbondale: Southern Illinois University Press, 1959).

——, *The Life and Works of D. H. Lawrence* (New York: Twayne, 1951).

——, *The Priest of Love: A Life of D. H. Lawrence* (New York: Farrar, Straus and Giroux, 1974).

Moynahan, Julian, *The Deed of Life: The Novels and Tales of D. H. Lawrence* (Princeton, NJ: Princeton University Press, 1963).

Parmenter, Ross, *Lawrence in Oaxaca: A Quest for the Novelist in Mexico* (Layton, UT: Gibbs M. Smith, 1984).

Siegal, Carol, *Lawrence Among the Women* (Charlottesville, VA, and London: University of Virginia Press, 1991).

Spilka, Mark (ed.), *D. H. Lawrence: A Collection of Critical Essays* (Englewood Cliffs, NJ: Prentice-Hall, 1963).

——, *The Love Ethic of D. H. Lawrence* (Bloomington: Indiana University Press, 1955).

Tedlock, Ernest W., Jr, *D. H. Lawrence, Artist and Rebel: A Study of Lawrence's Fiction* (Albuquerque: University of New Mexico Press, 1963).

Woolf, Virginia, "Notes on D. H. Lawrence," in *Collected Essays*, vol. I (London: Hogarth Press, 1966).

Worthen, John, *D. H. Lawrence and the Idea of the Novel* (London: Macmillan, 1979).

——, *D. H. Lawrence: The Early Years, 1885–1912* (Cambridge: Cambridge University Press, 1992).

James Joyce

Attridge, Derek (ed.), *The Cambridge Companion to James Joyce* (New York: Cambridge University Press, 1990).

Beja, Morris, *James Joyce: A Literary Life* (Columbus, OH: Ohio State University Press, 1992).

Blackmur, R. P., "The Jew in Search of a Son," *Virginia Quarterly Review*, XXIV (1948), 109–12; repr. in *Eleven Essays on the European Novel* (New York: Harcourt, Brace and World, 1964).

Brivic, Sheldon, *Joyce's Waking Women* (Madison: University of Wisconsin Press, 1995).

Budgen, Frank, *James Joyce and the Making of "Ulysses"* (Bloomington: Indiana University Press, 1960; orig. edn 1934).

Cheng, Vincent J., *Joyce, Race, and Empire* (Cambridge: Cambridge University Press, 1995).

Duffy, Enda, *The Subaltern "Ulysses"* (Minneapolis: University of Minnesota Press, 1994).

Eliot, T. S., "*Ulysses*, Order, and Myth," *Dial*, 75 (November 1923), 480–3; repr. as "Myth and Literary Classicism," in Richard Ellmann and Charles Feidelson, Jr (eds.), *The Modern Tradition: Backgrounds of Modern Literature* (New York: Oxford University Press, 1965).

Ellmann, Richard, "The Big Word in 'Ulysses,'" *New York Review of Books*, 31:16 (October 25, 1984), 31–2.

——, *The Consciousness of Joyce* (New York: Oxford University Press, 1977).

——, *James Joyce* (New York: Oxford University Press; rev. edn 1984).

——, *Ulysses on the Liffey* (New York: Oxford University Press, 1972).

French, Marilyn, *The Book as World: James Joyce's Ulysses* (Cambridge, MA: Harvard University Press, 1976).

Friedman, Susan Stanford (ed.), *Joyce: The Return of the Repressed* (Ithaca, NY: Cornell University Press, 1993).

Gifford, Don and Robert I. Seidman, *Notes for Joyce: An Annotation of James Joyce's Ulysses* (New York: Sutton, 1974).

Gilbert, Stuart, *James Joyce's Ulysses* (New York: Random House, 1930; rev. edn 1952; repr. 1955).

Goldberg, S. L., *The Classical Temper: A Study of James Joyce's Ulysses* (New York: Barnes and Noble, 1961).

Goldman, Arnold, *The Joyce Paradox: Form and Freedom in his Fiction* (London: Routledge and Kegan Paul, 1966).

Groden, Michael, *Ulysses in Progress* (Princeton, NJ: Princeton University Press, 1977).

Hayman, David, *Ulysses: The Mechanics of Meaning* (Englewood Cliffs, NJ: Prentice-Hall, 1970).

Henke, Suzette A., *James Joyce and the Politics of Desire* (New York: Routledge, 1990).

Herring, Phillip F. (ed.), *Joyce's Notes and Early Drafts for Ulysses* (Charlottesville, VA: University of Virginia Press, 1977).

Joyce, James, *The Critical Writings*, eds. Ellsworth Mason and Richard Ellmann (New York: Viking Press, 1959).

——, *Dubliners: Text, Criticism, and Notes*, eds. Robert Scholes and A. Walton Litz (New York: Viking Press, 1968).

——, *The James Joyce Archives: Ulysses* vols., ed. Michael Groden (New York: Garland, 1978).

——, *The Letters of James Joyce,* vol. I, ed. Stuart Gilbert (New York: Viking Press, 1957).

——, *A Portrait of the Artist as Young Man* (1916), text corrected Chester G. Anderson and ed. Richard Ellmann (New York: Viking Press, 1964).

——, *Selected Letters of James Joyce,* ed. Richard Ellmann (New York: Viking Press, 1975).

——, *Stephen Hero* (1944; rev. edn, ed. Theodore Spencer, New York: New Directions, 1963).

——, *Ulysses* (1922; rev. edn New York: Modern Library and Random House, 1961).

——, *Ulysses: A Critical and Synoptic Edition,* ed. Hans Walter Gabler with Wolfhard Steppe and Claus Melchior (New York and London: Garland, 1984).

Joyce, Stanislaus, *My Brother's Keeper: James Joyce's "Early Years,"* ed. Richard Ellmann (New York: Viking Press, 1958).

Kain, Richard, *Fabulous Voyager: A Study of James Joyce's Ulysses* (New York: Viking Press, 1947; repr. 1959).

Kenner, Hugh, *Dublin's Joyce* (1956; repr. Boston: Beacon Press, 1962).

——, *Joyce's Voices* (Berkeley: University of California Press, 1978).

——, *Ulysses* (London: Allen and Unwin, 1980).

Lawrence, Karen, *The Odyssey of Style in Ulysses* (Princeton, NJ: Princeton University Press, 1981).

Leonard, Garry, "Joyce and Lacan: The 'Woman' as a Symptom of 'Masculinity' in 'The Dead,'" *James Joyce Quarterly,* 28.2 (1991), 451–72.

Lernout, Geert, *The French Joyce* (Ann Arbor, MI: University of Michigan Press, 1990).

Maddox, Brenda, *Nora: The Real Life of Molly Bloom* (Boston: Houghton, 1988).

Mahaffey, Vicki, *Reauthorizing Joyce* (New York: Cambridge University Press, 1988).

McCormick, Kathleen and Erwin R. Steinberg (eds.), *Approaches to Teaching Joyce's "Ulysses"* (New York: MLA, 1993).

McGee, Patrick, *Paperspace: Style as Ideology in Joyce's "Ulysses"* (Lincoln, NE: University of Nebraska Press, 1993).

Norris, Margot (ed.), *A Companion to James Joyce's "Ulysses"* (Boston: Bedford Books, 1998).

——, *Joyce's Web: The Social Unraveling of Modernism* (Austin: University of Texas Press, 1992).

Pearce, Richard (ed.), *Molly Blooms: A Polylogue on "Penelope" and Cultural Studies* (Madison: University of Wisconsin Press, 1994).

Pecora, Vincent P., "'The Dead' and the Generosity of the Word," *PMLA,* 101.2 (1986), 233–45.

Rabate, Jean Michael, *James Joyce: Authorized Reader,* translation of *James Joyce, Portrait de l'auteur en autre lecteur,* 1984 (Baltimore: Johns Hopkins University Press, 1991).

Rader, Ralph W., "Exodus and Return: Joyce's *Ulysses* and the Fiction of the Actual," *University of Toronto Quarterly,* 48 (winter 1978/9), 149–71.

Restuccia, Francis L., *Joyce and the Law of the Father* (New Haven, CT: Yale University Press, 1989).

Reynolds, Mary, *Dante and Joyce* (Princeton, NJ: Princeton University Press, 1981).

Schwarz, Daniel R., *Reading Joyce's "Ulysses"* (New York: St Martin's; London: Macmillan, 1987).

——, *Reconfiguring Modernism: Explorations in the Relationship between Modern Art and Modern Literature* (New York: St Martin's, 1997).

Segall, Jeffrey, *Joyce in America: Cultural Politics and the Trials of "Ulysses"* (Berkeley: University of California Press, 1993).

Staley, Thomas F. (ed.), *Fifty Years: Ulysses* (Bloomington: Indiana University Press, 1974); repr. of *James Joyce Quarterly*, 10:1 (autumn 1972).

Stanford, W. B., *The Ulysses Theme* (Oxford: Blackwell, 1954).

Thornton, Weldon, *Allusions in Ulysses: A Line-by-Line Reference to Joyce's Complex Symbolism* (Chapel Hill, NC: University of North Carolina Press, 1968; repr. New York: Simon and Schuster, 1973).

Tymoczko, Maria, *The Irish "Ulysses"* (Berkeley: University of California Press, 1994).

Valente, Joseph, *James Joyce and the Problem of Justice: Negotiating Sexual and Colonial Difference* (Cambridge: Cambridge University Press, 1995).

Walzl, Florence, "Gabriel and Michael: The Conclusion to 'The Dead,' " *James Joyce Quarterly*, 4 (1966), 17–31.

Virginia Woolf

Beer, Gillian, *Virgina Woolf: The Common Ground* (Ann Arbor, MI: University of Michigan Press, 1996).

Beja, Morris, "Matches Struck in the Dark: Virginia Woolf's Moments of Vision," *Critical Quarterly*, IV (summer 1964); repr. in Morris Beja (ed.), *Virginia Woolf, To the Lighthouse: A Casebook* (London: Macmillan, 1970).

Bell, Quentin, *Virginia Woolf: A Biography*, 2 vols. (New York: Harcourt, Brace, Jovanovich, 1972).

Booth, Alison, *Greatness Engendered: George Eliot and Virginia Woolf* (Ithaca, NY: Cornell University Press, 1992).

DiBattista, Maria, *Virginia Woolf's Major Novels: The Fables of Anon* (New Haven, CT: Yale University Press, 1980).

DuPlessis, Rachel Blau, "Feminist Narrative in Virginia Woolf," *Novel*, 21:2–3 (winter–spring 1988), 323–30.

Fleishman, Avrom, *Virginia Woolf: A Critical Reading* (Baltimore: Johns Hopkins University Press, 1975).

Heilbrun, Carolyn, "The Androgynous Vision in *To the Lighthouse*," in *Toward a Recognition of Androgyny* (New York: Alfred A. Knopf, 1968); repr. in Thomas S. W. Lewis (ed.), *Virginia Woolf: A Collection of Criticism* (New York: McGraw-Hill, 1975).

Laurence, Patricia Ondek, *The Reading of Silence: Virginia Woolf in the English Tradition* (Stanford, CA: Stanford University Press, 1991).

Leaska, Mitchell, *The Novels of Virginia Woolf* (New York: John Jay Press, 1977).

Levenback, Karen, *Virginia Woolf and the Great War* (Syracuse, NY: Syracuse University Press, 1999).

Majundar, Robin and Allen McLaurin (eds.), *Virginia Woolf: The Critical Heritage* (Boston: Routledge and Kegan Paul, 1975).

Marcus, Jane (ed.), *The Unknown Virginia Woolf: New Feminist Essays on Virginia Woolf* (Lincoln, NE: University of Nebraska Press, 1981).

——, *Virginia Woolf: A Feminist Slant* (Lincoln, NE: University of Nebraska Press, 1983).

McLaurin, Allen, *Virginia Woolf: The Echoes Enslaved* (Cambridge: Cambridge University Press, 1973).

Poole, Roger, *The Unknown Virginia Woolf* (New York: Cambridge University Press, 1978).

Quick, Jonathan R., "Virginia Woolf, Roger Fry, and Post-Impressionism," *Massachusetts Review*, 26:4 (winter 1985), 547–70.

Richter, Harvena, *Virginia Woolf: The Inward Voyage* (Princeton, NJ: Princeton University Press, 1970).

Rosenfeld, Natasha, *Outsiders Together: Virginia and Leonard Woolf* (Princeton, NJ: Princeton University Press, 2000).

Rosenthal, Michael, *Virginia Woolf* (New York: Columbia University Press, 1979).

Silver, Brenda R., *Virginia Woolf's Reading Notebooks* (Princeton, NJ: Princeton University Press, 1981).

Spilka, Mark, *Virginia Woolf's Quarrel with Grieving* (Lincoln, NE: University of Nebraska Press, 1980).

Woolf, Leonard, *Beginning Again: An Autobiography of the Years 1911 to 1918* (New York: Harcourt, Brace and World, 1964).

——, *The Journey Not the Arrival Matters: An Autobiography of the Years 1939–1969* (New York: Harcourt, Brace, Jovanovich, 1970).

Woolf, Virginia, *The Diaries of Virginia Woolf*, 4 vols., ed. Anne Oliver Bell (New York: Harcourt, Brace, Jovanovich, 1977–82).

——, *The Letters of Virginia Woolf*, 6 vols., ed. Nigel Nicholson (New York: Harcourt, Brace, Jovanovich, 1975–80).

Zwerdling, Alex, *Virginia Woolf and the Real World* (Berkeley: University of California Press, 1986).

E. M. Forster

Bradbury, Malcolm (ed.), *Forster: A Collection of Critical Essays* (Englewood Cliffs, NJ: Prentice-Hall, 1966).

Colmer, John, *E. M. Forster: The Personal Voice* (London and Boston: Routledge and Kegan Paul, 1975).

Crews, Frederick C., *E. M. Forster: The Perils of Humanism* (Princeton, NJ: Princeton University Press, 1962).

Das, G. K., *E. M. Forster's India* (London: Macmillan, 1977).

—— and John Beer (eds.), *E. M. Forster: A Human Exploration* (New York: New York University Press, 1969).

Dodd, Philip, "England, Englishness, and the Other in E. M. Forster," in *The End of the Earth: 1876–1918* (London: Ashfield, 1992).

Forster, E. M., *Selected Letters of E. M. Forster*, eds. Mary Lago and P. N. Furbank (Cambridge, MA: Harvard University Press, 1983).

Furbank, P. N., *E. M. Forster: A Life* (London: Secker and Warburg, 1977).

Herz, Judith Scherer and Robert K. Martin, *E. M. Forster: Centenary Revaluations* (Toronto: University of Toronto Press, 1982).

Lewis, Robin Jared, *E. M. Forster's Passages to India* (New York: Columbia University Press, 1979).

Martin, Richard, *The Love that Failed: Ideal and Reality in the Writings of E. M. Forster* (The Hague: Mouton, 1974).

Martin, Robert K. and George Piggsford, *Queer Forster* (Chicago and London: University of Chicago Press, 1997).

May, Brian, *The Modernist as Pragmatist: E. M. Forster and the Fate of Liberalism* (Colombia, MO: University of Missouri Press, 1997).

McConkey, James, *The Novels of E. M. Forster* (Ithaca, NY: Cornell University Press, 1957).

McDowell, Frederick P., *E. M. Forster* (New York: Twayne, 1969; rev. edn 1982).

Rorty, Richard, "Love and Money," *Common Sense*, 1:1 (spring 1992), 12–16.

Rosecrance, Barbara, *Forster's Narrative Vision* (Ithaca, NY: Cornell University Press, 1982).

Schwarz, Daniel R., "The Importance of E. M. Forster's *Aspects of the Novel*," *South Atlantic Quarterly*, 82 (spring 1983), 189–208.

Shahane, Vasant A. (ed.), *Approaches to E. M. Forster: A Centenary Volume* (New Delhi: Arnold-Heinemann, 1981).

Stone, Wilfred, *The Cave and the Mountain: A Study of E. M. Forster* (Palo Alto, CA: Stanford University Press, 1966).

Trilling, Lionel, *E. M. Forster* (New York: New Directions, 1964; orig. edn 1943).

Index